Salience of Social Media in Hybrid Operations

Salience of Social Media in Hybrid Operations

Col Dheeraj Kumar

(Established 1870)

The United Service Institution of India
New Delhi

Vij Books
New Delhi (India)

Published by

Vij Books
(An imprint of Vij Books India Pvt Ltd)

(Publishers, Distributors & Importers)
4836/24, Ansari Road
Delhi – 110 002
Phones: 91-11-43596460
Mob: 98110 94883
e-mail: contact@vijpublishing.com
web : www.vijbooks.in

First Published in India in 2024

Copyright © 2024, United Service Institution of India, New Delhi

ISBN: 978-81-97691-35-5 (PB)

All rights reserved.

No part of this book may be reproduced, stored in a retrieval system, transmitted or utilized in any form or by any means, electronic, mechanical, photocopying, recording or otherwise, without the prior permission of the copyright owner. Application for such permission should be addressed to the publisher.

Disclaimer
The views expressed and suggestions made in the book are solely of the author in his personal capacity and do not have any official endorsements. Attributability of the contents lies purely with the author.

Contents

Foreword		vii
Abbreviations		ix
Chapter 1	Emerging Hybrid Threat Scenario	1
Chapter 2	Hybrid Warfare and Role of Social Media in Hybrid Operations	27
Chapter 3	Footprints of Social Media - Defining Contours of Hybrid Warfare	68
Chapter 4	Case Studies	103
Chapter 5	Impact of Social Media on Public Opinion and Decision-Making in Hybrid Warfare in Global and Indian Context	176
Chapter 6	Counter Measures to Mitigate Threats of Social Media	199
Chapter 7	Future Implications of Social Media on National Security	232
Chapter 8	Recommended Strategies and Counter Measures	243
Endnotes		269
Index		295

Foreword

In contemporary global conflict and competition scenario, nation states are increasingly embroiled in zero-sum political, legal, military and economic competitions to safeguard respective national interests, address security dilemmas and achieve balance of power. In predictable scenario, propensity of escalation in armed conflicts appears inevitable, wherein, competitors would leverage plethora of conventional and unconventional 'means' (i.e., kinetic, non-kinetic and non-contact) in innovative & radically different 'ways' to achieve the desired 'ends'. The trends of ongoing conflicts between state and/or non-state actors presage revolution in military and geo-political contestations. Recently, the world has witnessed involvement of all types of instruments of power and state & non-state actors in Ukraine-Russia conflict racing to seize physical, cognitive, economical and cyber battle spaces in a hybrid environment. Similarly, trends of violence and exploitation of myriad means by state and non-state actors in Israel-Hamas conflict, proxy war in J & K and cognitive operations during Doklam and Galwan incidents are reminders of prevalence of hybrid war over entire conflict spectrum. These incidents have revealed that security establishment and state actors have been contesting adversarial forces prosecuting their nefarious designs in kinetic and non-kinetic domains. Thus, emerging security scenario merits that security forces align their tactics & strategies to changing character of modern warfare i.e. Hybrid Warfare.

According to military thinkers and strategists, hybrid warfare entails an interplay of conventional & unconventional instruments of power and tools of subversion, blended in a synchronised manner to exploit vulnerabilities of an adversary and achieve synergistic effects. There are two distinct characteristics of hybrid warfare i.e. obscurity between war & peace time and ambiguity and attribution. As per Frank Hoffman, Hybrid warfare employs political warfare and blends conventional warfare, irregular warfare, and cyberwarfare with other influencing methods, such as fake news, diplomacy, lawfare and foreign electoral intervention to influence the outcome of the conflicts. Some common tools and tactics of hybrid warfare include Information operations, social engineering, cyber-attacks, political subversion, conventional military actions, proxy forces, and economic & political subversion. Recent trends have revealed social media also being exploited extensively to realise objectives of hybrid wars.

Evidently, owing to its wider access, affordability and ambiguous nature, social media emerges as an effective tool which would have relevance in all stages of hybrid conflict scenario. There are ample evidences in contemporary scenario wherein social media has proved to be a powerful tool of hybrid warfare, used to spread propaganda and disinformation to manipulate public opinion and destabilize societies. The major incidents of social media exploitation include Israel and Hezbollah conflict 2006, Arab Spring revolution of 2010, Yemen Crisis, Doklam Standoff in 2017, Ukraine Crisis and US Presidential Election of 2016.

Extant study by author is aligned to develop a comprehensive understanding of evolving concept of hybrid warfare and discern trends of social media exploitation in recent conflicts. In his book, author has also analysed range of social media warfare tactics and tools leveraged by actors to influence human minds, shape opinion and clog cognitive space so as to dominate information space and cripple objective decision making by strategic leaders. Book succinctly covers important case studies wherein social media platforms have played a pivotal role in influencing outcome of contestations. Analysing emerging trends of social media technology and evolving social media warfare, author has also endeavoured to assess impact social media platforms may have over future competitions and conflicts. He has recommended certain strategies and measures to mitigate threat to India's national security from battle of narratives and cognitive war prosecuted by adversarial forces and build credible capability to secure Indian information space and dominate critical space in cognitive war waged against hostile state and non-state actors.

New Delhi

Aug 2024

Major General BK Sharma,
AVSM, SM** (Retired)
Director General, USI

Abbreviations

BREXIT	British and Exit
CCP	Chinese Communist Party
COG	Centre of Gravity
DIME	Diplomatic, Information, Military and Economic
FCU	Fact Check Unit
FOMO	Fear of missing out
IM	Indian Mujahidin
IOR	Indian Ocean Region
IS Bangla	Islamic State Bangla
ISI	Inter Service Intelligence
ISIS	Islamic State in Iraq and Syria
ISJK	Islamic State Jammu and Kashmir
ISKP	Islamic State Khorasan Province
ISPR	Inter-Services Public Relations
JeM	Jaish-e-Mohammed
LeT	Lashkar-e-Toiba
MCDC	Multinational Capability Development Campaign
MEITY	Ministry of Electronics and Information
MENA	Middle East and North Africa
MPECI	Military, Political, Economic, Civilian and Informational
NATO	North Atlantic Treat Organisaton

OSINT	Open Source Intelligence
PESTLEM	Political, Economical, Social, Technological, Legal, Environmental and Military
PFI	Popular Front of India
QUAD	Quadrilateral Security Dialogue
SIMI	Students Islamic Movement of India
SMINT	Social Media Intelligence
SMPs	Social Media Platforms
SMW	Social Media warfare
VPN	Virtual Private Network
VUCA	Volatile, Uncertain, Complex, Ambiguous

Chapter 1

Emerging Hybrid Threat Scenario

Environment Scan

Consequent to unprecedented technological advancements and dynamic geo-political and geo-economical competitions amongst the nation-states aspiring to claim pole position in the emerging multi-polar world, the global arena presents a relatively complex, intensely contested and uncertain image of world affairs. The emerging contours of the great power game have revealed that in concert with the conventional military might, the contesting nations have leveraged geo-economical and geo-political influences to dominate the adversary and achieve their objectives. Consequent to race occupying the critical space in the world's economy, rise of neo-nationalists and radical hardliners, and relentless pursuit of global leadership, has manifested into potential flash points amongst nations. The world which appeared to have emerged out of the shadow of cold war, has seemingly engulfed with interstate and intrastate conflicts over myriad issues. Displaying a definitive departure from the traditional ways of settling the interstate conflicts, the nation-states are leveraging all instruments of national power i.e., diplomatic, information, military and economic (DIME) to dominate the adversary and gain a decisive advantage. The observation stands substantiated by the orchestration of geo-political, geo-economic and military responses by US and NATO signatories in the current Russia-Ukraine conflict. In the Indian Ocean Region (IOR), the Chinese geo-political overtures appear to have designs to intimidate and weaken India's dominance over her immediate neighbourhood. Based on the unfolding of these global incidents, it may be inferred that contemporary strategies of the competing nations have declared the arrival of 'Hybrid Warfare' in the conflict continuum. It is also argued that 'Hybrid Warfare' complements the overall effort to achieve the geo-political objectives. The wide array of the 'Ways' and 'Means' deployed to execute hybrid strategies exceed the military means; they involve manipulation of politics, psychology, economy, information, and diplomacy.

In the scholarly discourses, there is a tendency to compartmentalise military conflicts, political struggle and economic competitions in isolated bins; the approach may fall short of carrying out a comprehensive study of statecraft in hybrid scenario. In this rapidly evolving geo-political landscape, geo-economics, when used as a coercion tool to advance own economic interest to the detriment of adversary and to manipulate their behaviour, becomes a credible deterrence. Competing nations are increasingly leveraging economic coercion viz concessions/ foreign aid, sanctions, money power and trade volumes, to shape the behaviour of the adversary. Therefore, it can be deduced that economic coercion is an effective tool of hybrid strategies designed to shape the outcomes of competitions and conflicts. To corroborate the theoretical point of view, there are contemporary examples. The trade war between USA and China continues to intensify and its effects are transcending geo-economic boundaries. Resultant impacts manifest into regressive trade practices, supply chain disruption, tariff war, rising inflation, uncertain business environment, hindered business growth as well as strained bilateral relations. Some economists opine that the trade war between both economic power houses have benefitted other economies, however, these countries find themselves at the crossroads of geo-political engagements due to their affiliations with the US and China. Taiwan Strait, South China Sea and Red Sea have emerged as hot spots for future geo-political slugfest which has the potential for wider ramifications to include disruption of supply chain, global trade and even flare-up armed conflicts. Amidst these uncertainties and challenges, India is trying to negotiate troubled waters carefully to pursue its ambition to become a global economic and political power.

Current violence levels and armed conflicts are indicating an escalatory trend in fatalities and growing hot spots in almost all continents. While the major conflict hot spots in West Asia, Africa and South East Asia continue to simmer, the Russia-Ukraine and Israel-Hamas conflicts have pushed the world on the brink of a 3rd World War. Civil war conditions and internal conflicts which have plagued the peace and stability in various countries; these have caused humanitarian crises and displacements. As per a study published by Uppsala Conflict Data Program (2023), there have been approximately 2,36,992 fatalities in 2022 due to interstate, intrastate, extra systemic, non-state conflicts, and one-sided violence.[1] According to a report published by Julia Haines, compared to last four years, more people have died in deadly conflicts across the globe in 2023.[2] Amidst global trends of growing violence and turbulence, India continues to combat Pakistan abetted terrorism in J&K, however, there has been a visible decline in terrorist-initiated incidents (TIIs) in the Northern Union Territory (UT). A sudden spurt in violence in Manipur has created turbulence in the State and compounded the security challenges for the security forces. False news and propaganda in the social media domain have opened another front creating security dilemmas for India's security establishment. The impact of the narrative building and social engineering attempts were witnessed during wide spread protests in J&K post elimination of Burhan Wani in 2016. Rampant peddling of fake news and narrative building was also reported during farmer agitation (Aug 20- Dec 21), anti NRC/ CAA agitation held in Shaheen Bagh in 2019, the Manipur crisis in 2023 as well as during Lok Sabha elections of 2024.

Thus, in the realm of growing security challenges, there is a need to map the expanding footprints of technology and the positive and negative influence it may wield on human lives and shaping of world affairs. The imprints of unprecedented technological advancements in the recent past have been observed at multiple levels and in multi-domains. Expanding technological footprint has impacted all walks of life, triggering departure from era of gradual change to rapid transformation in multiple domains. Technological innovations have facilitated people to people connect beyond the immediate neighbourhood and have replaced conventional ways of doing business with e-commerce. The revolution in technological has also challenged the predominance of conventional means in competitions and conflicts; emerging trends indicate application of diverse means in simultaneity to realise objectives in multiple domains. Realising the capabilities of emerging niche technologies i.e., AI, nano technology, robotics, quantum computing etc, various countries have made substantial investments in Research and Development (R&D) so as to gain a stronghold over futuristic technology. In the backdrop of technological innovations, the proliferation of social media has transformed global landscape of business, statecraft, conflicts and social connect. Wide spread penetration of social media has led to shaping the opinion of world population and ushered in a new era of information warfare and social media warfare under the umbrella of 'Hybrid War'; a combination of conventional military tactics with unconventional methods, such as cyber-attacks, economic coercion, and propaganda. The emergence of Hybrid Warfare across the spectrum of conflicts has pronounced the challenges of VUCA (Volatile, Uncertain,

Complex and Ambiguous) environment of competitions and conflicts in foreseeable future. Thus, it is imperative to study the evolving character of warfare and understand the nuances of 'Hybrid Warfare' for development of comprehensive strategies aligned with dynamic threat environment.

Social Media 'A Weapon of Mass Manipulation'

Scenario Building 2030 – Hybrid Threat to India's National Security

Taking a cue from the prevailing security scenario, geo-political competitions and emerging threats to India's national security, a plausible conflict scenario is painted in the backdrop of hybrid threat to set a context to justify the purpose of this study. The situation simulated below is a reflection of current episodes of competition, violence and adverse internal situation, extrapolated for a foreseeable future in the Indian context.

> ➤ Having established its dominance over the 'Global Value Chain' and 'Global Economy', China rapidly consolidates its position as Regional and Global leader in the geo-political arena. Encouraged by support garnered for its political manoeuvres to negotiate peace and conflict termination during Russia-Ukraine and Israel-Hamas conflicts, China embarks on its ambitions plan to become a world leader and establish itself a hegemon. China's geo-economic might and influence over countries in West Asia, Africa, South America and other signatory countries of BRI embolden her to up the ante and challenge USA's dominance in world affairs. This race to secure leadership position at global stage leads to competition and conflicts in Asia also. In its immediate neighbourhood, China continues to feel threatened due to India's phenomenal rise as a strong geo-economic and geo-political power. Its active engagement with QUAD (Quadrilateral Security Dialogue) and other multinational alliances is perceived as a threat to Chinese hegemon.

> ➤ In the immediate neighbourhood, independent Taiwan continue to remain a bone of contention. The successful completion of general election in Taiwan in 2028 and rise of anti-China sentiments amongst the Taiwanese population irks the Chinese Dragon. Resultantly, to assert its dominance and achieve the objective of 'Unification', China exerts its might aggressively to compel Taiwan to concede to its coercive strategy. Her misdemeanours continue

in South China Sea; posing a serious threat to Brunei, Taiwan, Philippines, Vietnam, and Malaysia – each contesting to maintain respective territorial integrity.

- On the other hand, Pakistan, an all-weather ally to China, struggles to wriggle out of financial crises and to keep its democracy falling into the clutches of Islamic extremists. The national leadership fails to deliver stable governance and fulfil the aspirations of its people; resultantly the country slips into a state of chaos and economic depression. To tide over the financial crisis, the political leadership depends upon loans from IMF and China and imposes strict fiscal measures under compulsion from international financial institutions. The sectarian violence is at an all-time high and freedom movement by Baluchistan Liberation Army (BLA) gathers momentum amidst massive crack down by Pakistan's security forces. To divert public attention, political class, ISI (Inter Service Intelligence) and the Army continue to blame India for deteriorating internal situation and exploit social media to shape the perception of own citizens and of the world. Simultaneously, Pakistan government establishment abets terrorist activities in J&K and spread venomous agenda against India to create societal fissures, carries out social engineering to target minorities and attempts to achieve religious colonialism.

- By 2028, China embarks upon aggressive plans to intimidate India resulting in armed clashes along the India-China borders, disputes over China's maritime exploration in Bay of Bengal and Indian Ocean Region (IOR) and growing interference in India's internal issues in North East region and Kashmir. Avoiding risk of a full-scale war and assured destruction, China resorts to hybrid warfare (Three Warfare Strategy) achieve its geo-political and military objectives i.e., to weaken India's position globally, isolate by intimidating the allies and immediate neighbourhood and grab sensitive territory along India's Northern borders. To destabilise the internal environment, China covertly muddles in India's political affairs so as to colour opinion of Indian citizens against the ruling party and undermine people's trust in the government. In collusion with Pakistan, a social media warfare strategy is unleashed to smear the Indian Armed Forces and the government in J&K and NE states, spread regional and caste-based hatred and create societal fissures so as to incite violence. Cohort of Pakistani media, DGISPR and ecosystem of Pakistan sponsored trolls and pseudo accounts flood social media with negative narrative over the implementation of 'Uniform Civil Code and National Population Register'. They also give a negative spin to the apex court's decision on Gyanvapi Mosque and other religious institutes by portraying as an attempt to deny basic rights and religious freedom to minority population. Deep fakes are circulated to advance Pro-Khalistani narrative to provoke the people in certain border states and call for support for Khalistan Movement and Universal Brotherhood. India's amended 'Digital Media Guidelines and Policies' draws criticism from certain international organisation, who portray these policies as attack on freedom of speech and curbs on freedom of media. Alarming increase in cyber-attacks and cyber espionage on Indian industries, financial institutes and critical infrastructure results in substantial recurring financial losses. The deteriorating internal security environment and declining global ratings of security and human rights and uncertain political environment leads to a share market crash, wiping billions of dollars off the market.

- Externally, India faces multiple challenges such as coercive trade practices by Chinese companies and adverse global opinion over internal security situation created by misinformation campaign launched by Chinese and Pakistani hackers. Diplomatically, India is engaged on multiple fronts to maintain its sphere of influence; targeted misinformation campaign paints India as oppressor in J and K and a strong right-wing Hindu country. Amidst the turbulent situation, China mobilised its forces to capture value territory in Eastern Ladakh, the Lipulekh area, and the Doklam and Tawang sectors. To tie down Indian Forces, Pakistan in collusivity with China, launches attacks in J&K Sector to capture dominating heights along Line of Control and seize value real estate in IB sector. The social media is flooded with contradictory narratives about the state of affairs; both sides launch aggressive media warfare to dominate the cognitive space so as to create confusion, discredit the government/ establishment and influence public opinion and decision-makers.

- Rattled by the deteriorating situation along the borders and adverse internal security, financial losses and public anger and distrust, the ruling coalition alliance in centre, which lacked clear majority, comes under tremendous public pressure. Compelled by escalating tension along the borders and mounting internal pressure, Indian government mobilises the armed forces to Western and Northern Borders and deploys the strategic assets in IOR and Bay of Bengal.

> The conflict quickly spirals out of control, as both sides become increasingly reliant on Hybrid strategies to achieve their objectives. The use of social media in the conflict leaves a devastating impact on both countries, as it leads to widespread distrust, division, and violence. The belligerent states (China and Pakistan) ramp up the propaganda and narrative building through SMPs to dominate the information space, propagate exaggerated claims of progress on territorial gains and advance of forces, erode confidence of target population and break the will of strategic leadership and influence their decision making. Indian armed forces give a befitting response to Chinese hostile actions and successfully execute conventional operations to thwart 'Two Front Threat'. India's social media warfare strategy faces stiff competition to dominate critical space in cognitive domain. Aggressive social media campaign by Indian Armed Forces and intelligence agencies unmasks Pakistan's lies and mobilises the people of Pak Occupied Kashmir (Pok) and Baluchistan against the establishment. Astroturfing operations orchestrated by an Indian agency expose exploitative CPEC strategy and turn the Pakistani people against China. A popular people's movement in Xinxiang and Tibet gains traction in social media space and mobilises the minority population for 'call for action' against oppressive policies of Chinese Communist Party. People's movements in China and Pakistan receive a brutal deal from the respective establishments leading to human rights violation, atrocities and violent clashes.

The conflict eventually ends in a stalemate, with neither side able to achieve their objectives. But the damage has been done. The use of social media in this conflict erodes public trust in government institutions, exacerbated social divisions, and made it more difficult to resolve future conflicts peacefully.

Background and Context of Research

The scenario painted above reflects the prevailing trends of conflicts and competitions amongst the state and non-state actors and indicates plausibility of such scenario in the predictable future. Amidst the blurred peace and war scenario, the magnitude and intensity of hard power likely to be unleashed in future interstate and intrastate conflicts would remain unpredictable. During the Russia-Ukraine, Syrian and Israel-Hamas Conflicts, the world has witnessed emergence of a *'New Normal' of violence, destruction and use of new weapons and technology in the contested battle space.* The contesting global powers have exercised resilience to avoid direct involvement in kinetic operations to and prevent escalation. However, the world has been on the brink of a global war during these conflicts. Albeit, these incidents may not have triggered an armed conflict spreading to other regions, but application of other means has been escalated across the spectrum of conflict to gain an edge over the adversaries. The belligerent actors have displayed utter disregard to human rights, collateral damage, sufferings of humans and sovereignty of weaker nations. It appears that violating threshold for violence, circumventing international laws, subjugation of the international organisations and increasing influence of non-state actors/ organisations to determine the world order has become a new norm.

Various studies and think tanks have assessed that future battle space would be extremely complex, multi-dimensional, and non-traditional in both kinetic and non-kinetic form. Based on the study of recent conflicts, it may be deduced that future competitions and conflicts would occur in *'Volatile, Uncertain, Complex and Ambiguous (VUCA) Environment'* encompassing exploitation of myriad instruments of power to wrest control over the battle space and attain competitive edge over the adversaries. The trend analysis also indicates non-linearity of operations with blurring timelines and transcending battle spaces in physical and cognitive domain.[3]

Over the decades nation states have been embroiled in zero-sum military and politico-economic competitions to safeguard respective national interests, address security dilemmas and achieve balance of power. In the predictable scenario, the possibility of armed conflicts appears inevitable, wherein, competitors would leverage plethora of conventional and unconventional 'Means' (kinetic, non-kinetic and non-contact) in new, innovative and radically different 'ways' to achieve the desired 'ends'. The Ukraine-Russia Conflict has shattered the popular hype of superior military technology being capable of achieving asymmetric edge over the adversary and ensuring conflict termination in short duration wars. The world has witnessed involvement of all types of instruments of power and state and non-state actors in Ukraine-Russia Conflict racing to seize physical, cognitive, economical and cyber battle spaces in a hybrid environment. In the Indian context, examples of proxy war in J and K,

Doklam crisis, stand-off in Eastern Ladakh, security situation in Manipur and Assam and internal turbulence in urban centers and economic hubs are indicators of complexities of the evolving scenarios. These incidents have highlighted that the security establishments and government would be contesting overwhelming adversarial forces prosecuting their nefarious designs at multi-levels in kinetic and non-kinetic domains. Thus, the emerging security scenario merits that security forces align their tactics and strategies to changing character of modern warfare i.e., Hybrid Warfare.

Over the past decade, military thinkers and strategists have deliberated upon the concept of 'Hybrid Operations' in great detail. Hybrid warfare/ operations entail an interplay of conventional and unconventional instruments of power and tools of subversion, blended in a synchronized manner to exploit the vulnerabilities of an adversary and achieve synergistic effects. There are two distinct characteristics of hybrid warfare i.e., *obscurity* between war and peace time and *ambiguity* and *non-attributability*. As per Frank Hoffman, hybrid warfare is a theory of military strategy, which employs political warfare and blends conventional warfare, irregular warfare, and cyberwarfare with other influencing methods, such as fake news, diplomacy, lawfare and foreign electoral intervention to influence the outcome of the conflicts.

Hybrid warfare involves the use of a combination of different tools, techniques and tactics, depending upon the specific objectives and context of the conflict. Hybrid warfare strategies are designed to create confusion, degrade legitimacy and trust, promote chaos, and destabilize in such a way that the objective is achieved either through various coercive or manipulative means. Some common tools and tactics of hybrid warfare include information operations, cyber-attacks, political subversion, conventional military actions, use of proxy forces, and economic coercion. Recent trends have revealed social media also being exploited extensively to further the objectives of hybrid wars.

Evidently, owing to its wider access, affordability and ambiguous nature, social media has emerged as an effective tool which has relevance over the entire spectrum of hybrid wars. There is ample contemporary evidences wherein social media has proved to be a powerful tool, used to spread propaganda and disinformation to manipulate public opinion and destabilize societies. Certain global events are 2006 Israel and Hezbollah conflict, Arab Spring Revolution of 2010, Yemen Crisis, 2017 Doklam Standoff, Ukraine Crisis (2013 and 2023) and 2016 US Presidential Election. Thus, it is imperative that in the backdrop of increasing use of hybrid warfare, a holistic study be conducted to assess the potential of social media as an effective tool to manipulate human minds and shape the opinion of target population.

Hypothesis and Problem Statement

Amidst the prevailing hybrid warfare scenario, social media platforms have been extensively exploited by state and non-state actors to further their strategic aims. In the backdrop of rapidly increasing footprints amongst the masses, *social media platforms possess tremendous potential as low-cost option to shape the public opinion, spread ideological colonization and manipulate decision-makers and the target population.* Further, anonymity inherent in social media sources make it a dangerous tool and a serious threat to national security apparatus the world over. To establish the potential of social media warfare staged by the adversarial forces in influencing the outcome of conflicts and competitions, a study of various global events and incidents which have occurred in various parts of India has been carried out. This study would attempt to throw light on certain major cases and observations of subject matter experts to substantiate the above averment.

India has been combatting counter-insurgency and counter terrorism situation in J&K and North Eastern States under constant media glare. There have been numerous attempts by the inimical elements in the international forum to discredit the Indian Armed Forces and to paint a gruesome picture of alleged humanitarian crisis, HR violations and oppression. Since the advent of internet and social media, the occurrence of such smear campaigns and information warfare by the adversarial forces has been alarmingly high. The 2017 border stand-off in Doklam along India–China–Bhutan Trijunction, was a seminal moment for China to test its new information warfare strategy. The strategy combined radio, TV, newspaper, and social media messaging to push China's narrative at home as well as abroad. The stand-off in Doklam was marked by a multi-pronged messaging strategy. The objective was "*to fully integrate the publicity forces of public opinion, radio, TV, newspapers and social media, and carry out a multi-wave and high-density centralised publicity campaign in a fixed period to form favourable public opinion situation to allow for a final victory*" (Tu and Ge, 2018).[4] A similar dynamic played out three years later during the Galwan Crisis of 2020 in Eastern Ladakh, when China's media launched another multi-wave and high-density messaging campaign, which was successful at home, but arguably less so abroad. The Galwan Clash of 15 June 2020, was a bigger challenge for China's messaging. For eight months after the clash, Beijing kept mum over losses suffered in the clash. It was only in February 2021 that China's messaging strategy came into play. According to a Chinese media analyst based in Beijing, one possible reason for the delay may have been a desire to let the public passion in the aftermath of the clash subside.[5] A high-intensity media campaign was launched wherein a documentary about the clash, hosted on the official broadcaster CCTV, YouTube, Facebook, and Twitter platforms, portrayed India as the aggressor. The original documentary (produced presumably with the blessings of the People's Liberation Army) was part of a broader propaganda push that followed China's announcement that it had lost four soldiers in the clash. CGTN aired a subtitled version, titled 'Revealing truth on border clashes with India helps understand events', as part of Beijing's efforts to portray to the world its version of events. This version received 282,000 views.[6] The Chinese handlers attempted to reach out to Indian readers directly through various social media platforms. The social media campaign by the Chinese handlers resulted in Indian government facing a backlash and was questioned by the media and opposition parties about the incident.

As per reports, Pakistan has been involved in spreading disinformation and launching social media warfare against India. The Pakistani ISPR is known to have been running anti India social media campaigns. Citing fake news of HR violation by Indian Security Forces, thousands of handles pretending to be Hindus, incite the Muslim community in J&K and other parts of the country and spread communal hatred.[7] There are reports suggesting Pakistan running social media propaganda against the Indian government using fake Hindu, Christian and Arab identities. Further, security agencies and independent social media users after investigation have revealed that the recent hashtags such as '*#Islamphobia*' in India on Twitter were mostly sourced to bots, trolls and handlers in Pakistan.

During the recent Manipur crisis, narrative building and disinformation campaign on the social media added fuel to the fire. Manipur has seen worse ethnic clashes earlier. From 1992 to 1997, fighting between the Kuki and Naga communities reportedly caused greater loss of life, damage and destruction. However, what sets the recent violence apart is that this armed conflict in India was being fought hard on social media, as well. The narratives spread from each community closely followed the events on the ground, and sometimes provided the first evidence of incidents that later made it into the news. In at least two instances of violence – the first of two Kuki-Zo women being paraded naked, a video of which went viral, and the second of two Meitei students being killed, images of which also went viral – added to the vitriol being spread over social media. In both cases, the situation was aggravated with protests being held in the state. Disinformation campaigns by these social media warriors also reinforced existing hostilities.[8] For instance, in the early part of the conflict, a picture of a woman's body wrapped in plastic was shared widely with a claim that it was the body of a Meitei woman who had been sexually assaulted. Fact-checking websites like BOOM later reported that the body was of a woman killed by her parents in Delhi.[9] A month later, another video claimed that a Christian Kuki woman was assaulted by armed civilians. BOOM later found the video had originated in Myanmar.[10]

Thus, in view of the evident footprints of social media in creating a turbulent internal security situation in India, there is a need to study the relevance of social media in hybrid war scenario, analyse the recent trends and evolve a counter strategy. Considering the above, a plausible statement of problem is defined as under: -

> "Social-media poses a serious challenge to India's national security in hybrid threat scenario? Is India prepared to tackle this potent security threat? What should be India's response strategy to mitigate the threat and leverage social media as an effective tool to achieve its national security objectives?"

Considering the statement of problem enunciated above, the hypothesis for the extant research is as follows: -

> 'In the backdrop of Hybrid Warfare scenario, social media poses a serious challenge to India's national security in hybrid threat scenario? India is yet to formulate a robust strategy to mitigate the security threats posed by social media exploitation by adversarial forces and evolve an action plan to leverage social media to achieve its national security objectives?

Purpose and Objective of the Study

Hybrid warfare has emerged as a complex and dynamic security threat in the digital age, combining both traditional and non-traditional methods to deter National Security objectives. As a potent tool of hybrid warfare, social-media possess potential to manipulate perceptions, opinions, emotions and behaviours of a specific target groups, thereby impairing the target of the attack. In this backdrop, the purpose of this study would be as follows: -

- Discern the relevance of social media in hybrid warfare, with a focus on the role it plays in shaping public opinion, influencing decision-making, and achieving strategic outcomes.
- Recommend the strategy to leverage social media to prosecute hybrid operations to safeguard national interests and address/ create security dilemmas.
- Suggest strategy to execute social media warfare to exploit vulnerabilities of the adversaries/ competitors, seize critical space in cognitive domain, and attain decisive edge.

Significance of Research

The world in the recent past has witnessed threat posed by the social media warfare in multiple domains across the spectrum of conflict. To substantiate the averment and highlight the significance of the research, the study would focus upon global and national incidents related to threats to *national security* encompassing military, politics, economy, legal, information and society.

National Security - Colloquially, 'National Security' is perceived to be a military matter involving use of military means to safeguard the interests of the population/ citizens and the nation state. However, gradually the term has evolved to encompass all military and non-military threats to the interests of the nation. Thus, it is imperative to develop an explicit understanding of the term so as to discern the impact social media may have on national security issues. Various world views about the term are as elucidated below: -

- In scholarly realm, national security is defined as, "*absence of threats to acquired values and subjectively, the absence of fear that such values will be attacked*" (Arnold Wolfers, 1960).[11] As per Samuel Makinda, national security implies the *preservation of a society's values, institutions, rules, and norms.*
- In the backdrop of rapidly transformed global environment and emerging threat scenario, scholars also stress that national security implies the protection of a country from internal and external threats (*discredit military operations, economic crisis, energy crisis, environmental catastrophe, social engineering, political instability and cyber-attacks*) posed by adversarial forces/ actors using military and/ or non-military means.

➢ It may be inferred that prosecution of national security objectives mandate the capability to thwart overt and covert hostile threats (internal and external) orchestrated by state and/ or non-state actors, preserve the core values and sovereignty of the state and furthering national interests.[12]

➢ Nation states have continuously evolved their strategy and focused on capacity building to acquire credible military capability to tackle conventional kinetic threats. However, advent of technology and proliferation of cyber and social media dictates that impetus also needs to be given to develop capability to mitigate threats emanating from information warfare, cyber-attacks and weaponisation of social media. Amidst revolutionised threat environment, the nation states also need to formulate proactive strategy to prosecute social media warfare in concert with conventional/ sub conventional operations to seize the initiative, exploit vulnerabilities of adversaries and aggressively dominate the information sphere.

Impact of Social Media Activism on Military Operations – Amidst overarching digital revolution, the proliferation of social media has had profound influence over the operating environment of security forces. The effects of the social media penetration have been witnessed in information operations, intelligence generation and perception management as well. In the contemporary operating environment, the security forces are compelled to execute their operations under constant media glare. Omni presence of digital technology has facilitated security forces to reach out to the population in conflict zone, influence the local public and opinion shapers and defeat inimical designs of adversarial forces. However, they continue to face the challenges posed by perpetrators of violence and anti-national elements through negative social media campaigns. In the event of civilian casualties in operations, such elements upload edited contents, fabricate the false narrative and fake stories to give a negative spin to incite public anger and mount public pressure to cease ongoing tactical operations. In response, the security forces have to fight a long-drawn battle to do damage control, refute their false allegations and clear the perception of public based on correct facts. In the recent past, adoption of 'Generative AI' and 'Deep Fakes' in cognitive warfare have increased the challenges of military operations and national security manifold. Certain relatable trends of exploitation of social media in influencing the conflicts observed in the recent past are discussed below: -

- The ongoing Russia-Ukraine conflict has become an active ground of deep fake experimentation and execution. In March 2022, a deep fake video of Ukrainian President Volodymyr Zelenskyy asking his troops to surrender went viral. In another incident, a deep fake video of Russian President Vladimir Putin urging his troops to lay down their weapons had gone viral on Twitter (now 'X'). In the absence of credible reporting from the ground, such deep fake videos caused chaos and confusion for citizens on both sides. They also spread confusion and uncertainty around military operations.[13]

- In J&K, social media space has been used by anti-national elements to advance their inimical designs, foment separatism, to recruit local youth as terrorists and spread religious fanatism. As per a study, the slain terrorist Burhan Wani posted numerous videos on YouTube and Facebook to discredit the Indian Security forces, warn local police personnel to desist from participating in operations and urge people to provide intelligence about operations of the armed forces. This tactic led to ratio of local terrorists increasing vis-à-vis foreign fighters, who infiltrated from Pakistan; reportedly more local misguided youth joined terrorists organisations in valley.[14]

- Anti-India propaganda from China and People's Liberation Army (PLA) has been on rise since the Galwan Clash in June 2020. As per reports, China-linked elements used Twitter (now 'X') as a preferred tool to upload misleading reports related to the Galwan clash, aggressively pressing its territorial claims and disputing India's military preparedness. In some cases, their efforts were boosted by the Pakistani Twitter (now 'X") trolls, who amplified this propaganda through their own networks. Most recently, ahead of the third anniversary of the Galwan clash, Chinese handles posted graphic images and videos in an attempt to show the Indian Army in poor light.[15]

- US-based data analytics firm, New Kite Data Labs, recently claimed that a Beijing-based private AI firm, Speech Ocean, which has clients with ties to the People's Liberation Army, has been collecting voice samples from India. The voice samples have been collected primarily from sensitive border regions of Punjab and J&K. The firm adds that locals have been hired to record pre-scripted words, phrases, or conversations, which are then transferred to China-based servers. The exact purpose of this data harvesting remains unknown; however, the possibility of voice samples being used for machine learning to fabricate deep fakes cannot be ruled out.

Social Media and Shaping of Political Actions - Over last few years, the social media platforms have emerged as force multiplier for effective implementation of communication strategy for the government. The digital revolution has facilitated greater reach even in the remotest areas, instantaneous connect with the people and given a voice to convey concerns of marginalised sections. It has also afforded innovative ways to implement and monitor the projects. Many commentators suggest that the internet in general, and social media in particular, plays a key role in amplifying economic, political, and cultural grievances across the globe. Perhaps, digital platforms have gained more importance given to their capability to influence and independently impact politics in both established democracies and autocratic regimes. The apparent role of social media in coordinating protests and giving a voice to the opposition in autocratic regimes created high hopes for the internet and social media as a "Liberation Technology".[16] However, the concerns have also been raised on disruptive use of social media by autocratic regimes for surveillance and propaganda campaign, to manipulate perceptions and distract voters from politics and real problems. Of late, social media has come under serious criticism for the rise of populism, spread of xenophobic ideas, and proliferation of fake news in democracies. Considering the absence of gate keepers to filter the content being shared online, it may not be incorrect to infer that social media has been exploited extensively by governments, non-state actors as well as vigilantes and common public to pursue their agendas. To corroborate the above observations, various political events and social movements, wherein social media played a crucial role are discussed below.

> ➢ Certain peculiar features such as easy access, low barriers to entry, absence of regulation of contents, ambiguity and lack of attributability render these social media platforms a vital instrument for freedom of expression, garnering support for popular causes, to catch attention of wider audiences and initiate social activism. There have been abundant evidences in the recent years, wherein whistleblowers, citizen journalists, NGOs and common citizens have exploited the digital landscape to challenge authorities, expose atrocities and sufferings and demand equality and participation driven by grassroot movements. 'Arab Spring Revolution (2010-

11)' was a seminal political event, wherein the public driven activism on social media platform (predominantly Facebook and YouTube) led to toppling of authoritarian and autocratic regimes, ushered political transformations and compelled policy changes in the MENA (Middle East and North Africa) region. The ripple effect of the event transcended geographical confines, cultural silos and time zones.

- Researchers opine that social media has provided an opportunity to politicians to subvert traditional media outlets and outmanoeuvre the regulation and ethical codes and to launch outreach strategy to engage with the general public directly. Consequent to his loss in 2020 election, Donald Trump used social media platforms to question the legitimacy of the election process and demanded re-election. His online messages gained significant traction, presumably led to an attack on US Capitol on 6 January 2020 by his supporters.

- There have been numerous reports suggesting social media being used for meddling in electoral process of various countries. Alleged Russian influence footprints during 2019 election in USA and general elections of Ukraine in 2014 are testimony to the averment.

- Social movements have had a deep impact on the policies of government as well. It is reported that UK's 'BREXIT' decision was influenced to a great extent by the public emotional outpour in social media.

- *Impact of Social Media on Indian Elections* - 2014 Lok Sabha elections is considered to be a watershed moment in Indian politics. As per a study, Bhatiya Janta Party (BJP) leveraged social media platforms extensively to reach out to voters, especially youth and first-time voters. The elections resulted in landslide victory for BJP in the assembly elections. However, a similar strategy did not give BJP success in Maharashtra elections, presumably as other parties, having realised the potential of social media, also jumping into the fray.[17] The key findings of the study (based on survey done by digital marketing company) conducted by Dr Ambedkar University on impact of social media on general elections are as listed below: -

- Nearly 1/3rd of first-time voters were influenced by political messages on social media platforms. The survey report prepared based on the feedback of 25 lakh participants, revealed that around 15 crore first-time voters received political messages through various social media platforms.

- Political movement on social media was higher in 2019 Lok Sabha elections than in 2014, the report by ADG Online said. "30 per cent of 150 million first-time voters were engaged and influenced through social media platforms; political messages reached out to 50% of first-time voters through social media and rest 20% were aware of the developments in the country," the report said. Social media messages had a greater influence on youth; according to the report, more than 50 per cent voters influenced by social media were less than 25 years of age.

- As per the survey report, around 40% of youth (18-24 years) updated themselves about political developments through at least one social media platform i.e., Facebook, Twitter, Instagram, Share Chat or WhatsApp. Social media helped in amplifying engagement through comments, online interactions, trolls, posts and pictures showing support.

- Almost 50% of voters in 2014 were below 35 years of age and 40% of them were from urban areas. Political parties had been continuously reaching out the rural voters. However, today's youth, whether it is urban or rural, spends their maximum time on social media platforms. Therefore, in future elections, messaging and opinion shaping through SMPs would have greater impact on the decisions of the voters in urban and rural areas.

- Facebook users had a huge impact over the results of the polls in 160 of India's 543 constituencies; primarily due to young voters' profile. As per the report, 50% of population is below 25 years age group and secondly 65 % is below 35 years age group. This age group is either college students or employees in corporate houses (Information Technology (IT) companies, Business Process Outsourcing (BPOs), research centres and entrepreneurs, etc). The tech savvy younger generation relies on mobiles/ laptops and social media sites to keep themselves abreast with the political issues and to acquire or share information.

Influence of Social Media on Economic Matters - The study on impact of social media on markets and economy, a grey area in the past, is now gaining traction. The interconnectedness of social media and markets and influence of social media news in determining market trends and making financial decisions, is an area which requires detailed research. Certain studies having delved upon this issue point out that social media platforms are impacting markets in direct and indirect ways. According to a report, certain social media influencers with their limited knowledge are shaping the opinions of the investors. Influenced by such social media feeds, gullible investors are falling prey to such practices and making their investment decisions without much diligence and research. But a more serious matter is impact of false news spread on social media, which has greater effect on the market causing substantial damage owing to contagion and spillover effect over entire sector. A study suggests that misleading information is an emerging cyber risk and can cause enormous damage, especially to the financial sector and financial markets. In 2013, a fake news of two explosions at the White House caused the SandP500 index to lose more than $130 billion in market capitalisation in a day.[18] The important findings of the study on impact of misleading information are given as under: -

> ➢ The study amplifies that *negative messages elicit negative response and positive messages evoke positive reaction; however, impact of negative reports is greater than the latter*. Further, the information manipulation is achieved either through planting a fabricated messages bereft of truth or publishing an old report out of context pertaining to financial hardships of the targeted firm. The investors fall prey to such tactics leading to wrong decisions, e.g., in 2008, an article first published in 2002 about United Airlines' parent company bankruptcy resurfaced and was mistakenly believed to report a new bankruptcy filing by the same company. On the same day, the stock price of the company plummeted by more than 70% before Nasdaq Stock Exchange halted trading. When the "news" was declared to be false, the price rebounded, but it remained more than 10% below the initial price registered at the commencement of trading.

> ➢ J. Clarke and H. Chen, in their study titled 'Fake news, investor attention, and market reaction' assert that *fake news temporarily impacts stock price returns of small cap firms*.[19] The study also

suggests that financial markets, IT, infrastructure and pharma sectors are relatively more affected due to false news on social media.

➢ Mohamed Al Guindy, a researcher at Carleton University, has coined the relationship between social media and finance as 'Social Internetwork'. In his paper, he reveals that an *average company is connected to 600 other companies*. He asserts that by examining tweets about the most central and prosperous firms, the Social Internetwork (an AI Model) has uncovered that 92% of the economy is connected indirectly. *A single incident in one industry can trigger a ripple effect that spreads across seemingly unrelated sectors*. The negative news about core companies or central to constellation of interconnected networks, creates greater adverse and disproportionate effects to the entire eco-systems. However, any positive development/ news about peripheral companies does not have similar effect on the business of the core companies.

➢ During COVID-19 pandemic, a fake news stating, eating chicken caused COVID-19, has had an overwhelming and extensive impact on India's economy. As a consequence of this news, Indian poultry industry suffered staggering losses of Rupees 1,500-2000 crores a day with prices falling from 200 rupees per kg of chicken to just Rupees 70-60. Based on the predicted significant drop in demand, the drastic action by the farmers saw day-old chicks buried alive to avoid having to continue feeding them. The knock-on ramifications of the huge culling impacted India's maize and soya industries as the poultry industry was the biggest buyer of these crops. The incident of 'fake news' led to disruption of entire supply chain and huge numbers of farmers, small scales retailers, transporters and business getting badly impacted.

➢ A study done by Cybersecurity company CHEQ with the University of Baltimore found that the epidemic of online fake news costs *$78 billion annually of the global economy*. The report also analyses the direct economic cost from false news, it estimates that *fake news has contributed a loss in the stock market value of about $39 billion a year which is 0.05% of stock market values.*[20] Figure 1 below highlights certain incidents wherein fabricated news affected share market and financial impact of prevailing trend of fake news. The study further notes that while financial markets have been dealing with hoaxes, frauds and fake news for decades, technology advances and ubiquity of access to web-based information heightens the risks and costs of fake news by orders of magnitude. According to research of this study, the impact is likely to have a wider issue for smaller firms. Yale School of Management established that deceptive articles on investment websites appear to cause temporarily boost to stock prices, which may have a particular effect for small firms. Mike Paul, president of Reputation Doctor, comments that fake news are like a modern day tech suicide bomber in the world of communication, reputation and branding. It only takes one well-planned success to hurt a lot of people or an organization. Marko Kolanovic global head of macro quantitative and derivatives research, at JP Morgan Chase, points the modus operandi and dangers of fake news. He highlights that, "There are specialized websites that mass produce a mix of real and fake news. Often these outlets will present somewhat credible but distorted coverage of sell-side financial research, mixed with geopolitical news, while tolerating hate speech in their website commentary section. If we add to this an increased number of algorithms that trade based on posts and headlines, the impact on price action and investor psychology can be significant.

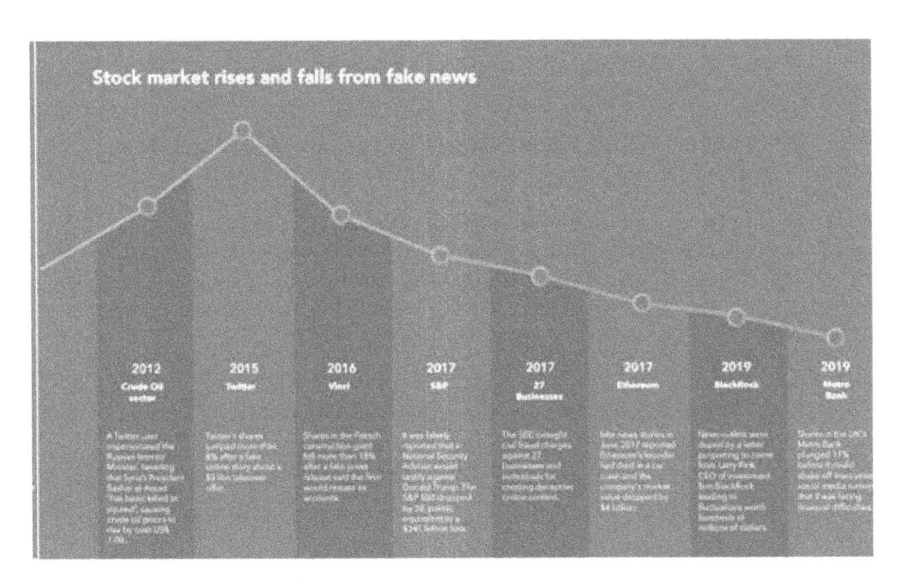

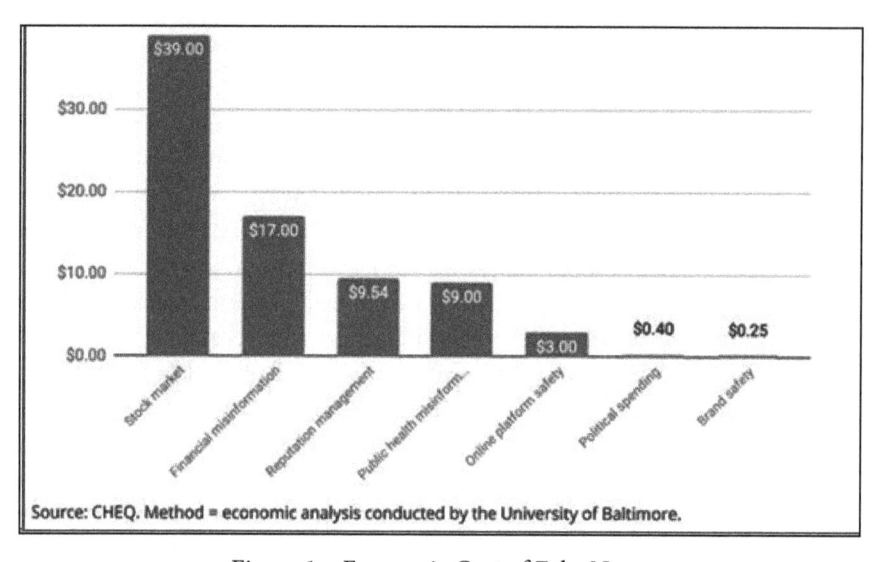

Figure 1 – Economic Cost of Fake News
Source – Study by Cybersecurity company CHEQ, University of Baltimore, priorityconsultants.com

- ➤ The Indian markets have also been subjected to turbulence created by such unverified and questionable speculations and fake news. The report published on Economics Times cautions about the enormity of threat Indian amateur investors are exposed due to social media scams and unregulated financial advice provided through WhatsApp and Telegram groups. According to a report, SEBI had shut down a Telegram channel called *"Bullrun2017"*, purported to specialize in *penny or small-cap stocks*. Group administrators bought shares of small companies, recommended them to their 50,000 or so subscribers, and then sold them for a profit.[21]

- ➤ Another example of effect of disclosure of audit report in media on the business is Hindenburg Report on Adani Group. On 24 January 23, Hindenburg accused the ports-to-renewable energy conglomerate of accounting fraud and stock price manipulation, which forced flagship Adani Enterprises to pull out of a ₹20,000 crore follow-on public offer (FPO) days later. The disclosure of report created panic amongst the investors, eroded their confidence in the company and wiped out $120 billion of shareholder wealth by late February 2023. Later in May 23, following the release of the Supreme Court-led panel's investigation report, Gautam

Adani's net worth soared to $55 billion placing him on 24th rank on Forbes' list of wealthiest people. Adani Group stocks rose over 13%, bringing its flagship company shares up by 159% from their 52-week low hit after Hindenburg's report. The aim of citing the example is to highlight the effect of messaging on shaping market behaviour and not to become jury on the matter.

- Thus, based on the examples cited above, it may be inferred with fair amount of confidence level that fake news, disinformation and manipulation of facts has tremendous potential to cause the harm/ turbulence in the financial markets. Such practices not only impact the market efficiency, but also erode the confidence of domestic and international investors. Lack of strict legal provisions and difficulty in detection and real time monitoring of such incidents have compounded the challenges of the financial markets and economic stability. It is assessed that interconnectedness and interdependence of various sectors can be exploited by actors to cause economic turbulence and financial loss to the target companies/ nations.

Influence on Judiciary and Media - The media and judiciary are regarded as integral components of modern democracies, their coverage and decisions affects the society and functioning of the government at multiple levels. Influence over these two pillars of the democracy is detrimental to a country's long-term interest and erode their credibility. However, at the same time both institutions need to be well aware of the upheavals in the society and to be situationally aware so as to remain just, transparent and unbiased in overall interests of their nation. In the contemporary scenario, there is a growing trend of media trial of the issues having greater impact on the society and government policies. These media trials afford platforms to various opinion shapers to voice their views and even pass unsolicited verdict on various sub-judice matters. But it is observed that contents of such debate, at times devoid of due deliberation and scrutiny, lack fairness and objectivity. The airing of such media trials and publishing of articles online is lopsided, depicting disregard to time sensitivity and is seemingly designed to twist the facts, build a narrative and trigger extreme public reaction so as to influence the judicial proceedings.

- Commenting on such trends, in their article Anurag Bana and Colette Allen observe that the reach of social media presents unprecedented opportunities for judges and lawyers to stay connected with the community. But there are risks and challenges inherent in the use of social media by the judiciary which highlight issues of integrity and ethics. Judges have to be extra vigilant and exercise selective restraint to perform their solemn duty in the 'Temple of Justice'. The study further points to the growing tendency among senior advocates to write articles in national newspapers, which are subsequently shared and commented on via social media, raising doubts about the Supreme Court's efficacy to deal with a particular case. Coincidentally, these articles are published the day the Supreme Court is scheduled to hear a particular case, presented to them by the very author of the article.[22]

- In 2011, International Bar Association Legal Policy and Research Unit (IBA LPRU), carried out a global survey to consider the impact of Online Social Networking (OSN) on the legal profession. 61 bar associations including the Bar Council of India (BCI), from 47 jurisdictions responded. The survey revealed that judges' use of social media raised specific concerns. While only 15% of respondents felt lawyers' use of OSN negatively affected the public image of the profession, 40% responded that judges' use of OSN negatively affected public confidence and undermined judicial independence.

- In October 2019, Justice **Arun Mishra** hearing an appeal against his own judgment, publicly condemned articles he believed to be sponsored by lobby groups. Consequent to a controversial article in social media, he rescued himself as lead judge of a Constitution Bench reviewing his own past judgment on interpretation of Section 24 of the Right to Fair Compensation and Transparency in Land Acquisition, Rehabilitation and Resettlement Act, 2013.[23] There are multiple instances wherein the interested lobbyist/ lawyers have attempted to post their comments and skewed perspective on social media platforms and in media to influence the court proceedings and mount pressure on the hon'ble judges.

Penetration of Social Media in Societal Matters - Social media platforms have provided an avenue to the marginalised sections of the society to voice their opinion, highlight their challenges and demand social justice, equality, and end to deprivation. Owing to huge user base, speed of transmission of messages and affordability, the communication platforms have also been utilised for generating awareness, educate and mobilise the masses for social causes. However, there are examples of social media being used for negative narrative painting, shaping perceptions and exploitation of societal fissures to create animosity and hatred, thus damaging the social fabric of the country. As discovered with movements like #BlackLivesMatter and #MeToo, social media gives opportunity to create online spaces where people come together and find support. Instances such as the 'Arab Spring' and 'Occupy Wall Street' showcased the global effect that can take place through the sharing of ideas online, such as massive gatherings that create unity for a cause.[24] Recently in 2024, pro-Hamas activists leveraged social media platforms to launch campaigns such as '#alleyesonrafah', to shape the global opinion and garner the support for their agenda.

> In the Indian context, the anti-corruption movement led by Anna Hazare in 2011 was largely fuelled by social media and gained support of the citizens for the social movement. Similarly, the digital space was leveraged to create a virtual public sphere to protest against the brutal gang rape of a young woman (Nirbhaya) in Delhi in 2012. The #MeToo movement in India, gained momentum through social media and led to mass mobilisation against sexual harassment at the workplace.

> On the flip side, the might of social media platforms has been manipulated by external state and non-state actors to spread disinformation/ misinformation, fake news and sow seeds of discord and hatred in the community. These strategies by inimical actors are aimed to cloud the cognitive space of target population, colour their perceptions and exploit reinforcing cycles to create 'Echo Chambers'. For example, in the real world of public discourse, the social media was used to mobilise the public for wide spread protest against 'Citizenship Amendment Act (CAA)' in 2019-20 in India. The digital space was also abuzz with substantial chatter and campaigning during Farmer's protest, Shaheen Bagh protests and Manipur Crisis.

In a nut shell, it may be inferred conclusively that Hybrid Warfare has gradually added complexities to the character of the war. This evolving form of warfighting have revealed usage of multiple means by various actors to prosecute war and to escalate the intensity of conflict. Social media has also emerged as an effective tool to influence the contours of the competition and shape the behaviour and attitude of the competitors/adversaries. In the digital realm, advent of AI and deepfakes would pose a serious threat to security of information owing to their potential to impair the rational thinking of the target population and leaders, thus, clogging their decision-making abilities. Therefore, it is imperative to study the world views of scholars about hybrid warfare and interplay of social media is execution of hybrid warfare strategies.

In the backdrop of the findings of chapter 1, in the next chapter, the research would explore the definition and key concepts of 'Hybrid Wars' and its characteristics given by various scholars and think tanks. The aim would be to develop a comprehensive understanding of the concept, identify the role of social media in hybrid wars and discern the trends with the help of case studies.

Chapter 2

Hybrid Warfare and Role of Social Media in Hybrid Operations

> "Hybrid warfare is not a new phenomenon, but the contemporary era has seen a significant increase in its use. It is a form of warfare that combines conventional and unconventional tactics, including cyber-attacks, propaganda, and other forms of information warfare. It is often used by state actors to achieve their objectives without resorting to direct military action. Hybrid warfare is a complex and evolving phenomenon that poses significant challenges to policymakers and military planners alike"[25]
>
> *—Williamson Murray*

Definitions and Broad Concept of Hybrid Warfare

There is no uniform definition of Hybrid Warfare, various scholars and military strategists have presented their world views about the evolving concept which has gained prominence in recent years. There is also a debate whether it's a de-novo concept or re-branding of the war-fighting practiced in history. Notwithstanding the debate and differing opinions about the concept, 'Hybrid War' is a reality which poses a significant challenge to nation states and demands a paradigm shift in the war fighting strategy of the security forces engaged in conflicts in different theatres. To develop a comprehensive understanding of the concept of 'Hybrid Warfare', the study would dwell upon the perspective of strategic thinkers and scholars of Western Countries i.e., USA and EU and Russia, China as well as India.

The term 'Hybrid War', a theory of military strategy, was first proposed by Frank G Hoffman in 2007. In his monograph titled 'Conflicts in 21st Century: The Rise of Hybrid Wars', Hoffman had discussed the emerging threat scenario for the USA and Western Countries in the 21st Century. He averred, 'Hybrid Wars can be conducted by both state and variety of non-state actors. Hybrid Wars incorporate range of different modes of warfare, including conventional capabilities, irregular tactics and formations, terrorist acts including indiscriminate violence and coercion and criminal disorder. These multimodal activities can be conducted by separate units or even by same units, but are generally operationally and tactically directed and coordinated within main battle space to achieve synergistic effects'.[26] The concept was depicted in hierarchical structure of grand strategy, refer figure 2 below. He averred that the concept amalgamates many schools of thought such as: [27]

- *Blurring nature* of conflict and loss of state's *monopoly of violence* from concept of '*4GW*'.

- Concept of *Omni-Dimensionality, Synchrony and Asymmetry* from Chinese theory of '*Unrestricted Warfare*'.

- '*Power of Networks*' from study of John Arquilla and TX Hammes.

- Concept of *synergy of conventional and unconventional capabilities* from theory of 'Compounded Wars'.

- *Growing complexities, disaggregated nature of operational environment and opportunistic nature* of future adversaries from Australian study.

Alluding to American Revolution, French invasion of Spain during Napoleonic era and Vietnam war and drawing an analogy with 'Compounded Wars', he highlighted synergy between regular and irregular forces wherein irregular forces were employed as *distraction or economy of force measure*. The employment of irregular forces lacked fusion and synergy at operational and tactical levels, and were largely employed in separate theatre or adjoining operational areas. He advocates that however, '*in Hybrid Wars, regular and irregular components of forces are blurred in its same battle space and are operationally integrated and tactically infused. The irregular component attempts to become operationally decisive rather than just protract the war, provoke over-reaction or extend the cost of the security for the defender*'. He emphasizes that Hybrid Wars would be fought in complex battle space i.e., '*Contested Zones*', encompassing urban centers and hub of economic activities.[28]

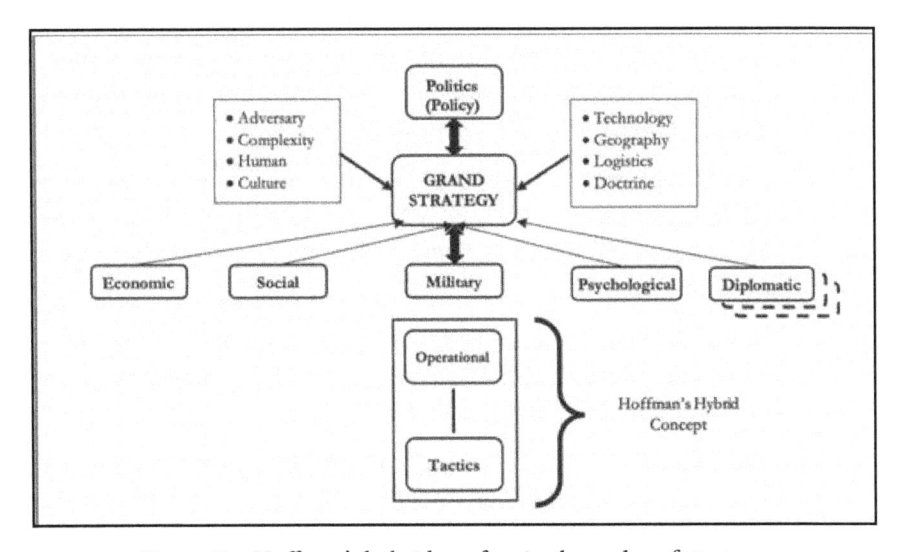

Figure 2 – Hoffman's hybrid warfare in the realm of strategy
Source - https://www.researchgate.net/figure/Hoffmans-hybrid-warfare-in-the-realm-of-strategy_fig3_332219970

In his paper titled *'Hybrid Warfare and Challenges'*, Hoffman emphasizes that hybrid wars blend lethality of state conflict with the fanatical and protracted fervor of irregular warfare. In such conflicts, future adversaries (states, state-sponsored groups, or self-funded actors) will exploit access to modern military capabilities, including encrypted command systems, man-portable air-to-surface missiles, and other modern lethal systems, as well as, promote protracted insurgencies that employ ambushes, improvised explosive devices (IEDs), and coercive assassinations. This could include states blending high-tech capabilities such as anti-satellite weapons with terrorism and cyber warfare directed against financial targets.

A study conducted by Multinational Capability Development Campaign (MCDC) 2017-18 provides clarity on 'Hybrid War Concept' and brings out a conceptual guidance and an analytical framework to study the evolving war fighting concept. MCDC is an initiative led by United States Joint Staff J-7 that partners with 23 countries and international organizations (IGO) designed to develop and assess non materiel (non-weaponry) force development solution. The study describes, 'hybrid warfare as the *synchronized use of multiple instruments of power tailored to specific vulnerabilities across the full spectrum of societal functions to achieve synergistic effects*'.[29] The study emphasizes that: -

- ➤ The uniqueness of hybrid warfare lies in the ability of an actor (state and non-state) to synchronize multiple instruments of power simultaneously and intentionally *exploit creativity, ambiguity, non-linearity and the cognitive elements of warfare*.

- ➤ Hybrid warfare is tailored to *remain below obvious detection and response thresholds*, and often bank on the *speed, volume and ubiquity of digital technology* that characterises the present information age.

- ➤ Hybrid warfare is designed to *exploit national vulnerabilities* across the *political, military, economic, social, informational and infrastructure* (PMESII) spectrum.

- ➤ Hybrid warfare uses coordinated *military, political, economic, civilian and informational (MPECI) instruments of power* that extend far beyond the military realm.

- ➤ Hybrid warfare is *asymmetric and uses multiple instruments of power along a horizontal and vertical axes*, and to varying degrees shares an increased emphasis on creativity, ambiguity, and the cognitive elements of war. This sets hybrid warfare apart from an attrition-based approach to warfare, where one matches the strength of the other, either qualitatively or quantitatively, to degrade the opponent's capabilities.

To amplify its findings, the study explains the concept with the help of figure shown below. The hybrid warfare actor can synchronize diverse instruments of national power (i.e., MPECI) vertically/ horizontally or both ways to escalate a series of specific activities so as to create desirable effects. It can be understood that the hybrid warfare actor can either vertically escalate by increasing the intensity of one or many of the instruments of power, and/or horizontally 'escalate' through synchronizing multiple instruments of power to create effects greater than through vertical escalation alone. The different instruments of power are used in multiple dimensions and on multiple levels simultaneously in a synchronized fashion, refer Figure 3. The innovative approach affords the hybrid warfare actor to exploit the different MPECI means to create synchronized attack packages (SAPs) tailored to strike the perceived vulnerabilities of the target system. The instruments of power used will depend on the capabilities of the hybrid warfare actor, perceived vulnerabilities of its opponent, political goals and planned ways to achieve those goals. The character of hybrid warfare would depend on the context of the conflict.

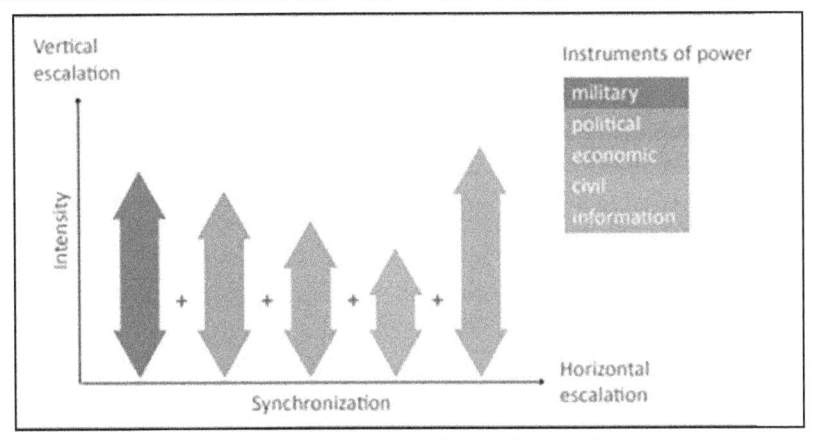

Figure 3 - Hybrid War Escalation (MPECI)
Source - https://www.researchgate.net/figure/Hybrid-War-Escalation-MPECI_fig2_373418977

In his article titled 'Hybrid Threat Concept: Contemporary War, Military Planning and the Advent of Unrestricted Operational Art', Brian P. Fleming suggests that *Hybrid threats translate strategic intent into unrestricted distributed operations*, representing the evolution of operational art and a potential paradigm shift as a doctrinal and organizational Revolution in Military Affairs (RMA).[30] The US Joint Forces Command defines hybrid threat as "any adversary that *simultaneously* and *adaptively* employs a tailored *mix of conventional, irregular, terrorism and criminal* means or activities in the *operational battle space*. Rather than a single entity, a hybrid threat or challenger may be a *combination of state and nonstate actors*.

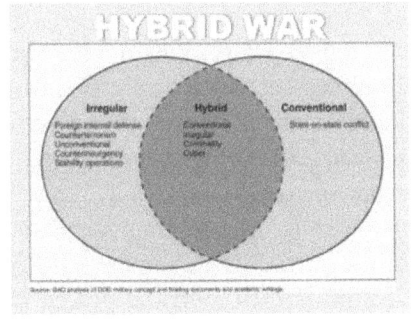

Figure 4 – Instruments of Hybrid Warfare
Source - https://www.researchgate.net/figure/Instruments-of-Hybrid-Warfare-Sehgal-2018_fig1_350711970, https://fabiusmaximus.com/2015/02/02/4gw-hybrid-warfare-innovation-77902/

NATO views, 'hybrid war as a very broad term thus rather than considering it as new type of war. Based on contextual complexity associated with current conflicts, this evolving concept of competition has been termed as 'Hybrid Threat' instead of hybrid war.[31] NATO describes 'Hybrid Threat' actors as, *'adversaries with ability to simultaneously employ conventional and non-conventional means adaptively in pursuit of their objectives'*.[32]

EU has defined the term as, 'Hybrid warfare can be more easily characterized than defined as a centrally designed and controlled use of various *covert and overt tactics*, enacted by *military and/or non-military means*, ranging from *intelligence and cyber operations* through economic pressure to the use of conventional forces. By employing hybrid tactics, the attacker seeks to undermine and destabilize an opponent by applying both coercive and subversive methods. The latter can include various forms of sabotage, disruption of communications and other services, including energy supplies. The aggressor may work through or by empowering proxy insurgent groups, or disguising state-to-state aggression behind the mantle of a 'humanitarian intervention'. Massive *disinformation campaigns designed to control the narrative are an important element of a hybrid campaign.* All this is done with the *objective of achieving political influence, even dominance over a country in support of an overall strategy.*'[33]

Mason Clark of Institute for Study of War (ISW), in his monograph titled 'Russian Hybrid Warfare' has studied the Russian philosophy of the evolving war fighting strategy. He avers that in Russian perspective, Hybrid war is a *whole-of-government activity, up to and including the use of conventional military forces*. He advocates that hybrid war is a strategic-level effort to shape the governance and geostrategic orientation of a target state wherein all efforts, including use of conventional military forces in regional conflicts, are subordinate to an information campaign.[34] He argues that Russian analysts frame the objective of a hybrid war as gaining the ability to determine the long-term governance and strategic orientation of a target state. In the Russian view, victorious states or coalitions in hybrid wars successfully impose their worldview, values, interests, and understanding of the 'fair' distribution of resources on a target state. Victorious states or coalitions then gain the power, and the right, to determine a country's future.[35] To support his findings, Mason has captured the world view of various prominent scholars on hybrid war. Important ones are mentioned below: -

- ➤ Senior Combined Arms Academy researcher Valery Kiselev asserts, *hybrid wars aim to fragment states and change their governments* as means to the end of *shaping a target state's orientation.*[36]

- ➤ The Russian military considers determining the *governance of a target state* a *political objective,* while the *broader objective* of a hybrid war—*gaining control* over the *fundamental worldview and orientation of a state*—is an information objective, requiring hybrid wars to, therefore, centre on information campaigns.[37]

- ➤ Russian analysts believe that hybrid wars are almost uniformly lengthy conflicts, as aggressors use a combination of *"crushing and starving"* to undermine the opponent, targeting both their resource base and political will.[38] He argues that these teachings find familiarities with approach of Russia's operations in Ukraine and Crimea.

Nils Peterson of ISW has analysed Chinese view point on Hybrid Warfare in his monograph titled 'The Chinese Communist Party's Theory of Hybrid Warfare'. According to his findings, Chinese Communist Party (CCP) military theorists predominantly view that prosecution of 'hybrid warfare' entails deployment of all aspects of physical and non-physical state power by nation state, including civil society, to indirectly confront an adversary.[39] The military theorist Gao Wei captured breadth of this concept when he provided CCP's first precise definition of hybrid warfare in a state-sanctioned Ministry of National Defense-affiliated press outlet in 2020. Gao Wei stated that: -

> "Hybrid warfare is 'a unified and coordinated act of war that is conducted at the *strategic level,* employing *political* (public opinion, diplomacy, law, etc.), *economic* (trade war, energy war, etc.), *military* (intelligence warfare, electronic warfare, special operations), and other such means'.[40]

Citing Han Aiyong, researcher at Central Party School's International Strategy Research Institute, Nils Peterson comments that in Chinese Schools of thought, goal of hybrid warfare is *destabilizing great powers along their peripheries* without directly targeting the great powers. *A hybrid war does not have to conquer territory but wins over the populace, slowly degrading surrounding security environment* of a great power. As per an article published on official PLA website, traditional military force forms the backbone of hybrid warfare even though large-scale battles are not the main avenue of competition.[41] Irregular units and fifth-column subversion of an enemy society mutually reinforce non-kinetic means to wage war.[42] The military section of the CCP media outlet People's Daily also wrote how non-kinetic means such as economic, diplomatic, cognitive, legal, cyber, and public opinion intertwine with kinetic activity to wage hybrid war. These articles demonstrate that the CCP's much-publicized *"Three Warfare" (public opinion, psychological, and legal warfare)* are means to conduct hybrid warfare.[43]

Benjamin David Baker in his article 'Hybrid Warfare with Chinese Characteristics', has shed light on Hybrid Warfare practiced in Chinese War Fighting concept. He avers that Sun Tzu's in his book 'The Art of War', stressed upon deception and intelligence, mixed use of regular and irregular troops, and emphasised on defeating the enemy's will to fight. To substantiate his observations, he sheds light on trends of Chinese Operational approach throughout the history as well as in contemporary times. Throughout China's history, elements of hybrid warfare have often been crucial components of its conflicts with its neighbours such as Mangolia. The amplification of Chinese strategy is as follows:-

> Imperial Chinese rulers often dealt with their 'barbarian' neighbours by following a recipe based on the *'four methods approach'*. Firstly, foreigners should be kept divided by 'using barbarian to fight barbarians'. This would entail using barbarian mercenaries and strategic alliances to ensure division among China's nomadic neighbours. Contemporary analogy would be *'diplomatic warfare'*; neutralising unfriendly states through public diplomacy, support for local insurgencies and pressure in international organizations. Secondly, if this failed, bribes and tribute would be presented to foreign leaders in order to dissuade them from attacking China. Current equivalent would be granting of lucrative trade and aid deals; a sort of *economic warfare combined with a 'soft power' approach*. Thirdly, China would *build fortifications* in order to deter outside attack. Finally, if all else failed, *military expeditions* would be deployed.

> Basics of this approach survived the fall of the Qing Dynasty. Perhaps the most famous practitioner of hybrid warfare is Chinese Communist Party. Although CCP and Mao Zedong are most famous for successfully using a combination of conventional and irregular troops to defeat the Nationalists under Chiang Kai-shek, CCP's real secret weapon was their mastery of propaganda, diplomacy, and information warfare. As Russia's annexation of

Crimea shows, these are some of the most effective tools in a hybrid warfare practitioner's arsenal, often more effective than conventional military superiority. By persuading the United States of the CCP's legitimacy among the Chinese people as well as its detachment from the Soviet Union, Mao was able to eventually defeat Chiang and exercise control over the mainland.

> ➤ The CCP today has not forgotten China's long tradition of hybrid warfare. The current pacification strategies in Xinjiang and Tibet employ many policies which are familiar to both students of Sun Tzu and Gerasimov. The government's propaganda, information, and cyberwar campaigns, coupled with use of irregular, local troops (i.e., Xinjiang Production and Construction Corps) and, as a last resort, conventional police and military units, represent a form of Hybrid Warfare with roots going back 2,500 years.[44]

The Indian armed forces are combatting externally abetted, hostile state sponsored insurgency and terrorism situation in J&K and North Eastern States. The trans-border and multi-domain collusive threat posed by regular and irregular forces to India's national security has explicit resemblance with hybrid threat scenario. Further, growing influence of ISIS, IM and SIMI network and exploitation of widening societal divide by hostile actors have compounded the complexities of security conundrum. Thus, it would not be an exaggeration to state that Indian security forces are operating in VUCA environment and increasingly exposed to challenges related to emerging hybrid war scenario. The security establishment, policy makers and think tanks have acknowledged the heightened threat situation and brain stormed to evolve an effective response strategy. The current doctrine and strategy framework of security forces are testimony to growing consciousness of state towards complex security scenario. The Indian Army's Land Warfare Doctrine 2018 exemplifies the changing character of future conflict scenario; "Future conflicts will be characterized by operating in a zone of ambiguity where nations are neither at peace nor at war - a 'Grey Zone' which makes our task more complex. Wars will be Hybrid in nature, a blend of conventional and unconventional, with the focus increasingly shifting to multi domain warfare varying from non-contact to contact warfare."

Characteristics of Hybrid Warfare

It is apparent that there is no unanimity over the definition of 'Hybrid Wars'; the concept is still debated in scholarly circles. Various scholars advocate that 'Hybrid Wars' are synonymous with 'Grey Zone' concept. The debate may settle in the foreseeable future, with scholars and strategists arriving at a consensus on this evolving warfighting concept. Notwithstanding the debate, footprints of 'Hybrid War' are visible in various ongoing conflicts across the globe, thus the relevance of the concept. However, based on the analysis of concepts and definition of Hybrid War proposed by Western, Russian and Chinese scholars, certain deduction can be drawn to list out plausible characteristics.

Combining world views of academicians and military strategists, it can be summarized that *Hybrid Wars entail unleashing all instruments of national power to simultaneously engage targets in physical, virtual, and cognitive battlefields and gradually escalate the conflict below the response thresholds. Under the ambit of strategic level efforts, it involves state and/ or non-state actors contesting in same operational and tactical battle fields employing a mix of conventional and irregular methods, such as professional soldiers, terrorists, guerrilla fighters, and criminal activities.* Lt General Ben Hodges (Retd) as commander of U.S. Army Europe contingent (2014-2017) in Wiesbaden, Germany was responsible for more than 30,000 U.S. soldiers and regularly exercised alongside NATO forces against conventional and hybrid threats. In interview to Center for European Policy Analysis, he shared his perspective about Hybrid Warfare. He argues that '*Hybrid warfare is the blending of conventional warfare, irregular warfare, and use of other capabilities such as cyber, disinformation, money, and corruption in order to achieve a political outcome that is always backed up by the threat or use of conventional weapons*'.

The plausible scenario for application of means of hybrid warfare across the spectrum of conflict is depicted at Figure 5 below. The diagram illustrates that players of hybrid warfare relentlessly pursue their goals in peace and war scenarios by deploying irregular tactics to leverage non-conventional and conventional means. For instance, psychological operations, social engineering and political influence are resorted to demoralise and destabilize target nation(s). Propensity to use these means as component of main effort may be dominant during peace or pre-war scenario, with escalation of conflict and deteriorating situation other relatively more aggressive means may be deployed. However, it does not imply that psychological operations, social engineering and political influence would no longer be effective during war. In fact, these efforts would work as force multiplier in tandem with conventional kinetic operations, coercive diplomacy and many other means to achieve strategic goals.

Means of Hybrid Warfare

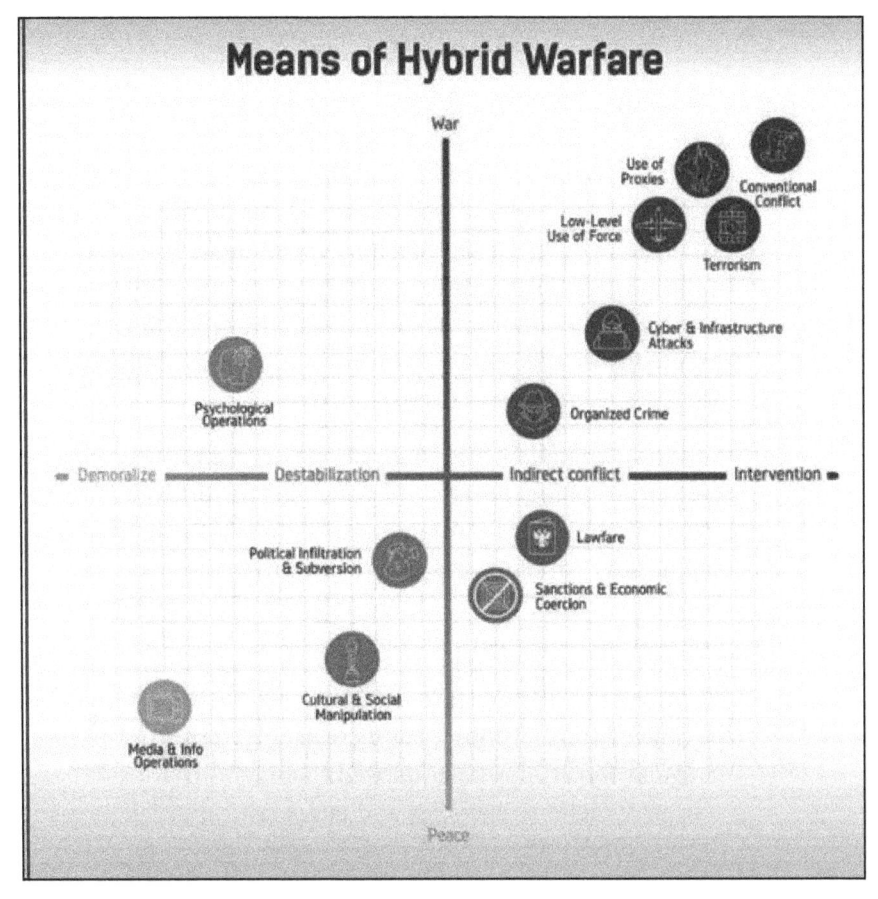

Figure 5 – Likely application of means of hybrid warfare across
the spectrum of conflict
Source - https://cepa.org/article/lt-gen-ben-hodges-on-the-future-of-hybrid-warfare/Hybrid Warfare Escalation Matrix

A flexible and quick response strategy is adopted to respond to the changing situations. The kinetic force may include conventional weapons as well as advanced weapons systems and other disruptive technologies. Non-kinetic means may involve extensive use of cyber and social media to spread mass communication for propaganda and create confusion and influence the Decision Makers.

The important characteristics of hybrid war may include *synergy, ambiguity, asymmetry, disruptive innovation, and battle over psychology.* [45]

- ➤ *Synergy* refers to use of various *MPECI* (Military, Political, Economic, Civil and Informational) spectrums to manipulate concentration of hybrid warfare. The aim of hybrid war is to exploit critical vulnerabilities of adversary to attain a competitive edge.

- Capitalising on own inherent capabilities and strengths and exploiting vulnerabilities of the adversaries, state actors may leverage economical and financial strategies to cause economic instability, affect social welfare and create internal turbulence. The state actors can also make large investments in strategically important projects, niche technology and rare minerals to dominate the international market and consolidate their hegemony as well as deny these technologies/ commodities to adversary or make it cost prohibitive.

- Political, diplomatic and international legal pressures may be exerted to gain a position of advantage in different forums and international organisations so as to garner international support to own cause and isolate the adversaries. The strategy may also be used to ban/ impose sanction on the belligerent non-state actors as per international laws.

- Regular and irregular forces may be deployed in synergy to tie down adversary's forces and create/ exploit vulnerabilities. Irregular forces may be employed to foment insurgency, take subversive actions, sabotage and target critical installations of the target country.

➤ *Ambiguity* explains the blurred periphery between peace and war. Although peace and war are opposite phenomenon but hybrid warfare has made this distinction vague through use of such techniques, tactics and strategies that defy categorisation between the two terminologies.[46] Through intensified use of AI technologies and spreading propaganda on social media, civilians also become warfighters in disguise.

➤ *Asymmetry* is the feature of hybrid warfare which discusses that capacity of state and non-state actors is unequal. State actors are more equipped with advanced training skills and high-end technological weapons as compared to non-state actors. However, state actors are duty-bound and confined by law and war ethics thus usually not able to launch counterattacks while ignoring the legal norms. On other hand, non-state actors use violent extremist ideologies, criminal and illegal means to launch terrorist attacks and achieve their objectives. The argument may not be sacrosanct; ongoing Russia-Ukraine conflict and Israel-Hamas war point towards increasing tendency of state actors to operate outside the purview of international laws and leverage all means (legal or illegal) to decimate the adversary and seize decisive edge.

> *Disruptive innovation* involves actions at operational and tactical levels to achieve strategic objectives. This is done by state actors through disinformation campaigns in cyber domain and media, mobilization of non-attributable forces, and manipulating opinion of the public especially social media users. This disruptive innovation can be exploited either to foster cooperation or exacerbate tensions amongst the nation states. The strategy necessitates strategic directions, unified approach and application of diverse means through out conflict continuum.

- Non-state actors use this characteristic by repetitive use of terrorist attacks, bombings, using advanced commercial technology and amplified levels of military sophistication i.e. UAVs (Unmanned Aerial Vehicles), command and control system, and secure communication.[47]

- The objective is to achieve a degree of internal instability that again would negatively influence the management of the conflict. Propaganda, destabilizing impact of terrorism, and creating insecurity through organized crime cause destabilisation, heightening of ethnic, religious, or social tensions.[48]

> *Battle over psychology* involves target population including the conflict zone population, home front population and the international community.[49] Both state and non-state actors use such technologies and strategies to win this battle by presenting their loyalty, ideologies and agendas to the target population. The non-state actors use propaganda and disinformation campaigns innovatively through wide range of social media and other platforms. Conversely, state actors tend to threaten but economize the military equipment usage to create psychological pressure on the target population.

Hybrid War v/s Grey Zone

While the study navigates towards exploring the role of social media in Hybrid Wars, however, to ascertain areas of convergence and divergence, it is pertinent to touch upon concept of 'Grey Zone' which has increasingly gained attention of military strategists and scholars worldwide.

- As per subject matter experts, *'Grey Zone'* refers to *'Operational and Conceptual Space'* between peace and war wherein State and Non-State actors contest to occupy the critical space. The competing forces exploit coercive state craft actions to prosecute operations below the threshold of full-fledged war and avoid legitimate conventional conflict.

- Conversely, 'Hybrid Wars' employs political warfare and blends conventional warfare, irregular methods and cyber warfare coupled with diplomacy, lawfare and economical influence to shape the behavior of the adversary. All *instruments of national power are unleashed simultaneously across the spectrum of conflict with unified strategy.* The Hybrid War is executed in Grey Zone.

- Grey Zone campaigns involve an *incremental application* of vectors of CNP (Comprehensive National Power) to achieve desired results without triggering a decisive military response.[50] Grey Zone Warfare can be segregated from other categories of conflict. *Hybrid Warfare*, in Frank Hoffman's concept, is a form of conflict in which unconventional types are mixed with traditional *conventional warfare. Grey zone competition falls into the space of measures short of armed conflict. It can involve coercion and some minimal violence but is generally non-kinetic and non-contact in character.* Despite conceptual overlap of 'Grey Zone' and 'Hybrid Warfare', they are surely not synonymous. Hybrid Warfare is combined use of conventional and unconventional tactics that do cross the line of warfare. Some of the hybrid tactics used, such as disinformation, may be in the grey zone. *Grey zone conflict is only the tactics that does not cross the line of state-level aggression.* Some academia opines that hybrid warfare is focused on events at the tactical level, while the grey zone encompasses the long-term strategic considerations of C5 continuum.

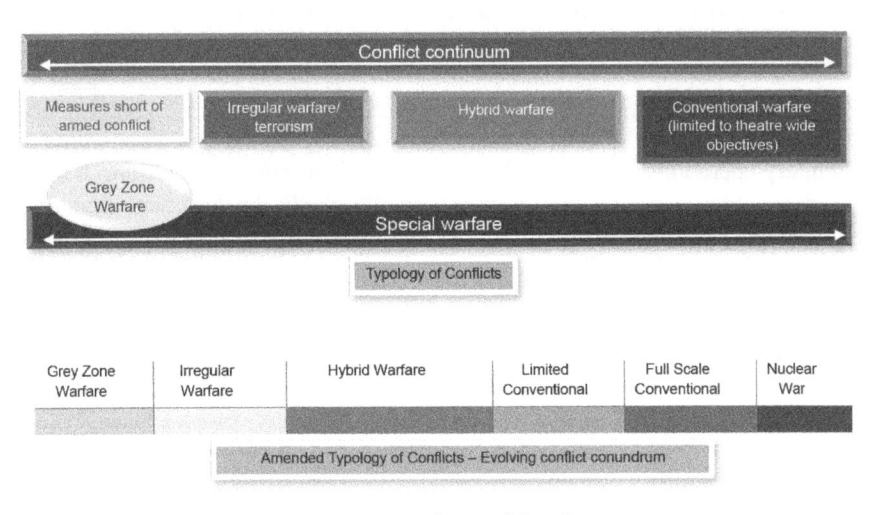

Figure 6 – Typology of Conflicts

David Carment and Dani Belo advocate that grey-zone conflict may incorporate conventional and non-conventional techniques or rely entirely on non-conventional tactics. *Complete reliance on unconventional tools is likely to be less effective at fully and rapidly compelling relatively strong opponent(s) into specific avenues of desired action.* Thus, in the event of unconventional techniques perceived to be insufficient to achieve a desired outcome, the *states engaged in grey-zone conflicts are likely to use hybrid techniques and relatively greater conventional resources.* Incorporation of conventional forces against an opponent would be more likely in cases of asymmetric conflict in which the cost of applying conventional techniques against a weaker opponent is much lower. However, in cases where opponents are in a symmetric conflict, states are likely to rely heavily on unconventional tools and covert operations.[51] The comparative analysis presented by both, in the event of predominance of asymmetry, is as tabulated below: -

Characteristics	Grey-Zone Conflict	Hybrid Warfare
Level	Tactical, operational, strategic	Tactical and operational
Use of conventional military operations	Used alongside non-conventional operations	Used alongside non-conventional operations. Usually, the dominant element
Use of non-conventional military operations	May be used standalone or alongside conventional operations	Used alongside conventional operations as auxiliary tactics
Protracted engagement	One of the dominant characteristics	May be protracted or short
Global and/or regional revisionist ambitions	One of the dominant characteristics	Out of scope as the concept pertains to operational and tactical levels
Symmetry between opponents	Used under both symmetric and asymmetric conditions	Largely used under asymmetric conditions

Table 1 – Characteristics of Grey Zone and Hybrid Warfare
Source - War's Future: The Risks and Rewards of Grey-Zone Conflict and Hybrid Warfare - Canadian Global Affairs Institute (cgai.ca)

Both argue that need to exploit hybrid warfare may emerge when military decision-makers are able to largely circumvent weak international legal regimes governing unconventional warfare tactics. Cyber-warfare, for example, which both democratic and authoritarian states use, has been a grey area for international law. Cyber-operations can seldom be considered an armed attack that warrants an immediate military response by the target as deaths and infrastructure destruction are rarely immediate, reliably measurable or directly attributable to state actors.

To a large extent, the findings of these studies resonate with global view point on Grey Zone and Hybrid War concepts. However, it is assessed that these concepts of war fighting are rapidly evolving with unfolding trends of competitions and changes in the character of war and conflicts. Contrary to viewpoints endorsed by studies mentioned above, it is argued that Grey Zone and Hybrid War are both orchestrated at strategic levels instead of notion suggesting hybrid concept being pitched at operational levels and below. This point view is substantiated by the following observations: -

- The discussion on applicability of Hybrid Warfare at strategic/ operational level should not be driven by conservative thought process as the operations are non-linear and conducted in multiple domains in simultaneity. The application of force and execution of operations is not confined to clearly distinguishable bins of military hierarchy, rather they transcend to multiple levels and multiple domains. It is not the size of military force (corps/ divisional level) applied in the contested zones which should define the level, but wide array of instruments of power (DIME construct), effects and end state should be the governing factors. It is emphasised that in contemporary scenario, the hybrid wars have been orchestrated collusively by state and non-state actors at strategic levels and the conflicts have led to far reaching effects.

- The Russia-Ukraine Conflict and Israel-Hamas Conflict explicitly demonstrate that ongoing hybrid conflict are fought to achieve long term strategic goals such as subverting political will, forcing regime change, shaping perceptions of target population and triggering social engineering in target nation states. The effects of ongoing conflict are transcending tactical and operational battle fields and altering the regional balance of power.

- Further, multi-layered application of instruments of national power i.e., *MPECI* necessitates planning and coordination at strategic levels. The conduct of such campaigns mandates strategic direction, unified goal and unity of efforts to terminate the conflict(s) in concert with overall strategic objectives.

- It creates long term implications for national security and may even upset the regional stability. The footprints of multi order effects over multiple domains are suggestive of hybrid war strategies being conceived at apex levels and executed in simultaneity in all/ more than one level/ domain of the conflict.

- The counter measures and response strategies against hybrid threat are also planned and coordinated at strategic levels involving deployment of myriad means across the spectrum of conflict.

Role of Social Media in Hybrid Wars

With the proliferation of internet and world wide web, vast network coverage, greater access, affordable services and cheap smartphones, the number of internet users have increased exponentially across the globe; the internet has penetrated users of all age groups and strata. Consequently, social media platforms thriving on growth of internet, have witnessed a substantial growth both in terms of number of platforms and variety of services provided as well as quantum of users. Resultantly, social media platforms have emerged as reckoning force capable of spreading information instantly to large population across geographical borders and influencing minds of the people. Thus, it is important to ascertain growing user base of internet and social media users globally, and in India in particular. It is also important to discern the emerging trends of social media usage so as to gauge its global reach and potential to influence the cognitive space of world population.

Growing Internet Footprint. As per a report published by Statista, as of October 2023, there were *5.3 billion internet users worldwide which accounts for 65.7% of global population.* Out of these internet users, *4.95 billion or 61.4 % of world's population, were social media users.*[52] In Indian context also, internet has strong users base which is expanding its footprints rapidly. As per reports, in 2023, India had over 1.2 billion internet users across the country. This figure is projected to grow over 1.6 billion users by 2050. The assessment of social media and internet proliferation predicts future potential of digital platforms in generating situational awareness amongst the users and controlling their cognitive space.

Around 20 years back, the phenomenon of 'Social Media Warfare' was initially coined as *'NETWAR'.* Unlike cyber warfare, it was not intended to focus on the attack on IT or communication systems. In fact, the idea of network warfare was conceived to orchestrate *deliberate manipulation of perceptions of target population/ institution to cause damage to specific target entity.* This concept appears to be inherent in trends of conflicts in the information age. It is stated that in digital age, blood no longer needs to be shed to eliminate a competitor and win a war. In fact information itself becomes the most powerful and low cost weapon that can be used by state, companies, small groups and individuals alike.[53]

In the contemporary era, the concept of 'NETWAR' is no longer fiction, but rather a reality. Various actors have internalised the core concept of network warfare and increasingly rely on using manipulation tactics rather than physical attacks to drive through their agenda. In the realm of hybrid warfare unleashed in contested battle space between Russia-Ukraine and Israel-Hamas and the prevailing security situation in J and K and North Eastern states of India, the concept of 'NETWAR' or 'Social Media Warfare' appears relatable, undeniable reality and a viable tool to gain and maintain a competent edge over adversaries/ competitors. It has been emphasised in the previous chapter that operations within the framework of hybrid warfare are carried out undercover and without an official declaration of war. Covert physical attacks, cyber-attacks, communicative and psychological tactics such as propaganda and disinformation are used throughout the conflict-even well before the commencement of hostilities as well as the post-conflict resolution stage.

In overall concept of Hybrid Warfare, social media is used as a weapon to cause lasting damage to certain actors such as governments or institutions and build a narrative to shape opinion. Various micro-targeting strategies and tactics as well as technological means (social bots) are exploited to push through a political, economic, social or cultural agenda to manipulate perceptions, opinions, emotions and behaviours of the target group. The range of participants of hybrid warfare is diverse, their modus operandi is unpredictable and terminal objectives lies in varied domains aligned to secure campaign goals.

Thomas Elkjer Nissen has illustrated the effects and activities undertaken through weaponised social media space, refer Figure 7 below. The diagram highlights potential role social media can play to augment effectiveness of wide range of operations viz., targeting, intelligence collection (Social-media listening and intelligence gathering), shaping of opinion and dominating information space and assist in decision making by leadership. The flow chart also depicts mutual dependence and complementarity of role of social media in weaponised information space. For example, targeting operations would directly and indirectly aid in intelligence collection (through social media listening and social media intelligence operations) as well as influencing target audience and shaping operations.

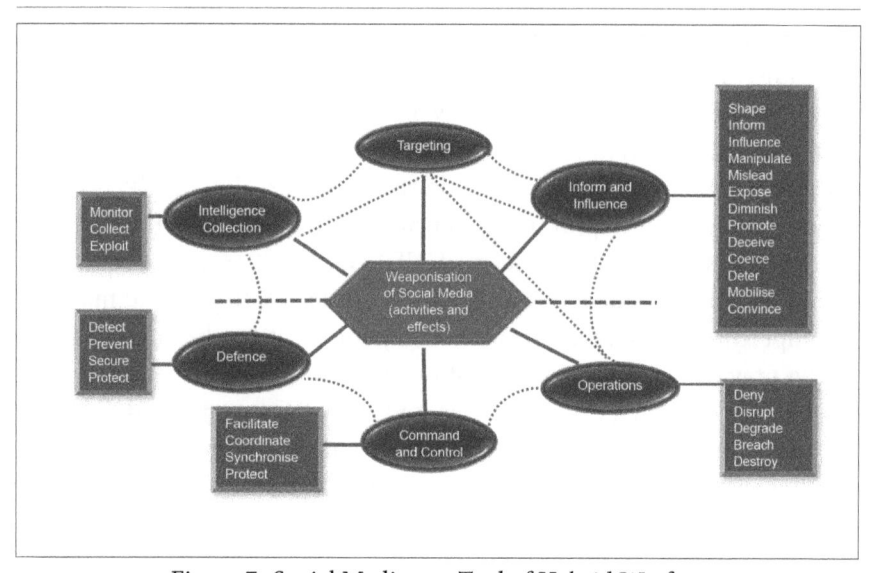

Figure 7- Social Media as a Tool of Hybrid Warfare
Source – Thomas Elkjer Nissen, Social media as tool of Hybrid Warfare, NATO Strategic Communications Centre of Excellence, Riga, Jul 16, pg 11.

Typology of Prominent Actors/ Players in Social Media Slugfest. Despite cognitive dissonance amongst scholars and military strategists over the very concept of 'Hybrid Warfare', there is still certain level of consensus over relevance and broad contours of this evolving concept of warfighting. According to scholarly discourses, 'Hybrid War' encompasses overlapping battlespaces, range of operations (military or non-kinetic) and a blurring of actors with scope of achieving strategic objectives by creating 'exploitable ambiguity'.[54] There exists a lack of clarity over the extent to which operations are combined across battlespaces and key players/ actors. The recent conflicts such as Russia-Ukraine Conflict, Israel-Hamas Conflict and Sino-India stand-off have demonstrated that hybrid war has the capacity of combining armed actions across all five domains of space, cyber, maritime, air, and land within wider campaigns construct involving politico-economic, socio-cultural, and informational dimensions.[55] Yet, we know very little about the types, roles, and relationships involving actors both within and across these layers, outside claims about their regular-irregular nature and the synergy of their actions (Hoffman 2007). For the purpose of this research, the articles by various informed authors have been studied to arrive at a uniformly acceptable categories of the players and actors of 'Social Media Warfare' and 'Hybrid Warfare'.

In the article titled, 'What is Social Media Warfare?, which was selected for final round of '2021 NATO Innovation Challenge', the author has elaborated the concept of 'Social Media Warfare'. It is emphasised that social media warfare is a subset of hybrid warfare. Both are closely related but not the same. He has stressed that battle in social media, initially limited to political arena, is now being exploited by various actors as a strategic weapon. Thus, both attackers and targets can be found in many areas of society. As per the author, the actors can be roughly divided into four categories viz; *political actors, economic actors, actors with special interests and actors with mixed interests.*[56]

In another article titled, 'Towards a typology of non-state actors in 'hybrid warfare': proxy, auxiliary, surrogate and affiliated forces, Vladimir Rauta has presented four different categories of actors/ players of hybrid warfare, namely *proxy, auxiliary, surrogate and affiliated forces.*[57] The author has arrived at classification based on two considerations viz; *relational embeddedness* and *relational morphology*. He has amplified the classification in following manner: -

> *Relational Embeddedness* – implies way of pursuit of coercive goals solely 'by/through' the irregular or in cooperation 'with/ alongside' regular forces.

- The distinction between 'by/ through' and 'in cooperation with/ alongside' has been explained by referring to the emerging model of *collaborative fighting involving local armed non-state actors,* conceptualized by the US armed forces as the 'by, with, and through' (BWT) approach. As General Joseph L. Votel explains, the approach involved operations *"led by [our] partner, state or non-state, with enabling support from the US led coalitions, and through US authorities and partner agreements"* (Votel and Keravuori, 2018).

- Embeddedness is the logic of describing and pursuing relationships through functional identification. Embeddedness becomes a *measure of the interactivity of the mode of operations employed towards reaching the desired strategic ends*. It is neither an indicator of the complexity of relationship nor of the control mechanisms underlying it (Bowen 2019).

- Simply put, *embeddedness* describes the *structural relationship* between regulars and irregulars, and the *'by/ through'* and *'in cooperation with/ alongside'* pairing enables distinguishing between direct and indirect embeddedness, which forms the first classificatory criterion, hindered by the application of Principal-Agent Theory and its logic of delegation.

> *Relational morphology* – distinguishes between *supplementary* and *delegatory* pathways of relationship constitution.

- Supplementary morphology identifies a relationship in which the *non-state actor element provides a complementary, additive value through combination.*

- This is in contrast to the delegatory one in which the irregular replaces the regular entirely through substitution. Together, relational embeddedness and relational morphology delineate four patterns of interactions i.e. 'proxy', 'auxiliary', 'surrogates', and 'affiliated'.

To arrive at a tacit understanding of the actors and key players and identify commonalities or to distinguish the perpetrators, the summarised description of the above-mentioned actors of Social Media Warfare and Hybrid Warfare is as tabulated below: -

Political Actors	**Proxy Forces/ Actors**
Uses social media to push through a certain political agenda such as *influence election* results, *destabilize political systems*, or *dismantle society's trust* in a government. Political actors include *alliances of states, individual states, parties* or even *military units*.	*Armed groups*, not part of regular forces, but fight for and on behalf of states wishing to alter the strategic outcome of a conflict while remaining external to it. The proxy is *indirectly embedded with the external state* as their conduit of armed violence on the basis of state's provision of a range of support. They *operate by entirely replacing regular forces* on the battlefield. This strategic relationship results from the regulars' delegation of war to the irregulars (Salehyan 2010). This *relationship is by no means linear and unidirectional, it can diverge.* In Russia-Ukraine conflict, *non-state actors* (political fronts such as Ukrainian Front) played *military and politico-strategic roles* to fight for various degrees of *autonomy, independence, and unification* with Russia in *Luhansk and Donbas* regions.

Economic Actors	Auxiliary Forces/ Actors
Primary focus is to target *financial gains*. Industrial groups or sectors *assert their interests to gain an advantage or harm* others. Companies also use social media to *discredit their competitors*, to *gain a competitive advantage* and ultimately to assert themselves on the market.	*Armed groups*, not part of the regular forces, *directly embedded into structure of operations* in collaboration with or alongside regulars. Act as *supplementary force* and provides additive value to regulars through combination. Combination underlines a pattern of *strategic collaboration* and association: non-sequential arrangement and rearrangement of militia activities in support of and with regular forces. Act as *force multipliers*, in defensive or offensive roles, accompanying or being accompanied by regulars in operation. They identify a collusion pathway of *working jointly towards coercive ends*. Local self-defence militias played auxiliary role during annexation of Crimea by Russia in 2014; involved in acts of disinformation, political disruption and propaganda.

Actors with Special Interests	Surrogate Forces/ Actors
Besides political and economic, there are other motivations to participate in social media warfare. Lobby groups, for example, try to *influence public opinion* in order to *obtain certain regulations* and *religious or political groups* try to *recruit more followers* for their purposes.	Armed groups *through which regular forces of the state involved in the ongoing conflict, prosecute the operations* (either by being partially supplemented or wholly replaced). *Indirectly embedded in operational-tactical interaction* with the regulars: takes over the burden of fighting as a response to the inability of the state to assert the monopoly of violence. *Employed by a state in any external conflict where the employment of its own forces may be deemed undesirable. These may be pro-governmental groups or militias 'utilised in an internal war* between a government and armed opposition' and that were 'aligned with the government but not formally part of it' (Hughes and Tripodi 2009, 4/5).

	Surrogates are different to the other aforementioned categories because they observe a *relationship with the very state whose authority is contested through violence.*
	Ukraine used volunteer paramilitary formations, crowd funded privately by Volunteer Council under MoD to supplement the Army and the National Guard. The *Ukrainian Volunteer Army, the Aidar battalion, the Azov and Donbas battalions, Right Sector, Dnipro-1, and the Organisation of Ukrainian Nationals* are some of the most famous surrogate forces.
Actors with mixed interests	**Affiliated Forces/ Actors**
Ultimately, not all actors can always be assigned to a specific group, because some attackers *pursue several goals* at the same time or *merely work on behalf of other actors.* The group of hybrid actors includes exactly these attackers. One of the best-known examples of such an actor is the *Internet Research Agency* – a Russian company that has been involved in various information operations in the past to enforce the interests of both the Russian government and individual Russian companies.	*Armed groups*, unofficially part of the regular forces, fig*ht for and on behalf of states* wishing to alter the strategic outcome of a conflict while remaining external to it. Affiliated forces are an invisible arm of states having a *symbiotic, formal, yet legally dubious relationship*. These are *violent non-state actors* (mercenaries, shadowy private military and security contractors) who *exploit opportunities in battle field for profit-maximisation and revenue accumulation*. These may be '*private business entities* that deliver to consumers a *wide spectrum of military and security services*, assumed to be exclusively inside the public context' (Singer 2003, 8). These are private armies that can '*conduct autonomous military campaigns, offensive operations, and force projection*' (McFate 2017, 14).

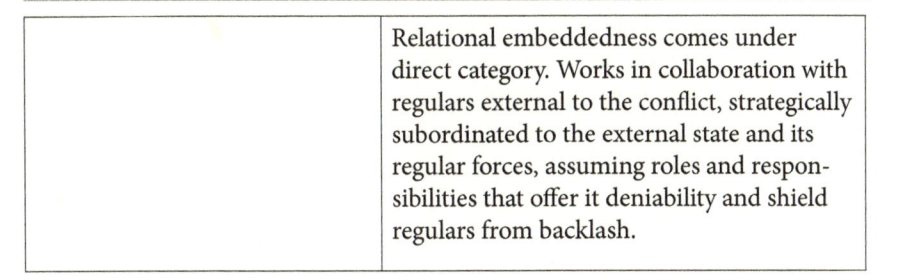

	Relational embeddedness comes under direct category. Works in collaboration with regulars external to the conflict, strategically subordinated to the external state and its regular forces, assuming roles and responsibilities that offer it deniability and shield regulars from backlash.

Table 2 – Actors and Key Players of Hybrid Warfare and Social Media Warfare

Consequent to the study of description of actors as tabulated above, it is established that there may be certain amount of overlap in roles/ tactics adopted by actors of social media warfare as well as hybrid warfare. But owing to range of their actions, the actors of social media warfare can be distinguished with substantial confidence level. Consequent to analysis of scholarly articles by various think tanks, there can be some more additions to the categories of actors of Social Media Warfare as illustrated above.

➢ *Organised Cyber Criminals.*[58] These actors target financial and/or data rich institutions and businesses for *financial gains*. These are orgainsed groups who orchestrate *cyber heists or use ransomware to extort*. Their acts cause *substantial economic losses* to businesses and the states. Cyber organised criminals execute variety of cybercrimes to include fraud, hacking, malware development and distribution, distributed denial of service (DDoS) attacks, blackmail, and intellectual property crime.[59] Examples of organised cyber criminals are as follows:-

- 'Zeus', a banking Trojan, captures users' banking details to log into online accounts.

- 'Shadowcrew', an international organisation of approximately 4,000 members, allegedly promoted and facilitated a wide variety of criminal activities [online] including, electronic theft of personal identification information, credit and debit card fraud, and the production and sale of false identification documents.

➢ *Hacktivists - Cyber Activism with a Dark Side.* Hacktivism is defined as *"the nonviolent use of illegal or legally ambiguous digital tools in pursuit of political ends"*. These actors are known to have *strong political affiliations or social ideologies* coupled with expert hacking skills. They demonstrate vulnerabilities in systems/ networks or advance socio-political agendas. Engaging a wide range of targets and ethical hacking, they focus on *exposing secrets and disrupting organisations* perceived or painted as evil. The tools of the hacktivist can include holding virtual sit-ins, website defacement, mass emailing, Denial of Service (DoS) or Distributed Denial of Service (DDoS) attacks, Domain Name Service (DNS) hijacking, or any of a number of other methods.[60] The most widely known hacktivist group is 'Anonymous' and its affiliated groups. Certain recent examples of Hacktivism include attack on financial site during G8 summit and DDoS on the internet infrastructure in Estonia in reaction to the plan to move a Soviet-era statue in Tallinn.

➢ *Insider Threats.* These actors circumvent the cyber security protocols and authorized access privilege provided by their companies/ organisations to steal the data. Their actions are driven by motivation to gain financial benefits or sharing propriety information/ classified information with the competitors. These actors pose a significant challenge for the organizations owing to difficulty in detection and prevention of such intrusion.

➢ *Cyber Extortionists - Holding Data Hostage.* These actors reportedly target businesses, state machinery and important services to capture critical data, cause damage and destruction. They demand ransom payments for release of data. Cyber extornists exploit ransomware attacks to encrypt valuable data, jeopardize critical systems and cause major operational disruptions with significant financial consequences. Cyber extortion methods include *ransomware attacks, DDoS attacks, doxing, and sextortion.*[61] Certain recent incidents of cyber extortion are as follows: -

- *Colonial Pipeline Attack (2021).* DarkSide, a cybercrime group, perpetrated a ransomware attack on the Colonial Pipeline, the largest pipeline system for refined oil products in the U.S. The attack led to shutdown of pipeline, sparking widespread fuel shortages and price hikes. This ransomware attack yielded nearly $5 million in ransom paid by Colonial Pipeline to regain control over their systems.

- *Atlanta Ransomware Attack (2018).* In March 2018, Atlanta was exposed to a ransomware attack that crippled several critical systems, affecting various city services. The attackers demanded a $51,000 ransom, which the city reportedly did not pay. However, the recovery and mitigation costs following the attack were estimated to be over $2.6 million.

> *Script Kiddies - Amateur Threat Actors.* These actors lack sophisticated techniques and expertise in hacking skills, but they orchestrate attacks to vandalize and cause significant damage to relatively easy to penetrate and vulnerable systems and networks. They are like new kids on the block, usually rely on pre-written scripts and tools developed by other types of threat actors to penetrate a network or system. Despite their less sophisticated approach, their actions can still cause significant damage and financial losses.

> *State Sponsored Hackers - A Nation's State Arsenal.* Presumably backed by nation states, government organisations and influential leaders, they are considered as most dangerous type of threat actors capable of inflicting devastating damage to businesses and government run institutions/ installations. By virtue of their access to significant resources, they are equipped with formidable capabilities to orchestrate sabotage and disrupt networks and critical computer systems. These actors are potent tools of state sponsored information warfare, social engineering, narrative building and carry out espionage, theft and wide range of disruptive activities to further interests of their countries/group of countries and organisations. Examples of state-sponsored cyberattacks include the 'Stuxnet Worm', which targeted Iran's nuclear program, alleged Russian interference in the 2016 U.S. presidential election, and the 2017 WannaCry ransomware attack, which was linked to North Korea.[62]

> *Internal User Errors/ Gullible Social Media Users.* These actors are usually ignorant/ gullible users within the target systems/ organisations, who either fall prey to cyber espionage attempts by adversaries or inadvertently compromise the data. They may be employees, contractors, outsources workers or social media activists who may not have malicious intent but their actions can cause extensive damage.

In the light of overlapping interests, target profiles, tactics adopted and blurring lines of direct and indirect consequences, it is a complex task to deduce explicit categories of actors of social media. However, considering motives and objectives of Social Media operations in the overall construct of hybrid threat environment, the key players of Social Media warfare can broadly be categorised under four categories viz; *state and non-state actors, political actors and actors with special interests and actors with mixed interests (online influencers and opinion shapers)*. For the purpose of the extant research, the suggested sub categorisation is as follows.

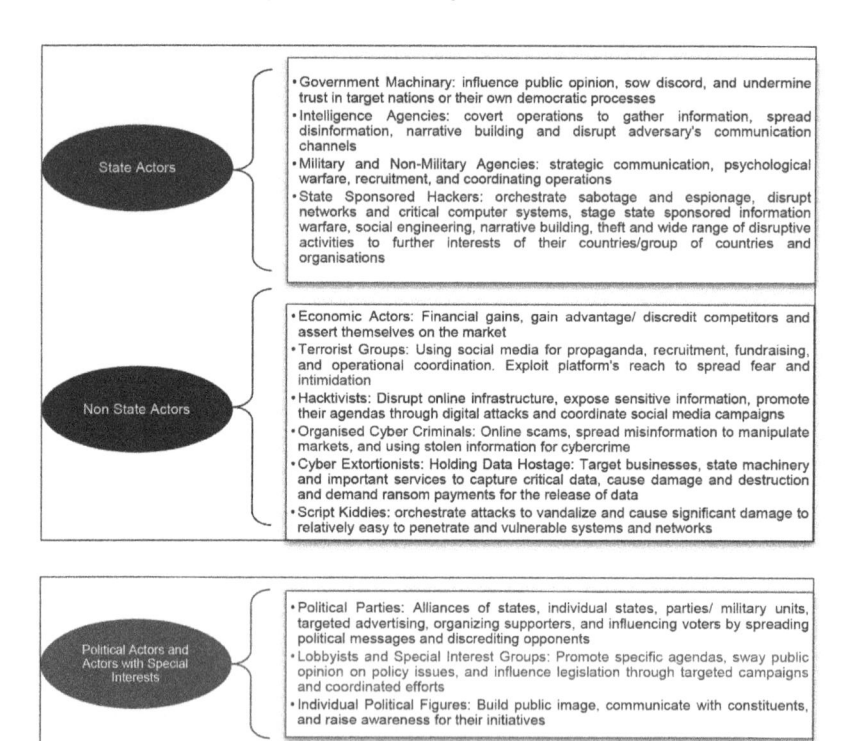

State Actors
- Government Machinary: influence public opinion, sow discord, and undermine trust in target nations or their own democratic processes
- Intelligence Agencies: covert operations to gather information, spread disinformation, narrative building and disrupt adversary's communication channels
- Military and Non-Military Agencies: strategic communication, psychological warfare, recruitment, and coordinating operations
- State Sponsored Hackers: orchestrate sabotage and espionage, disrupt networks and critical computer systems, stage state sponsored information warfare, social engineering, narrative building, theft and wide range of disruptive activities to further interests of their countries/group of countries and organisations

Non State Actors
- Economic Actors: Financial gains, gain advantage/ discredit competitors and assert themselves on the market
- Terrorist Groups: Using social media for propaganda, recruitment, fundraising, and operational coordination. Exploit platform's reach to spread fear and intimidation
- Hacktivists: Disrupt online infrastructure, expose sensitive information, promote their agendas through digital attacks and coordinate social media campaigns
- Organised Cyber Criminals: Online scams, spread misinformation to manipulate markets, and using stolen information for cybercrime
- Cyber Extortionists: Holding Data Hostage: Target businesses, state machinery and important services to capture critical data, cause damage and destruction and demand ransom payments for the release of data
- Script Kiddies: orchestrate attacks to vandalize and cause significant damage to relatively easy to penetrate and vulnerable systems and networks

Political Actors and Actors with Special Interests
- Political Parties: Alliances of states, individual states, parties/ military units, targeted advertising, organizing supporters, and influencing voters by spreading political messages and discrediting opponents
- Lobbyists and Special Interest Groups: Promote specific agendas, sway public opinion on policy issues, and influence legislation through targeted campaigns and coordinated efforts
- Individual Political Figures: Build public image, communicate with constituents, and raise awareness for their initiatives

Actors with Mixed Interests - Online Influencers and Opinion Shapers
- Social Media Personalities and Celebrities: Use large followings to amplify messages, promote agendas, and manipulate public opinion for various purposes
- Activists and Grassroots Movements: Organise protests, raise awareness for their causes, and mobilizing supporters
- Individual Opinion Leaders and Experts: Share expertise and shape public discourse on specific topics, potentially being manipulated or used to spread misinformation
- Internal User Errors/ Gullible Social Media Users: Employees, contractors, outsources workers or social media activists fall prey to cyber espionage attempts by the adversaries or inadvertently compromise the data

The identification of key actors, preparators and warriors of social media warfare would be instrumental in determining the role and impact of social media in hybrid warfare. Social media has become a crucial battleground in modern hybrid warfare, wherein state and non-state actors manipulate information, sow discord, and influence public opinion to achieve their strategic goals. The global trends of social media exploitation indicate that various actors are using this potent tool for defensive and offensive purposes in intensely contested hybrid environment. The plausible roles of social media in the hybrid environment are discussed in succeeding paras.

Plausible Roles: Social Media as Tool of Hybrid Warfare in Digital Realm

Weaponisation of Information - In the era of digital connectivity, internet and social media platforms have facilitated ease of sharing of ideas and information, greater awareness of contemporary issues and improved connectivity even to the remotest areas across the globe. By virtue of relative better affordability, global reach, penetration and speed of dissemination of information, social media platforms have emerged as force multipliers to establish and strengthen a global connect for the people. However, the attributes of social media assessed to be capable of delivering dividends for the humanity, have also been exploited to wage war by state and non-state actors alike. A study by Mercy Corps has noted that social media has created new, highly accessible channels for spreading disinformation, sowing divisiveness and contributing to real-world harm in the form of violence, persecution and exploitation. The impact social media has on real-world communities is complex and rapidly evolving. It stretches across international borders and challenges traditional humanitarian aid, development and peacebuilding models.[63] Various studies have identified the following trends of weaponisation of information globally: -

> *Disinformation and Propaganda.* Fake news, fabricated stories, and manipulated videos are amplified through bots and targeted campaigns to mislead the audiences and cloud their cognitive abilities, undermine trust in legitimate sources and discredit the adversaries/ competitors. Albeit, the practitioners of warfighting and statecraft have been resorting to various tactics to achieve surprise and deception so as to mislead the enemy and to create confusion in minds of decision makers. However, owing to ambiguity and deniability, social media has been misused by various actors to spread disinformation and propaganda to influence target population in contested battle space across the spectrum of contemporary conflicts. Certain examples of disinformation and propaganda are as appended below: -

- Alleged Meddling in US Elections of 2016. During the 2016 US election, Russian intelligence campaign allegedly penetrated social media space with fabricated contents to spread disinformation about Hillary Clinton and promote Donald Trump. The US agencies accused that Mr Prigozhin's (referred as Chef of Putin) two companies i.e. Concord Management and Consulting and Internet Research Agency (IRA), and 12 other Russian nationals, allegedly coordinated the online rabble-rousing.[64]

- In the digital realm, the terrorism in J&K has moved beyond traditional battle space; the radical groups and terrorist organisations are extensively exploiting social media platforms to spread their propaganda. Resultantly, the unchallenged radical use of social media coupled with radical content has changed the landscape of J&K in last 30 years. Many radical ideological groups, terrorist groups and their leaders are surviving on the social, political, and economic weaknesses of population.[65] Terrorist organisations, like *Hizbul-Mujahideen (HM) and Lashkar-e-Taiba (LeT), are using social media platforms such as YouTube, WhatsApp, Facebook, Twitter (now 'X'), Telegram, and others to spread anti-India propaganda* through videos of terrorist training sessions and alleged harassment of locals by security forces to fuel enmity between security forces and local youth.[66] In J&K, Social media platforms have been used extensively by the terrorist organizations and mushrooming network of unauthorized online news platforms to spread misinformation and fake news. Burhan Wani, portrayed as poster boy of terrorist organisations, used to post photographs on Facebook to spread fake news and recruit gullible and misguided local youths for the terror outfit. Post abrogation of Articles 35A and 370, Pakistan has continuously used social media platforms (Facebook and Twitter *(now 'X')*) to project Indian government and security forces as anti-people and authoritarian in Kashmir. Old videos and clips of violence and unconnected incidents were hosted on these platforms to depict the current situation in Kashmir portraying that Indian Muslims opposed the move[67]. Consequent to crack down against online hate mongers, the terrorists have changed their strategy. To elude the security agencies, they are posting propaganda contents with fake identities, avoiding posting own photos and using other platforms such as 'Nand Box' and 'TamTam'.

> *Nand Box – a Canadian no-code mobile app development platform, can be used to create native, host ready mobile app for Android and IOS with no coding expertise. It includes a wide range of capabilities for people, groups, and organizations to satisfy their various needs.*
>
> *TamTam – launched by Russian company Mail.ru Group in May 2017, an encrypted and safe messaging app with channels, video calls and geolocation services.*

- There are umpteen incidents highlighting the susceptibility of Kashmiri public to these unsubstantiated fabricated contents hosted to trigger angst and unrest even on trivial issues. For instance, in 2016, a fake news depicting the death of an infant due to polio vaccination was circulated on social media. The rumour stated, "thousands of children who were administered pulse polio drops were rushed to the hospitals across Kashmir… by their parents (Ganai, 2016)." Consequent to wide spread rumours, the anxious parents with their infants chocked every road that led to medical facilities in Kashmir. Authorities were caught unaware by the swelling of hospitals and roads by people. At some places people vandalized hospital furniture and equipment and beat doctors in anger.[68] It took sustained efforts by the government and local administration to dispel the rumors and calm the public. Though, the rumors were proven false subsequently, however, the incident provided an opportunity to anti-national elements to test their weapon of mass dis-information, manipulate public sentiments and mobilizing the crowd.

- In another incident, the propaganda machinery of adversarial forces, attempted to malign development and welfare initiative by the Indian government. According to reports, free LED bulbs under Ujala scheme were disturbed by Power Development Department in 2017 and 2018 to every household in Kashmir.

Soon a rumor spread that these bulbs were fitted with spy camera, used by government forces to maintain surveillance on militant activities in the region. As rumor gained ground that several militants hiding in civilians' homes were killed after government forces spied on them using 'surveillance cameras' fitted in the bulbs of these houses, people started destroying the 'spy bulbs'. A video circulated on Facebook, claiming that an engineering student has found a spy camera fitted in the bulb, garnered more than 2 lakh views in few weeks. The rumour having first originated in South Kashmir was soon believed to be untrue (Nazir, 2017).

➤ *Cyber Trolling and Harassment.* Cyber/ Internet Trolling and Harassment is defined as *coordinated campaigns of online harassment* and *abuse* aimed to *silence dissent, intimidate opponents,* and *disrupt online discourses.* As per article published by Social Media Victims Law Centre, trolling, a category of cyberbullying, is an *act of posting damaging or harassing comments* on social media to purposefully *insult or humiliate* the recipient.[69] Internet users often point to any controversial opinion or disagreeable interaction as trolling. The trolls lob insults and slurs, spread false or misleading information, or disrupt genuine conversations with offensive or nonsensical memes. The goal is to annoy, to malign, to push a particular message, and to negatively affect experience of a person or specific group.[70]

- In late 1980s and early 90s, the term trolling, part of internet culture, was used to define behaviour of users and mock new arrivals. Online communities such as *4chan* and other internet forums emerged where trolling was part of expected behavior. With the advent of social media and expansion of internet, governments and political officials 'weaponized' trolling to attack their enemies, opposition and media. In 2014, there was a leak of emails that exposed creation of an army of internet trolls by the Chinese regime; '*50 Cent Army*' supposedly employed at least 500,000 internet trolls to leave fake comments on news articles and social media. By 2017, the estimate of troll army increased to two million people. The goal of massive operation was to drown out conversations and information deemed undesirable to the regime while cheerleading for the government and Chinese Communist Party.

- *Trolling has emerged as a component of information operations and military strategies across the world.* Troll farms and troll factories prevalent in small European countries and parts of Asia can produce fake content at a large scale. A similar model exists in Latin America, where digital agencies create troll factories for electoral purposes, as seen in Mexico's presidential election held in 2017.

- As per study published by Luis Assardo on Global Investigative Journalism Network, the tactics employed by the trolls to spread the messages and contents are as follows: -[71]

    - *Amplification Through Social Media.* To amplify their contents, 'Trolls' use social media platforms to spread their messages through *multiple accounts* or by employing *automated bots.* By generating *likes, shares and comments,* trolls can manipulate platform algorithms to make their content more visible and reach out to larger audiences.

    - *Hashtag Hijacking.* Trolls monitor *trending hashtags* or create their own hashtags to spread disinformation, gain traction for own fabricated narratives or harass targeted individuals and groups. This enables them to inject their messages into popular conversations and gain more exposure.

    - *Emotional Manipulation.* Trolls often use emotionally charged language, slurs and provocative content such as texts, photos, short videos and memes to elicit strong reactions from the users. The trend of *'Rage Farming'* is very common wherein manipulators leverage the *'Read, Anger and Response Cycle'* to rile the readers up and evoke strong response.[72]

    - *Astroturfing.* Trolls *create illusion of grassroots support* for a particular cause, idea, or narrative *by coordinating a large number of fake accounts.* This tactic is resorted to make their disinformation campaigns appear more credible, and create an aura of popular support.

- *Targeting Influential Individuals.* Trolls may target celebrities, politicians, or high-profile individuals to capitalize on their followings, gain more attention and peddle lies through their compromised accounts and credentials.

- *Memes Mania.* Humorous or provocative memes are hosted on the social media platforms to spread disinformation or offensive content. Since Memes go viral quickly, they facilitate reaching out to larger audiences and amplify the message.

- *Deepfakes and Manipulated Media.* Trolls may use advanced technology i.e., Artificial Intelligence (AI) and Machine Learning (ML) to create fake videos, images, or audio recordings to spread disinformation, discredit individuals, or fuel conspiracy theories. Owing to difficulties in differentiating between deep fakes and real contents, the normal social media users fall prey to deep fakes and circulate contents in respective groups thereby making them viral. By the time authenticity of such contents is investigated, such contents are seen by millions of users who perceive them as truth. Exploitation of AI and Generative AI to create Deep Fakes and manipulation of contents on social and digital media has emerged as grave threat to national security and raised concern amongst the government agencies world-wide.

- *Exploiting Existing Divisions.* Trolls are designed to capitalise on societal divisions, such as political, ethnical, social, ideological, religious, or cultural differences, to amplify discord and polarise online discussions. Skillfully designed troll campaign may entice vulnerable sections of societies into degenerative online discussions and fuel discontent and disharmony in target nations.

- *Modus Operandi – Troll Campaigns.* The study has also presented modus operandi of troll factories to make their messages and manipulated contents viral, gain wider readership and elude detection by social media app control mechanism. Troll factories produce fake social media accounts and websites to spread their narratives. As part of their strategy, trolls target specific platforms and communities to spread their narrative. Their operations show resemblance with functioning of any digital marketing agency; creating messages and content and strategically targeting them across multiple social media platforms and channels to achieve their goals. To illustrate the nitty gritty of harassment campaign, the study has deliberated upon the *amplification ecosystem*, and their role in an *attack operation*.

- *Amplification Ecosystem.* Encompasses inventory of assets, accounts, channels, pages, or spaces used to disseminate and amplify messages part of any strategy. The example of elements of a media amplification ecosystem used to manipulate public opinion is given at Figure 8 below: -

Influencers — Allied and hired influencers to spread fabricated content.

Website(s) — One or many websites in parallel or cascade to be used as source.

Brigading — Accounts use to flood comment section or reply in social media.

Social Media — Fake Accounts in any social media platform. Hybrid or bot.

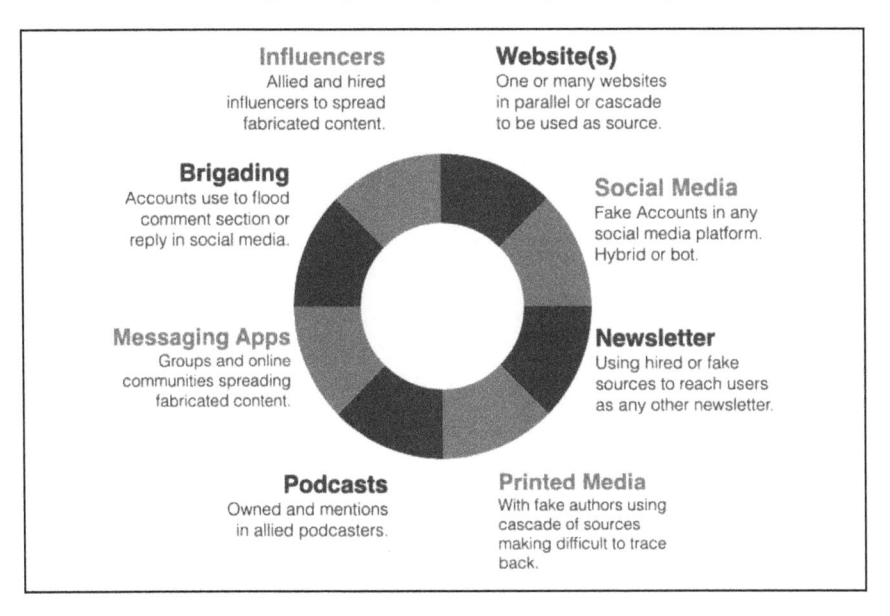

Messaging Apps — Groups and online communities spreading fabricated content.

Newsletter — Using hired or fake sources to reach users as any other newsletter.

Podcasts — Owned and mentions in allied podcasters.

Printed Media — With fake authors using cascade of sources making difficult to trace back.

Figure 8 - Different elements of a trolling campaign's amplification ecosystem. Image: Courtesy of Luis Assardo, Source - https://gijn.org/resource/investigating-digital-threats-trolling-campaigns/

- *Attack Operations.* The modus operandi of attack operations envisages use of multiple disposable fake accounts, online radicalised supporters and target audience. The diverse *disposable fake accounts* (shown in yellow in flow chart, refer Figure 9) *post fabricated false and doctored contents* online to target larger audiences.

The *trolls and manipulated public figures (shown in red)* would distribute *doctored contents to specific audiences* (supporters or radicalised users). These red accounts provoke adversaries and engage with the supporters using the content. In case social media platforms receive reports for malicious contents, only yellow accounts would be subjected to suspension. The red accounts would be able to evade any problem or suspension since they 'only' shared something posted by other accounts. This will avoid trolls being shut down. Once viral provocative contents are received by the accounts in green group, it will spread organically and reach a larger audience. Subsequently, another set of accounts in yellow (or the same if they are not suspended yet) will amplify the posts from green accounts, thereby gaining greater credibility and create reinforcing cycle.

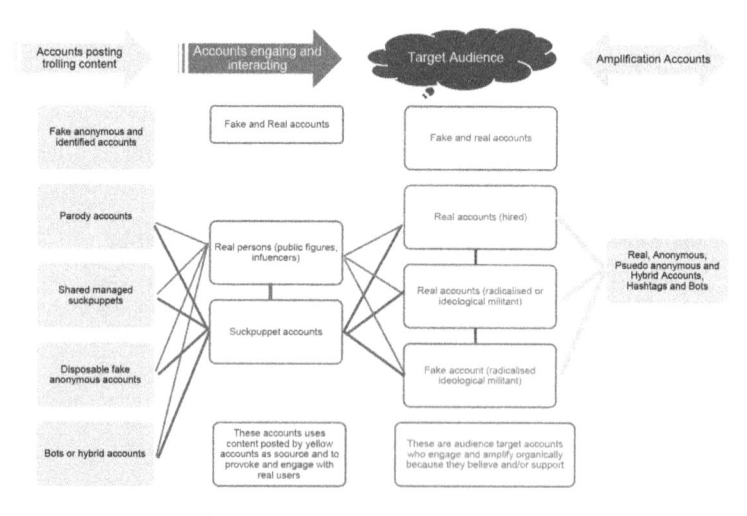

Figure 9 - Flow chart of the rollout strategy of a trolling campaign.
Image: Courtesy of Luis Assardo
Source - https://gijn.org/resource/investigating-digital-threats-trolling-campaigns/

Shaping Public Opinion and Perceptions. By virtue of its innovative potential, global reach, ambiguity and non-attributability, social media provides a virtual space for the global community to respond, analyse and debate various current issues.[73] The exploitation of these platforms affords a medium for sharing viewpoints, perception and influence broader audiences. Thus, with this kind of constellation, social media becomes more than just a means of communication; it becomes an active force that has a significant role in shaping, directing, and even changing public opinion which in turn can steer the direction of broader social, political, and economic events. The state and non-state actors with innovative and covert use of various tactics and strategies can execute their plans to dominate the intellectual discourse and may even achieve *cognitive colonization/ imperialism* or *colonization of minds*. The strategy to shape public opinion and perceptions may involve the following: -

> *Echo Chambers and Confirmation Bias.* Involves algorithms and targeted advertising to create *closed information ecosystems* and *self-reinforcing cycles*, wherein users are exposed to selective viewpoints that *reinforce their existing beliefs*. It facilitates polarization of societies, clog their objective thinking, sow dissent and make it harder to reach consensus on important issues.

- The opinion shaping during 2016 United States presidential election was described as an echo chamber effect, wherein information pertaining to the campaigns was exchanged on Twitter primarily among the individuals with similar political and ideological views. A study conducted by Guo et. al. showed that Twitter communities supporting Trump and Clinton differed significantly. Relatively more vocal online groups and communities were assessed to be responsible for creating echo chambers within their followers.[74] A Washington Post report claimed that Facebook's algorithms were criticized for creating echo chambers which contributed to the spread of misinformation and political polarisation during US Presidential elections in 2016.

- The impact of echo chambers and conformation bias is not restricted to shaping the opinion of unsuspecting voters and influencing electoral process. The social media activism has had tangible influence on decision making by government and policy formulation which had greater ramification for national interests and even global issues. The decision of UK government on proposal for 'BREXIT' is an apt example. A 'New Statesman' essay argued that echo chambers were linked to the United Kingdom Brexit referendum.[75] The study of sequence of events and trends of public discourse on social media platforms, revealed that capitalizing on public sentiments, vested groups launched an online campaign to garner public support, create pressure on UK government and influence decision-making. Various reports on the matter speculate that the 'Leave' campaign, advocating for Brexit, placed a major emphasis on online outreach. Led by strategist Dominic Cummings, significant portion of resources were employed for targeted social media advertising and digital communication to initiate 'Digital Opinion Movement'. These opinion movements gathered momentum on account of democratic deficits, a lack of political representation and low levels of trust in government and established political parties.[76] The 'Leave' campaign deployed automated bots to inflate perception of their popularity. Further, micro-targeting strategy involved propagation of tailored messages to specific demographics, potentially influenced voters more than traditional media campaigns.

> *Moral Manipulation and Framing.* Emotional appeals, fear mongering, and manipulative framing of events are used to influence public opinion, create moral dilemmas and mobilise support for specific agendas. Moral manipulation and framing tactics may fall under the ambit of strategies used in psychological warfare to influence the perception, opinions, emotions, and behavior of a specific target group.[77] Moral manipulation could involve challenging the moral values of the competitors so as to influence the behaviour of targeted group of their sympathisers/ supporters/ followers. Framing may involve distorting and selective disclosure of facts so as to present doctored information in conformity with own agenda and influences the target group's perception of the issue. During the Syrian Civil War, both sides used social media to share graphic images and emotionally charged narratives to garner international support for their cause and occupy moral high ground.[78]

Mobilisation and Coordination. Social Media networks (Facebook, 'X' etc) complemented the traditional organization such as unions, political parties, socio-political and socio-ethnical groups and mass media in recent global events. The strategy was observed during 2010 Arab Spring Revolution, mass political protests in Spain in 2011, pro-Russia and anti-Russia protests in 2013 and 2014 and seize of Capitol Hill in USA in 2020. In Indian internal security context also, social media has played a major role in mobilization and coordination of anti-establishment protests, riots and violence in J and K and Manipur as well as in various parts of country. Owing to ambiguity and non-attributability, various actors exploited social media platforms undetected for painting narrative, colour opinion of target population, garner support for their cause and recruit and mobilise the cadres/ activists to voice their dissonance and stage protests. The display of discontentment and dissent orchestrated through online activism may materialize in virtual space and/ or in the physical domain. The study of political and social movements occurred in past decade reveals a pattern in exploitation of social media by the actors. Notably, various social media platforms such as Facebook, YouTube, 'X', Telegram and Twitter etc, are used to advance the agenda, garner public support and mobilise their followers to 'call for action' campaigns. These trends are briefly discussed below: -

> *Recruitment and Radicalization.* Extremist groups, terrorist organizations and political groups use social media to *recruit new members, organize crowd funding, spread their ideology, and coordinate their activities.* For instance, ISIS utilized social media platforms like Twitter and Telegram to attract followers, spread propaganda, and plan attacks.[79]

> *Organizing Protests and Civil Unrest.* Social media can be used to *mobilize supporters, communicate plans, and share information during protests* and *demonstrations.* Social media played a pivotal role in mobilizing protesters during the Arab Spring uprisings in 2010 and anti-corruption demonstrations led by Anna Hazare in India in 2011.[80]

Intelligence Gathering and Targeting. Targeting may involve selection of targets (individuals/ groups/ institutions), designing modus operandi and defining desired end state i.e., extent of damage/ influence on the target audience as a direct/ indirect consequence of the action. For this purpose, social media could be used to identify potential targets for attacks in multiple domains. In a military conflict scenario, it may imply locating enemy troops by investigating social media behaviour of the troops by means of *geo-tagging* or by *gaining access to social media accounts.* In geo-political and geo-economical conflict scenario and corporate competitions, the probable target profile may include prominent leaders, think tanks, opinion shapers, decision makers and people in the organization. The aim would be to discern their pattern of *social behaviour, affiliation, linkages, alliances, moral values* and *vulnerabilities* which could be targeted to gain competitive edge and put the adversary in dis-advantageous position. This aspect is closely linked to the possibility of using social networks to gather as much information as possible about the target and the stakeholders.[81] For example, to manipulate opinion of a certain group (political institution, government body, customers, business partners, etc.), social media profiles are first identified and analysed. The information then helps to design precisely tailored tactics and content in order to manipulate the target group as effectively as possible. In addition, the misconduct of individual stakeholders such as business partners, leaders, opinion shapers or suppliers can also be instrumentalised to damage the reputation of the stakeholders as well as actual target of the attack. This procedure is also known as *'Discreditation by Proxy'*. The tactics employed for intelligence gathering and targeting can be categorized as 'Social Media Intelligence (SMINT)' and 'Social Listening and Data Analysis'. Both are amplified in succeeding sub paras.

> *Social Listening and Data Analysis.* Social media platforms offer a wealth of data on public opinion, sentiments, and trends, which can be used for intelligence gathering and targeting specific audiences. Social listening involves monitoring online conversations to understand people's viewpoints, stereotypes and perceptions and areas of interests/ trends which may be relevant to overall operation. Governments and intelligence agencies use social media analytics to track potential threats, monitor public sentiment, and identify potential targets for online and offline operations.[82] Monitoring of traffic on social media and internet also provide valuable open source intelligence (OSINT).

> *Social Media Intelligence (SMINT).* SMINT which is sub branch of OSINT, encompasses information gleaned from publicly available data as well as data for which court orders are required. It involves gathering data from social media conversations and communications to identify and gain information critical for target profiling and anticipate future actions/ options of target audience.

  • Unlike social Listening, which involves simply monitoring conversations, social media intelligence takes it a step further and uses patterns and trends in data for inform decision-making.[83] For example, marketers looking to leverage social data intelligence might track Instagram, Facebook, and Twitter conversations to measure sentiment around their brand or products. They could later use this data to target their ads more effectively or change the topics they write about on their blog. Social media intelligence can also be used to analyze demographic data, uncover trends in customer behaviour, and track competitor's activities. Such information can subsequently be used to inform campaigns, modify strategies, create more effective content, build narrative and increase influence and penetration of social media efforts.

- In this process, multiple social networking sites used by target audience are constantly monitored to collect data, undertake in depth analysis and make informed decision making. The data set can range from *demographic information* (such as age and gender), *users' behaviour, sentiment analysis, trends,* and *predictive analysis* to tailor the campaign. Interpretation of data, whether through manual analysis or automated tools, allows to uncover insights into target audience behavior and trends in conversations. Consequent to detailed analysis, the actionable steps are brainstormed, designed, and validated prior to putting into action. This could involve things like A/B testing, content validation, optimising landing pages, creating targeted campaigns, or making changes to overall strategy.

Thus, based on study of various global events driven by online public activism, which caused a deeper and broader impact on geo-politics and altered the power dynamics, it may be inferred that social media has been instrumentalised as potent weapon by various actors. Social media may play increasingly greater and decisive role in shaping the contours of global competitions and influencing their outcomes by providing asymmetric advantage to actors, who gain and maintain initiative to dominate the cognitive space. Therefore, it is prudent to study the penetration of social media platforms and evolving social media warfare strategy. The next chapter would delve upon the trends of social media usage and diverse techniques and tactics deployed by various actors to leverage the potential of weaponised social media space.

Chapter 3

Footprints of Social Media - Defining Contours of Hybrid Warfare

Trends Analysis: Exploitation of Social Media

The analysis of statistics pertaining to social media users and various platforms presents an interesting picture pointing towards quantum jump in the social media foothold over the world population. As per reports, the numbers of social media users have surged to *4.95 billion amounting to 60.49%* of world population (8.1 billion). By end of 2024, global social media users are appreciated to reach 5.17 billion.[84] The statistical trends of social media exploitation are as follows: -[85]

Social Media Users (in billions)

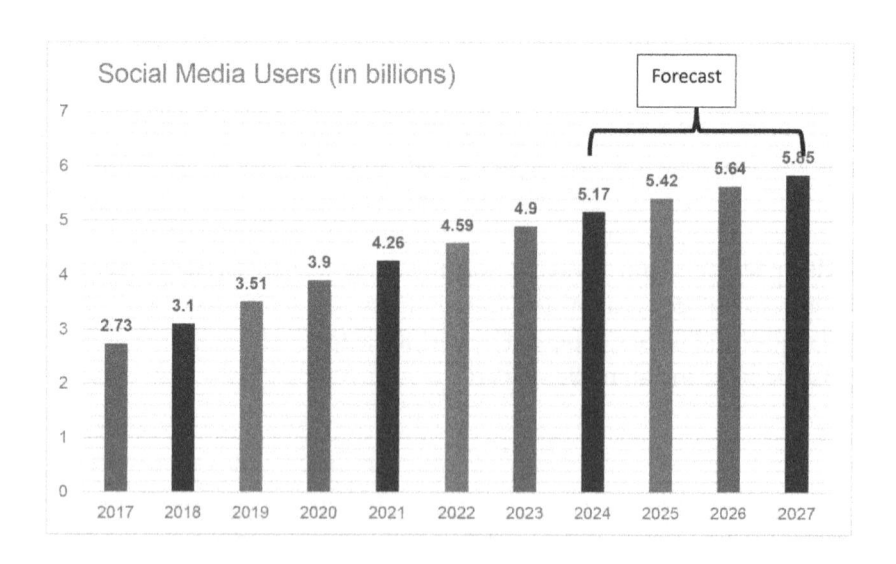

Year	Users
2017	2.73
2018	3.1
2019	3.51
2020	3.9
2021	4.26
2022	4.59
2023	4.9
2024	5.17
2025	5.42
2026	5.64
2027	5.85

(Forecast: 2024–2027)

Figure 10 – Trends of Social Media Exploitation
Source - Statista

Evidently, compared to user base in year 2022, there has been an increase of approximately 300 million social media users in year 2023. The statistical data also suggests that 85% of world's 5.27 billion mobile phone users are exploiting various social media platforms. On an average, a social media user interacts on 6.6 different social media platforms. Facebook is the biggest social media platform, with 3.03 billion users. TikTok/Douyin, Instagram, Snapchat, Pinterest and Twitter are steadily emerging as leading social media platforms.

As per latest data, BeReal, a French app is the fastest growing network with user base skyrocketing 313% from May 2022 to January 2023.[86] Facebook and Instagram are most surfed social media platforms in India. China, with 1.02 billion users, has highest number of social media users. India and USA make it to the top three with 755.47 million and 302.25 million users, respectively. Millennials and Gen Z are the most frequent users of social media platforms.[87] The graphical representation of statistical data and a plausible inference is as given below: -

> Social media platforms such as Facebook, WhatsApp and Facebook Messenger, owned and controlled by Meta Platforms, a US based company, dominate the global customer base. Owing to their strong footprint, these platforms wield significant influence over cognitive domain and possess potential to shape perceptions and behaviour of the population as direct consequence of the contents hosted online. YouTube and Instagram are also the prominent leaders in competition. By virtue of their unique features, they are suitably poised to exert influence over the users. The assessment corroborates the exploitation trends by state and non-state actors racing to dominate and control the contested battle space in virtual and cognitive worlds. Figure 11 below depicts the quantum of market share in terms of customer base of leading social media platforms.

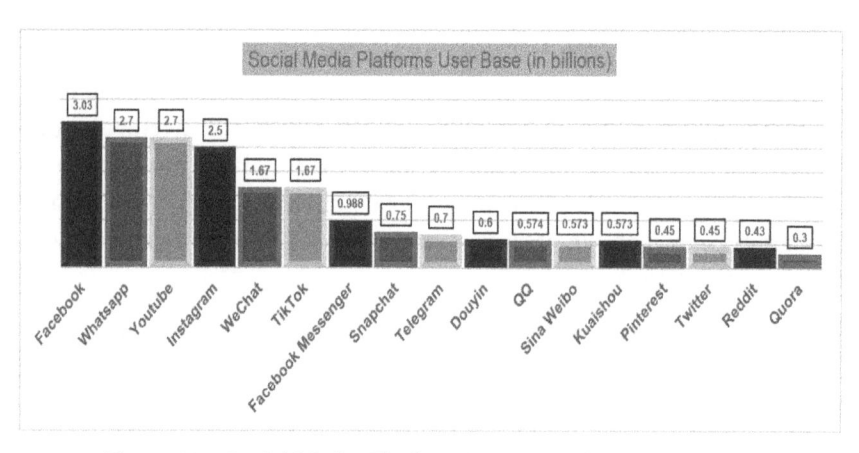

Figure 11 – Social Media Platform User Base, Source – Statista

> Statistically, Facebook has the highest number of users across the globe, closely followed by WhatsApp, YouTube and Instagram. Reportedly, WhatsApp, TikTok, Telegram and Mastodon are few social media platforms which are gaining popularity exponentially owing to features like end-to-end encryption, decentralised and user-controlled alternatives and captivating short videos and reels. The content regulation policies of these platforms have denied control of governments. However, the loopholes of privacy policies of social media platforms have been exploited by various actors to conduct influence operations in conflict prone/ unstable regions. The customer base data as shown above and low barriers for content regulation offer a plausible justification for exploitation of Facebook, YouTube, WhatsApp, Twitter and Telegram in various conflicts in recent past.

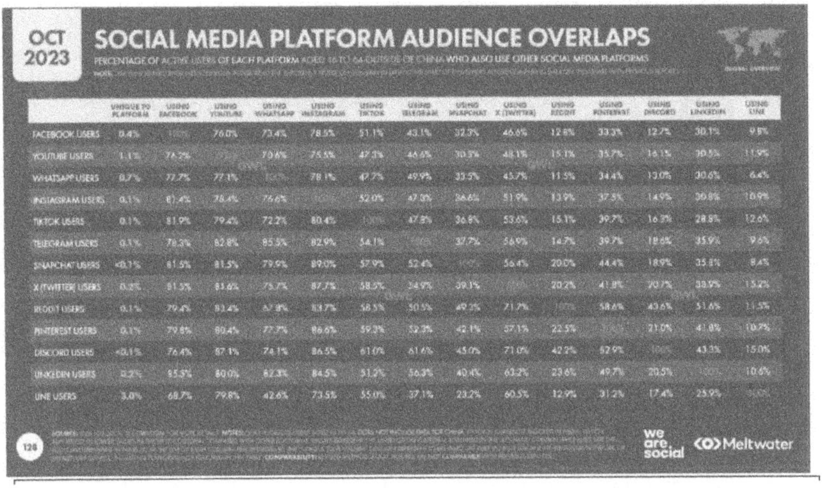

Figure 12 – Multiple accounts of the users on social media platforms
Social Media Source – Global Media Statistics, https://datareportal.com/social-media-users

- Relatively higher clientele in Gen Z indicates potential impact of social media in shaping the perception of impressionable young minds with consequences in multiple domains viz; society, politics and governance etc. Refer Figure 12 above, presence of users on multiple social media platforms offers them opportunity to engage with diverse contents and a viable alternative, however it also makes them vulnerable to narrative building and conformation biases. It is assessed that incidence of same content going viral in near simultaneity on diverse platforms may make it appear authentic and credible to the audiences, thereby leading to conformation biases and reinforcing cycles.

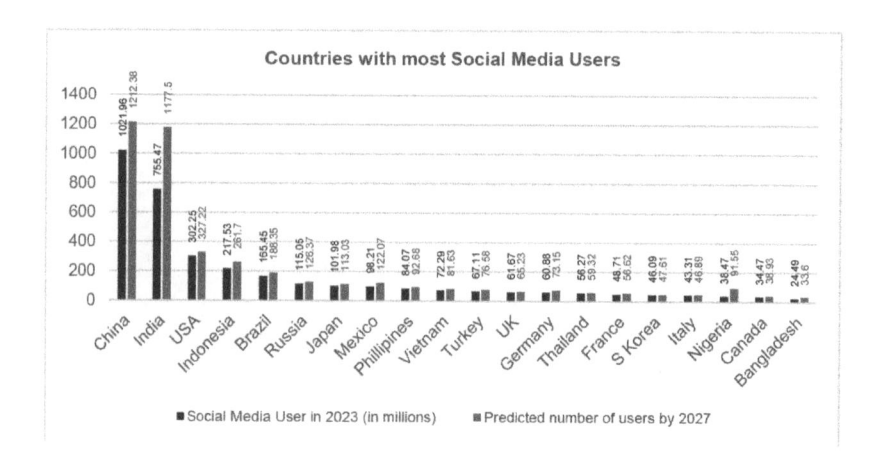

[Chart: Countries with most Social Media Users — showing Social Media User in 2023 (in millions) and Predicted number of users by 2027 for: China 1021.96 / 1212.38; India 1177.5 / 755.47; USA 302.25 / 327.22; Indonesia 217.53 / 281.7; Brazil 165.45 / 186.35; Russia 115.06 / 126.37; Japan 101.98 / 113.03; Mexico 96.21 / 122.07; Phillipines 84.07 / 92.68; Vietnam 72.29 / 81.63; Turkey 67.11 / 76.58; UK 61.67 / 65.23; Germany 60.88 / 73.15; Thailand 56.27 / 59.32; France 48.71 / 56.62; S Korea 46.09 / 47.61; Italy 43.31 / 48.89; Nigeria 38.47 / 91.55; Canada 34.47 / 36.93; Bangladesh 24.49 / 33.6]

Figure 12A – Country Wise data of social media users
Source - Global Media Statistics, https://datareportal.com/social-media-users

> Refer Figure 12A above, China, India and USA have highest concentration of social media users. However, China has banned Western social media platforms (SMP) in the country, which leaves India and USA becoming leading global trend setters. Countries with greater internet and SMP penetration have witnessed phenomenal growth in multiple sectors. However, higher SMP penetration is also linked to increasing trends of polarisation, radicalisation, spread of extremists' ideas and externally driven mobilisation of masses.

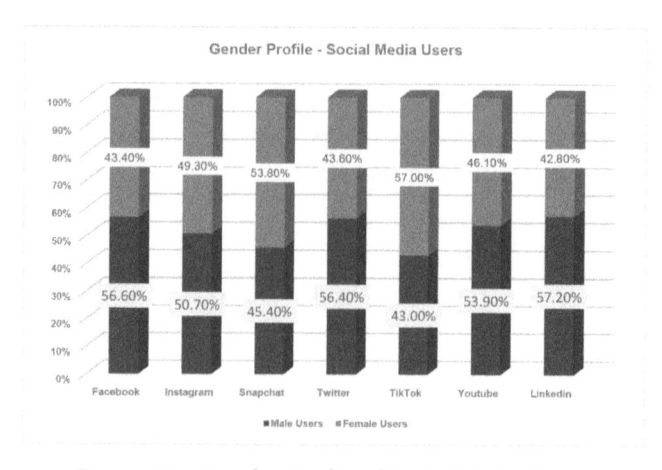

[Chart: Gender Profile - Social Media Users — Male / Female Users:
Facebook 56.60% / 43.40%; Instagram 50.70% / 49.30%; Snapchat 45.40% / 53.80%; Twitter 56.40% / 43.60%; TikTok 43.00% / 57.00%; Youtube 53.90% / 46.10%; Linkedin 57.20% / 42.80%]

Figure 13 – Gender Profile of Social Media Users

➢ Figures 14A and 14B below reveal that apart from making social connect, users exploit social media platforms for accessing news (34.3%), exploring trending topics of discussions (28.8%) and contents (30%) and sharing/ discussing opinion with others (22.6%). The usage pattern varies for different age groups.

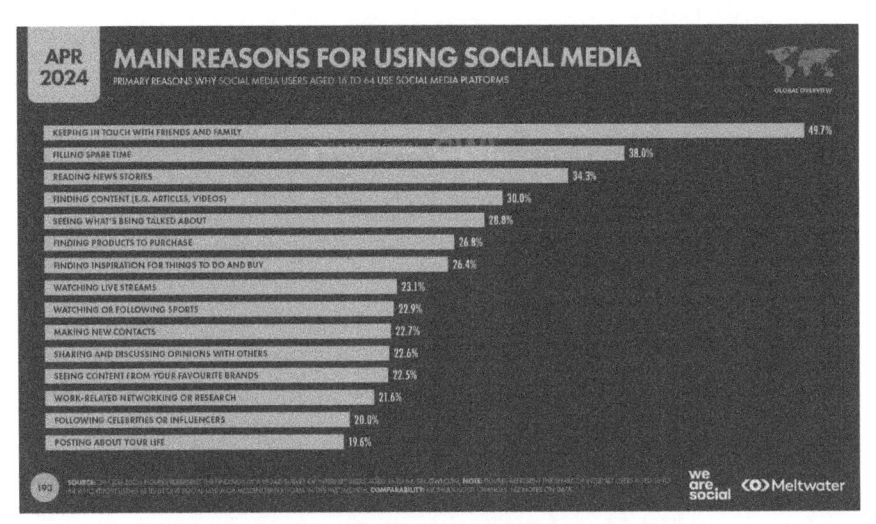

Figure 14A – Reasons for using social media
Source – Global Media Statistics, https://datareportal.com/social-media-users

Figure 14B – Reasons for using social media for different age groups
Source – Global Media Statistics, https://datareportal.com/social-media-users

➢ Refer figures 14C and 14D below, analysing survey data GWI's comments that younger generation is more likely prefer (at least in most Western countries), whereas older generations tend to prefer Facebook and WhatsApp. Delving deeper into data reveals that preference pattern also vary for different countries. Data in Figure 14D reveals that messaging friends and family is a particularly popular topic on Facebook, however TikTok primarily explore platform to look for funny and entertaining videos.

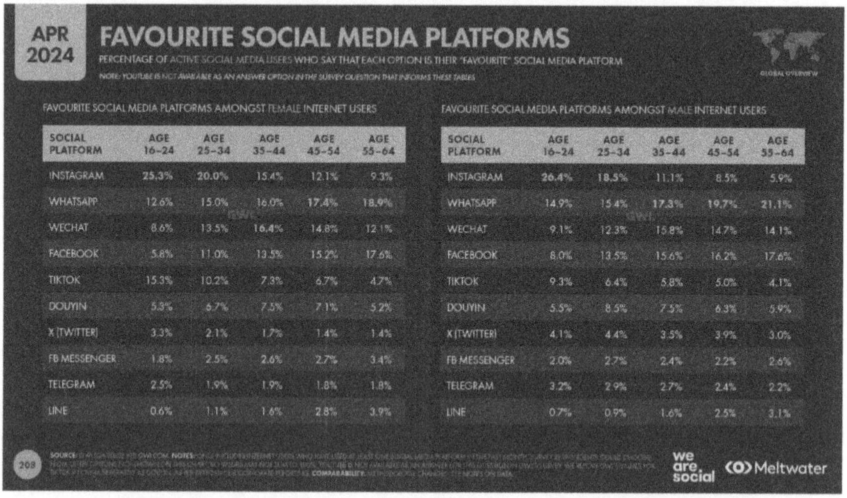

FAVOURITE SOCIAL MEDIA PLATFORMS
APR 2024
PERCENTAGE OF ACTIVE SOCIAL MEDIA USERS WHO SAY THAT EACH OPTION IS THEIR "FAVOURITE" SOCIAL MEDIA PLATFORM
NOTE: YOUTUBE IS NOT AVAILABLE AS AN ANSWER OPTION IN THE SURVEY QUESTION THAT INFORMS THESE TABLES

FAVOURITE SOCIAL MEDIA PLATFORMS AMONGST FEMALE INTERNET USERS

SOCIAL PLATFORM	AGE 16–24	AGE 25–34	AGE 35–44	AGE 45–54	AGE 55–64
INSTAGRAM	25.3%	20.0%	15.4%	12.1%	9.3%
WHATSAPP	12.6%	15.0%	16.0%	17.4%	18.9%
WECHAT	8.6%	13.5%	16.4%	14.8%	12.1%
FACEBOOK	5.8%	11.0%	13.5%	15.2%	17.6%
TIKTOK	15.3%	10.2%	7.3%	6.7%	4.7%
DOUYIN	5.3%	6.7%	7.5%	7.1%	5.2%
X (TWITTER)	3.3%	2.1%	1.7%	1.4%	1.4%
FB MESSENGER	1.8%	2.5%	2.6%	2.7%	3.4%
TELEGRAM	2.5%	1.9%	1.9%	1.8%	1.8%
LINE	0.6%	1.1%	1.6%	2.8%	3.9%

FAVOURITE SOCIAL MEDIA PLATFORMS AMONGST MALE INTERNET USERS

SOCIAL PLATFORM	AGE 16–24	AGE 25–34	AGE 35–44	AGE 45–54	AGE 55–64
INSTAGRAM	26.4%	18.5%	11.1%	8.5%	5.9%
WHATSAPP	14.9%	15.4%	17.3%	19.7%	21.1%
WECHAT	9.1%	12.3%	15.8%	14.7%	14.1%
FACEBOOK	8.0%	13.5%	15.6%	16.2%	17.6%
TIKTOK	9.3%	6.4%	5.8%	5.0%	4.1%
DOUYIN	5.5%	8.5%	7.5%	6.3%	5.9%
X (TWITTER)	4.1%	4.4%	3.5%	3.9%	3.0%
FB MESSENGER	2.0%	2.7%	2.4%	2.2%	2.6%
TELEGRAM	3.2%	2.9%	2.7%	2.4%	2.2%
LINE	0.7%	0.9%	1.6%	2.5%	3.1%

Figure 14C – Favourite social media platforms different age groups and gender profile
Source – Global Media Statistics, https://datareportal.com/social-media-users

➢ Instagram and Snapchat clientele are particularly interested in publishing their own content, but this activity is significantly less popular on TikTok, Reddit, and LinkedIn. This survey observes that Pinterest users are particularly interested in following or researching brand-related content on the world's most popular online pinboard.

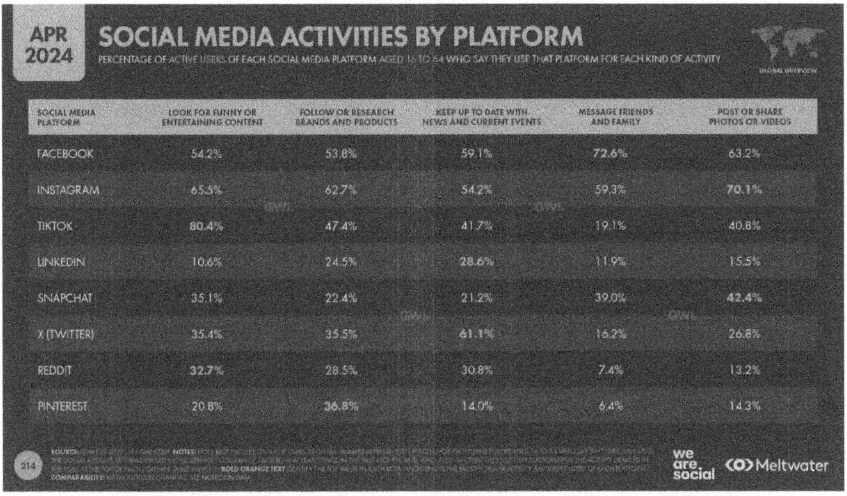

SOCIAL MEDIA ACTIVITIES BY PLATFORM
APR 2024 — PERCENTAGE OF ACTIVE USERS OF EACH SOCIAL MEDIA PLATFORM AGED 16 TO 64 WHO SAY THEY USE THAT PLATFORM FOR EACH KIND OF ACTIVITY

SOCIAL MEDIA PLATFORM	LOOK FOR FUNNY OR ENTERTAINING CONTENT	FOLLOW OR RESEARCH BRANDS AND PRODUCTS	KEEP UP TO DATE WITH NEWS AND CURRENT EVENTS	MESSAGE FRIENDS AND FAMILY	POST OR SHARE PHOTOS OR VIDEOS
FACEBOOK	54.2%	53.8%	59.1%	72.6%	63.2%
INSTAGRAM	65.5%	62.7%	54.2%	59.3%	70.1%
TIKTOK	80.4%	47.4%	41.7%	19.1%	40.8%
LINKEDIN	10.6%	24.5%	28.6%	11.9%	15.5%
SNAPCHAT	35.1%	22.4%	21.2%	39.0%	42.4%
X (TWITTER)	35.4%	35.5%	61.1%	16.2%	26.8%
REDDIT	32.7%	28.5%	30.8%	7.4%	13.2%
PINTEREST	20.8%	36.8%	14.0%	6.4%	14.3%

Figure 14D– Users activities pattern on social media platforms
Source – Global Media Statistics, https://datareportal.com/social-media-users

- Analysing Figures 13 and 14 (A to D) above, it is assessed that survey report depicts popularity of various SMPs, clientele preference and SM usage patterns and variation in users' choices for different age groups. Based on statistics, the study has established that Facebook, Twitter, Instagram, WeChat, WhatsApp and Snap Chat are the most popular platforms amongst Gen Millenium and Gen Z. Apart from entertainment and engaging with friends, the users have fair amount of dependence over the SMPs for news, information and situational awareness. It is pertinent to highlight that in contemporary scenario, the conflict prone and conflict-stricken nation states, owing to absence of strong traditional/ digital media and dependence on SMPs for news and information, are vulnerable to social media driven narrative building and perception shaping. For instance, majority of Ukrainians had heavy dependence on social media platforms owing to absence of strong network of indigenous traditional media, which was exploited by Russia to seize the critical space in the cognitive domain.

- Refer Figure 15 below, the data related to social media penetration reveals that global penetration rate is 59.4%. UAE has highest penetration rate of 106.1% whereas India (second highest social media user) has 61.5% social media penetration rate as Government of India (GoI) data of 2024. USA has 80.9% social media penetration rate.[88] The investigation to explore any possible connect between social media penetration rate and prevalence of radicalization and extremists' ideology throws some captivating perspective. Certain cases are discussed in the succeeding paras to draw logical inferences. The graphical representation of the statistical data of social media penetration rate is as follows:- [89]

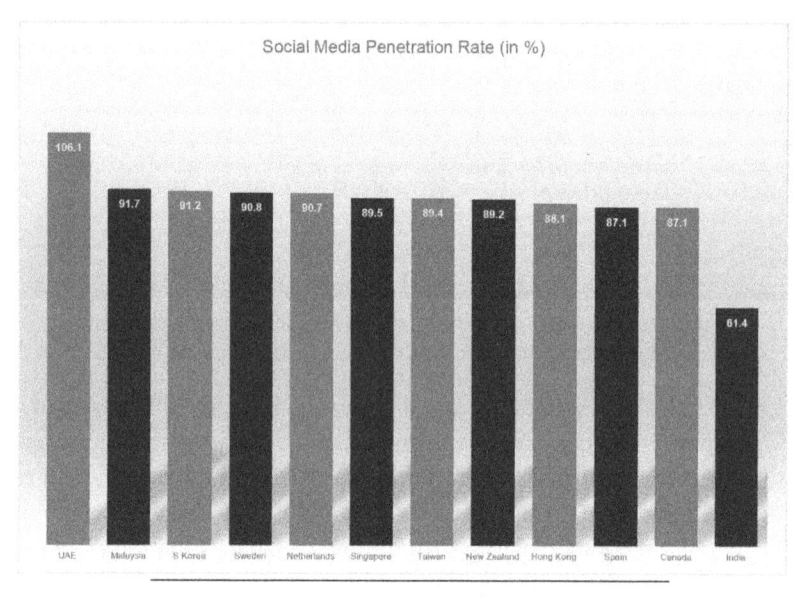

Figure 15 – Social Media Penetration Rate

- It is interesting to note that in recent years, social media penetration has seen a phenomenal increase in West Asia; making it highest in the world. According to a survey published by Sawab Centre (Global Coalition against Daesh, established jointly by US and UAE), 53 % of participants in survey assessed social media as the most important source of spreading extremist ideas. The recruiters from terrorist groups viewed social media a highly effective tool to garner support. Further, 42% of Arabs opined that websites are effectively used by terrorist groups to radicalize individuals[90].

- Malaysia which has 91.7% social media penetration rate, is also combatting the challenges of rising radicalization and extremists' ideology. According to a report published by Counter Extremism Project, a non-profit international policy organization, Kumpulan Mujahidin Malaysia (KMM) aspires to create an Islamic state comprising of Malaysia, Indonesia, and Southern Philippines. There are also reports of Malaysian citizens participating in Soviet-Afghanistan war and Al-Qaeda cadres trained in Muslim dominated country. Further, report reveals that ISIS has been able to gain a foothold in Malaysia. The terrorist organization is exploiting social media platforms especially Facebook to radicalize and carry out recruitment in Malaysia. According to Malaysian Home Minister, Ahmad Zahid Hamidi, social media comprises 75 % of ISIS recruitment efforts. ISIS is operating a web site 'Isdarat Daulah Islamiyah' to upload radical contents in malay language and motivate them to join ISIS supporters in Philippines. Malaysians radicalized and recruited by ISIS appear to come from diverse backgrounds. Some are religious, some are secular who sought to redeem themselves for a religious cause, and others joined for thrill-seeking reasons. The report also claims that ISIS ideology has fascinated even the personnel of Malaysian Defence Forces[91].

- Europe has significantly high internet and social media penetration rates. Many European nations are facing increasing threats of hate crimes, spread of radicalization and ISIS ideology. Terrorists' organisations such as ISIS have made inroads in the vulnerable sections of the society to spread their ideology, garner support, carry out recruitment and lure their supporters to join their terror acts globally.

- It is important to note that social media platforms are linked to spread of extremists' ideology owing to encryption, lack of stringent policies for content regulation and policies framework promulgated by the concerned nation regarding utilisation of social media. The inimical actors exploit the loopholes in the policies and weak legal measures to advance their agenda, upload intimidating and inflammatory messages and carry out perception shaping of the target audience through social media space.

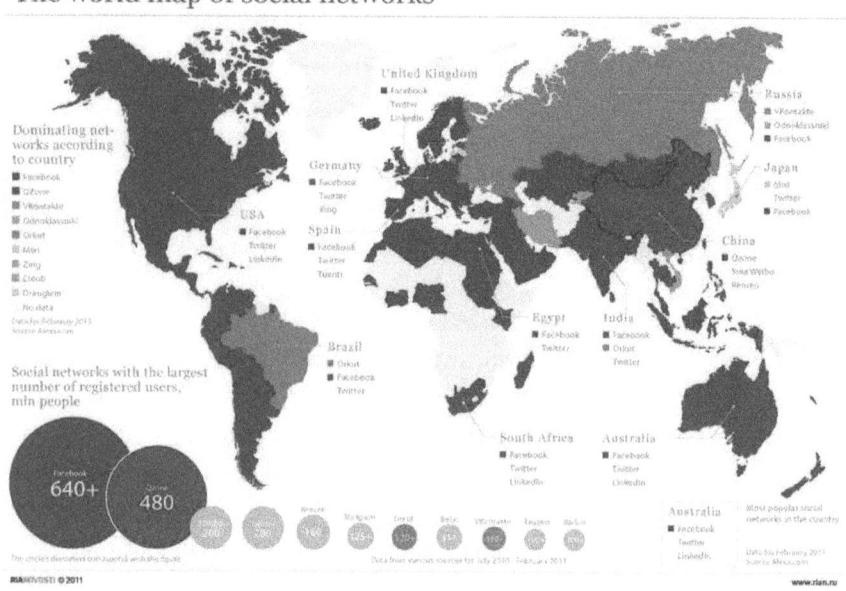

The world map of social networks

Figure 16 – Dominance of various social media platforms across the globe
Source - https://sputnikglobe.com/20110228/162792394.html

Figure 16 above indicates the dominance of Facebook across the continents. Africa, except Northern and Southern parts, has relatively low penetration of social media seemingly attributed to low internet coverage, inadequate digital literacy and lack of infrastructure. Data at Figure 17, depicts social media usage pattern amongst the users beyond 13 years of the age. Except Africa, Central Asian region and South East Asia, social media usage rate is more than 60% amongst the population beyond 13 years of age.

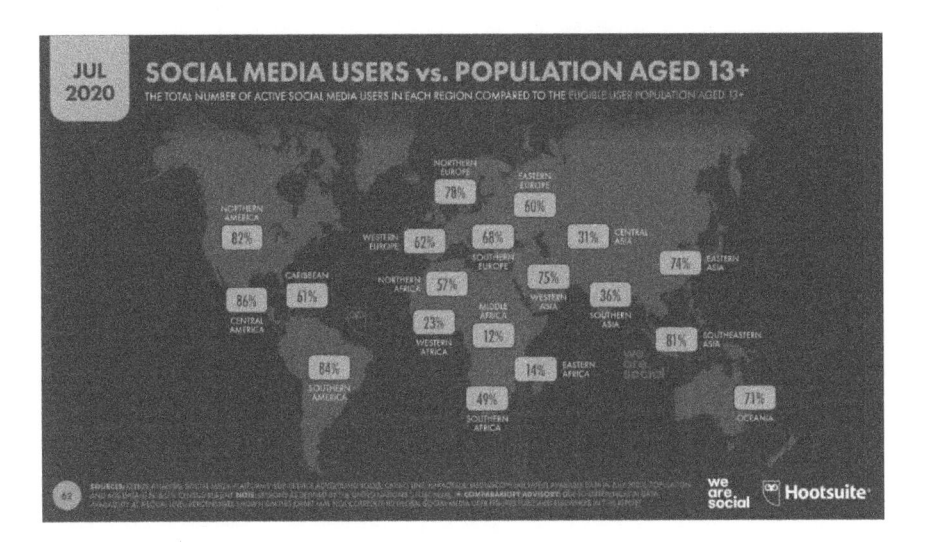

Figure 17 – SM Users' age profile
Source – Kepios Analysis: Social Media Platforms 'Self Service' advertising tools, CNNIC, Line; Kakaotalk; Mediascope

The analysis of India specific statistics provides an interesting insight about expanding social media footprints in the country. The important facts are listed below along with graphical representation of the data: -[92]

➢ In 2023, there were 1.2 billion internet users in India. According to recent statistics, social media penetration in India is around 66.85%. Further, 67.5% of internet users (regardless of age) are subscribing to atleast one social media application.[93] The statistics at Figure 18 below, depicts current trends and forecast of growth of internet in India. By 2028, social media users are estimated to become 83.16% of total population.

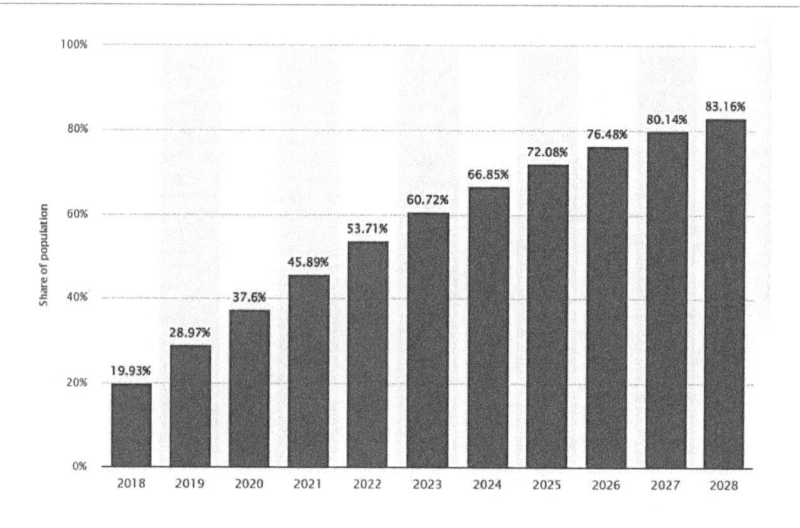

Figure 18 – Current status and forecasting of internet penetration in India, Source - Statista

> It is pertinent to note that in 2023, approximately 74.70% of internet users in India subscribed to most popular network Instagram. As per reports, there are 516.92 million active Instagram users in India comprising of predominantly younger generation. Amongst 492.70 million active internet users, Facebook is the second most popular platform in India. Trends suggest that 71.20% of internet users have profiles on Facebook. Further, the statistics also claim that Facebook continues to be the leading social media application with 398 million users in age group of 18 years and above, which is 40.2% of total population. It is important to note that YouTube and Twitter also have significant users' base in India. TikTok which had exploding growth in India, was banned by Government of India on account of data privacy issues. Consequent to their large customer base especially amongst Gen Z and Gen Millenium, these SMPs dominate the information space and wield power of influence over Indian population. It would be prudent to deduce that consequent to significant foothold of these SMPs across the geo-graphical and socio-political spaces, the ripple effects of social media driven influence operations and activism are witnessed in multiple spheres in India. According to various analyses, Facebook was extensively exploited to influence elections in 2019. The reports also suggest that the contents uploaded on the

YouTube channels played a major role in influencing the voters. The fabricated messaging cast aspersion on Indian democracy and criticized the government agencies during the recently concluded Lok Sabha elections in 2024.

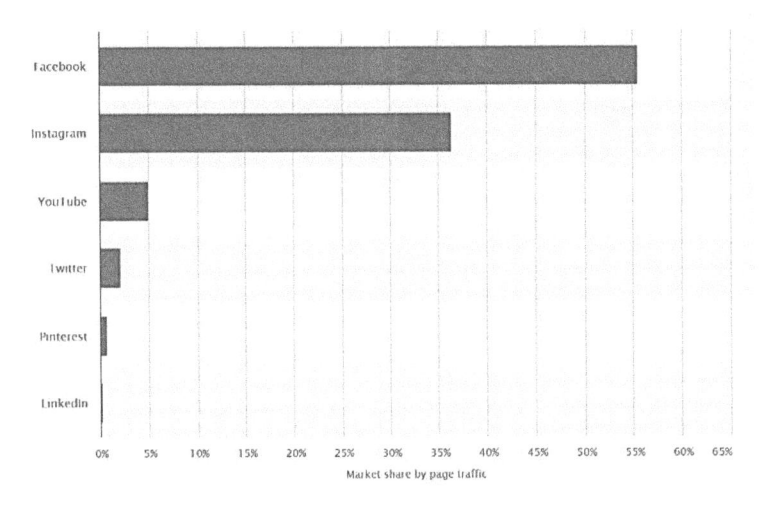

[Bar chart showing market share by page traffic:
- Facebook: ~57%
- Instagram: ~37%
- YouTube: ~8%
- Twitter: ~3%
- Pinterest: ~2%
- LinkedIn: ~1%]

Figure 19 – Percentage share of SMPs in Indian Market based on the traffic, Source – Statista2024

- Other popular social media applications include Twitter (42.90% penetration), LinkedIn (35.7% penetration), Moj (29.50% penetration), a short video community created locally, and Pinterest (29% penetration). A short video app called Moj Lite Plus (26.20% penetration) is one of the few newcomers.

- The most engaging type of content on social media is short-form videos (less than a minute) capturing attention of 66% of subscribers. Highly shareable, these bite-sized videos are 2.5 times more engaging than longer videos.[94]

SALIENCE OF SOCIAL MEDIA IN HYBRID OPERATIONS

[Bar chart showing age profile of social media platform users in India by number of platforms used]

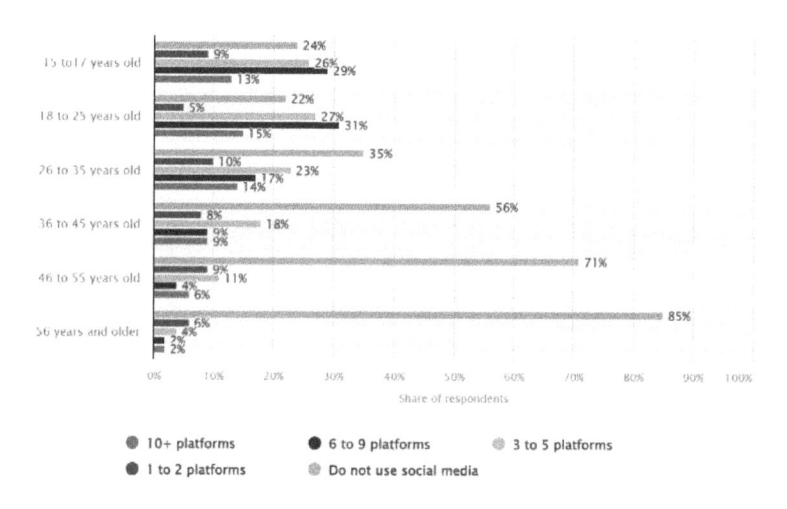

- 15 to 17 years old: 24%, 9%, 26%, 29%, 13%
- 18 to 25 years old: 22%, 5%, 27%, 31%, 15%
- 26 to 35 years old: 35%, 10%, 17%, 23%, 14%
- 36 to 45 years old: 56%, 8%, 9%, 18%, 9%
- 46 to 55 years old: 71%, 9%, 4%, 11%, 6%
- 56 years and older: 85%, 6%, 4%, 2%, 2%

Legend: ● 10+ platforms ● 6 to 9 platforms ● 3 to 5 platforms ● 1 to 2 platforms ● Do not use social media

Figure 20 - Age Profile of SMP users India (January 2022), Source - Statista 2024

➢ The statistics at Figure 20 depicts age profile of the Indian users. The survey conducted in January 2022 revealed that 18 to 25 year age group constituted the largest share of social media users in India, with 31 percent using six to nine social media platforms at a time. The survey highlighted that people residing in urban areas were using more social media platforms than those in rural areas.

➢ According to Nielsen's India Internet Report 2023, India had over 700 million active internet users aged two years and above as of December 2022. A survey conducted from November 2022 to January 2023 found that 425 million people in rural India, or 48% of the rural population, are active internet users. Further, total smart phones users in country own 450 million smartphones; video watching and video calling are top two online activities of smart phone owners. It is interesting to note the growth of internet; a survey by 'Datareportal' titled 'Digital 2024 – India', revealed that total social media users in India soared to 462.0 million by January 2024, equating to 32.2 percent of total population. Further, this report suggests that a total of 1.12 billion cellular mobile connections were active in India in early 2024, figure is equivalent to 78.0 percent of total population.

Characteristics of Trending Social Media Platforms

The positive aspects of social media platforms in improving the people to people connect across the globe, creating awareness and sharing of ideas remain undisputed. However, lack of regulation and content sharing, code of ethical conduct and misuse of platforms for misinformation and creating turbulence remains a cause of concern. It is therefore important to glance through the characteristics of certain most trending social media platforms having substantial customer base and penetration rates. A brief overview of social media platforms shortlisted for the extant study are elucidated in the succeeding paras.

Facebook. Founded in 2004 by Mark Zuckerberg, Eduardo Saverin, Dustin Moskovitz, and Chris Hughes, the social media platform is owned by US based company Meta Platforms. The servers and data centers of the platform are located at Oregon, Lowa and North Carolina cities in US, Luleå in Sweden and Singapore. A social networking platform, it is used for connecting individuals, communities, and businesses through various features to include profiles, news feed, messaging, groups, events, marketplace, advertising, live streaming etc. The platform offers phenomenal *'Network Effect'* implying greater the number/ subscriber of a particular group/ communities greater would be its influence thus stronger network effect. *As per a report, an average Facebook user has 330 friends; implying the user can share a message to 330 other users.*[95] The multiplying effect of the platform can be well imaged considering the network of users. The concerns related to Facebook are as under: -

- ➢ The social media platform recommends *tailored news feeds and contents* in accordance with the user's data, search activities and digital footprints.

- ➢ The algorithms of the platform create *'Echo Chambers'* capable of potentially reinforcing existing biases.

- ➢ Facebook collects user data and analyses vast user data leading to concerns related to *privacy, security and targeted* advertising. The New York Times report published on 03 Jun 2018 revealed data-sharing partnership between Facebook and at least 60 device makers including Apple, Amazon, BlackBerry, Microsoft, and Samsung. These companies were even allowed to capture data belonging to users' friends without their explicit consent. Subsequent to disclosure of *Facebook-Cambridge Analytica episode,* the social media giant had issued apology in response to notices issued by Government of India over sharing of data pertaining to Indian citizens.[96]

- The platform's structure can facilitate the spread of *misinformation and fake news*, impacting public discourse and decision-making. A study published in the journal 'Nature: Human Behavior', established that compared to Google, Twitter and webmail providers (AOL, Yahoo and Gmail), Facebook is the worst perpetrator of spreading fake news.[97] The algorithm of social media platform, which determine viewers' search tendencies and preferences, was found to amplify fake news and hate speech. Though Russia kept Facebook under scanner in the country, but took advantage of the platform to prosecute social media warfare against its adversaries such as USA and Ukraine. As per reports, the Russian hackers reportedly weaponized the information to sway the election in Trump's favour.[98] As per AP News, in November 23 Facebook deleted around 4800 accounts reportedly created in China, designed to appear owned by Americans and used to spread polarizing political content in an apparent effort to divide the U.S. electorates ahead of 2024 elections. These accounts pushed the contents shared by politicians (Liberals and Conservatives) on Twitter to make them appear authentic. The report also reveals that later these accounts started to appear originated in India. The report also cautions that these accounts may have been created to influence the upcoming national elections scheduled in India, Mexico, Ukraine, Pakistan, Taiwan and other nations in 2024.[99]

- The footprints of Facebook have been observed in *impacting politics and election worldwide*; it has been used extensively for campaigning, organizing, and spreading information, raising concerns about manipulation and voter's influence.

- Facebook is also exploited for *'Social Movements and Activism'* for organising and mobilising supporters for protests and raising awareness or spread agenda. The inference is corroborated by analysis of 'Arab Spring Revolution' wherein Facebook was used by the activists to mobilise the crowd for demonstrations and protests and garner global support to their cause.

'X' or formerly Twitter. With 280-character limit, Twitter has carved a unique niche in the social media landscape. Twitter thrives on *real-time information, fleeting engagement,* and *bite-sized updates*. Initially founded in 2006 by Jack Dorsey, Noah Glass, Biz Stone, and Evan Williams, the platform is currently owned by Elon Musk and four renowned institutional investors i.e., Vanguard Group, Morgan Stanley, Black Rock, and State Street.

A microblogging platform, it's features include *profiles, tweets, hashtags, mentions, retweets, direct messages, polls, spaces (audio chat), communities, and trending topics.* Facilitating real-time information, the platform serves as pulse for breaking news, live events, and rapid-fire discussions. The tweets, public by default and ephemeral, disappear quickly from trending topics and contents thus create a sense of immediacy and fleeting conservations. Hashtags act as digital threads connecting conversations on specific topics, fostering shared interests and communities. The concerns related to the regulation of content shared and security challenges pertaining to Twitter functioning are summarised below: -

- *Data Security and Privacy Concerns.* 'X' uses the subscribers' data to include email addresses, phone numbers, and location information, to target users with advertisements. The social media platform has received criticism for *lack of transparency* about handling users' data. There are concerns that the data collated may be used for other purposes viz., *tracking users' online activity* or *selling their personal information to third parties.* Consequent to investigation into these allegations, the platform was fined by the Federal Trade Commission (FTC) for misusing user data[100]. The ephemeral nature of contents may also make it difficult to trace the objectionable contents and compound the task of regulation difficult.

- *Fake News, Hate Mongering and Propaganda.* As per reports, Twitter's *algorithms can amplify toxic content*, leading to several problems, including users being driven off the platform and spreading misinformation and hate speech.[101] In the recent past, the social media platform has been used by certain groups and actors for misinformation, propaganda and hate mongering. The fall out of these actions resulted into aggravation of conflicts, communal hatred and violence in various regions of the world.

- *Influencers and Opinion Leaders.* Groups/ organisations, celebrities, journalists, and experts can wield significant influence, shape narratives and drive public opinion on myriad issues such as religious, ethnic, environment, economic, and various other contemporary agendas. As per the reports, one of the mediums through which *ISIS targets Saudi Arabia is the use of Twitter to exploit Saudis obsessive Twitter use.*[102]

- *Bots and Automation.* Automated accounts can manipulate trends, spread misinformation, and amplify specific voices, thus may raise concerns about authenticity and manipulation.

- *Echo Chambers and Conformation Bias.* Twitter algorithms can create personalized information ecosystems, potentially *reinforcing existing biases* and *limiting exposure to diverse viewpoints.*

- *Cyberbullying and Harassment.* Public nature of the platform can facilitate online abuse and harassment, impacting mental health and fostering negative online environments. Another weakness of Twitter is its toxicity due to the prevalence of *trolling, harassment, and abuse* on the platform. The *anonymity of Twitter users* makes it easier for them to engage in toxic behaviour and harass the users having differing viewpoints. The 280-character limit on tweets can make it difficult to convey complex ideas, leading to misunderstandings and even conflicts.

- *Political Activism and Mobilization.* Platform can potentially be used for organizing *protests*, launching *awareness campaigns*, astroturfing and *mobilizing and recruiting* supporters for various causes and agendas.

Instagram. Founded in 2010 by Kevin Systrom and Mike Krieger, Instagram is currently owned by Meta Platforms, a US based company. Unlike Twitter's fleeting tweets and Facebook's comprehensive profiles, Instagram offers *captivating visuals, curated feeds* and *visual storytelling.* Owing to its focus on creating a world of *aesthetics, micro-influencers,* and fleeting *trends*, the platform has emerged as a dominant force in the social media landscape. The prominent features of the platform include *profiles, posts* (photos and videos), *stories* (disappear after 24 hours), *reels* (short-form video format), *direct messages, live videos, shopping features and hashtags.* The security and personal safety related challenges posed by Instagram are as follows: -

- *FOMO (Fear of Missing Out).* Highly curated feeds and the constant influx of new content can create a sense of missing out, potentially impacting self-esteem and mental health.

- *Body Image and Comparison.* The reports suggest that focus on idealised images and curated lifestyles has led to body image insecurities and social comparison amongst the users. As per report published by UK's Royal Society for Public Health based on

'The Status of Mind Survey', Instagram was rated as worst social media platform for mental health. The report stated that while this photo-based platform is widely liked for its unique features facilitating self-expression and self-identity, it was also associated with high levels of anxiety and depression.[103] The constant glare of thousands of social media users and peers, the users developed an inferiority complex about their looks, body shape and personality thereby, forcing them to resort to use various filters, special effects, aesthetics and editing tools.

- ➤ Other concerns are related to *'Echo Chambers and Conformation Biases'*, *'Cyber Bullying and Harassment'* and *tracking of users' location* through the GPS on their device.

YouTube. Founded in 2005 by Chad Hurley, Steven Chen, and Jawed Karim, social media platform was acquired by Google in 2022. YouTube facilitates users to upload, view, share, and comment on videos. Prominent features of platform include channels, video uploads, comments, likes/ dislikes, subscriptions, playlists, live streaming, community features (polls and super chats) and monetisation options for creators. The vast content library containing videos on wide range of topics, caters for diverse interests and audiences. User-Generated Content (UGC) i.e., videos facilitate random users to create and upload contents. Algorithms and user interaction can propel videos to viral fame, shaping culture and online trends. Micro-celebrities, influencers, YouTubers and creators can build immense fan followings and wield significant influence, shape perceptions and promote their ideas and agendas. The concerns related to YouTube are discussed in the succeeding sub paragraphs: -

- ➤ *Echo Chambers and Conformation Bias.* 'Recommendation Algorithms' of the platform can create *personalized content bubbles*, potentially reinforcing existing biases and restrict exposure to diverse viewpoints.

- ➤ *Misinformation and Fake News.* The *open nature* of the platform can facilitate spread of misinformation and fake news. Protection against manipulation of intellectual space by state and non-state actors necessitate critical thinking and verification skills from viewers. As per reports, terrorists' organisations have primarily relied on Facebook, Twitter and YouTube to spread their propaganda, carryout online indoctrination and actively recruit their members. Facebook and Twitter remain to be most crucial platforms as both allow people to stay updated with different issues. Owing to features such as, share, comment, react, and retweet information, it becomes easier for terrorist groups to maximize their propaganda publicly. YouTube also plays an important role for propaganda purposes to politicise support and create powerful terror networks. The social media platform has allegedly been exploited by influencers to share their prejudiced and skewed views on wide range of issues such as politics, finance and social issues. The unfettered messaging may cause confusion and chaos in the minds of the users.

- *Copyright Issues and Content Regulation.* Balancing user-generated content and copyright protection remains a challenge, leading to content removal and ongoing debates about platform.
- Youtube has emerged as an alternative platform for news content, independent journalism, and citizen reporting, offering diverse perspectives and challenging traditional media narratives. However, *unregulated sharing of extreme views*, radicalism, and engineered narrative remains a potential challenge for security establishments.
- *Political Activism and Mobilisation.* This social media platform has also been used for organising protests, raising awareness, and sharing political statements, playing a role in political discourse and social movements.

TikTok – The Short-Term Sensation. Founded in 2016 by Zhang Yiming, owner of ByteDance in China, TikTok is the international version of 'Douyin'. With its catchy tunes, addictive dances, and bite-sized content, the platform gained massive fan following amongst Gen Z users. A *platform for hosting short-duration videos (15 seconds to 10 minutes)*, offers options to upload music, dance, comedy, and entertainment. TikTok has multiple features such as video uploading and editing with extensive tools and effects, challenges and trends, duets and reactions, live streaming, interactive features like comments, shares, and virtual gifts, and monetisation options for creators. Its algorithm ('For You' page) enables personalised content based on user engagement, thus making users addicted to the platform. Owing to its micro-influencers and creators, TikTok gained global reach and became leader in cultural exchange transcending geographical boundaries, facilitating cultural exchange and showcasing diverse content from around the world. The security concerns related to the social media platform are as follows: -

- ➢ *Privacy Concerns and Data Security.* There are serious concerns pertaining to data collection practices and potential vulnerabilities about user privacy and security risks.

  - The application collects sensitive information without user's explicit knowledge. The information collected includes *email addresses, phone numbers, content uploaded, keystroke patterns,* battery levels, audio settings, mobile carrier, *wireless connections,* device brand and model, operating system, *browsing history,* ways of consuming data, time spent on watching posts, *searches,* apps, *filenames and filetypes,* and *location.* Information contained in data collated includes contents of messages and time of uploading, receipt and reading by the users.

  - A paper by cybersecurity firm 'Internet 2.0' claims that TikTok app uses *"excessive" data harvesting,* reaping information on *user location,* the contents of direct messages, and more.[104] The paper claims this information is *stored on servers located in mainland China.* TikTok admitted in November 2022 that Chinese staff could and did access user data, however they denied sharing user data with the Chinese government officials.[105]

  - A Forbes report claimed ByteDance planned to *"monitor the personal location of some specific American citizens".*[106] TikTok denied the claims made in the article, but *later sacked four employees* for accessing personal data of journalists in an attempt to track down sources.

  - The investigation by US agencies observed that *ByteDance was responsive to requests by the CCP officials to promote and remove certain posts.* The user data was also provided to Chinese official through a back door channel; an allegation which was denied by the company.

  - Consequent to wide spread security concerns, TikTok has been banned in around 22 countries to include UK, EU, Canada, India, Bangladesh, Denmark, Belgium, Netherlands and many other countries. USA has banned use of TikTok on official mobile phones and computers.

- *Misinformation, Fake News and Spreading Hatred.* The platform's open nature and rapid content spread can facilitate the circulation of misinformation and fake news. TikTok has also been demonstrated to be a hive of misinformation. In September 2022, Newsguard found that when searching "2022 election", "mRNA vaccine", and "Uvalde tx conspiracy", 20% of TikTok posts contained false or misleading information.[107] Further a study reveals that TikTok has become favourite medium for extremists to sow seeds of hatred exploiting the platforms' young audience and lax security measures to prey on the vulnerable audiences. The hate speech found on TikTok ranges from neo-Nazi to Boogaloo (far right anti government movement in USA) with a range of antisemitic and racist contents. Until 2019, the hate speech on TikTok had gone virtually unnoticed until *Motherboard* reported that it had found examples of "blatant, violent white supremacy and Nazism", including direct calls to kill Jews and black people.[108]

- *Potential Mental Health Impacts.* Addiction to platform, unrealistic beauty standards, and cyberbullying can pose potential mental health challenges. The researchers claim that TikTok will show children harmful content as soon as they show an interest in related topic. During the research, accounts were generated in the US, UK, Canada, and Australia on behalf of fictional 13-year-olds, these accounts were shown videos related to mental health and body image. The accounts were exposed to self-harm or eating disorder content every 206 seconds on average. More extreme content was shown to accounts intended to represent vulnerable youths, with references to weight loss in their usernames.[109]

- *Social Activism and Movements.* Constructively the platform can be used for raising awareness about social issues, organizing protests, and mobilizing supporters for various causes. However, considering vulnerabilities of algorithm and echo chamber effect, the platform presents potent threats of social engineering and manufactured political dissent by the adversarial forces through their staunch supporters and naïve users. In April 2021, Israeli forces evicted Palestinian families from their households in Sheikh Jarrah neighbourhood. In response, Palestinians used the power of social media, especially TikTok, to support a *'call for action'* on the hashtag #SaveSheikhJarrah.[110] The content on TikTok, being viral and free from limitation, inspired the emergence of a new term, *"TikTok Intifada"*, using the Arabic term for previous Palestinian uprisings.[111]

Telegram: Beyond Basic Messaging. Telegram was founded in 2013 by Pavel and Nikolai Durov (founders of Russian social network VKontakte). This *Cloud-based instant messaging platform* offers private and group chats, file sharing, and various additional features. The key features are text and voice messaging, *encrypted 'Secret Chats', large group chats* (may have upto two lakh members), channels for broadcasting information, self-destructing messages, bots for automation, media sharing with generous limits, cloud storage for saved messages and files, cross-platform functionality, and open API for third-party development. Telegram prioritises users' privacy through features like *optional end-to-end encryption, two-step verification,* and *self-destructing messages.* This makes it popular amongst users seeking secure communication channels. The encrypted data feature has proved Telegram most effective platform during ongoing Russia-Ukraine war for communication and sharing the information. The prominent security concerns related to Telegram are flagged as under:-

- *Bots and Automation.* The open Application Programming Interface (API) allows creating diverse bots, offering functionalities such as news aggregation, reminders, and games, which extends the platform's capabilities.

- *Potential for Misinformation and Spam.* Openness, self-destructing messages, encrypted 'Secret Chats', large group chats and larger group sizes can facilitate the spread of misinformation and spam. Owing to exposure to unregulated contents and difficulty in detecting the source of information, the users need to exercise caution and government needs to ensure responsible platform management.

- The open API feature of the application fosters a thriving developer community and creates potential for innovative integrations. However, owing to lack of safety mechanism, the open-sourced API may expose the platform to exploitation by hackers, radical elements and extremists to host deep fakes, engineered contents and propaganda messages.

- *Limited Content Moderation.* Compared to stricter platforms, Telegram has less stringent content moderation, which can attract users seeking open expression but also raise concerns about harmful content.

> *Data Privacy Concerns.* While Telegram emphasises privacy, some concerns remain regarding data storage. Owing to end to end encryption and data security feature, which favours the users, the platform presents a serious challenge for the security agencies to carry out monitoring of online chatter, detect false news and propaganda and ascertain the source of fabricated contents detrimental to security and safety.

> *Social Movements and Activism.* Channels and group chats offer efficient communication medium for organizing protests, raising awareness, and mobilizing supporters for various causes.

WhatsApp. The social media platform was founded by Jan Koum and Brian Acton in 2009. WhatsApp as group communication offers cross-platform for instant text, voice, and video calls with strong encryption and privacy. It's **features include** Individual and group chats, voice and video calls, media sharing (photos, videos, documents), voice messages, end-to-end encryption (optional), status updates, location sharing, contact synchronisation, web/desktop app integration, and business-oriented features for WhatsApp Business. The issues related to security of information are as follows: -

> *Misinformation and Spam Potential.* Its popularity and open nature can facilitate the spread of misinformation and spam, requiring users' caution and responsible platform management. Introduction of chat group features presents the challenges of sharing of sensitive contents in the closed groups undetected.

> *Privacy Concerns and Data Collection.* While emphasizing privacy, concerns remain regarding data collection practices of the platform and potential access by law enforcement agencies.

> *Social Movements and Activism.* Platform can also be used for organizing protests, sharing information in closed groups, and mobilizing supporters/ sympathizers for various causes.

Reddit. Founded in 2009 by Steve Huffman and Alexis Ohanian Reddit, the majority stake holders are US based companies. The social media platform is a vast network of online communities, or subreddits, each dedicated to a specific topic or interest. Users can submit content like text posts, links, images, and videos, which are then voted up or down by other users, determining their visibility within the subreddit and potentially on the front page. Its functions are democratic voting system, user-generated content, social news aggregation, content rating, and discussion website. The important features are Subreddits (user created communities), posts (text, links, images, videos), up votes/ down votes, comments, private messaging, user profiles, Karma system (reflects user's contributions), awards, live streams, and various community-specific features. Major issues related to security concerns are as under: -

- *Anonymity and Pseudonymity.* Users can choose usernames, allowing for varied levels of anonymity and expression, which may be exploited by certain users to spread their nefarious agenda and colour the opinions while concealing own identity.

- *Misinformation and Echo Chambers.* Platform algorithm can discern users' online search pattern and can recommend the content/ channels according to the preferences. Resultantly, the users may become part of certain subreddits which can lead to creation of closed information ecosystems, potentially reinforcing biases and spreading misinformation.

- *Cyberbullying and Harassment.* Anonymity and pseudonymity can embolden some users to engage in cyberbullying and harassment, requiring active moderation and community vigilance.

WeChat. The platform was developed by Allen Zhang in 2011 and owned by Tencent, a Chinese technology and entertainment conglomerate. It's a multifaceted platform that has woven itself into the fabric of daily life for over 1.3 billion users in China and beyond. The multipurpose platform offers messaging, social media, mobile payments, online shopping, transportation booking, food delivery, government services, and more. It's features include Chat (individual and group), Moments (newsfeed), Official Accounts (branded channels), Mini Programs (embedded apps within WeChat), Payments (integrated digital wallet), QR code scanning for payments and connections, ride-hailing, food delivery, government services, games, and various other functionalities. The security concerns flagged by various researchers are as follows: -

- WeChat Pay has become the dominant mobile payment method in China, significantly impacting cash dependence and consumer behaviour.

- > *Social Currency and Influence.* Reportedly social connections and reputations built on WeChat can impact user access to services, employment opportunities, and even social credit scores.

- > *Censorship and Privacy Concerns.* The platform is subject to Chinese government censorship and data collection practices, thus raising concerns about user privacy and freedom of expression.

- > Social Mobility and Inequality. Access to WeChat's functionalities and social networks can impact personal and professional opportunities, potentially contributing to inequalities.

- > *Social Control and Surveillance.* The platform's integration with government services and data collection raises concerns about potential social control and surveillance mechanisms.

Tools, Tactics and Social Media Strategies Employed by Hybrid Actors

In Chapter 2, based on the analysis of various studies, it has been highlighted that Hybrid warfare entails blend of conventional and unconventional methods. The state and non-state actors would explore a complex toolkit to achieve their objectives. The tools, tactics and strategies prevalent in contemporary 'Hybrid' conflicts are summarised in the succeeding sub paragraphs.

- > **Tools.**

  - Conventional Military Means. Application of conventional military means would be corresponding to escalatory matrix. The conventional forces may be used for intervention tasks as well as conflict resolution in low intensity/ full scale war.

  - *Unconventional Warfare.* Imply dovetailing guerrilla warfare, proxy and auxiliary forces, sabotage, terrorism, assassination, etc along with application of instruments of nation's power (DIME) to create instability, diversion and chaos without direct attribution.

  - *Information Warfare.* Leveraging internet, social media and other traditional communication channels, the state and non-state actors can launch cyberattacks, propaganda, disinformation campaigns, fake news, social engineering, etc.

to manipulate public opinion and decision makers and sow discord within the target society.

- *Economic Warfare.* In the contemporary conflict scenario, economic sanctions, trade restrictions, financial manipulations and cyberattacks on critical infrastructure have been exploited to cripple the target state's economy, weaken its resolve and war waging capability.

- *Diplomatic and Legal Tools.* Utilising international law, alliances, and treaties to pressure the target state, isolate state and non-state actors in regional and global forums, deflect attribution and garner support to own agenda.

> **Strategies.**

- *Blurring Contours of Conflict.* Apply varied 'means' to orchestrate the contest and calibrate horizontal and vertical escalation of violence, so as to maintain the competition below the threshold of war, making it difficult to identify the aggressor and deter retaliation.

- *Ambiguity and Deniability.* Utilizing proxies and non-state actors, employing irregular forces, mercenaries and criminal organizations, the aggressors can evade from direct responsibility while still achieving their goals. This facilitates ambiguity, elude involvement and creates plausible deniability and complicates the responses.

- *Strategic and Operational Deception.* Propagate engineered false narratives, misinformation, and fabricated evidence to obfuscate actions and intentions and mislead the adversaries.

- *Exploiting Vulnerabilities.* Targeting societal, ethnical and religious divides, political discord, economic weakness, and technological dependence to compound the existing tensions.

- *Violence Escalation Control.* Carefully calibrating the intensity of attacks to avoid open war while maximizing pressure in multiple domains and achieving objectives.

- *Leveraging Networks of Actors.* Forging alliances with non-state actors, proxy and auxiliary forces, criminal organizations, and sympathetic groups within the target country to amplify effects.

- *Leverage Geo-economic Influence.*
  - Imposing economic sanctions and trade restrictions would cripple the target nation's economy through financial pressure, weaken its resolve, limit its resources, and force concessions. This can be particularly effective in dealing with resource-dependent nations.
  - Manipulating energy supplies and controlling access to vital resources like oil, gas, or food can create economic instability, fuel discontent, and give the aggressor leverage in negotiations or power struggles.
- *Diplomatic and Legal Maneuvering.*
  - Exploiting legal loopholes and international treaties, aggressors may exploit legal technicalities, escape routes and international treaties, existing agreements, or even fabricate evidence to justify their actions and deflect blame. This can delay international intervention and provide time to solidify gains.
  - Through diplomatic pressure, propaganda campaigns, and strategic alliances, aggressors can aim to isolate the target nation and weaken its international support, making it more vulnerable.
- *Exploiting Internal Fissures and Sensitivities.*
  - Hybrid warfare thrives on pre-existing fault lines within a society. Aggressors can exacerbate social, ethnic, or religious divisions to create internal conflict and weaken national resolve and unity.
  - Disrupting power grids, transportation systems, and communication networks can create chaos, panic, and dependence on the aggressor for assistance, potentially leading to concessions.

➤ **Tactics.**
  - *Cyber Attacks and Hacking.* Embedded and sponsored hackers may be employed to launch cyber strikes to disrupt critical infrastructure, steal sensitive data, create online clutter and conduct cyber espionage campaigns. Such attacks can cripple

essential services, sow panic, and provide valuable intelligence for further operations.

- *Propaganda and Weaponised Disinformation Campaigns.* It entails synergised application of multiple channels to shape public opinion through fake news, social media manipulation, and targeting vulnerable groups. Spreading false narratives, manipulating news, and flooding social media with fabricated content can sow discord, undermine trust in institutions, and sway public opinion in favour of the aggressor's agenda.

- *Psychological Warfare.* Targeting individuals and communities with fear, intimidation, and emotional manipulation can break morale, erode social cohesion, and create an environment ripe for exploitation.

- *Infiltration and Subversion.* Recruiting proxies to sow dissent within government and institutions, and manipulate electoral process.

Social Media Strategies. In the contemporary conflict scenarios, state and non-state actors have used social media extensively to dominate and influence the virtual and cognitive battle space and shape the perception of target population. The Russia-Ukraine and Israel-Hamas Conflicts and Doklam and Galwan incidents have demonstrated the efforts by both sides to carefully weave a narrative to own advantage, dominate the adversary and influence the decision-makers and masses. The trends of social media strategies put into action by various actors in hybrid warfare context are as follows: -

➢ **Disinformation and Propaganda.**

- Spreading *fabricated or misleading information* disguised as legitimate news can sway public opinion and undermine people's trust in established institutions and leaders. *Deep Fakes and manipulated videos* compound the challenges by blurring the lines between truth and fiction.

- *Weaponising Existing Narratives.* Exploiting pre-existing societal divisions, prejudices, and anxieties through targeted messaging can exacerbate existing tensions and fuel the conflicts.

- *Bot Amplification.* Utilizing automated accounts (bots) to artificially *amplify specific narratives,* create *online noise* and *muffle the dissenting* voices can engineer the illusion of widespread support for a particular agenda.

➢ *Astro-turfing and Online Trolling.*

- To create a plausible impression of grassroots movements (based on manufactured narrative), multiple campaigns can be orchestrated using fake accounts to mimic organic support for a particular cause/ agenda or create perception of widespread public backing.
- *Trolls and Harassment Tactics.* Unleashing abusive and inflammatory tactics can silence or intimidate opponents, discourage their participation in online discussions/ public debates and create a hostile atmosphere.

➢ *Hijacking Hashtags and Trends.*

- *Infiltrating Trending Online Chatter.* Multiple fake accounts can be used to host malicious content or propaganda material into trending hashtags and discussions with a view to manipulate online discourse and control the narrative surrounding a particular event.
- *Fabricating Fake Trends.* Popularity of specific hashtags or topics can be inflated artificially to create diversion from real issues or promote alternative narratives.

➢ *Targeting and Micro-targeting.*

- The personal data gleaned from social media activities and other sources can be exploited for achieving targeted manipulation. Tailored messages and contents can resonate more effectively with target population and achieve desired impact.
- *Exploiting Emotional Vulnerabilities.* The analysis of social issues and public sentiments can facilitate identification of sensitivities and fears, anxieties, and biases of the public. Based on findings of sentiment analysis, the actors can inundate the virtual and cognitive battle space with emotionally charged contents to render the target population more susceptible to manipulation.

> *Disrupt and Muzzle Dissent.*

- *Mass Reporting and Censorship.* The state agencies can resort to imposing the curbs to restrict the access of people to alternate viewpoints or/ and censor and silence critical voices. This can be achieved by flagging such alternative/ differing views and content as abusive or misleading.

- *Doxing and Online Threats.* To deter the dissent and create a climate of fear, certain actors may resort to exposing the identities of individuals/ competitors online with an aim to subjecting them to harassment or threats.

Narrative Designing

In the contemporary times, the world is witnessing an increasing trend of exploitation of internet and social media by various actors to wage the battle of narrative, create societal fissures and furthering their inimical agendas. The fabricated narratives are pushed by these actors in simultaneity with the kinetic actions and violent tactics as a low-cost option. The objective of narrative campaigns is to break the linearity of operations, erode trust of target population in values and institutions and achieve desired result while keeping escalatory matrix below the conventional war. In Indian context, Pakistan sponsored separatists and terrorists' outfits, troika of ISIS, SIMI (Students' Islamic Movement of India) and IM (Indian Mujahidin), insurgents in North Eastern states and anti-national elements have glamorised the methods of recruiting youth to their cause by leveraging the power of social media and internet. The quality and scale of their output is growing and they are increasingly pioneering new ways of spreading malicious content. They produce compelling content delivered by influencers which can add to the allure of their messages and effectively appeal to their target audiences. Thus, there is a need to develop alternative approaches to tackle battle of narrative beyond online censorship. In a world where it is impossible to completely silence extremist narratives, developing "counter-narratives", is a necessary alternative.

Narrative Designing. Institute of Strategic Dialogue (ISD) has taken out a handbook to guide social media campaign planners and strategists to formulate an effective counter narrative. As per handbook, articulation of narrative revolves around four fundamental questions i.e., who is the audience, what is the message, which medium to be used and who is the messenger?. Narrative contents vary whether messages are being designed for 'Upstream' prevention and 'Downstream' intervention.

'Upstream Prevention' messages are designed to target broader population to guard against influence of radicalization, whereas 'Downstream Intervention' is designed to reach out to audience with extremists' views. The impact of narratives would depend upon themes, ability to establish emotional connect/ evoke reaction of target audience, timing of uploading the content, language and coverage of social media platforms amongst the population.

> Types of Narrative. According to a study conducted by International Centre for Counter Terrorism, there can be five types of narratives relevant to Al-Qaeda and related organizations. 'Positive/ Alternative' narratives are designed to counter violent extremist narratives, 'Strategic counter narratives' are designed for wider audiences and used by governments and institutions, 'Ethical counter narratives' are aimed to achieve moral high ground and discredit the 'ways and means' of extremist violent ideology. Similarly, 'ideological and religious counter-narratives' are best suited to be delivered by a messenger having religious authority over the community and are aimed to counter the negative messaging using religious teachings. Tactical counter-narratives emphasize that violence in the long run is often less effective when compared to more peaceful methods, and not useful to an organizations' overall reputation and objectives. This type of narrative can be used by a variety of messengers, including governments and community-based organisations.[112]

> The Message. A story is conceived with a message with a subtle purpose and should be thought provoking. Fundamentally, the message should speak with the audience, not at them. According to Institute of Strategic Dialogue (ISD) Handbook, the most effective messages do not lecture the audience, they offer an alternative idea and compel them to reflect on. The messages may contain facts from credible sources to deconstruct, discredit and demystify fabricated narratives. It may also be constructed around emotional appeals, satire and humour to de-glamorise and undermine agenda of extremist groups. Even the positive stories and messages from people within the audience, or whom the audience admires leave a lasting impact. Some messages may include a "call to action", seeking audiences to do something immediately.

> Medium. The narratives can be made in multiple forms such as Videos (short films or animations), texts (slogans, hashtags or

open letters), images (photos or memes) and online literature (brochures or informative posters). Any content, online or offline, is likely to be misconstrued by the audiences due to differing perception and intellect. Thus, it is important to ascertain as to how the content or message could be misinterpreted or cause offense to some audiences. Conducting research about the audience can help to gauge the potential reaction. Directly making fun of or humiliating members of an extremist group can also have the unintended effect of emboldening their extreme stance or increasing feelings of alienation.

- Messengers. Credibility and acceptability of messengers is key to effective messaging and narrative building. It is observed that factual campaigns are potent tool to counter misinformation, undermine extremist narratives and encourage critical thinking. Government-run information campaigns encounter difficulties with credibility and legitimacy; however, incorporation of former/ survivor extremist/ terrorists, victims, local influential personalities, artists and media persons may enhance the effectiveness of campaigns.

- Style and Tone of Contents. As per Institute of Strategic Dialogue Handbook, counter-narrative content can have a wide-range of tones, engaging and resonate with the audience, viz; reflective, antagonistic, scholarly, mournful, regretful, cool, exciting, adventurous, provocative, humorous, or satirical. It may be a personal story to directly engage an ideology or one component of an ideology. It can feature real-life people e.g., former terrorists/ extremists and survivors/ refugees, in an engaging documentary-style. It can also involve cartoons and created characters; or fictionalised dramas or scenarios.

Based on the findings of extant study and observations of various thinks tanks, it can be concluded that social media platforms have gained a strong foothold over the world population. By virtue of their accessibility, features and engaging contents, social media platforms have emerged as a potential alternative to traditional media and a platform for the common public to voice their concerns. Resultantly, social media platforms have gained prominence in strategic communication and have become a powerful tool for moulding thoughts, behaviours and attitudes of the population. While the growth of social media and internet has offered a viable solution to many problems in governance, communication and socio-political space. The unfettered spread of information, anonymity and non-attributability has been exploited to weaponise information, carry out social engineering and control the cognitive space. The issues discussed in extant chapter, provides a conceptual framework to study social media warfare. The analysis of certain global events in next chapter would facilitate a comprehensive understanding of strategies employed by various actors to leverage the influence of social media in controlling outcomes of the conflicts.

Chapter 4

Case Studies

(Israel- Hamas Conflict, Russia-Ukraine Conflict, India-China Standoff, Pakistan's Battle of Narrative and Radicalisation Campaign by ISIS, SIMI and IM)

Evidently social media platforms have made considerable inroads in societal and political engagements; the digital platform retain potential to shape opinion of the masses, influence the decision-makers and mobilize the netizens beyond geo-graphical borders. Owing to their extensive reach, affordability and speed of transmission of content, social media platforms can act as driving force to spread awareness over social issues, improve governance and lives of human beings. However, there is also a dangerous side of this technological innovation. The prevailing ambiguity, absence of globally recognized ethical code of conduct and anonymity make social media platforms vulnerable to exploitation by state and non-state actors to further their ulterior motives and wage 'Social Media Warfare' against target nations/ competitors. There are no credible and irrefutable empirical data to establish direct linkage between ongoing conflicts between nation states and/ or between state versus non-state actors. However, it would be logical to state that social media platform's global reach, speed of dissemination, non-attributability, ambiguity and absence of a legal frame work has been exploited by various actors to advance their agendas and prosecute hybrid war. Having analysed the penetration rates of various social media platforms, their strengths and vulnerabilities and tactics and strategies of social media warfare, this study would attempt to connect the dots to discern the ways in which social media warfare have manifested the proliferation of conflicts/ competitions and may dominate emerging spectrum of conflict in the foreseeable future. To steer the study further, an analysis of Global Risk Report 2024 by World Economic Form (WEF) has been carried out. The important aspects of the report are discussed in the succeeding paragraphs.

The Global Risks Report explores some of the most severe risks world may face over next decade, against a backdrop of rapid technological change, economic uncertainty, a warming planet and conflicts. 2023-2024 GRPS results highlight a predominantly negative outlook for the world over next two years which is expected to worsen over next decade. The majority of respondents (54%) anticipate some instability and a moderate risk of global catastrophes, while another 30% expect even more turbulent conditions. The outlook is appreciated to be more negative over 10-year time horizon, with nearly two-thirds of respondents expecting a stormy or turbulent outlook.

> As per 2024 Global Risk Report, *'AI generated disinformation and misinformation'* has been ranked at 2nd place (in short term scenario i.e., two years) amongst 34 economic, environmental, geopolitical, societal and technological risks shortlisted for global risk categories. In this report, societal and political polarization and cyber-attacks are ranked at 3rd and 5th places. In the risk severity index for short term and long-term scenarios i.e., 'two and 10-years' time stamps, 'disinformation and misinformation', 'societal and political polarisation' and 'cyber-attacks' are placed at 1st, 3rd and 4th and 5th, 9th and 8th positions respectively.[113]

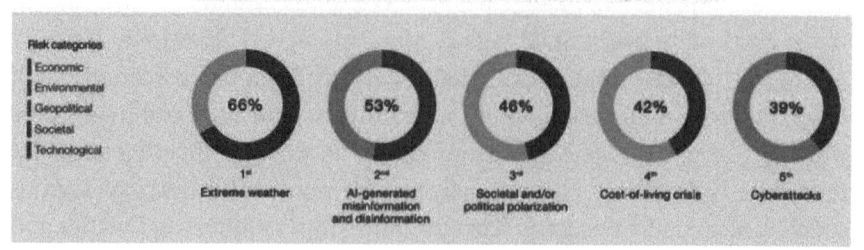

FIGURE B Current risk landscape
"Please select up to five risks that you believe are most likely to present a material crisis on a global scale in 2024."

Risk categories
| Economic
| Environmental
| Geopolitical
| Societal
| Technological

66% — 1st — Extreme weather
53% — 2nd — AI-generated misinformation and disinformation
46% — 3rd — Societal and/or political polarization
42% — 4th — Cost-of-living crisis
39% — 5th — Cyberattacks

CASE STUDIES

FIGURE C	Global risks ranked by severity over the short and long term

Risk categories	2 years		10 years	
Economic	1st	Misinformation and disinformation	1	Extreme weather events
Environmental	2nd	Extreme weather events	2	Critical change to Earth systems
Geopolitical	3rd	Societal polarization	3	Biodiversity loss and ecosystem collapse
Societal	4th	Cyber insecurity	4	Natural resource shortages
Technological	5th	Interstate armed conflict	5	Misinformation and disinformation
	6th	Lack of economic opportunity	6	Adverse outcomes of AI technologies
	7th	Inflation	7	Involuntary migration
	8th	Involuntary migration	8	Cyber insecurity
	9th	Economic downturn	9	Societal polarization
	10th	Pollution	10	Pollution

Figure 21 – Global Risk Report
Source – World Economic Forum Survey 2023-24

As per this report, 'Societal Polarisation' and 'Economic Downturn' would be the most interconnected and influential risks in global risks network. Further it is speculated that 'Misinformation and disinformation', emerged as most severe global risk, would be leveraged by state and non-state actors to widen societal and political divides. The onslaught of information manipulation would impact more than three billion population who would be participating in electoral polls over two years across several economies i.e. Bangladesh, India, Indonesia, Mexico, Pakistan, UK and USA. Resultantly, world may witness tools of information and media manipulation undermining legitimacy of newly elected governments and pushing these nations towards unrest, violent protests, hate crimes, civil confrontation and terrorism. Consequently, people's perception and public discourse on issues ranging from public health to social justice may end up turning extremely polarised. The governments may resort to censorship and imposing more control measures to contain information manipulation thereby resulting into domestic propaganda and curbs on freedom related to internet, press and access to wider sources of information.[114] The causal loop diagram given below represents interconnection between various risk categories: -

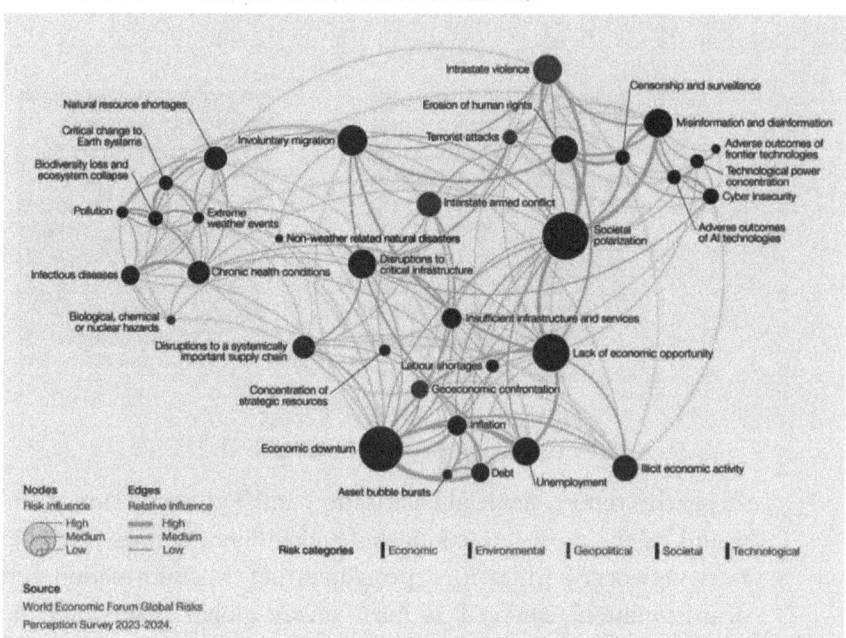

FIGURE D Global risks landscape: an interconnections map

Figure 22 – Causal Loop Diagram of Risk Categories,
Source – WEF Survey 2023-24

➢ Decoding 2024 Global Risk Report, Anna Fleck in her article published on Statista has opined that in the backdrop of upcoming elections, *'false information'* is the biggest threat looming large on the world population. Further as per this report, *India is the most exposed nation to this menace*. Circulation of fake news had been on rife since 2019 elections wherein various political parties *"weaponised social media platforms such as WhatsApp and Facebook to spread incendiary messages, heightening fears of online anger spilling over into real-world violence."* More recently, misinformation also became an issue during the COVID-19 pandemic in India, again via WhatsApp. Other countries facing a high risk of the impact of misinformation and disinformation are El Salvador, Saudi Arabia, Pakistan, Romania, Ireland, Chechnya, USA, Sierra Leone, France and Finland. All these countries are facing threat considered to be one of the 4th to 6th most dangerous risks facing the concerned country out of 34 in the coming two years. In UK, risk related to misinformation and disinformation is in rank 11 of the perceived threats.[115]

CASE STUDIES

Where False Information Is Posing the Biggest Threat

Rank of "misinformation/disinformation" among 34 risks for the following countries

GB 11th

US 6th

MX 11th

IN 1st

ID 18th

- 1st
- 4th-6th
- 7th-10th
- 11th-15th
- 16th-20th
- 22nd or lower

Based on 1,490 expert opinions across academia, business, government, the international community and civil society collected Sep. 4-Oct. 9, 2023
Source: World Economic Forum

Figure 23 – Countries most effect due to 'False Information',
Source - Statista

The comparative study of Conflict Monitoring Report Map: Sep 2023, Global Risk Report 2024 (survey by World Economic Forum) and global social media footprints reveals the following: -

> False news, media manipulation and propaganda (tools of social media warfare strategies) pose the most severe threat to global security and stability in immediate time span. These issues would continue to dominate the threat matrix even in long term scenario i.e. next decade.

> Weaponisation of Social-media would act as force multiplier for Hybrid Warfare; creating an environment of uncertainty and trust deficit, discrediting the establishment, clouding people's perception, sowing discord, hatred and animosity and triggering social engineering. Though, social media is neither a driver nor directly responsible for triggering the conflicts, however, it has

been leveraged by various actors to advance their agendas, recruit and mobilize the forces/ supporters and exert coercion against the adversary.

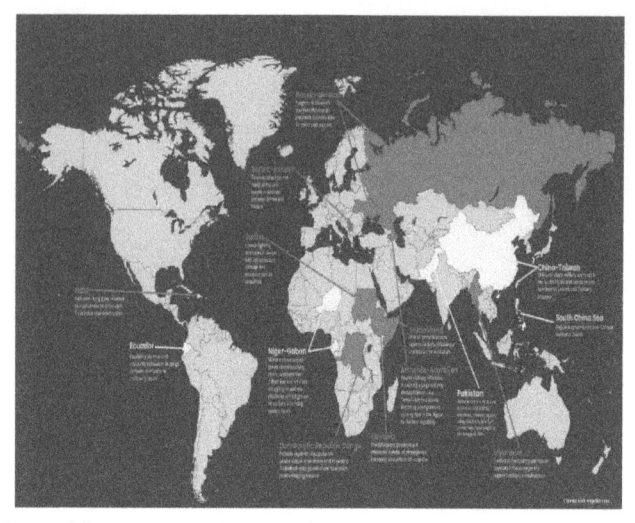

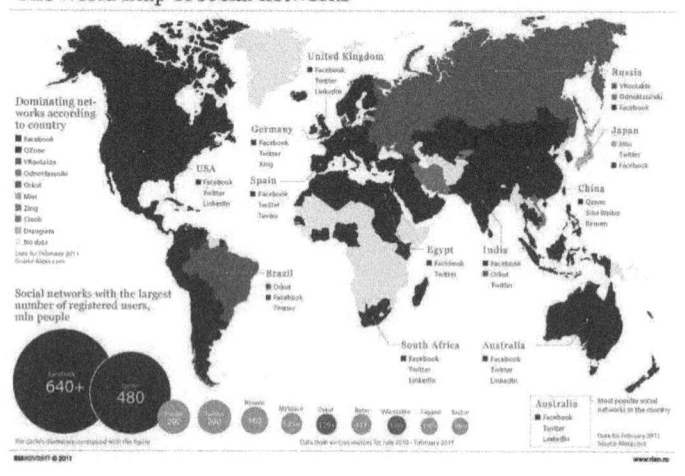

Figure 24 - Conflict Monitoring Report Map: Sep 2023
Source – Dyami Security intelligence services, By Jacob Dickinson, Roos Nijmeijers, Sara Frisan, Mark Bruno, Conflict Monitoring Report: September 2023, *https://www.dyami. services/post/conflict-monitoring-report-september-2023*

> ➢ Conflict Monitoring Report - September 2023, has mapped 14 regions/ nations combating intra/ inter-state conflicts. The affected regions/ countries are Russia-Ukraine, Serbia-Kosovo, Sudan, Democratic Republic of Congo, Azerbaijan-Armenia,

Haiti, Pakistan, South China Sea, Ethiopia, Somalia, Niger-Gabon, Ecuador, China-Taiwan and Myanmar. In addition, Israel-Hamas conflict in Gaza and Syrian Crisis are also creating serious threats in geo-political arena. Consequences of these conflicts are felt across the globe, e.g., EU is facing acute crisis arising out of massive influx of migrants' and spread of radical ideology. India has had serious conflict situation with China during Doklam and Galwan Crises, whereas Pakistan abetted terrorism continue to pose considerable threat to internal security in J and K. The North Eastern states of India have also encountered episodes of violent clashes and tension in the recent past over societal issues. Other parts of India have also been subjected to violence, protests and hatred propelled by inimical forces by exploiting difference of opinion and fomenting communal divide.

➢ The regions facing conflicts of varied nature have significant penetration of social media and internet. Ukraine an epicenter of power game, has internet and social media penetration rate 79.47% which is likely to increase to 89.65% by 2027. Facebook and Telegram are the prominent social media platforms used by the public.[116] Reportedly, Ukrainian information space has been exploited extensively by Russia during ongoing Ukraine Crisis.

➢ As per report published by Statista, in 2023, there were 1.2 billion internet users (49.15% of population) in India. Social Media penetration in India is around 66.85%. As highlighted above, India is ranked 1st amongst the countries facing threat of false news and propaganda. Indian social media market is dominated by Facebook, WhatsApp, Twitter, YouTube and Telegram. In the recent years, there were numerous reports of spread of manipulated and fabricated stories and narratives on Facebook, WhatsApp, Twitter and YouTube resulting in societal division and tension. In immediate neighbourhood, Pakistan and Bangladesh have 37.75% and 39.52% internet penetration rate respectively.[117] Both nations are facing serious issues related to false news and propaganda spread by various actors with vested interests.

➢ These challenges are not alien to developed nations also. For example, internet penetration rate in USA and UK is 93.7% and 98.19% respectively; social media penetration rates of both countries are 92% and 87% respectively.[118] USA is placed at 6th rank and UK stands at 11th position amongst the countries facing the highest risks of fake news. These countries have witnessed adverse effect of social media manipulation in recent past leading to protests, riots and unrest. The trend was prevalent during US Presidential election of 2019, Capitol Hill riots and protests against racism (e.g., #Black Lives Matters). Similarly, EU nations having strong internet and social media foothold are exposed to threats posed to internal security on issues related to migrants' issues, racism, ethnical and religious divide.

> The situation in the conflict-stricken regions in the world is not likely to improve and hopes of conflict stabilization and resolution are no longer in immediate sight. Rather, the intensity of conflict may increase thereby presenting threat of escalatory matrix and a relatively more unstable world. Visualizing the emerging trends of increasing polarisation, neo-nationalism and radicalization, it is inferred that manipulation of social media may continue to have significant impact on global security environment.

Considering these insights, the analysis of certain major conflicts would be carried out wherein impact of social media in the backdrop of Hybrid Warfare would be assessed. The examination of other aspects related to application of kinetic force and other instruments of war waging would not be deliberated upon to keeping in sight the purpose and objective of extant study.

For the purpose of extant study, certain inter-state and intra-state contests, wherein exploitation of social media tools manifested into major conflicts with regional and global ramifications, have been selected. The objective of analysis of case studies would be to discern emerging trends of social media usage in shaping the contested battle space, to coerce and exert influence, escalate/ de-escalate the friction and prosecute hybrid warfare. To formulate an analytical frame work, the studies by Multinational Capability Development Campaign (MCDC), Countering Hybrid Warfare Project and Mercy Corps have been deliberated upon. Certain concepts have been incorporated in the extant study to develop a broad frame work and heuristic model to conduct a holistic analysis and deduce logical inferences.

Analytical Framework. The aspects being examined would include brief scan of conflict space, strategic culture, critical functions and vulnerabilities, target system, means, synchronisation of attack, effects and end state.

These aspects are amplified in the succeeding paragraphs to arrive at an explicit understanding.

> *Environmental Scan.* Environment scan of the contesting nation states, non-states actors and organisations would encompass internal and external factors acting as fertile ground for conflict trigger and having tangible impact on respective influence power over outcome of the competitions. For the purpose of this study, political, social, economical, legal, information and internal security environment would be examined.

> *Strategic Culture.* Strategic culture is a set of shared *beliefs, assumptions*, and modes of *behavior* that shapes collective identity and relationships to other groups, and which *determine appropriate ends and means for achieving security objectives*. It is derived from common experiences and accepted narratives, both oral and written. Strategic cultures are *dynamic and ever-evolving notions* and understanding of a country's history and place in the world, often negotiated and re-assessed across generations.[119] Jack Snyder in his article titled 'The Soviet Strategic Culture: Implications for Limited Nuclear Options', has defined strategic culture as the "*sum total of ideals, conditional emotional responses*, and *patterns of habitual behaviour* that members of the *national strategic community* have acquired through instruction or imitation and share with each other with regard to [...] strategy".[120]

> *Critical Functions and Vulnerabilities.* Critical functions are activities/ operations distributed across the *PMESII spectrum* which, if discontinued, could lead to *disruption of services* that a working system (for example, a state, its society or a subsection thereof) depends on. Critical functions can be broken down into a combination of *actors* (individuals, groups, societies, institutions, or organizations), *infrastructures* ('critical' national power grids, communication architecture, commercial and economic hubs/ institutes, industrial bases etc) and *processes* (legal/ jurisdictional, technical, political).[121] Critical functions are necessary to the agency being able to effectively perform and maintain control of its mission and operations.[122] All critical functions have vulnerabilities that present a hybrid warfare opponent/ actor with the possible conditions for exploitation, depending on the means at its disposal. However, it is important to realize that not all

vulnerabilities necessarily present themselves as opportunities for an opponent to exploit.[123]

➤ *Target System.* In the realm of Hybrid Warfare, the target system of social media warfare would invariably fall into PMESII spectrum. These targets would be selected carefully across multiple domains so as to synchronise attacks and calibrate intensity of the competition or conflict.

➤ *Means.* The actors would exercise discretion in exploiting the instruments of national power i.e. MPECI and legal depending upon own capabilities and perceived weaknesses/ vulnerabilities of the adversary. Use of selected mean(s) would also be determined by stated political goals and ways to actualize these goals. These means would be applied simultaneously in diverse domains and synchronised in time, space and purpose continuums to avoid detection and calibrate intensity to remain below response and international legal thresholds.[124] As per a study conducted by MCDC, ability to synchronise both military and non-military means simultaneously within the same battlespace is considered a key characteristic of a hybrid warfare actor. Synchronisation allows hybrid warfare actor to 'escalate' or 'de-escalate' horizontally rather than just vertically, thus generate wide range options for attacker to leverage force multiplier effects. The study suggests that the actors in hybrid warfare would launch Synchronised Attack Packages (SAP) tailored to exploit the vulnerabilities of adversary's systems, calibrate intensity and escalation and avoid detection and response/ retaliation.[125]

➤ *Effects.* The effect may be a direct consequence in immediate/ near future and indirect consequences in time and space with certain time delay. The effects are divided in three categories for study of 'Game Theory' viz; as 'First Order Effects', 'Second Order Effects' and 'Third Order Effects'. An explanation of these categories are as follows[126]: -

- *First-Order.* The most *immediate results* of an action/ decision.

- *Second-Order.* The *longer-term effect* of an action/ decision. Implies *compounded and non-visible* effects.

- *Third-Order.* The *significant long-term impact* of the decision and eventual outcome.

The analytical framework elucidated above would be applied to study various case studies and deduce the inferences to determine the effect of social media in shaping the contours of opinion shaping, mobilisation and coordination of protests and in impacting the decision making of strategic leadership and rationale thinking of the population.

Anecdotes – Media as Tool of Disinformation and Narrative Building

During invasion of Iraq, the US forces capitalised the reach and power of the Internet to provide live feed on combat operations and achieve an absolute information dominance. The live feeds on TV channels facilitated near real time reporting of progress of the US military operations. It also had a significant psychological effect on the Iraqi forces as well as population whether in the contested zone or otherwise elsewhere in the region. It provided a platform to promote the narrative of perceived righteous battle and supremacy of US military might. Though, social media was still not in deployable state, but "war blogs" gained significant traction and offered alternative narratives to mainstream media coverage. The operation established the importance of information dominance and advantages of leveraging technology in propaganda and influence operations.

In opinion of certain think tanks, Israel-Palestine war of 2006 can be termed as first 'War of Attention and Narrative Building', wherein Hezbollah advanced its narrative through various media channels (predominantly Al-Jazeera and Al-Arabiya) and journalists reporting from the conflict zone. Hezbollah highlighting its asymmetry in force level, weaved its narrative to shape a favourable opinion amongst the Palestinians and population in extended neighbourhood, gain sympathy of Arab brethren, glamourise its operations and portray IDF operations as an 'disproportionate' response. Influenced by narrative and opinion shaping, the media outlets emphasised upon 'Disproportionate' theme.[127] Resultantly, this incident evoked strong reaction from the global organization and Hezbollah emerged as victorious.

This was the era when social media platforms were not prevalent. However, in subsequent years, keeping pace with transformation in information and communication technology, Hezbollah adeptly changed its modus operandi. The change may have been triggered by net driven social activism during 'Arab Revolution of 2010' and use of social media by Russia during annexation of Crimea in 2014.

It is interesting to note that around 2015-16, ISIS and Al Qaeda started using social media to carryout indoctrination, recruitment and advance pan-Islamist vision. Seemingly, inspired by these groups, Hamas and Hezbollah also enmeshed social media in their strategy to further their aim and dominate the information space. Both groups are exploiting SMPs such as Facebook, WhatsApp, Telegram, and Instagram for their propaganda and influence operations. As per a report, Hamas uses SMPs and TV channels to legitimate its governance in Gaza and demonize Israel through plays, dramas and children's entertainment programs. Hezbollah uses social media to shape perceptions of friends and foes alike and to advance its propaganda emphasising upon theme of resistance, martyrdom, military success and spread stories of provision of public services and other good public relations.[128] The trends of past few years indicate a steady increase in use of social media by the terror outfit to recruit Arab Israeli and West Bank-based Palestinians to carry out attacks on Israel. The modus operandi encompasses contacting potential recruiter on Facebook, disseminating instructions through encrypted email and plotting terror attacks on encrypted social media platforms. Taking advantage of technology, the group has been able to recruit new members, generate funds and orchestrate terror attacks undetected through pro-Palestine members.

In the opinion of strategists and think tanks, exploitation of social media by Hamas is limited. Even, Hezbollah also does not rely significantly on social media. According to a study, both groups use social media and information technology to recruit and, at times, support operations. However, their primary focus remains on utilising more traditional media to gain support from Arab and Muslim populations. Social media space is leveraged to bolster morale within their organizations, with their constituents in the Palestinian territories and Lebanon comprising their most important audiences. According to a study, it may be deduced that avoidance to use social media space by both organisations is presumably attributed to their strategy to evade counter attacks by Israel on IT infrastructure.[129] According to an article published by Yousef al-Helou in an online magazine 'Middle East Eye', contrary to restraint exercised by Hamas and Hezbollah due to reasons cited above, younger generation of Palestinians spearheaded campaign on social media platforms. The author remarks that 'Twitter' has emerged as one of the most preferred platforms by Palestinian citizen journalists and amateurs to post visuals of collateral damage and casualties, upload comments, blogs and content. The report suggests that some of content were repackaged, commented and redistributed on SMPs in innovative ways through hashtag accounts such as #GazaUnderAttack and #PrayforGaza[130].

The response strategy of Israel to counter claims of Hamas, Hezbollah and their ecosystem has evolved as an effective weapon to shape information sphere. The strategy is seemingly aimed to shape favourable global opinion and generate support within external and internal environment. Israeli efforts are also directed to legitimize own actions in Gaza, strengthen own perspective on conflict, denounce actions and ideology of Hamas and Hezbollah and silence claims of human rights violations made by Palestinians. It is assessed that social media strategy of Israel has matured post 2006 Israel–Hezbollah conflict. An article by Antony Loewenstein suggests that Israeli perception shaping capabilities were at display during 2008-08 Israeli 'Operation Cast Lead' in Gaza, wherein around 1,400 Gazans lost their lives. However, Israel's revolutionised and well-coordinated Instawar portrayed their operations as battle against hardcore militants so as to win battle of perception shaping. These social media campaigns dovetailed both domestic and global supporters in military operations, who posted tweets, Facebook posts, or Instagram images to support Israeli operations. In addition, Israeli Defence Force (IDF) created IDF Social Media Unit, wherein approximately 70 officers and 2000 soldiers were employed to design, process, and disseminate official Israeli propaganda, on almost every social media platform. Israeli social media themes were centered around to link their operations to western values, weaponised Jewish trauma in the service of perpetuating occupation and portray Israel as part of Islamophobic hegemonic coalition that positions Israel as eastern-most front of USA's 'global war on terrorism'[131]. Antony Loewenstein in his article also reveals that seemingly to gain greater popularity and followership, IDF Instagram pages also tagged pro-gay and pro-feminists messaging alongside its hardline militaristic iconography. The impact of Israeli social media strategy can be gauged by the fact that this strategy has been adopted by many other countries including CIA to launch its recruitment drive. However, during the ongoing conflict with Hamas, Israel is facing a collusive social media offensive launched by hackers, activists, citizen journalists and bloggers presumably supported covertly and overtly by Iran, Hamas and Hezbollah. As per various experts, ongoing Israeli-Palestinian social media war is characterized by guerrilla, asymmetrical nature of attacks. Activists can warp events, images, and videos around their agenda without any accountability. The weapons of this asymmetrical social media warfare are TikTok, Reddit, YouTube, Twitter, Facebook, Instagram, and Wikipedia. According to American University's Thomas Zeitzoff, Israel appears to be losing social media war, with Palestinians garnering sympathy worldwide[132].

In the contemporary scenario, there are global and regional events wherein social media has played a crucial role. The case studies pertaining to these events and groups are discussed in detail.

Arab Spring Revolution – 2010 to 2012

Conflict Typology. The conflict has been termed as '*Popular anti-government protests and Riots*' i.e., popular demonstrations, involving a spontaneous action by unorganized and unaffiliated members of the society.[133] During this period wide spread uprising, riots and armed rebellion against the monarchy and authoritarian governments were reported. The conflict triggered in early 2010 in Tunisia (termed as *Jasmine Revolution*) consequent to self-immolation by Mohd Bouazizi a street vendor, rapidly gripped the majority of *MENA* (Middle East and North Africa) region. Sustained protests were reported in Morocco, Iraq, Algeria, Lebanon, Jordan, Kuwait, Oman and Sudan. Minor protests took place in Djibouti, Mauritania, Palestine, Saudi Arabia and the Moroccan-occupied Western Sahara.[134]

Environment Scan. The 'Arab Spring' was a reflection of people's feelings and angst against oppressive autocratic regimes, failing governance, rampant corruption, HR abuses, rising unemployment and their shattered dreams of financial stability, better future and acceptable living standards. The revolution unfolded as series of pro-democracy protests and uprisings in the MENA Region in 2010 and 2011.[135] The *political environment* was characterized by authoritarian regimes accused of power abuse for decades, suppressing political opposition, limiting freedom of speech, and using security forces to quell dissent. The *economic landscape* was eclipsed by high unemployment rates, rising inflation, and corruption. In the backdrop of conservative outlook, the *social space* was heavily contested by divergent pro-democratic and religious radicalism ideologies. The expanding 'Youth Bulge', which dominated the social landscape, was frustrated with the lack of opportunities and political representation. The

CASE STUDIES

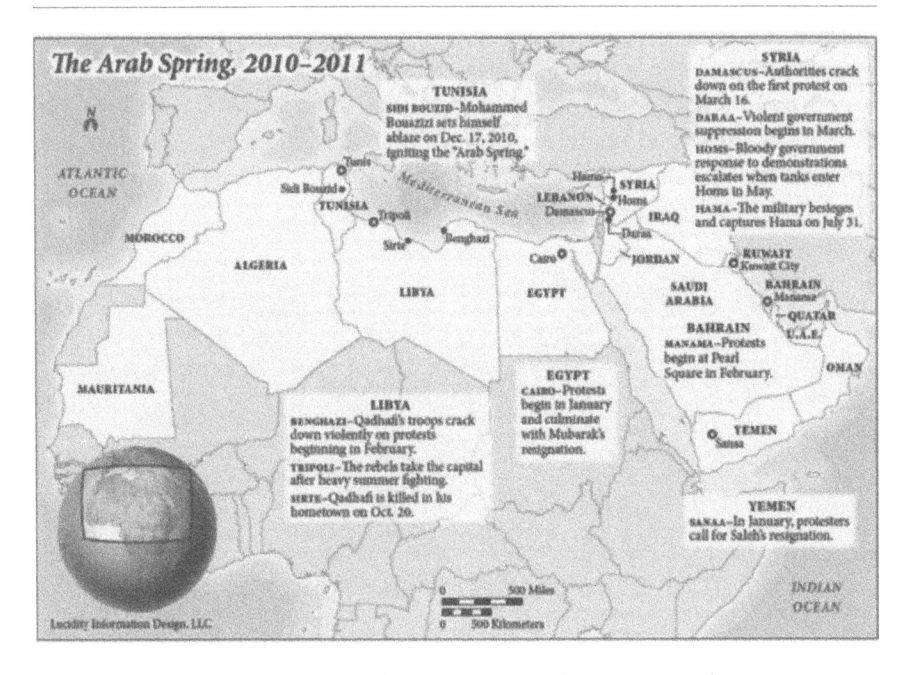

Figure 25 – Countries affected during Arab Spring Revolution

countries in the region have a diverse demographic profile. Gulf states of Saudi Arabia, Qatar, and Oman are sunni dominant with smaller Christian and Jewish communities. North African countries Egypt, Tunisia, and Algeria have predominantly Sunni Muslim populations with small Shia minorities. The countries in the Levant Region i.e., Lebanon, Syria, and Jordan, has a more diverse religious landscape, with significant Christian and Druze communities alongside Muslim majorities. The *legal framework* i.e. judiciary and executive (law enforcement agencies), drew criticism for being arbitrary, devoid of transparency and discriminatory. *Information environment* was subjected to strict state control and censorship by the government agencies thereby curbing freedom of expression, dissent and voices of population. *Internal security* environment was turbulent and opaque; the citizens were subjected to repression, surveillance, and censorship. The security forces and law enforcement agencies were used by many governments to suppress dissent. A retrospective reading suggests that a decade of turmoil was triggered mainly by the demands for political transformation, transparency, inclusive growth, greater opportunities and social justice. The broader transitions in the international order also significantly accelerated the pace and direction of regional restructuring.[136]

Strategic Culture. Owing to vast diversity in social, political, cultural and historical hues, the strategic culture of countries of the MENA region was divergent and complex. However, certain trends can be discerned to determine the broad contours of prevailing strategic culture. The type of governance in affected countries is depicted at Figure 26 below.

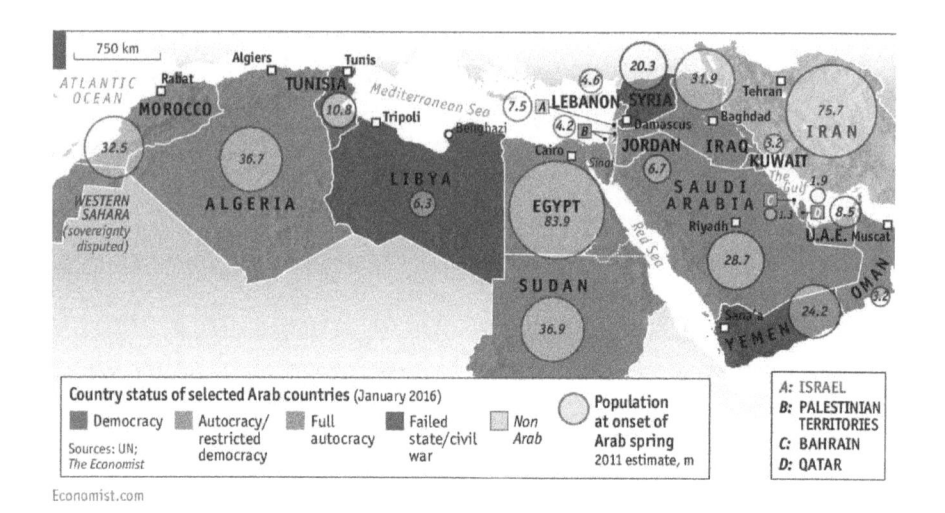

Figure 26 – State of Governance
Source - https://www.semanticscholar.org/paper/The-political-participation-of-the-diaspora-of-the-al-Khulidi-'Hondt/a0c68f12e8f51b7d08f6fd5697c9171a65c2a9c7

> The prevalence of authoritarian regimes with strict control over information flow, media reporting, and functioning of civil society created an environment of extremely limited public discourse and fostered a culture of obedience and deference to authority. Restricted political participation and absence of democratic practices left limited or no room for dissent and public influence on decision-making. The political architecture stifled social change movements and fostered a sense of alienation among certain segments of society. Various studies assert that rigid and inflexible approach of some regimes hindered their ability to adapt to the demands of the protesters and contributed to an escalation of conflicts. The prevailing political structure of affected countries at the time of the revolution is given at Table 2 below: -

Case Studies

North African Countries				
Tunisia	**Egypt**	**Libya**	**Algeria**	**Morocco**
Authoritarian one-party state under President Zine El Abidine Ben Ali (Constitutional Democratic Rally)	Authoritarian regime under President Hosni Mubarak (National Democratic Party)	Authoritarian dictatorship under Muammar Gaddafi (Jamahiriya system)	Semi-authoritarian regime under President Abdelaziz Bouteflika (National Liberation Front)	Constitutional monarchy under King Mohammed VI

Middle East Countries			
Syria	**Yemen**	**Bahrain**	**Saudi Arabia**
Authoritarian regime under President Bashar al-Assad (Ba'ath Party)	Republic led by President Ali Abdullah Saleh (General People's Congress)	Constitutional monarchy under King Hamad bin Isa Al Khalifa (Al Khalifa family)	Absolute monarchy under King Abdullah
Oman	**Qatar**		**Jordan**
Absolute monarchy under Sultan Qaboos bin Said	Absolute monarchy under Emir Hamad bin Khalifa Al Thani		Constitutional monarchy under King Abdullah II

Table 2 – Political Structure of Arab Spring Revolution affected countries

➢ Strong influence of religion, traditional values and social hierarchies played a significant role in cultural and social fabric of the region, influencing political discourse and social norms.

➢ Encumbered by national security concerns, with countries facing internal and external threats (terrorism, regional rivalries, and foreign intervention), resorted to militarised approach to problem-solving and emphasised on maintaining order. The oil-rich Gulf states, with their relative stability and prosperity, differed from non-Gulf states facing economic hardship and political unrest, thus failed to formulate an inclusive and coherent strategy to address the evolving dynamics and change management.

Critical Functions and Vulnerabilities. Owing to peculiar internal dynamics, politico-social structures, economic state, the critical functions crucial to functioning of nation states of the MENA Region differed on many accounts. However, certain common trends and threads can be described as critical functions. The prominent critical functions include political leaders, religion, society and indigenous population and youth (*actors*), economy (*infrastructure*) and judiciary, legislature and executive (*process*). The vulnerabilities of these critical functions which were exploited include unemployed youth, economic disparity and lack of opportunity, autocracy and lack of governance and curbs on freedom of speech. For example, in Tunisia, the government's crackdown on political dissent and civil liberties was a major vulnerability that contributed to the Jasmine Revolution.[137] In Egypt, the government's failure to address economic inequality and political corruption was a key vulnerability that fueled the protests.[138] In Libya, country's weak institutions and lack of a strong central government made it vulnerable to political instability and violence. In Syria, government's brutal crackdown on protesters and opposition groups was a major vulnerability that led to the country's ongoing civil war.[139]

Target System. Arab Spring was a complex and multifaceted event, and social media played a significant but not singular role in uprisings. The uprising demonstrated potential of digital technology and social platform to stir up political activism and mobilise the population undetected. Subject matter experts have commented that protests took place in countries with significantly high internet penetration such as Bahrain (88%) as well as countries with abysmal internet access e.g., Libya and Yemen.[140] The social media platforms were leveraged by both the government and protestors to advance their agendas and execute their plans. The targets of social media warfare were as follows: -

> *Protestors.* Using *Facebook* and *Twitter* (now 'X') as part of internet war, the protestors actively engaged with domestic audiences through awareness campaigns and mobilization drive. The information about protests, government abuses, calls for action and mobilisation of large crowd to protest sites were shared through the social media platforms. Students, workers and marginalized communities were targeted through digital platforms to garner support and seek their participation. For example, in Egypt, *"We Are All Khaled Said"* page resonated with young people facing police brutality. Leaked videos and photos were used to demoralise the security forces and influence defections in the state forces by

exposing their brutalities and HR violations. The impact of social media reach was not confined to domestic environment only. The protestors reached out to international media outlets, government organisations and international organisations to attract global attention, build pressure to condemn actions of repressive regimes and intervene in the state of affairs. Live-streaming from besieged cities like Misrata in Libya effectively showcased plight of civilians. Hashtags like *#YemeniSpring* and *#SidiBouzid* reached a global audience and put pressure on international actors.

➢ *Government.* The government and security organisations exploited social media platforms to control the narrative, divide and demoralize protestors and carry out surveillance and intimidation. The government agencies flooded social media platforms with pro-establishment content to suppress dissent, sow discord to weaken unity and resolve of the protestors and spread counter narrative with propaganda, disinformation and censorship. The online activities were monitored to identify and arrest active players and launch crackdown on protestors. With a view to influence international forums, legitimize their actions and counter international pressure, the government agencies launched an online offensive to justify their actions to impose law and order, portray demonstrators as extremists and lobby against intervention and claims of HR violations.

➢ In Egypt, when protesters used Facebook event pages to organize the '*25th January Revolution*', the government responded by blocking access to the platform. Syrian government flooded the platform with pro-government hashtags and fake accounts as a counter to campaign launched by the activists on Twitter to highlight the brutal crackdown in Homs. Yemeni protesters' attempt to reach out to international supporters through '*#YemeniSpring*' hashtag, was met with pro-government tweets flooding the digital space aimed to muzzle their voices.

Means. The unfolding of uprising in the MENA Region witnessed various elements of instruments of national power (MPECI) coming into play. The existing regimes unleashed whole or some part of military, political, economic, civil and information tools to crush the protestors and control the spread of protests and public sentiments. The protestors exploited political and information domains to advance their agenda, mobilise crowd and garner international support. However, since analysis of military, political, economic and civil means is outside the purview of this study thus not being deliberated upon. The trends of exploitation of information space envisaged cyber-attacks, hacking, psychological warfare and manipulation, crowdsourcing and online fundraising and collaborations with international media and NGOs. The key trends observed during the uprising are as listed at Table 3 below: -

Protestors		
Mobilization and Coordination	Amplifying Grievances and Sharing Evidence	Bypassing Censors and Surveillance
Hashtags #SidiBouzid, #WeAreAllKhaledSaid, #YemeniSpring *Facebook Event Pages* Egyptian 25th January Revolution event *Livestreaming* Videos from besieged cities like Misrata in Libya *Geolocation tags* Pinpointing protest location	Photos and videos of human rights abuses and brutality Personal stories and testimonials Satirical content and humour to critique regimes Live *blogs and online diaries* documenting event	Proxy servers and VPNs (virtual private networks) Encrypted messaging apps Alternative platforms and decentralized networks Creative use of humour and metaphors to evade filtering
Government		
Censorship and Surveillance	Propaganda and Disinformation	Counter-Mobilization and Manipulation
Blocking access to specific platforms and websites Internet blackouts and throttling (*Kill Button*) *Monitoring* online activity and tracking dissidents	Spreading *fake news and rumors* to discredit protesters *Bots and troll* accounts to amplify pro-government messages	Organising *pro-government rallies* and online campaigns Exploiting existing *social divisions* and *sectarian tensions*

CASE STUDIES

Targeting and arresting online activists	Hacking and manipulating online content Intimidation and harassment of online dissenters	Infiltrating opposition groups and spreading discord Using social media to identify and target key activists

Table 3 – Trend of exploitation of social media space during Arab Spring Revolution

Social Media Strategy. Albeit, social media played a vital role in the Arab Spring, however, it wasn't the sole driver of change. In fact, prevailing political grievances, economic hardships, and social movements laid the groundwork for the uprisings. Social media platforms provided tools to protestors for communication, coordination, and information dissemination, but successes and failures of the revolution stemmed from complex political and social dynamics. During days of mass protests in 2011, governments in Bahrain, Egypt, Libya, and Syria ordered telecommunication companies to shut down internet to disrupt flow of information and keep protestors in dark.[141] The Arab Spring uprisings across the Middle East in 2011 saw social media (especially Facebook) emerging as a vital tool for activism and mobilization. The penetration rate of Facebook in various affected nations during this turbulent period is shown at Figure 27. Diverse strategies adopted by affected countries had their own nuances and effectiveness.

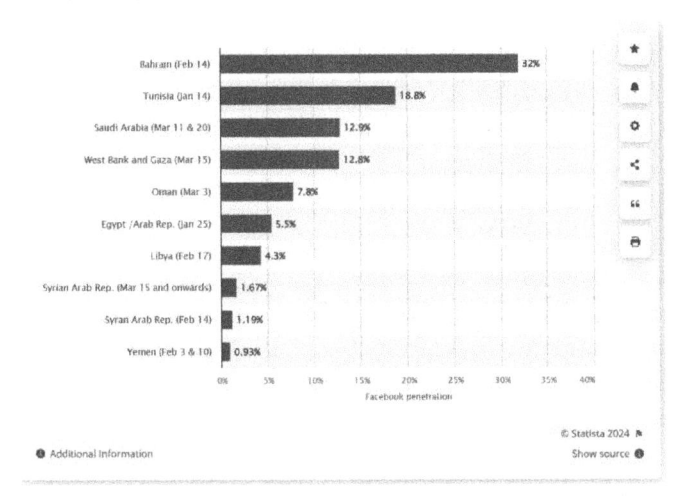

Figure 27 – Facebook Penetration in MENA Region during Arab Spring Revolution, Source – Statista 2024

123

The summary of the social media strategies peculiar to affected nation is as follows: -

> *Tunisia.* Facebook and Twitter (now 'X') platforms were used extensively by opposing sides to further their operations. The strategy involved using digital space for Ddsseminating updates on protests, sharing government abuses, and coordinating actions. As per a study titled 'Twitter and the Tunisian Revolution: The Power of the Nudged Network' by Philip N. Howard, '*#SidiBouzid*' hashtag sparked national awareness of Mohamed Bouazizi's self-immolation, a key trigger for the uprising.

> *Egypt.* Omar W El-Ghazawy in case study titled 'The Egyptian Revolution and Social Media: A Case Study of Facebook and Twitter as Tools for Social and Political Change', highlights that Facebook and Twitter ('X') dominated digital and information battle space during the 'Arab Spring' uprising in Egypt. Social media strategy envisaged hosting video footage of police brutalities to evoke public sentiments and fuel anger, create communities to generate nationwide debate and discussions and mobilise protests through event pages. The social media page titled '*We Are All Khaled Said*' drew attention to a young man beaten to death by police and led to national outrage. Networks formed online were crucial in organizing a core group of activists, specifically in Egypt.[142] The protestors exploited reach and impact of digital platforms to share information undetected about location and timings of protests with the public and upload footage to create an impact on the minds of the people. The government agencies also used these platforms for propaganda, spread counter narrative, to create confusion and sow discord amongst the protestors. In certain cases. Fake news about protests were also spread to lure the protestors resulting into crack down by police.

> *Libya.* Despite relatively low internet penetration rate, the country witnessed innovative employment of social media platforms by the protestors. The information space was dominated by Facebook and YouTube during uprising in Libya. The trends of social media exploitation included sharing eyewitness accounts and protest imagery, countering government propaganda, and coordinating logistics for armed resistance. One of the key examples of social media use was live-streaming from rebel-held Misrata which showcased the city's plight under siege. The live streaming had

CASE STUDIES

a major impact on opinion shaping and garnering international support.

> *Syria.* In Syria, Facebook, YouTube, and Twitter (Now 'X') were on the centre stage of social media warfare during anti-government protests. The social media strategy encompassed documenting human rights violations, mobilising protests, and fostering local coordination amidst fragmentation. The Facebook page titled *'Syrian Revolution 2011'* served as a central hub for information and activism.[143]

> *Yemen.* Exploiting Facebook and Twitter (Now 'X'), the protestors launched online campaign to build solidarity among diverse opposition groups, organize demonstrations, and garner support for international intervention. *'#YemeniSpring'* hashtag connected activists across the country, amplifying demands for political reform.

Effects. The effects of social media warfare during the Arab Spring were unprecedented, unexpected, far reaching and multifaceted. Social media propelled revolution impacted the momentum of uprising, altered regional dynamics and emboldened people driven activism for equality, social justice and participative governance through internet freedom. The key effects are summarized below: -

> *First Order Effects.* These included global attention towards issues faced by people of the MENA Region, garnered local support and channeled people's sentiments, mobilisation of citizens for social cause and coordination of protests. The protestors could bypass traditional media censorship, share tactics, rally crowds and amplify their grievances. The existing state regimes responded with censorship, internet blackouts, and surveillance tactics. This also led to ouster of Tunisian President Zine al-Abidine Ben Ali on 14 January 2011 followed by free election. Egypt also witnessed change in regime, wherein President Hosni Mubarak had to step down after 30 years of rule.

> *2nd Order Effects.* In the midterm, revolution empowered marginalized groups and individuals to participate in political process, giving rise to new political parties and social movements. Increased media attention and international involvement led to support for democratisation efforts in some cases. By 2014, the Tunisian Government introduced new constitution. In Yemen,

in November 2011 President Saleh signed an internationally mediated agreement calling for a phased transfer of power to the Vice President, Abd Rabbuh Mansur Hadi. Hadi took over governing responsibility immediately and formally assumed the presidency after standing as the sole candidate in a presidential election held in February 2012. Unable to improve conditions and maintain stability, however, Hadi's government faced armed confrontation and rebellion leading to civil war in 2014.

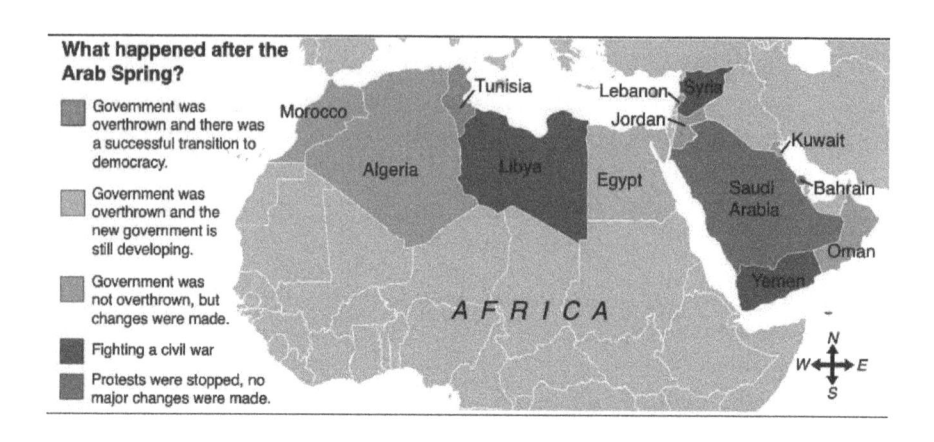

Figure 28 – Fallout of Arab Spring Revolution,
Source – https://inspirecitizens.org/the-arab-spring-and-syria

> 3rd *Order Effects.* In the longer term, Tunisia successfully completed transition of power and restored peace. In Egypt, immediately after ouster of President Mubarak, the military took over control of the government, however failing to meet people's aspiration, drew serious criticism. The country continued to face uncertainty and instability for a prolonged period. The uprising led to stricter curbs on social media and freedom of speech. Even after a decade, the MENA Region is still struggling to restore peace and stability. The key finding by Kali Robinson and Will Merrow, in their article titled 'The Arab Spring at Ten Years: What's the Legacy of the Uprisings?', published on Council on Foreign Relations on 03 Dec 2020 are as follows: -

- *Democracy.* During uprising, representation in governance, democracy and right for dignity and human rights was common demand. However, much to chagrin, long-term outcome has been disappointing for the people. Figure 29 represents democratic progress in the affected countries post people's driven movement. In some countries, existing religious tensions being a dominant factor led to Islamist parties gaining power e.g., in formerly secular Tunisia and Egypt (although only temporarily in the case of latter). Meanwhile, sectarian divides facilitated rise of the anti-government movements in Bahrain, Syria, and Yemen. Only Tunisia made a lasting shift to democracy, whereas Egypt backslid, and Libya, Syria, and Yemen spiraled into protracted civil wars.[144]

No Lasting Democratic Progress, Except in Tunisia
Countries' political rights and civil liberties scores

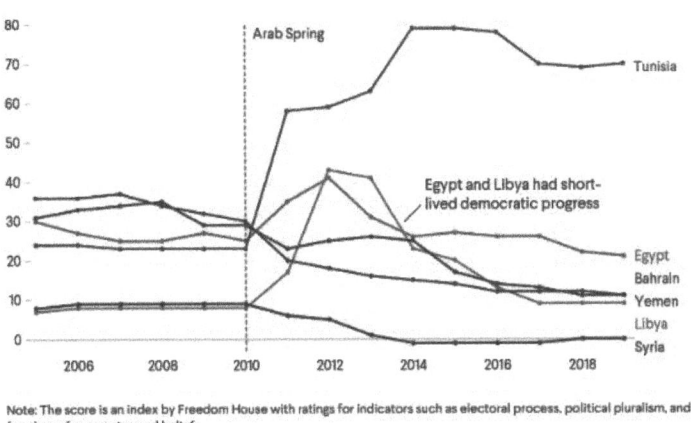

Note: The score is an index by Freedom House with ratings for indicators such as electoral process, political pluralism, and freedom of expression and belief.

Source: Freedom House.

COUNCIL on FOREIGN RELATIONS

Figure 29 – State of Democratic Process post Arab Spring Revolution, Source – Freedom House

- *Standard of Living.* A revolution which started due to high inflation, rising food prices and preference to ethanol production over farm produce, did not meet the objective of the people's struggle. The statistical representation of average income given at Figure 30 represents decline/ no improvement in standard of living of the populace. A significant percentage of the population in the Middle East struggled financially due to declining oil prices, high unemployment, and corruption among political elites who thrived at the expense of ordinary citizens. Poverty rates were high, especially in rural areas. Presently, in no country has the standard of living significantly improved since the revolutions. It has declined in some conflict-ravaged areas especially Libya, Syria and Yemen.

Standard of Living Has Fallen in Libya, Syria, Yemen
Index of countries' average incomes (gross national income per capita)

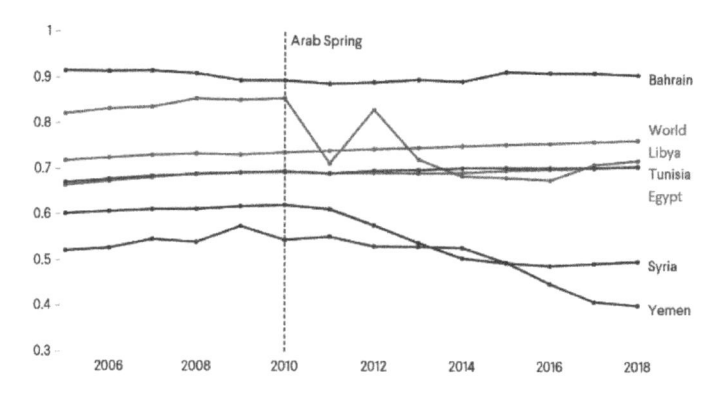

Note: Created by the UN Development Program, the income index is scaled to reflect the fact that an income increase in a lower-income country is more consequential for people there than the same increase for people in a higher-income country.

Source: UN Development Program.   COUNCIL on FOREIGN RELATIONS

Figure 30 – Standard of Living Index,
Source – Freedom House

- *Youth Unemployment.* Unemployment in the region remains the highest in the world and has even worsened in several countries, rekindling protests in some cases. As per analysis, Tunisia and Libya had shown slight improvement in employment index, however gradually employment rate declined in both countries, refer statistical data represented at Figure 31 below.

CASE STUDIES

Youth Unemployment Remains High
Unemployment among people ages 15 to 24

Note: Data not available for 2007 to 2010.
Source: International Labor Organization via UN Development Program.

COUNCIL on
FOREIGN
RELATIONS

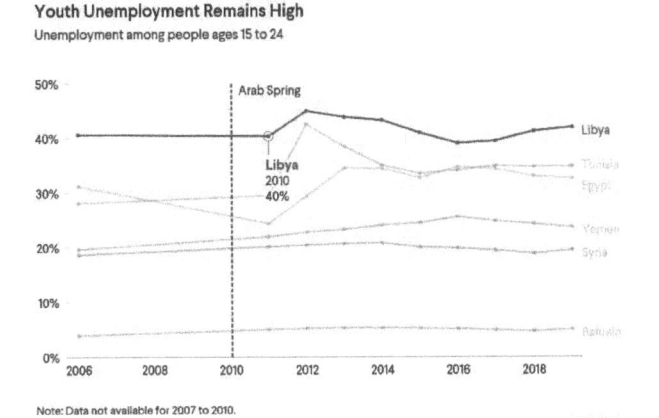

Figure 31 – Youth Unemployment Rate,
Source – Freedom House

- *Press Freedom.* Press freedom in the region is worse today than in the years before the revolts, refer Figure 32 below. Many governments aggressively suppressed any criticism in media, leading to imprisonment/ death of foreign and local journalists. Egypt had resorted to strict action against press and journalists; cases of imprisonment of journalists saw a visible rise since President Abdel Fatah al-Sisi took power in 2013.

Jailing of Journalists Has Increased
Number of journalists imprisoned as of December 1 of each year

26 journalists were imprisoned in Egypt at the end of 2019

Source: Committee to Protect Journalists.

COUNCIL on
FOREIGN
RELATIONS

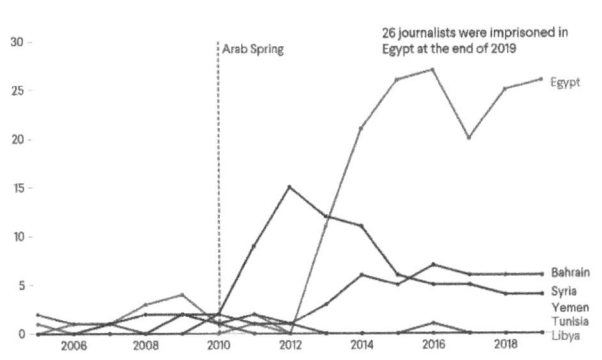

Figure 32 – Press Freedom Status,
Source – Freedom House

129

- *Internet Freedom.* The internet and social media were vital tools for mobilising Arab Spring protesters and documenting some government injustices. In subsequent years post revolution, countries such as Egypt have tightened their grip on cyberspace by restricting internet access, enacting laws that facilitate censorship, and jailing people over their online anti-government posts. Only Tunisia has increased internet freedom, particularly by protecting free expression and the press under its 2014 constitution.

Internet Freedom Mostly Stagnant or Declining
Countries' internet freedom scores

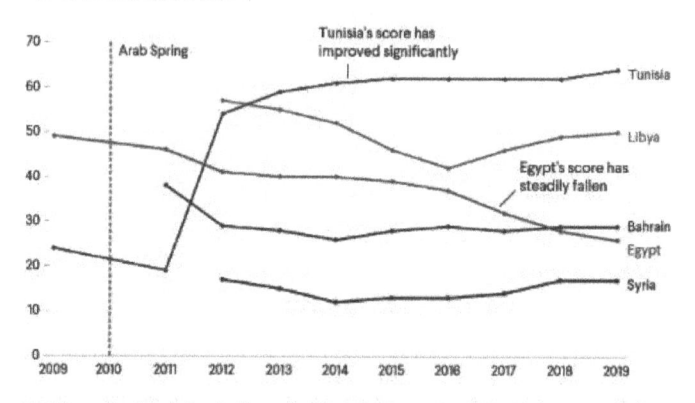

Note: The score is an index by Freedom House with ratings for indicators such as obstacles to internet access, limits on content, and violations of user rights. Data is not included for Yemen.

Figure 33 – Internet Freedom Status,
Source – Freedom House

- *Corruption.* Some countries, such as Tunisia, have attempted to respond to protesters' calls for better governance, created anticorruption agencies and introduced new laws to protect whistleblowers. However, corruption persists and is worsening regionwide. It is particularly daunting in the countries fragmented by civil war.

Government Corruption Unchanged or Worsening
Countries' perceived government corruption scores (higher numbers indicate less corruption)

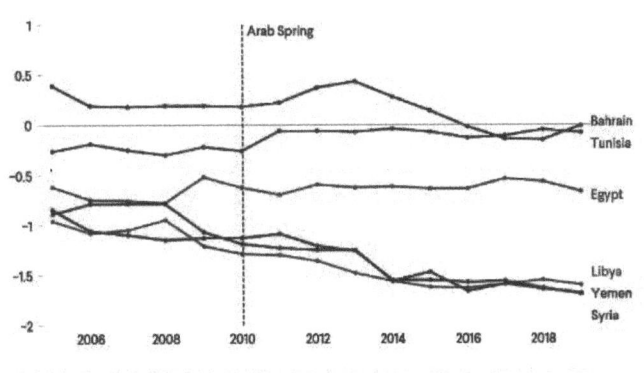

[Chart showing corruption scores from 2006 to 2018 for Bahrain, Tunisia, Egypt, Libya, Yemen, and Syria, with Arab Spring marked around 2011]

Note: The score is the World Bank's Control of Corruption Indicator, which ranges from approximately -2.5 to 2.5, represents the perceived level of government corruption based on surveys of citizens, enterprises, and experts.

Source: World Bank.   COUNCIL on FOREIGN RELATIONS

Figure 34 – Corruption Scores,
Source- Freedom House

To conclude, it can be stated that social media platforms played a pivotal role in generating awareness amongst marginalised sections of oppressed population of the MENA Region and garnered support of citizens of diverse strata and demography. It also provided them platform to voice their concerns, highlight sufferings and expose predatory practices of the prevailing autocratic regimes. It would not be incorrect to infer that social media and internet acted as facilitators for emergence of people led revolt against injustice, inequality, deprivation and lack of representation in autocracy. The messaging and content uploaded on these platforms resonated with the people's sentiments and gave strength to their movements despite multiple odds. A storm created in the virtual space turned tsunami in physical space, drew attention of international community to ordeal of people in the MENA Region and compelled them to intervene in deteriorating situation. The coordination of protests through social media platforms helped in circumventing the censorship and restrictions imposed by government agencies and mobilise people to mount pressure on the governments. Resultantly, governments had to pay heed to people's grievances and initiate measures to meet their demands. It would be fair to assess that social media and internet emerged as harbinger for the 'change'. The revolution did achieve some goals partially and some fully. However, failed to achieve objectives in certain areas in entirety wherein Islamic ideology and hardliners prevailed over the people's aspirations. This led to silencing of people's voice and momentary pause in revolution before people's rousing anger took the region by storm and forced the change.

NATO- Russia Conflict in Ukraine

In February 22, Russia launched 'Special Military Operation' to conquer Ukraine. It is perceived that Russia launched a full-scale offensive under pretense of securing Ukraine's eastern territories and 'liberating' Ukraine from alleged 'Nazi' leadership. In the opinion of military strategists and scholars, during current conflict, Russia has leveraged wide range of instruments of national power to prosecute hybrid war against Ukraine. Non-state actors, social media and cyber space have been exploited extensively along with the kinetic operations to maximise effects of its war waging efforts. The world has witnessed intense competition between Russia and NATO supported Ukraine to dominate information space. It is estimated that Russia's information campaign unleashed during the current 'Special Military Operation' is a manifestation of its social engineering and propaganda strategy evolved in concert with trends of geo-political competition. A report published by NATO Centre of Excellence (COE) has highlighted that *"Before Russia got to implement its information campaign against Ukraine, it learned lessons from its own mistakes during previous years. The first Chechnya war (1994-1996), the second Chechnya war (1999-2009), the sinking of the Kursk submarine in 2000, the Beslan hostage crisis in 2004 and the Georgia-Russia war of 2008 were some of the important events which formed the Russian power elite's understanding of how information campaigns should be organized"*.[145] These lessons were apparently dovetailed into the strategy applied to annex Crimea in 2014. It is also observed that Russia has meticulously enmeshed legal warfare with overall hybrid campaign strategy to create grounds to justify offensive launched against Ukraine. Thus, to analyse the Russian strategy to exploit social media in dominating the information space and influencing the opinion and decision making by the leaders in Ukraine offensive, it is imperative to study the Russia -Ukraine conflicts of 2014 and 2022. It would assist the arriving at pragmatic inferences and develop a comprehensive understanding of Russia's social media warfare strategy.

Conflict Typology. The conflict between Russia and NATO-supported Ukraine falls into the category of 'Inter-State Warfare' or may be termed as 'Global Cold War', wherein social media emerged as a potent vector for state orchestrated information operations. Evidently, social media platforms have been exploited to execute coordinated disinformation/ information operations, propaganda and narrative building designed to achieve multiple objectives. It is assessed that both Russia, Ukraine and presumably NATO have leveraged the social media to influence target public perception, discredit the leadership and erode people's support and faith in the institutions. The offensive social media warfare strategy of the belligerent nations has also attempted to create cognitive dissonance, confusion, and weaken internal and external relationships of the target nation states/ institutions. During this conflict, evidently state and non-state actors have connived to further their campaign objectives and dominate the contested space. The contesting nation states have applied diverse instruments of national power to impact the entire spectrum of conflict.

Russia's Tryst with Social Media Exploitation - Crimea's Annexation

Environment Scan – The Russia-Ukraine conflict in 2014 was preceded by episodes of political differences, internal turmoil and upheaval in Ukraine's socio-political landscape, growing tensions between both belligerent states over NATO's influence and geo-strategic pulls. The 'Orange Revolution' between November 2004 and January 2005 briefly demonstrated that there existed an active civil society in Ukraine which could hold the elites accountable. The election of the pro-European candidate Viktor Yushchenko in January 2005 instilled hope for improvement in situation in the country. Instead, the Yushchenko-Tymoshenko government was marred by political infighting, and in February 2010 the candidate who had been defeated in the Orange Revolution, Viktor Yanukovych, was elected as president.[146] Between Yanukovych's election and onset of EuroMaidan Revolution, Ukraine's democracy was unraveled, rule of law undermined, and economy severely mismanaged. In 2013, political manoeuvre by Ukrainian regime to forge closer ties with the West and seek membership of NATO drew strong Russian's reaction. Russia perceived this step as infringement of its sovereignty. The external environment was thus volatile and uncertain. It exposed wide ranging threats eclipsing the entire spectrum of geo-political spectrum. The internal environment in Ukraine was polarised, emotionally charged and stiffly contested and presented triggers for internal conflicts and societal divide. The regime of 'Party of Regions' led by President Viktor Yanukovych and Prime Minister Mykoly Azarov perceived as Pro-Russian, faced mounting pressure at home front over joining NATO. Reportedly in November 2013, their decision to reject the agreement of association to join NATO fueled public anger and set the stage for protests by three opposition parties and students. The protest mobilised through call made on social media (hashtag on Twitter (X)) was termed as 'EuroMaidan (Euro Square)'. The initial demand of the protestors was to compel the President to review his decision and sign agreement on 29 November 2013 at a summit in Vilnius, Lithuania.[147] However, post 29 November 2013, deadline to accept agreement of association, the protestors raised demand for removal of 'Party of Regions' from power. As per analysts, protest gained significant momentum post laws passed by government on 16 January 2014 imposing restriction on freedom of speech. However, Russia's political and social scene underwent a significant shift marked by a strong nationalist sentiment, mobilising the citizens to rally around Russian Flag and triggering a strong anti-West and anti-US sentiment, who were perceived to be interfering in Russian sphere of influence and threatening national security. Economically also, Ukraine was unstable; amidst bankruptcy situation prevailed in late 2013, President Yanukovych and Prime Minister Azarov decided to ask the Russian Federation for financial support rather than the EU or IMF.[148] Socially, internal environment in Ukraine was extremely polarised and divided between pro-Europe (mostly Western and Central Ukraine) and pro-Russia (mostly Eastern and Southern Ukraine).

Strategic Culture – In Russian geo-politics, Ukraine forms part of inner crescent of main land Russia and is central to Russia geo-strategy to safeguard to their national interests and keep expanding Western influence at bay. Aiming to regain it's global geo-political influence and global leadership under neo-nationalist Putin's leadership, Russia perceived NATO influence in its extended neighbourhood, especially Ukraine's drift, as threat to national security. It is presumed that strong military and coercive politics were main stay in Russian strategy to exert and enhance its influence. Ukraine, despite gaining independence in 1991, was still struggling to carve its strategic culture; caught between Russia's influence and aspirations for European integration. The national identity was still in nascent stage; the ideological differences and emotional overtone influenced by legacy of past relations with Russia and aspiration to forge tie with West, dominated political discourse and impacted response to the conflict. The regime under President Viktor Yanukovych and Prime Minister Mykoly Azarov, was perceived as pro-Russia, corrupt and incompetent to handle the precarious internal situation and address people's aspirations.

The analysis of various papers and studies point out that Russia's strategic communication to dominate the information space and cloud decision-making during Russia-Ukraine conflict of 2014 was a manifestation of enduring vision. It is observed that the significance of secure information space to realize national security objectives was identified by the Russians decades ago. According to a report published by NATO COE, Russia's National Security Concept 2000, emphasised upon increasing threats to its national security in the information sphere. The concept paper alluded that growing dominance of Western Countries in the global information space and endeavour to oust Russia from external and internal information market poses a serious danger. To dominate information space, the Russian Foreign Policy Review of 2007 recommended increase in foreign broadcasting by Russian state news agencies and expanding their foothold abroad. The Russian strategists also promoted the concept of creating a 'Russian World' and 'Russian Information Sphere'.

Russian Compatriots and Russian World - The tenets of legal warfare were seemingly leveraged to legitimize Russian operations and weave a narrative to augment the effectiveness of its information operations. In this regard, it is prudent to delve upon the concept of 'Russian Compatriot' coined by the Russians, which was used to justify operations in Ukraine. In the chapter titled "The Humanitarian Direction of Foreign Policy", Russian Foreign Policy Review 2007 defined the 'Compatriots'. The policy states that 'Compatriots are considered to be the 'tens of millions of our people' artificially separated from their historic homeland (Russia) after collapse of the USSR'.[149] According to policy document, creation of the 'Russian World' was perceived as 'a unique element of human civilisation', supporting the idea of uniting compatriots abroad, maintaining their strong links with homeland, encouraging their loyalty to Russia, its government and policies, thus enabling them to 'act in the capacity of an authoritative intellectual, economic and cultural-spiritual partner of Russia in world politics'. The sections on 'Consular Work' and 'Cooperation in Culture and Science', list out the elements supporting execution of Compatriots' Policy. In this regard, address of President Putin on 02 July 2014 at the Conference of Russian Federation Ambassadors and Permanent Representatives on Protecting Russia's National Interests is relevant to decode the concept of compatriot diaspora. Putin regarded compatriot diasporas as a potential supporting force for Russia's foreign policy. He emphasised that when he speaks of Russians and Russian-speaking citizens, he is 'referring to those people who consider themselves part of the broad Russian community, they may not necessarily be ethnic Russians, but they consider themselves Russian people'. 'Russian speakers' is mainly used as a term for persons whose first language is Russian. These can be ethnic Russians or those ethnic groups who underwent enforced Russification during the Soviet period.

Information Sphere - Russia's new State Security Strategy-2009 resonated with 'Foreign Policy Review-2007' and influenced the handling of Ukraine crisis in 2013-14. The strategy delineates the expanse of common information sphere of Russian speaking communities which included Russia, Commonwealth of Independent States and neighbouring regions. The common information sphere is maintained and enhanced by applying the Compatriots' Policy which is viewed as a way of exerting soft power on neighbouring countries. It is important to note that this policy serves as an efficient tool for geopolitical influence in the post-Soviet sphere, helping Russia attain specific foreign and security policy goals.[150]

It is assessed that by creating the concepts as discussed above, the Russian strategists meticulously planned their narrative building campaign as part of their cognitive warfare strategy. The Russian leadership carefully created legal framework to justify their claims and actions, shaped public opinion, fomented societal divide in Ukrainian community and devised diverse means to execute their information operations.

Critical Functions and Vulnerability – It is assessed that Russia conceived multi-pronged strategy to realise its objectives. The overall strategy was to degrade Ukraine's combat potential and simultaneously orchestrate escalation across the DIME construct. In the realm of calibrated strategic framework, Russia directed its social media offensive towards discrediting Ukrainian government, institutions and leadership by creating trust deficit amongst the public on account of corruption, incompetence and being West leaning. Ukrainian national unity and social fibre also became casualty of Russian strategy which exploited ethnic and linguistic divisions. Vulnerability to cyber threats and weak cyber defence capability, limited coverage and lack of credibility of Ukrainian media outlets in Eastern part of the country and inadequacy to deal with contestations in social media and digital space were also effectively exploited by the Russia.

Target System – The narrative campaign and social media offensive launched by Russia targeted the population of East and South Ukraine citing historical and linguistic connects under the overall construct of 'Russian Compatriot' and 'Russian World'. This was seemingly planned to gain ground support, trigger social engineering and turn local populace against the Ukrainian government as well as West. Simultaneously, the efforts were directed to create confusion amongst the leaders and strategists of NATO nations and Ukraine. The Ukrainian leadership and security forces faced relentless propaganda, fake news and dis-information attacks. Ukrainian media outlets were also subjected to cyber and social media offensive.

Means – The overall information and social media warfare strategy was executed by Russia through state-controlled media outlets, social media platforms (Twitter/ now 'X'), Cyber Berkut and Russian Special Operations Forces (SPETSNAZ) or 'The Green Men'.

Social Media Strategy- Based on the various studies, it is assessed that the Russian social media strategy was formulated around legal construct propagated to promote the idea of 'Russian Compatriots' and 'Russian World'. The narratives and themes designed to substantiate Russian claims and legitimise their actions, were communicated through multiple state-controlled media outlets and TV channels. These state-controlled media outlets spread news reports prepared by political technologists (a legacy of the Soviet period) and gained prominence as potential opinion shapers. According to NATO StratCom COE's research, Russian mass media (especially TV channels) were instrumental in disseminating key narratives, thematic frames and messages outlined in strategic policy documents of the Russian Federation (or channeled via political elite or Kremlin-affiliated experts). Messages such as *'brother nations', common history, the Orthodox religion and common culture* were used to encourage the inhabitants of East and South Ukraine to think about a joint future destiny with Russia. It is noteworthy that according to a survey, majority of Ukrainian population watched TV channels for news; though Ukrainian TV channels were dominant players, however Russian TV channels also had a significant viewers' base especially amongst Russia speaking population in Crimea and East Ukraine. According to GALLUP research, in 2012 the viewers in Crimea accessed news and information through five TV Channels which were all Ukrainian. However, by 2014 the pattern had changed, Russian TV Channels i.e. Russia 24, NTV, ORT (Channel One), and RTR (Russia-1) and Russian social media giant VKontakte emerged as most dominant source of information for the Crimean public.

The strategic narrative was curated to cultivate fear and anxiety amongst the Ukrainian population about their future and economic stability post forging association with West. The apprehensions of Russia speaking population in East and Southern Ukraine regarding their historical, cultural and linguistic identities were also exploited through narrative building. This facilitated garnering support for actions of the rebels demanding re-unification with Russia. As per various studies, amongst multiple themes of Russia's Strategic Communication, the dominant ones were cultural differences between West and the Orthodox Christianity of the East, concept of Eurasianism, unity of Eastern Slavs, common history of Russia and Ukraine and Orthodox religion as a uniting element.

Simultaneously, Russia deployed social media bots and troll farms to amplify pro-Russian narratives, harass Ukrainian supporters, and spread disinformation on SMPs e.g., Twitter (Now 'X') and Facebook. As per Russian analytical portal 'The Insider', the Domestic Policy Department of Presidential Administration controls the work trolls and bloggers, tasked to publish and distribute fabricated material, create fake accounts on SMPs for dissemination of information and send spam messages and persecute opponents on the Internet. Russia's independent investigative newspaper Novaya Gazeta reported on the work 'troll farm' in September 2013. According to newspaper, mass recruitment of trolls had started in August 2013. Reportedly, each account holder was expected to post 100 internet comments per day. Trolling also involved maintaining multiple Facebook and Twitter (X) accounts, gaining new followers, participating in discussions. Pro-Russian Twitter (X) users frequently used active forms of tweeting – sharing opinions, commenting, calling for action, using propaganda, getting involved in discussions. Social media was also used for the recruitment of pro-Russian fighters to be sent to East Ukraine and mobilisation of the rebels. Resultantly, Russia gained initiative, dominated cognitive space and created decision dilemmas and confusion for the adversaries.

Effects – The first order effect of social media manipulation resulted in opinion shaping, confusion and reinforcing biases which impacted decision making and created societal divide between East and West Ukraine. The narrative building and proliferation of concocted facts created a pretense of public dissent against the Ukrainian regime and portrayed as ground movement against association with Western countries, especially NATO. It also created confusion in the international arena and rendered it difficult to ascertain true picture of the situation. Indirectly as second order effect, it afforded an opportunity for Russia to evade international scrutiny and deny its involvement in turning people against the plan to join NATO and annexation of Crimea. As third order effect, in the long-term Russia evolved its strategy to leverage social media to orchestrate influence operations and opinion shaping during Russia-Ukraine conflict in 2022.

Russia Ukraine Conflict - 2022

There is a unanimous opinion amongst scholarly circles that information operations encompassing opinion shaping, propaganda and disinformation have been integral to Russian campaign strategy in various conflicts in past. In Russian lexicon, 'Hybrid Warfare or GIBRIDNAYA VOYNA', largely described as informational warfare, designed to amplify social, political, and ideological divisions to create and exploit vulnerabilities of the adversaries. The concept has been put into practice by army of Russian influencers and actors in various conflicts and contestations.[151] The discussions on Russia's warfighting strategies in contemporary scenarios have frequently found mention of article by Russia's Chief of the General Staff, General Valery Gerasimov in 2013. In his article, the General stressed upon the growing role of non-military means towards achieving political and strategic objectives. He viewed that in an armed conflict automated, robotic, and artificial intelligence tool can be exploited in conjunction with asymmetric actions to dominate information spheres with a view to offset an enemy's advantage. The asymmetric actions may range from guerilla warfare to terrorist attacks, and from creation and stoking up of mis-/disinformation to direct state propaganda coupled with proactive diplomacy. In this context, it is important to refer to the views of the late head of the Russian Academy of Military Sciences, General Makhmut Gareev. He had argued that one of the lessons that Russia could draw from 2014 invasion of Crimea was to perfect the use of soft power, politics and information to achieve strategic goals.[152] Russia's military doctrines of 2010 and 2014 also referred to integrated use of military and non-military resources and mean. A critical look at Russia's security policy reveals that in the recent years, non-military means have been employed extensively to complement the hard power. There are several examples that illustrate this combination, including fanning disinformation, sponsoring non-state actors in Russia's European neighbourhood and beyond, launching cyberattacks, interfering in the electoral processes of Western countries, and using energy as a weapon. It would not be incorrect that annexation of Crimea and Russia-Ukraine Conflict in 2014 was a test case to practice this strategy. In subsequent years, Russia seemingly refined its strategy to dominate the information sphere and cyber space. The broad theme of the narrative battles has centered around historical linkages between Russia and Ukraine, exploiting apprehension related to growing influence of NATO in extended neighbourhood and claims about neo-Nazi infiltration in the Ukrainian government.

Evidently, launch of Russia's 'Special Military Operations' against Ukraine on 24 March 2022, were preceded by persistent cyber-attacks, narrative building, opinion shaping and propaganda since annexation of Crimea in 2014. These cyber-attacks and social media warfare gained momentum just prior to 2022, presumably to weaken the will to fight and denude the combat potential of Ukraine and create grounds to justify Russian actions. Consequent to these acts of hybrid warfare, Ukraine's public, energy, media, financial, business and non-profit sectors suffered the most due to disruption of services and critical infrastructure[153]. The analysis of various studies reveal that Russia initiated various measures to enhance its capability to conduct effect-based operations in digital space to dominate cognitive space, strengthen its 'information sphere' and exploit vulnerabilities of the external environment. Concomitantly based on the lessons drawn from pattern of Russian operations in 2014, the US, NATO and Ukraine also developed their capabilities to counter Russia in multiple domains including cognitive space and prepared a counter strategy. Thus, to develop a comprehensive understanding of Information Operations and exploitation of social-media by Russia post 2022, it is imperative to analyse the prevailing situation in the Ukraine and Russia.

It is interesting to note that even prior to imposition of ban on Facebook and Twitter (Now 'X') by Russia, majority of Russian populace (2/3rd population) had predominant reliance on news-papers and TV channels as source of information. The statistics is based on the evidence from the latest World Values Survey, conducted in Russia in 2018 and in Ukraine in 2020. Younger and tech savvy Russians have demonstrated inclination to gain access to internet through VPNs, however this process demands technical expertise and is effort intensive. In contrast to trends of Russia information ecosystem, the Ukrainians had greater dependence over the internet and social media for gaining access to information. Though, it facilitated diversity in information sources for the Ukrainians and gave them relatively greater freedom vis-à-vis Russians but it also exposed them to greater risks of external influences and dis-information through unfiltered information propagated on internet and SMPs. To substantiate the inference, it is pertinent to refer to data of 'World Value Survey' at Figure 35, which presents a skewed picture of the accessibility to diverse channels of information to Russians vis-à-vis Ukrainians.

The press freedom in Russia has come under severe criticism by the various think tanks and organisations. 'Varieties of Democracy' project publishes a freedom of expression and alternative sources of information index. According to project report, since 2000 state control over media has increased significantly in Russia under President Putin. It is learnt that Russia has exercised the control of media to favourably shape opinion of its own population and presumably counter any external influences presenting alternate perspectives. Efforts to control the information space in prevailing scenario can also be seen via increase in budgetary spending for state media in the run up to mobilization and mounting to offensive. Government spending on 'mass media' for the first quarter of 2022 was 322% higher than for the same period in 2021, reaching 17.4 billion rubles (roughly EUR 215 million). According to a report published in The Moscow Times in 2022, almost 70% of Russia's spending on mass media in Q1 2022 was spent in March, immediately after the invasion. The outlets which received these funds, included RT and Rossiya Segodnya, which owns and operates state-linked and state-owned outlets Sputnik and RIA Novosti.

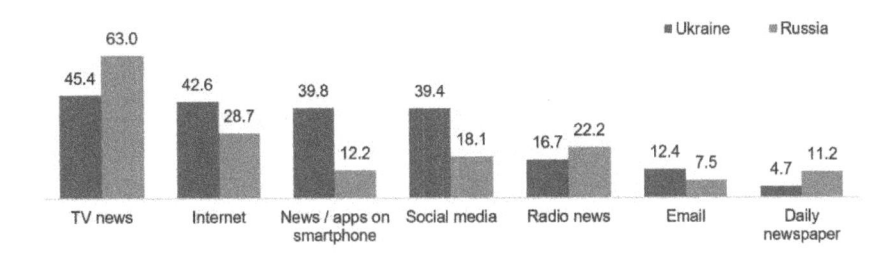

Figure 35 – Dependence of Russian and Ukrainian population for news and information
Source - World Values Survey wave 7 (2018-2021), N=1289 in Ukraine; N=1810 in Russia. What do ordinary Russians really think about the war in Ukraine? | EUROPP (lse.ac.uk)

During the current crisis, Russia has enacted a law banning publication/sharing any information about military operations deemed false by the state. The law stipulates that violation of these orders would invite jail for 15 years. Resultantly, many international news corporations such as CNN and BBC suspended their operations in Russia. Independent media outlets in Russia, such as newspaper Novaya Gazeta and independent TV channel Dozhd have been closed.[154] The step may be justified by the Russian state as a measure to safeguard its national security interests but it is detrimental to citizens' right to have an alternate perspective. Such steps may have resulted in Russia sliding down in global index of Press Freedom. According to a survey conducted by Reporters without Borders, Russia is ranked 150th amongst 180 countries in Press Freedom Index. The comparative analysis of alternate sources of information and press freedom index of Russia and Ukraine is depicted in Figure 36 below. The dataset depicts a steady decline in Russia since 2000. However contrary to portrayal by West leaning think tanks, Ukraine has also not performed well to safeguard the freedom of expression. Presumably, freedom of speech has been victim of collateral damage caused by the race to dominate cognitive space by both sides.

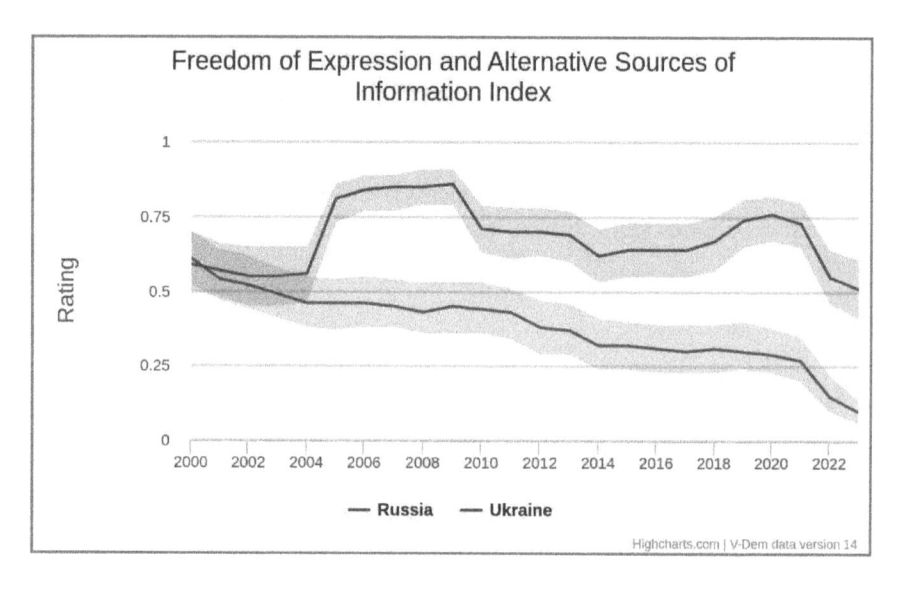

Figure 36 - Freedom of expression and alternative sources of information index scores for Russia and Ukraine
Source - Varieties of Democracies dataset 2024, What do ordinary Russians really think about the war in Ukraine? | EUROPP (lse.ac.uk)

Penetration of Internet and SMPs – Russian government and agencies synergistically activated plethora of communication channels to present their perspective to world about ongoing conflict with Ukraine. Through multiple international forums and social media communication, Russians presented their argument to justify annexation of Crimea compelled by threats to their national interests owing to perceived growing NATO influence in extended neighbourhood especially in Ukraine. Evidently, Russia leveraged state-controlled media outlets and digital media channels such as RT, to execute its information operations within the country as well as to reach out to 'Russian World' and 'Compatriots' in break-away nations of the erstwhile USSR. Simultaneously, Russian communication strategy manipulated Ukrainian population and targeted NATO member nations. The strategy facilitated domination over information space of the neighbouring countries devoid of strong network of indigenous media outlets and channels. Simultaneously, internet and SMPs such as Facebook, Twitter (X), TikTok, YouTube, and Telegram, have also been leveraged to influence the diverse audiences, gain greater circulation for narratives and messages and shape the opinion of target audiences across the globe. As per various reports, Ukraine learning from its past experiences dovetailed SMPs into Strategic Communication to counter Russian propaganda and narrative building. Reports suggest that at the onset of Russia-Ukraine conflict, Russia imposed restriction over internet and banned Facebook and Twitter (X). Ironically, Russia denied access to both SMPs for its own citizens, presumably to protect its own information sphere, but used these platforms to disseminate curated messages for target audiences and intrude in the Ukrainian's cognitive space. Within Russia, YouTube and TikTok are still accessible to everyday citizens, but with heavy censorship. The most popular social media platform used within Russia is VKontakte (VK), which hosts 90 percent of internet users in Russia, according to the company's self-reported statistics. It was previously available and widely used in Ukraine until 2017, but the Ukrainian government blocked access to VK and other Russian social media such as Yandex in an effort to combat online Russian propaganda.[155] The statistics of clientele base of SMPs in Russia and Ukraine in 2022 are depicted at Figure 37 below: -

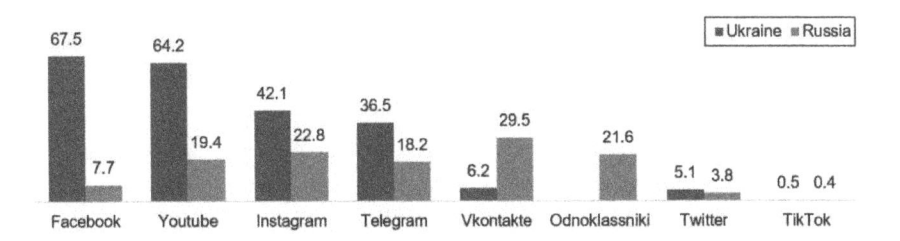

Figure 37– Use of social media in Ukraine and Russia
Source - Eurasia Barometer wave 3 (Nov 2021), What do ordinary Russians really think about the war in Ukraine? | EUROPP (lse.ac.uk)

It emerges from the graph above that Instagram, YouTube and TikTok had significant hold over market in Russia, whereas in Ukraine, social media space was dominated by Instagram, Facebook and YouTube. The report also suggests that Vkontakte (VK) was the most popular Russian social media platform with 100 million monthly users, and 50 million daily users. Yandex, Russia's most popular search engine with a 60 % market share, sold its news division to Vkontakte in April 2022. Since the start of Russia-Ukraine Conflict, Telegram's use increased rapidly; in the first three weeks of the war, Telegram users increased by 46 % and from February to April 2022 it was Russia's most downloaded application with 4.4 million downloads. The significant increase in popularity and usage of Telegram is attributed to encrypted messaging service which renders it difficult to enforce content regulation and detection of source of information. This platform created and owned by Russian tech billionaire Pavel Durov, has been used extensively for multiple tasks such as connecting with Ukrainian refugees, circulating fabricated contents and providing near-real-time videos of events on the battlefield. It is important to note that Telegram has no official policies to censor or remove content of any nature. The platform circulates majority of content posted by users, regardless of its nature. Resultantly, Telegram emerged as unfiltered source of disinformation within Russia and Ukraine with access to audiences devoid of access to Western SMPs. Owing to its software designs, Telegram is not suitable for AI tools to effectively boost disinformation, whereas on other platforms such as Twitter (X) and Facebook, AI is enabling rapid spread of disinformation about the war.

Social Media Warfare Tactics - It is observed that Russians have exploited sophisticated network of fake accounts, proxy servers and VPNs to circumvent the ban imposed by Ukraine and Western countries. This modus operandi has facilitated rapid dissemination of the messages and targeting of diverse global audience without being detected. It is learnt from OSINT that Russia invested significant resources and time to develop an effective propaganda ecosystem of official and proxy communication channels, to launch wide-reaching disinformation campaigns. For instance, '*Operation Secondary Infektion*' one of Russia's longest ongoing campaigns, has spread disinformation about issues such as COVID-19 pandemic across over 300 social media platforms since 2014.[156] The trend analysis of the tactics adopted to execute a synergised narrative building and information dominance operation reveals simultaneous exploitation of AI, Chat Bots, Deep Fakes, hashtags, spams, buffer/ fake accounts and multitude of dis-information sites to gain maximum traction and speedy dissemination of fabricated contents. To compound the woes of security establishments and social media watchdogs, Russian improvised their tactics to leverage 'Fact Check Sites'/ 'Fact Check Tropes' to spread true or partially true fact-checks, fake fact-checks of real news and debunks of 'Ukrainian disinformation'.[157] According to a report published by DFRL Lab, multiple Russian Fact Check organisations portrayed as apolitical entities, released analytical contents created based on borrowed tropes from legitimate fact-checking organizations and open-source researchers. These fact-checks contents in multiple languages are amplified by Russian media pundits, state television, or government through overlapping web of outlets such as Telegram channels, websites, Vkontakte accounts, and Russian government social media accounts. The overlapping network and information sourced from legitimate fact check organisations facilitated wider audience reach, achieved greater legitimacy and acceptability through endorsement and created cognitive biases. For example, 'War on Fake' channel on Telegram with seven lakh subscribers was promoted by Russian diplomats and government officials. The content uploaded by the channel was gradually circulated in Western circles also. Subject matter experts opine that by leveraging manipulated fact check contents, Russia could mould the perception of its population, distort opinion of global audience and erode confidence of people in credibility of fact check news. Russian government accounts have also been linked to "typo squatting" (registering websites with deliberately misspelled names of similarly named websites) of popular news organisations containing false information.[158]

In the run up to Russia's invasion on 24 February 2022, disinformation themes were designed to demoralise Ukrainians, sow division between Ukraine and its allies and bolster public perception of Russia.[159] Certain claims and assertions propagated through multiple channels are as under:[160]

- ➢ Military build-up prior to invasion was for training exercises only.

- ➢ Messages focused on historical revisionism to delegitimise Ukraine as a sovereign state. It was argued that Ukraine has no historical claim to independence as the country was created by Russia.

- ➢ Claims about neo-Nazi infiltration in the Ukrainian government were aggressively pushed.

- ➢ Fear psychosis was created through assertion regarding threats to Russian populations in Ukraine and Ukrainian government committing genocide in those parts of Donetsk and Luhansk oblasts which were under control of Russian-backed separatists since 2014.

- ➢ Spreading "whataboutisms" that downplayed Russia's large-scale invasion by drawing attention to alleged war crimes by other countries.

While non-kinetic operations were directed to dominate the virtual space and create online noise to muzzle the alternate perspective. Kinetic operations were conducted to destroy Ukrainian TV towers to disrupt broadcasting. In early March 2022, TV towers were attacked in Kyiv and Kharkiv. The broadcasting tower was seized by the Russians in Kherson, with local TV and radio channels switched to Russia-promoting video and audio messages. The Russian-appointed new 'acting mayor' of Melitopol urged local people to switch to Russian TV channels for 'more reliable' information. These strategies were designed to enforce a fabricated narrative around Russia's invasion into Ukraine, as well as revising the whole history of Ukraine-Russia relations.

In the second year of conflict in 2023, consequent to international sanctions, dented reputation and ban on state-sponsored RT and Sputnik in many Western countries, Russia shifted toward more targeted and tailored influence operations. Russian influence operations commenced exploiting TikTok, Telegram, and other social media platforms to expand its international audience, especially in the Global South, where Russian state media are still big players. Russia also deepened its cooperation in media and information spheres with sympathetic countries.[161] Unfolding of Russian actions revealed tightening of state control over use of digital space by Russian citizens and stricter rules for scrutiny of online contents. Surveillance measures and censorship of communication over internet persisted, access to information remained restricted and legislation introduced to prevent use of VPNs by circumventing online scrutiny. Russia's Federal Service for Supervision of Communications, Information Technology and Mass Media, the state telecommunications regulator commonly known as Roskomnadzor, also rolled out an internet surveillance system known as Oculus designed to detect content that the Kremlin considers undesirable.[162]

A study by Atlantic Council and DFRL argues that Russia's social media strategy was a meticulous work to address diverse audiences (internal and external) through specially curated narratives and themes. The study observes that to weaken the resolve, create trust deficit and erode Ukraine's reputation amongst its Western allies, Russia continued to carry out influence operations by uploading contents discrediting Ukrainian leadership, flagging corruption in government practices, labelling Ukrainian as unreliable ally and amplified its internal conflicts. The Kremlin's propaganda apparatus conducted the largest known influence operation on TikTok to disseminate rumours about Ukrainian political corruption. To drive a wedge, weaken the resolve and undermine EU support to Ukraine, persistent attempts were made to red flag alleged sale of weapons by Ukraine in black market and highlight the consequences of non-availability of Russian gas. Simultaneously, Maldova and South Caucuses were subjected to targeted messaging to foment societal divide, gain local support and undermine support for Ukraine. The opinion and perception of leadership and masses in Azerbaijan, Georgia and Maldova were influenced through war mongering, coercion and energy blackmail. The external audiences in MENA and Latin America were influenced through synergised efforts to justify Russian actions, assert claim of dominance in the conflict, garner pro-Kremlin support and propagate anti West and anti-colonial sentiments.

Response by Ukraine. Based on the analysis, it may not be incorrect to establish that Russia leveraged penetration of internet in Ukraine to carry out its 'Battle of Narrative' and enhance impact of information operations. It is important to note that since 2015, the percentage of Ukrainians using television, radio and print media to receive news has steadily declined, while on average, social network usage and viewership of news websites have grown. Indeed, the start of Russia's war of aggression against Ukraine saw a large increase in use of social networks as a source of news. According to a study conducted in May 2022, the top sources of news in Ukraine were social media networks, used by 77% of Ukrainians, followed by television (67%) and internet excluding social networks (61%). Particularly striking was increase in importance of social media as a source of news, which rose from 62% in 2020 to 77% by May 2022. The platforms that people use have also changed: since the start of the war, Telegram has become the leading source of information for Ukrainians, followed by YouTube, whereas Facebook has moved from first to third place.[163] Ukraine's efforts to strengthen its media sector since 2014 has been an essential pillar of its resilience to mis-information and disinformation. In January 2017 public broadcaster UAPBC (Public Broadcasting Company of Ukraine, rebranded as Suspilne in 2019) was established meeting European standards and practices. Suspilne focused on capacity building, ensuring transparency and independence and devised strategy to execute operations in the event of Russian hostilities.[164] In May 2021, Ukraine established 'Centre on Countering Disinformation (CCD)' under National Security and Defense Council (NSDC), tasked to monitor and analyse information threats to Ukraine's national security. Since February 22, it has conducted fact-checking and debunking activities on Telegram and Twitter (X)[165] In addition, Ukraine's Ministry of Digital Transformation developed a chatbot on Telegram that allows citizens to send videos and locations of Russian forces, which Ukraine's army can use to supplement other sources of intelligence. Ukrainian President has also leveraged social media space (Telegram channel with 1.4 million subscriber) to establish direct connect with citizens. He shares videos of daily update on the war, motivational speeches, pictures of Russian destruction, and appeals to the international community, at times shot seemingly spontaneously on a smartphone, directly to the Ukrainian population.

The media outlets have also adapted to the challenging conditions wherein reporting in war zone is fraught with life risks due to precise targeting by Russian forces using geo-tagging features of social media feeds related to battle zone. In addition, Russian cyber-attacks on media websites have also been frequent impacting their functioning and at times using their sites for peddling fake news. UAPBC relocated from Kyiv to Lviv and continued to broadcast national news on Telegram and Viber. Three largest private media organisations of Ukraine (Star Light Media, 1+1 Media, and Inter Media Group) joined public broadcasters UA: First and Ukrainian Radio to provide unified round-the-clock coverage under the 'United News' project. The consciousness towards national interests and functioning and autonomy in reporting by the Ukrainian private media houses was governed by the political leanings of the owners and investors. After the heads of the broadcasters met amongst themselves at the start of the war, President Zelensky signed a decree on 18 March 2022 requiring all national TV channels to broadcast through one platform, funded by the government. While effective for providing access to information and important for controlling narratives around the war in the face of Russian disinformation campaigns, this approach raises questions over direct state intervention in media. Each channel produces a segment of news for a slot of 24-hour news cycle, which is then broadcast by the other channels. In this case, coverage could continue should one provider lose its ability to broadcast. Some regional providers have also joined the initiative, and all fees have been waived to make access to news free.[166] Similarly, difficulties with accessing television and print media led to development of application 'RadioPlayer.ua', which provides free access to United News output in Ukrainian, English and Russian, also available through state's e-services application DIIA. Ukrainian mobile operators do not charge or deduct from allowances for connecting to it. Removing financial barriers to information in this manner is essential to help ensure citizens can access news in extremely challenging circumstances.[167] In addition to supporting efforts to increased access to news, Ukraine has also limited access to Russian state-linked media in an effort to reduce its influence. On 16 January 2022, one month before the Russian attack, a law came into force requiring all national print media to be published in Ukrainian, the country's official language. The aim was to push back against the use of the Russian language (and influence) in the public sphere. The law stipulated that a least 90% of airtime on national TV should be in Ukrainian and that local channels were allowed no more than 20% of non-Ukrainian language content.

Amidst the challenging circumstances and intense war, the Ukrainian public has gainfully used SMPs to showcase their courage, boost morale of their soldiers, highlight alleged war crimes by Russian soldiers and provide battle field intelligence about Russian military movements. The heart-wrenching glimpses of life in Ukraine since the Russian invasion have become powerful ammunition in an information war playing out on social media. The messaging has become a crucial battleground complementing the Ukrainian military's performance on physical front lines, as images and information ripple out on Instagram, Facebook, Telegram and TikTok. The proliferation of pictures showing human toll of the war has helped Ukraine project an image of a country of stalwart survivors with the moral high ground, while casting Russia as a merciless aggressor, an impression reinforced by global condemnation and sanction.[168]

Social media space has also been cultivated by the Ukrainians to ascertain precise locations of the Russians troops in tactical battle areas and launch strike to inflict damage. On 12 October 2022, a Russian soldier Aleksey Lebedev logged onto VKontakte, Russia's social media network, and uploaded a photo of himself in military fatigues while being located at Svobodne village in Southern Donetsk. Though, he did not disclose his face but his post was picked up by a Ukrainian military investigations company called Molfar. Subsequently, analyst in OSINT branch, and investigators ascertained the target location through geo-tagging analysis, which was believed to be a training base for Russian and pro-Russian separatist troops. Molfar passed its findings to Ukrainian intelligence to carry out an attack on the facility resulting in Russian fatalities as reported by Security Service of Ukraine (SBU) on its Telegram Channel.[169] The analysis of social media posts and media reporting also facilitated in revealing locations of various Russian Forces location and involvement of Chechen in Rubizhne. The location was targeted by HIMARS system later, however casualties to Chechen soldiers could not be ascertained. Like Russia, Ukraine has learned this the hard way and has suffered through its own OPSEC blunders, such as when Russian OSINT researchers successfully identified location of a tank repair facility in Kyiv from a report on 7 April 23 by Ukrainian TV channel 1+1. Local media reported that the facility was targeted shortly after, on 15 April 2023, by a Russian missile, reportedly resulting in destruction and casualties. Learning from these experiences, speculating precision targeting by Russia forces based on geo-tagging of the posts, reportedly Ukrainian government has prohibited its journalists to operate in front line in the war zone.

To summarise, the ongoing Russia-Ukraine conflict has been seminal event in social media warfare. The impact of manipulation of social media has been witnessed in multiple domains viz; psychological warfare, social engineering, kinetic operations and geo-politics. Rampant use of propaganda, fabricated messaging and manipulated fact checking by belligerent nations has sowed the seeds of distrust amongst the native population as well as global audiences. Manipulation of tropes from legitimate sources has also led to erosion of credibility of Fact Check News and organisations. The state control over media imposed by both Russia and Ukraine has infringed upon press freedom, right to freedom of speech and denied alternate perspective/ opinion to citizens. The legislation introduced by Ukrainian government imposing restriction on media coverage in non-Ukrainian language content is also a violation of rights of ethnic Russian minority residing in fractured and fragile Ukrainian society.

Three Warfare Strategy and China's Social Media Maze

'Propaganda' and 'dis-information' tactics have been mainstay of the Chinese war fighting strategies evolved over the years. The CCP and Chinese security forces have honed their manipulative skills significantly and have leveraged the art to shape opinion of target minds to attain a decisive edge against the competitors in geo-political arena. Many strategists and China watchers opine that in past decades China has exploited 'Three Ws Strategy' encompassing 'Media, Psychological and Legal Warfare' to weaken and dominate its adversaries and competitors in core interests' areas. India has been a target of Chinese propaganda campaigns since long; during Doklam and Galwan stand-off, the Chinese propaganda machinery unleashed well-coordinated attacks against India. These attacks were designed to discredit the Indian government and malign image of the security forces amongst the Indian public as well as shape global opinion. The trend of Chinese tactics also reveals the design to create trust deficit, sow seeds of discord and trigger panic amongst the Indian public. A study was undertaken by India Today OSINT group, to understand the objectives and effects of

Chinese propaganda campaigns. The analysis was conducted based on SCAME framework i.e., source, content, audience, media and effects, to understand its efficacy. The study reveals that Chinese dis-information tactics encompass utilising wide variety of media such as print, digital and social media platforms. The sources for information peddling can be categorised as 'White' (whose source is known), 'Grey' (source unknown) and 'Black' information attributed to someone other than the source)[170]. The study points out that propaganda classification based on source generally refers to the methods employed to carry the message rather than its content. White, grey and black classification provides identification of the source, which in turn gives out purpose and aim of the messages. Sources could be individuals propagating narrative on the behest of Chinese government or even government organisations itself uploading messages on Chinese platform Weibo. The scrutiny of social media uploads during Galwan stand-off reveals that fabricated facts related to incidents were linked to white sources i.e., inputs from PLA troops deployed along the borders. The targets of Chinese social media campaigns included Indian public, media houses and political leaders, who were concerned about developments along the borders but had no or limited access to latest credible update. In addition, intelligentsia and army personnel were also part of Chinese targeting strategy. The messaging and narratives designing for each segment of target groups was carried out meticulously to trigger fear, evoke sentiments and sow trust deficit for Indian government and erode morale of armed forces. The analysis of social media communication also indicates that China adopted a separate strategy to target indigenous population to shape their opinion, hide Chinese casualties and paint a fake narrative about their actions.

The 2017 border stand-off in Doklam, along the India–China–Bhutan Trijunction, was a seminal moment for China in testing out a new information strategy. As PLA's Western Theatre Command put it following the stand-off, the strategy combined radio, TV, newspaper, and social media messaging to push China's narrative at home, as well as abroad[171]. As per a study, Chinese social media platforms emerged as a useful outlet for authorities to not only monitor local issues and protests and gauge public sentiment but also to disseminate propaganda through a layered apparatus, comprising official government accounts, official media, individual journalists, and a network of tens of thousands of pro-government accounts that are sometimes disparagingly called the '50 cent party' in China, as that is the amount they are supposedly paid per post.[172] These multiple agencies and account handlers promoted government's agenda and targeted Indian media houses, general public and security forces through meticulously curated narratives.

Amidst emerging social media landscape, the focus of China's information strategy has evolved from restricting sensitive information to a more sophisticated approach of 'guiding public opinion'. This was applied to both internal and external messaging. As Xi Jinping put it in an ideology work conference in 2013, "China's media needed to prioritise 'telling China's story well' while meticulously and properly conducting external propaganda, innovating external propaganda methods, working hard to create new concepts, new categories and new expressions that integrate the Chinese and the foreign, telling China's story well, and communicating China's voice well" (Bandurski, 2020). To carryout the task of 'telling China's story well', China's 'big four' Party media—China Central Television (CCTV), People's Daily newspaper and English website, Chinese and English editions of *Global Times*, Xinhua News Agency, and China Radio International (CRI)—all play key roles in external messaging.[173] To influence intellectuals and media houses, there were also reports of Chinese hosting the Indian journalists on scholarship cum internship programs.

The stand-off in Doklam was marked by a multi-pronged messaging strategy. The objective was "to fully integrate the publicity forces of public opinion, radio, TV, newspapers and social media, and carry out a multi-wave and high-density centralized publicity in a fixed period to form favourable public opinion situation to allow for a final victory" (Tu and Ge, 2018). An analysis by Tu Ling and Ge Xiangran, strategists with Joint Staff Department of the People's Liberation Army's (PLA) WTC, reflects upon the line of strategic thought on leveraging social media to dominate the cognitive space. They state that, "On this 'no-smoke battlefield, we comprehensively used various communication platforms…and always maintained the absolute superiority of the legal struggle against India… initiative is the key of public opinion struggle and whoever grasps it will have an advantage, and whoever loses it will fall into passivity… To disclose the truth in time and seize the legal high ground, is the key to grasp the initiative of the legal struggle of public opinion". In their analysis they have highlighted seamless coordination and synchronisation of messages and statements released by MoD, Ministry of Foreign Affairs, Chinese Embassy in India, People's Daily (Renmin Ribao), PLA Daily (Jiefangjun Bao), and Xinhua on 3rd and 4th August 2017. Subsequently, various media outlets such as Global Times amplified and re-posted the messages uploaded by People's Daily thereby formed a wave of public opinion and disseminated photos and videos to support their claim of Indian Army crossing the border. According to an article published in The Diplomat, on 7 August 2017, China's Defense Ministry invited a delegation of Indian media for face-to-face dialogue with high-level officers of the People's Liberation Army. The Chinese media did not cover the visit, however selectively picked the news published in Indian Media to present the distorted facts. The People's Daily mobile version published an article — "A slap in the face! Bhutan acknowledges that Doklam is a Chinese area and finds it strange that the Indian troops are on the Chinese soil"- based on the report- "Bhutan acknowledges that Doklam is a Chinese area: Chinese official"- of Press Trust of India (PTI). It is apparent that People's Daily intentionally deleted the most important part of the headline -Chinese official. People's Daily downplayed the fact that the Chinese official is the only source of the information and highlighted the Bhutan part. In the end, People's Daily even claimed that "Bhutan acknowledges that Doklam is a Chinese area" was widely reported by Indian media. Soon, the article was reposted by the Global Times (the most hawkish Chinese state-run newspaper) and grabbed attention there.[174]

During Galwan Stand-off of 2020, the dynamics had changed, China did try to exploit its network of publicity forces to spread lies and shape the domestic and global opinion. However, Chinese success was restricted to domestic audiences only. Seemingly, Indians could seize initiative and unmasked the truth about Chinese setbacks and casualties in front to world which took the Chinese by surprise. Consequent to a well-coordinated social media campaign by the Indian government, security forces and national media, the Chinese social media account handlers could not achieve the desired effect. While the Indians were transparent in sharing the details of casualties suffered in the stand-off, the Chinese authorities remained silent about their losses. Its only after a year Chinese came up with documentary on the incident. As per a study, Chinese social media strategy post Galwan stand-off extended the cross-platform coordination to global social media platforms on a scale that exceeded the trend observed during the Doklam crisis. Many 'unofficial' voices were also incorporated in the messaging, unlike during Doklam, when it was limited to official media. During the Galwan stand-off, unverified images, first shared on Chinese social media such as Weibo and WeChat, were subsequently posted on Twitter (X) by social media handles that had somewhat unclear links with the Chinese government. The use of social media during the Galwan stand-off allowed China to share its message directly with the Indian audience also. The Chinese social media handlers uploaded photos of an Indian soldier in captivity and a Chinese soldier hoisting flag in an unknown location which was portrayed as Galwan. Both these imaged were widely circulated and created heated debate in Indian political circles.

On analysis of multiple comments, studies and analysis, it can be inferred that in the realm of 'Three Warfare Strategy' China has meticulously created a potent force of diverse actors to carry out social media attacks, create confusion and cloud opinion of the target population. The capability of the Chinese ecosystem of social media warriors was at display during Doklam and Galwan stand-off and in the subsequent period.

Weaponised Social Media Space: Pak Orchestrated Threats to India's National Security

As per military strategists and many think tanks, Pakistan has executed its meticulously planned anti-India 'information operations' in an effective manner. The theme of Pakistan's information operations and battle of narratives revolves around alleged oppression and ill treatment of Indian Muslims, 'Azadi' for Kashmir and alleged atrocities by Indian security forces on India.[175] Recently, Pakistani social media handles have also been making desperate attempts to stoke controversy and create a hype over perceived Hindu superiority, governance and abrogation of Article 370. The unfolding of events surrounding Pulwama Terrorist Attack and Balakot Airstrike, witnessed coordinated information operations and narrative building by social media handles controlled by cohort of inimical forces. The propaganda warfare prosecuted by Pakistan supported forces forms part of larger conspiracy to alienate the Kashmiri populace, cloud their cognitive thinking and negative portrayal of Indian government and security forces. The eco-system of Pakistani propaganda machinery and social media warfare extends beyond geo-graphical borders. It comprises ISPR, Pakistan government's official accounts and network of intellectuals, certain media houses and think tanks organisations. The sphere of influence of eco-system is augmented by covert and overt support of separatists' organisations, terrorists and over ground workers/ hybrid terrorists operating in valley, and netizens influenced by fabricated narrative. To prosecute the 'Battle of Narratives', discredit Indian government and establishment and cripple cognitive capabilities of target population, Pakistan has exploited various incidents and events occurred in India in recent years and has presented a concocted version of the historical facts. The study of certain incidents exemplifies the pattern of manipulation tactics deployed by Pakistani establishments.

> During Delhi riots in late February 2020, multiple social media accounts traced back to Pakistan, amplified fear and anxiety, uploaded hate messages and fake stories, pictures and videos to enrage and colour opinion of the target population. There was a massive surge in tweet traffic from accounts linked to Pakistan, with hashtags like #Hinduterrorism and #RSSKillingMuslims.[176] The fabricated and edited media reports on various social media platforms were synchronised through accounts handled from different countries with varied timestamps, but claiming to be from India. The investigation of incident has revealed that Pakistani political parties were actively involved in spewing venom against India through their online propaganda campaign. As per a report compiled by Delhi Police, Insaf Students Federation (ISF), student wing of Imran Khan's Tehreek-e-Insaf party, had activated around 100 accounts mostly created under Hindu names. Using these accounts, ISF operated numerous anti India hashtags and portrayed the riots as genocide against Muslims.[177] Further to make their false narrative as legit and portray the Indian government in negative shade, these handles shared old photos of incidents of destruction and excessive use of force pertaining to Syria and Bangladesh, claiming them as pictures of Delhi riots.[178]

> The Pakistani media and political establishment have also spun narratives and propagated twisted messages to intimidate specific target population in India on various internal matters. The prominent incidents include Citizenship Amendment Act (CAA) and National Residents Census (NRC), Uniform Civil Code (UCC), debate over illegal immigrants and controversy over religious places.

> Kashmir and Indian armed forces have been central to Pakistan's disinformation campaigns. Pakistan has consistently accused armed forces of committing war crimes in Kashmir using verified Twitter handles, including that of ISPR, the PM's Office, Ministry of Foreign Affairs (MOFA) website, foreign media, and social media trolls. MOFA's website has a separate section called 'Indian Illegally Occupied Jammu and Kashmir', which contains heavily edited and misleading media portraying Indian Army as a threat to the Kashmiri population.[179] Foreign media, too, has contributed to Pakistan's information warfare (IW) against India. For instance, Stoke White, an independent UK-based investigative unit,

published a report in collaboration with Legal Forum Kashmir, a Pakistan-based law firm alleging war crimes and human rights violations by Indian Army in Kashmir.[180] Pakistan's anti-India propaganda witnessed hyperactivity following India's decision to abrogate Article 370 in August 2019. The ISPR went so far as to claim that 1947 Instrument of the Accession of Kashmir was 'illegal'. Further, the Pakistani Prime Minister repeatedly alleged persecution of Kashmiri Muslims and militarisation of the Valley.

> Retaining initiative to execute inimical plans at time and place of own choosing, Pakistan and cohort of terror organisations have been able to synchronise the acts of terror and violence followed by social media warfare to propagate conspiracy theories and create confusion. It is evident that sensational terror attacks in valley by Pakistan sponsored non-state actors are immediately followed by online tirade against Government of India; naming and shaming security forces, shifting the blame of act(s) of violence to Indian establishment and alleging the Government of India of plotting such incidents to hide own failures and falsely implicating Pakistani agencies. The fact can be corroborated with occurrence of terror incidents in recent past followed by barrage of social media offensive undertaken by Pakistan sponsored social media account handlers. Terror strike in Pulwama by terror organisation (non-state actor) was carefully planned coinciding with election campaign in India. The Pakistani establishments through aggressive manoeuvre on social media were quick to shift blame of incident to Indian establishment as diversionary tactics and could create confusion in the minds of Indian public. The incidents witnessed a state response by Indian side, wherein IAF carried out Balakot Strike. To discredit IAF and downplay Indian response, Pakistani media handles once again flooded the internet with fake narrative and fabricated visuals and pictures. Pakistani social media warfare was at display again during PAF attempt to intrude in Indian airspace resulting into Wing Commander Abhinandan Varthaman destroying Pakistan Air Force's F-16 fighter jet before his MiG-21 Bison crashed in Pakistan-occupied Jammu and Kashmir. Pakistan has used this episode on numerous occasions to reiterate its narrative and reinforce belief of its citizens and international audiences. In 2023, social media was abuzz with flurry of tweets and messages related to this incident.

Consequent to study of pattern of social media traffic post Pulwama incident and Balakot Strike, it was perceived that Pakistani agencies enjoyed an edge over their competitors on the Indian side. Many think tanks opine that over the decades Pakistan has created a complex ecosystem to further its objectives of narrative building, foment discontent, keep the agenda of 'Azadi' alive and peddle lies to tarnish image of government of India and security forces. The Pakistani propaganda machinery has capitalised on vicious network of separatists' organisations in the valley, India based radical organisations and various Western thinks tanks and media to advance their agenda and spread doctored contents on social media. The simultaneous activation of vicious web of Pakistani state actors and non-state actors on both sides of Line of Control, launched an aggressive influence operation on multiple social media platforms, thereby gaining advantage in time and cognitive space. Exploiting absence of verified and genuine online reports supported by facts, Pakistani handlers could cloud rationale thinking and objective opinion of Indian media and certain sections in political circles. The media and political parties who were surfing digital space to glean information about the incident, faced the challenge of gaining first hand access to information and fell prey to designs of Pak sponsored propaganda machinery.

Spread of ISIS (ISIL) or ISKP Tentacles – The reports suggest that over past decade, the ISIS (K) has been making overtures to gain a strong foothold in India. In recent past, the intelligence agencies have gathered credible evidences of recruitment drive undertaken by ISIS in India, hatching a conspiracy to foment unrest and carryout terror attacks in India. Decoding of ISIS operational manual indicates that terror outfit has weaved its anti-India narrative around Kashmir conflict and alleged oppression of Muslim minorities in India. The outfit has also been attempting to fuel anti-government sentiments by spreading the manipulated narrative painting CAA, NRC, UCC, Ram mandir temple in Ayodhya, contestation over Gyanvapi Mosque as threats to Islam. The negative spinoff and fabricated falsehood propagated by this terror orgainsation is aimed to fuel anger amongst the Muslim population, create societal fissures and damage communal harmony. The intensity and occurrence of such propaganda attacks have been on rise especially during the election campaigns.

The broad trends of modus operandi and tactics deployed by the terrorist organization are discussed in the succeeding paras.

- *Environment Scan.* India's has been battling with internal security challenges posed by jihadi ideology and Pak sponsored separatist movement for long. It is pertinent to highlight that country was the birthplace of Deobandi and Barelvi movements even before the independence. The Deobandi sect is believed to be source of ideas for creation of Taliban and other terrorist organisations. The mushrooming of unauthorised madrasas under the umbrella of Deobandi sect in Muslim dominated states accelerated spread of fanaticism and radical ideology and acted as jihadi labs for indoctrination and recruitment by such organisations. Further, external influences and narrative building exploited the religion as motivation for jihad and mobilise misguided youth to join or support terrorists' organisation. Prolong conflict in Kashmir Valley, externally doctored societal divide based on communal hatred, perceived oppression and threat to Muslim minority created environment conducive for ISIS influence operations in India. Availability of radicalised material on internet and social media platforms and 'Syrian Conflict' emerged as turning point in spread of jihadi ideology in Indian Subcontinent.[181] In 2021, ISKP, having close links with Pakistan, announced its new wing "Wilayah of Hind" or India Province to be functioning from Kashmir.[182]

- *Ideology/ Driving Force.* ISIL (Islamic State of Iraq and Levant) and ISKP (Islamic State Khorasan Province) follow Salafi or hybrid of Wahabi, Salafi and Sunni Jihadist ideologies, a branch of Sunni Islam, incorporating legal opinions of ancient Iraqi schools of Kufah. ISKP, a transnational jihad movement loosely affiliated with Islamic State in Iraq and Levant (ISIL; also called ISIS), operates primarily in Afghanistan.[183] Whereas ISIL operates in Iraq and Syria primarily. Recently, ISKP carried out a major terror attack in a mall in Russia in Mar 2024, which is seen as demonstration of its ability to strike across the globe. Both terror organisations (ISKP and ISIS) aim to establish the Caliphate, enforce Sharia law, denounce Western thoughts and oppose other religious beliefs. The geographical confines of their respective areas of operations have not precluded both the terror organizations from commanding their influences over their staunch and radicalized followers in multiple regions across the globe. Both terror outfits have exercised their influence through propaganda strategy deployed through dark net and social media platforms. Certain radicalised and vulnerable sections of the Indian population have also been trapped/ lured by their extremist ideology and indoctrination strategy. Some relevant observations by subject matter experts on ideology of ISIS/ ISKP are elucidated in succeeding paragraphs.

- As per some analysts, a major attraction drawing young men and women to jihadism has always been the idea of participating in a transnational religious movement and an epic global struggle.

- A major turning point in Indian and Central Asian involvement in the global jihadist movement was Syria. A cauldron that continues to draw people in, it is a clear and significant marker in the international jihadist story. The battlefield was one that drew in Muslims from almost 100 different countries and from every continent. This included Indians and Central Asians, though their experiences were markedly different.[184] It is pertinent to highlight that according to account narrated by some of ISIS recruits escaped clutches of terror organization or arrested by NIA, the recruits from Indian subcontinent are looked down upon by the Arabs and they are ill-treated and used for menial jobs by the terror outfit. However, despite these revelations certain misguided and indoctrinated individuals continue to remain attracted towards ISIS ideology.

➢ *Social Media Strategy* - It is noteworthy that the terror outfit has exploited digital space to spread its propaganda and gain support of misguided and vulnerable sections towards its agenda. There are various evidences of use of social media by ISIS in radicalising the target population in India as well as in other parts of the world especially in MENA Region. Leveraging growing internet footprint, vast social media customer base and phenomenal rise in mobile phones, ISIS has been able to add approximately 40,000 foreign nationals from 110 countries to its cadre base.[185]

- According to a report published by RAND Europe in 2018 for United Nations Development Program, ISIS is using social media platforms like Twitter (X), Telegram, YouTube and online propaganda magazines to recruit, radicalize and coordinate attacks in Africa.

- Taking advantage of feasibility to hide identity on Twitter (X) accounts and ease in activation of new accounts, ISIS has maintained Twitter accounts for its several official media outlets. It includes Al-Hayat media (distributes polished propaganda pieces in Arabic as well as Twitter feeds in various other languages, including English), Al-Medrar (publishes in multiple languages), Platform Media (tweets news updates in Arabic) and Al-Battar media (deals with English and Arabic feeds that tweet news, graphics, official statements, and videos). In addition, multiple ISIS regional groups maintain Twitter feeds posting news, images, and video of their activities. ISIS official Twitter accounts are augmented by supporters, with quasi-official status, who upload the contents in multiple languages and on diverse SMPs such as Twitter, Facebook, Instagram, and 'Question and Answer' service 'Ask.FM'. For example, Markaz-al-Islam Twitter feed, which promoted ISIS propaganda primarily in English, simultaneously also directed supporters to its English-language Facebook pages to generate propaganda content in English. This is the counter strategy to maintain circulation and visibility of such pages through multiple accounts thereby making it difficult to contain spread and removal of such manipulated messages by Facebook for content violation.

- Another strategy by IS involves luring the supporters to sign up for an Android app through Google Play called "Dawn of Glad Tidings" to receive information from ISIS on smart phone. In the process, ISIS gains access to users' accounts to post messages from their Twitter accounts, which become de-facto ISIS propaganda outlets facilitating amplification of their messages and creating astroturfing effects.

- ISIS also encourage supporters to repeatedly Tweet various hashtags such as #AllEyesonISIS or #CalamityWillBefallUS to vastly increase the visibility of tweets with ISIS's message. Similarly, ISIS encourages tweets of 'active hashtags' or hashtags that are already trending. Thus, it will encourage its supporters to tweet ISIS messages with popular hashtags (a tactics referred as hashtags hijacking) such as #worldcup so that people searching for those hashtags will inadvertently come across pro-ISIS posts.[186] A Brookings Institution study of ISIS propaganda on Twitter, found that group puts out 18 media releases a day and has upto 90,000 dedicated twitter handles, which helped it recruit over 20,000 followers including 3,000 teenagers and over 200 women. These numbers may have shot up since the study was released in March 2015.[187]

- The themes of such social media posts center around showcasing military might/ hard power of IS, guardian of sharia and painting the image of a goodwill organization through posting images, videos, graphics and messages. To shape the opinion and perception on its followers and global audiences, this outfit deliberately craft online content displaying ISIS cadres playing with kids, carrying out relief operations, making donations, spreading messages for Muslims to attend Friday prayers and even carrying out operations against armed forces. Social media strategy of ISIS has similarity with corporate marking strategy. To outplay their competition, they change the target audience by replacing the older cadres with young faces; ISIS social media messages engage with teenage recruits to gain traction, generate craze amongst the young impressionable minds and encourage them to popularise outfit brand. A report published by Brookings Institution revealed that in 2014, ISIS managed around 45000 Twitter accounts to tweet approximately 90,000 to 2,00,000 messages every day. The study further states that there were approximately 2000 accounts which used to upload 50 or more tweets per day as part of deliberate strategy.[188]

- Social media strategy of ISIS has got significant traction globally including in India. A report published by two Indian firms after analysis of over 60 million social media posts in 2019, especially on Facebook and Twitter, revealed that there are growing pockets of ISIS-related Islamist extremism in Andhra Pradesh, Tamil Nadu and Kerala. Refer Figure 38 below, reportedly ISIS modules have attempted to gain string hold in various Indian states; the trends reflect a relatively higher penetration in Kerala. The report claims that the content populated on social media platforms (SMPs) is not generic Islamist fundamentalism but is in the form of sophisticated propaganda built around themes peculiar to ISIS ideology. Reportedly, strategy of pro-ISIS individuals encompasses

SALIENCE OF SOCIAL MEDIA IN HYBRID OPERATIONS

securing positions in elected management committees in masjids, madrasas and other Islamic teaching centres as part of a deliberate and premeditated approach to increase the reach, influence and power of ISIS networks in these states.[189]

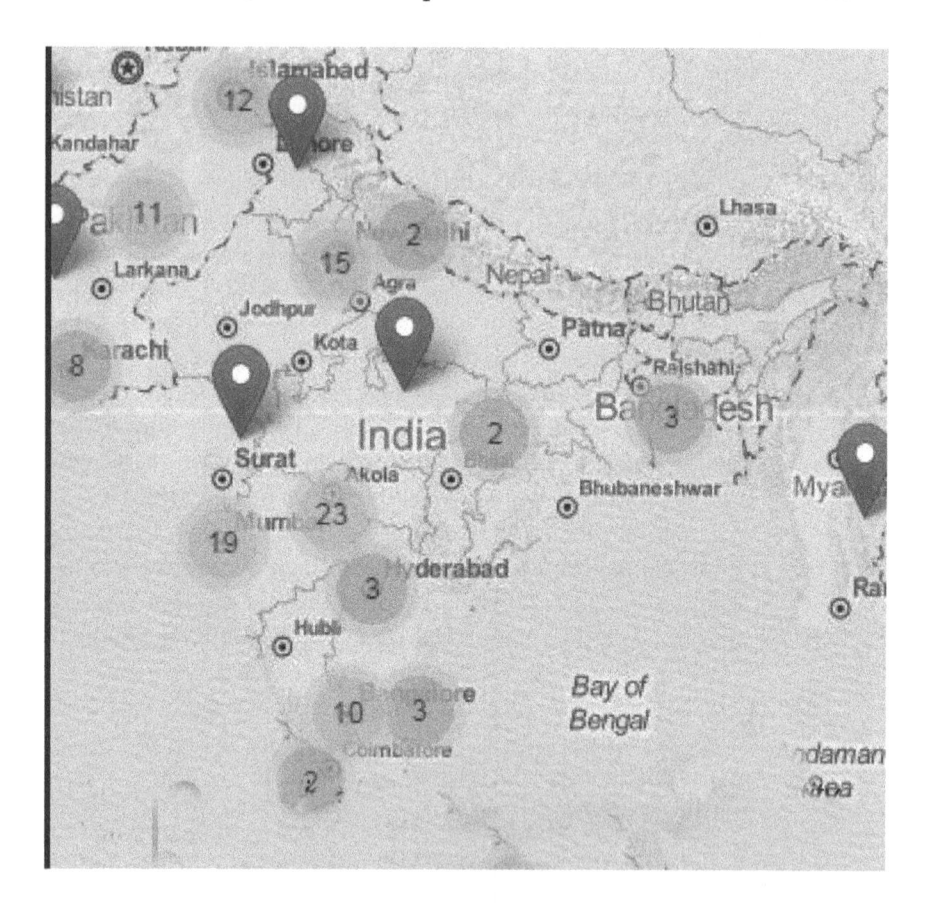

Figure 38 – ISIS High Influence-High Indoctrination Entity Distribution in India
Source - https://theprint.in/india/isis-influence-growing-in-south-india-particularly-kerala-social-media-monitoring-firms/234953/

- The report also claims that a lot of propaganda are originated from the MENA Region, Syria, Iraq and Saudi Arabia included. ISIS has demonstrated a sophisticated capability to translate the content it creates in the Middle East languages into local Indian languages. The quality of translations and sophistication of messages is indicative of involvement of dedicated PR teams with local language capabilities for India.[190] In December 2014, Bangalore police arrested Mehdi Masroor Biswas for operating a pro-ISIS *Twitter account @ShamiWitness.*[191] Reportedly, Biswas communicated with English-speaking members of IS and his account had viewership from multiple countries. He was was also in touch with one of the perpetrators of July 2016 terrorist attack in Dhaka, Bangladesh.[192]

- As per report published by Moran Yarchi in 'Sage Journal', the ISIS uses various platforms and media products to promote its messages. The details compiled by Moran Yarchi as per Table 6 given below, reveals that ISIS social media strategy encompassed engaging diverse target audience through varied propaganda material propagated through multiple channels of communication. The themes revolved around projecting warrior like image to catch imagination of own cadres, champion the agenda of self-proclaimed protector of Islam for larger Muslim population and power projection to intimidate Western Media: -[193]

Summary of the Organisation's Media Products

Media Product	Salient Themes	Target Audience	Image Projection tools	Notes
Audio Statements	Fighting and Violence, power projection, Islamic religious messages	All Muslims, supporters/ fighters, and enemies	A presentation of a clear and decisive image— through the usage of salient themes and metaphors	Changes according to circumstances
Videos	Violence and warfare, power and deterrence	Mostly ISIS members and supporters	As the most visual media platform, videos are used by ISIS frequently in its Image war in an attempt to promote its narrative	

Media Product	Salient Themes	Target Audience	Image Projection tools	Notes
Magazines	A shift from the emphasis on power projection to more religious based messages	Mostly the organization's supporters, potential supporters and fighters	Usage of Images (both visual images and texts) in an attempt to empower the organization, attract supporters, and present a threat to its enemies	The lengh of magazine allows for various messages to be promoted
Nasheeds	Islamic religious messages	Only Muslim audiences—fighters, supporters and potential supporters	Heavy usage of metaphors	The messages contain many visual descriptions that assist in the creation of the organization's image
News Reports	The reports are brief and informative presenting power projection	Western Media	Pictures or infographics	The news reports try to appear objective

ISIS: Islamic State of Iraq and al-sham

Table 6 – Use of media platforms for various type of contents by ISIS
Source – Sage Journal

- As per OSINT, various social media accounts have been found to be associated with ISIS recruits in India involved with online spread of radicalization, recruitment, indoctrination and mobilization. Mohammed Shafi Armar, resident of Bhatkal, Karnataka, important ally of Abu Bakr al-Baghdadi and Chief recruiter of ISIS, was in touch with around 600 youths through Facebook groups and messaging platforms such as WhatsApp, Trillion, Surespot and Skype. He reportedly recruited 30 personnel and had formed outfit named 'Junud-al-Khalifa-e-Hind (Soldiers of the Indian Caliphate)'. As per reports, ISKP launched an online magazine 'Sawt-Al-Hind' (Voice of Hind), propagating translated excerpts in Hindi, Bengali and Malayalam. ISKP propaganda tried to leverage Delhi riots and Babri Masjid case judgement to rile up emotions on Indian Muslims[194]. In December 2017, IS in its Telegram channel used hashtag 'Wilayat Kashmir' wherein Kashmiri militants stated their allegiance with IS. Around same time frame, Shajeer Mangalassery Abdullah, a resident of Kerala who fought with ISIS in Afghanistan, launched a social media group, 'Ansar ul-Khilaaf-Kerala' and "The Gate', on Telegram to radicalise the people in South India. He formed a group which communicated through Telegram's encrypted messaging software or the Tutanota secure, encrypted e-mail.[195]

> *Targeting Patterns* – Replying to a question in Rajyasabha in August 2020, Minister of State of Home G Kishan Reddy claimed that as per NIA report, ISIS, a sunni jihadist group has been most active in Kerala, Karnataka, Andhra Pradesh, Telangana, Maharashtra, Tamil Nadu, West Bengal, Rajasthan, Bihar, Uttar Pradesh, Madhya Pradesh, and Jammu and Kashmir. He highlighted that ISIS having links with other terror outfits like Lashkar-e-Taiba and Al-Qaeda, is using various social media platforms to propagate its ideology in India. The intelligence reports have revealed that apart from southern states like Telangana, Kerala, Andhra Pradesh, Karnataka and Tamil Nadu, wherein Iran and Syria-based terrorist outfit penetrated years ago, the terrorist group has penetrated other states as well.[196] Most importantly, the sympathisers and recruits of the terror outfit in India are predominantly educated youth (Engineers, MBBS and MBA graduates), which is a cause of concern for the security establishment. As per reports, Kerala has become a likely hotspot for ISIS recruitment overdrive due to some self-radicalized individuals who joined ISIS and travelled to Iraq, Syria, or Afghanistan. These people after returning back to Kerala reportedly indulged in spreading the ideology of terror outfit and recruited vulnerable youth to join ISIS. As per statement given by Indian Home Minister in June 2017, out of 90 ISIS recruits apprehended in India 21 recruits were from Kerala. As per an article on emergence of ISIS footprints in state, *Kerala's strong undercurrent of radicalisation could be one reason for this; between 1977 and 2006, the state has seen emergence of Islamist groups like Student Islamic Movement of India (SIMI), banned Islamic Sevak Sangh floated by Abdul Nasser Madani and National Development Front, now rechristened as Popular Front of India (PFI).*[197]

> *Territorial Entity and Ecosystem* - The reports published in ISIS magazine 'Dabiq' suggest that Islamic State organizes territorial entities under "wilayat" or administrative divisions. The group has declared one division in Indian subcontinent i.e., 'Wilayat Khurasan', consisting of Afghanistan and Pakistan. Apart from this provincial unit, group's magazine *Dabiq* regularly features operations and fighters from a second area, simply termed Bengal (i.e., Bangladesh) often branded 'the Khilafah's soldiers in Bengal'. There is no specific mention of a separate administrative unit or chieftain operating from within India as yet.[198] An article published in The Diplomat in Juen 2017 proclaimed that *"India faces an increasing domestic threat from virtual recruitment and self-radicalization, which has resulted in some Indians officially joining ISIS and fighting in Iraq and Syria. Also of concern is the external threat from Bangladesh's rising extremist population and radicalized individuals from Bangladesh that might plan and execute attacks in India if ISIS were to grow larger in the region".[199]* The author argues that preoccupation of jehadi elements with insurgency in J and K may have precluded a catastrophe in rest of India, but ISIS's unique online media exploitation has allowed individuals and small groups to garner significant attention. The author argues that increasing influence of ISIS in Bangladesh, vulnerability of porous Indo-Bangladesh borders to infiltration and illegal migration and rising tensions in refugee camps concerning Rohingya migrants provides a viable nexus for ISIS to strengthen its foothold in India. The media reports claimed that ISIS attempted to plant the seeds of unrest in India in June 2014 by including India in a map of its planned caliphate. Six months later, ISIS even named former Tehrik-e-Taliban commander Hafiz Saeed Khan as the 'Wali (Governor)' of the "Khorasan Province," which reportedly includes India. However, propaganda about Khorasan apparently has not gained significant traction in India. It is assessed that ISKP/ ISIL is appreciated to make inroads through home grown terrorists' groups IM and SIMI. Reportedly, strong presence of Indian Mujahideen (IM) in Kerala and links between ISIS and IM were revealed after a known IM militant, Muhammed Sajid, was killed in Syria. The reports also hint that both IM and Students' Islamic Movement of India (SIMI), another radical Islamic organization with a strong presence, could help push already radicalized youth toward ISIS or serve as direct recruiting platforms.[200] Reportedly a certain

section of groups, especially an Islamist extremist cell located in South India, have also been influenced by the sermons of Indian prominent extremist preacher Zakir Naik, whose speeches have helped radicalize numerous different jihadists around the world.

> *Effects* - ISIS operations, except one odd isolated incident, have not succeeded in carrying out any major incident in India. However, given the growing influence of radicalism and ISIS ideology, the possibility of a major incident by ISIS cadres operating independently or in collusion with IM and SIMI cannot be ruled out. It is noteworthy that ISIS cadres of India origin were reportedly involved in terror attacks executed by the outfit abroad. In 2019, ISIS officially announced creation of an Indian affiliate hinting its involvement in operations in Kashmir. Al Naba, the Islamic State's regular publication, also listed the martyrdom notices of three Kashmiris who died while fighting for the group. These individuals join the growing numbers of Keralites and other Indians who reported to have died or fought alongside the cadres of Islamic State. The effects of ISIS ideology and its indoctrination operations are assessed to be deeper and far reaching capable of posing a significant threat to global peace and security of nation states.

- First order effect of influence of ISIS social media can be on Indian working in West Asian countries as well as radicalised youth back at home. IS cells operating in Telangana, Kerala, Andhra Pradesh, Karnataka and Tamil Nadu may be desperate to recruit more youth to beef up declining cadre strength of terror outfit. The groups of indoctrinated Indian youth along with IM/ SIMI may orchestrate isolated terrorist incident(s) in India to demonstrate their solidarity and gain popularity. The possibility of such a strike appears imminent in light of call by IS spokesperson Hudhayfah al-Ansari to 'Lone Wolfs' to carryout strikes globally in month of Ramadan in Apr 2024.[201]

- Second order effect may entail increased followership and recruitment amongst radicalised and indoctrinated Muslim youth driven by hatred and portrayal of certain policies of present government as pro-Hindu and anti-Muslims. The IS ideologist may continue to gain a foothold in J and K in collusion with separatists' organization and terrorists' outfits operating in valley viz; JeM, HM, LeT, United Liberation Front of Kashmir (ULFK), The Resistance Force (TRF), Kashmir Tigers, and People's Anti-Fascist Force (PAFF).

- Third order effects may be the manifestation of geo-political situation in Middle East, spillover of Israel-Gaza conflict and feeling of alienation and alleged victimization of Muslim population and implementation of CAA, UCC and NRC in India. The situation may also be exploited by Bangladeshi extremists/ ISIS recruits infiltrating into India to carryout terrorist strikes. There is a likelihood that third order effects may unfold as collusive threat from IS, IM and SIMI in long term, which may be a consequence of strategy adopted by these radical organizations to regain/ strengthen their resurgent/ declining influence. Further, Indian citizens working in West Asian countries are increasingly exposed to IS ideology. Indoctrinated by IS ideology and radical elements during their stay in West Asia, these individuals or groups may become instrumental in giving momentum to ISIS operations in India, spread radical ideology, lure vulnerable youth to join ISIS and may even act as sleeper cells.

Penetration of Social Media Space by IM and SIMI

The pattern of social media exploitation by SIMI and IM presents a complex interconnected web; both terror outfits have used social media or internet in a limited manner to address Indian media, engage with their followers & vulnerable sections of society and make their presence felt. Devoid of a substantial source of motivation and explicitly linked and ideologically aligned Indian Muslim following, they have used sermons of radical clerics and IS/ AQIS videos to influence their followers and mobilise them for global jehad and spread terror in India. In this regard, it is pertinent to understand the trends of recruitment by both terror organisations. In a study published by ORF, the author has highlighted that cadres recruited by IM (Indian Mujahideen) and SIMI (Students Islamic Movement of India) are predominantly highly educated individuals with engineering, medical and management backgrounds. It needs no emphasis that the terrorists' organizations having cadres with sound educational backgrounds in technical and medical fields make them a formidable force to contest. The terror outfits such as ISIS/ ISKP, SIMI and IM are not alien to this fact and have extensively leveraged technical expertise of their cadres to enhance their influence in physical and digital space as well as threat potential. ISIS/ISKP has primarily depended upon social media and internet to reach out to target audience and carryout virtual indoctrination and recruitment. However, IM and SIMI by virtue of being home grown outfits have exploited existing societal fissures and religious polarization to their advantage to expand their influence and increase their followings.

The ORF study further makes an important observation that major Islamist terror cells in India have drawn their cadre mostly from SIMI. The origin of these cells can be traced back to the founders of TIM (Tanzim Islahul Muslimeen), founded in 1985, suspected to be involved in multiple blasts after Babri Masjid demolition. SIMI emerged as student wing of Jamaat-e-Islami-e-Hind (JIH) in April 1977.[202] From the onset, SIMI made explicit declaration that practice of Islam was 'a political project' and in the long term, caliphate would have to be re-established as without it practice of Islam would remain incomplete. SIMI's propaganda found appeal amongst a growing number of lower-middle and middle-class urban men who felt deprived of their share of the growing economic opportunities.[203] Resultantly, some radicalised elements among students' community developed fascination for SIMI's ideology and goals. The predominance of educated youth with easy access to internet and social media gives a plausible explanation for some of the SIMI cadres being influenced by online radicalisation and drift towards terror organisations like ISKP/ ISIS. OSINT also suggests that SIMI has become main line feeder for providing recruits for terror outfit viz; ISKP/ ISIS, AQIS and IM.

Indian Mujahideen (IM), a loose coalition of jihadists rather than a structured organisation, has drawn many of its cadres from SIMI. These IM jihadists are connected through ideological similarities and personal linkages and have been found to be mostly under the age of 40. As per reports, they are often trained in Pakistan by Lashkar-e-Toiba (LeT) and many of them have been highly educated professionals before being recruited. IM recruits tend to be lower and middle-class Muslims who either have been fuelled with anti-Hindu nationalism or driven by hatred for Western values and polytheism. Many high-profile SIMI and IM members are computer-literate and in certain cases have an impressive background with private-sector employment. It is pertinent to note that IM has used internet as a tool to send messages to media, communicating amongst members and spreading propaganda.[204]

Consequent to crackdown by Indian security agencies, IM and SIMI network had gone into disarray, however in recent past there have been attempts to unite and reorganise both outfits. As per a report published by Jamestown Foundation in April 2016[205], IM has developed linkages with the IS leadership in Syria and Iraq. Shafi Armar, a former IM militant, along with his elder brother, Sultan Armar founded 'Ansar-ut-Tawhid fi Bilad al-Hind (AuT)', an India-centric militant group based on Afghanistan and Pakistan borders. They were the first to pledge support to IS. By joining hands with IS and pledging 'bayat' to its leader, Abu Bakr al-Baghdadi, they hoped to unite IM and sympathizers of SIMI. Through its media arm called 'al-Isabah Media', AuT has focused on recruiting Indian-origin fugitives in Pakistan to participate in fighting in both Syria and Afghanistan. Shafi Armar took the reins of AuT and 'al-Isabah Media', with the intention of expanding group's network inside India. He pumped money and mobilised online resources into recruiting operatives to form JKH (Janood-ul-Khalifa) i.e., Caliph's Army of India. According to reports, AuT has been using internet chartrooms and messaging applications such as Trillian and Facebook to recruit mostly former IM cadres and members of SIMI.[206]

As per a report published by Animesh Roul, Director of Research at Society for the Study of Peace and Conflict (SSPC), New Delhi, JKH's (Janood-ul-Khalifa) use of internet has been significant. Following NIA-led raids, the intelligence agency confirmed that online involvement of arrested terrorists had led to physical meetings at different locations in Hyderabad, Bangalore, Tumkur, Saharanpur, Lucknow, and Pune. Nafees Khan of Hyderabad and Rizwan of Uttar Pradesh were recruited via Facebook and accessed bomb-making knowhow from publishing platforms like 'justpaste.it'. From social media accounts of Obeidullah Khan of Hyderabad, investigating agencies found IS videos and images that were frequently shared by him with his followers. It is also clear that group's members used the internet to connect with Shafi Armar who was based in Syria at that time. JKH also made use of teachings and sermons of senior Islamic scholars like Mufti Abdus Sami Qasmi, a resident of Delhi and an alumnus of infamous Darul Uloom Deoband Islamic institution in Uttar Pradesh. According to a news article published in Indian Express, Qasmi as a preacher of IS ideals, often gave incendiary, anti-India sermons and lectures on Islam at madrasas across India. As per certain reports, the clerics have played a crucial role in influencing the minds of Muslim youth. The findings are corroborated by inputs shared by apprehended IS cadres in India. Reportedly. a majority of 127 arrested IS sympathizers from across India revealed that they were following speeches of controversial Indian preacher Zakir Naik of Islamic Research Foundation (IRF).[207] The leaders of these organisations have frequently manipulated the emotions of radicalised and/ or innocent Muslim youth on various issues such as

Hindu Nationalism, CAA, NRC, UCC, triple talaq, ban on burqa and controversies related to religious places viz; Ayodhya Temple, Gyanvapi Mosque etc.

Patterns of Social Media Usage and Narrative Building by Separatists Forces in J&K

J&K has witnessed onslaught of Pakistan sponsored terrorism and proxy war since long. The separatists' organisations, terrorists' outfits and external forces have sowed the seeds of discord, indoctrinated and radicalised the Kashmiri population and created an atmosphere of anti-India sentiments. Distorting historical facts, obliterating vibrant religious and cultural lineage, discrediting ancient Kashmiri Sufi culture, the adversarial forces have spread the idea of Jehad and Azaadi to shape opinion and mindscape of Kashmiri population. Mushrooming madrasas network in valley targeted minds of Kashmiri people and have lured them to align Salafi/Wahabi and hard-liner ideology propagated by Islamic clerics. Amidst extremely radicalized environment created by separatist elements and sponsored by Pakistan, advent of internet and social media platforms and phenomenal proliferation of mobile phones have exposed the Kashmiri populace in general and youths in particular to dark world of extremist ideology and radical Islam propagated by AQIS, ISIS/ ISKP and Taiban on deep dark web and internet. While, we examine impact of social media in opinion shaping in Kashmir, a distinct issue can be highlighted comparing the character of terror network in valley vis a vis other Indian states influenced by radical ideology. The radicalisation in J&K is directly attributed to Pak-sponsored proxy-war and spread of Wahabi/ Salafi ideologies, whereas radicalisation in West and South India is driven by IS ideology and motivation to establish Caliphate. Consequently, while radicalised local Kashmiris unite with Pak-backed terror groups for 'Azadi' or other fabricated local issues, the indoctrinated sections of society in Southern States are fascinated/ mobilised by controversies over Hindu Nation ideology, contestation over UCC/ NRC/ CAA and Global Jihad.

The history of use of technology to spread rumours and xenophobic ideology in Kashmir can be traced back to 2003-2004. As per OSINT, initially, Kashmir based 'Jaish-E-Mohammad' (JeM) distributed audio cassettes of Masood Azhar's speeches across India. Later in 2003-04, this terror outfit circulated downloadable materials through anonymous links/ emails. Subsequently, it started weekly e-newspaper, 'Al-Qalam' and a chat group on Yahoo. Gradually, JeM shifted from mainstream online platform to social media sites, blogs and forums to gain access to larger section of target population and expand its sphere of influence.[208]

The trend depicts that usage of social media in spreading separatist ideology, fuelling unrest by planting fabricated stories and doctored contents and lure misguided and indoctrinated Kashmiri youth to join terrorists' outfits has gained momentum gradually and progressively in a planned manner. 2014-15 can be termed as a watershed period, wherein slain Hizbul Mujahideen (HM) terrorist 'Burhan Wani' portrayed as a poster boy on Facebook and YouTube, caught the imagination of impressionable Kashmiri youths. Burhan and his cohort posted multiple photos and videos brandishing guns and exhorting false bravado to entice local population and instigating them against security forces and government forces. The period witnessed a new trend of use of social media in coordinating mass agitation and protests against security forces and mobilise the crowd to disrupt operations against terrorists. Post elimination of 'Burhan Wani' in an operation conducted in Tral region, HM and separatist elements leveraged social media influence for crowd sourcing during funeral procession, orchestrate valley wide violence and agitation and disrupt law and order situation in valley. Simultaneously, multiple social media accounts handled by operators abroad and within country flooded internet with doctored videos and fabricated false narrative to garner global attention, tarnish image of security forces and gain traction for their separatist's ideology. This led to spurt in recruitment of local youth in cadres of terrorists' outfit; a visible departure from past trends of predominance of foreign militants.

To gain mileage, the terrorists used innovative methods such as targeted productions e.g., rap music videos promoting Kashmiri Azaadi ('freedom') on YouTube, to garner support from Kashmiri youth.[209] Organisations such as LeT and JeM spread their anti-India images, videos, memes and misinformation through WhatsApp groups comprising of around 100 members (majority of numbers were not Indian) so as to spread content faster. This was a well thought of strategy to evade interception and detection by security agencies due to WhatsApp encryption policy. To evade targeting by security agencies and circumvent internet ban imposed by the authorities, terrorists, over ground workers and their supporters started using mobiles on VPNs and uploaded videos and images from neighbouring areas. This period also witnessed a significant increase in mobile phone users in valley. According to a report published in Greater Kashmir in February 2022, from 95,73,852 mobile subscribers in 2016, the figures have soared 15 to 20% per annum. As per TRAI, by year 2017, there were 1,04,28,635 mobile subscribers registered in Kashmir; more than 60 per cent contribution to the total subscriber base of J&K was from Kashmir. As per reports, by Dec 2021 total mobile subscribers soared to 1,18,00904 which was 97% of total household wherein 58% had access to internet. The phenomenal increase is attributed to cheap Chinese made mobile phones and introduction of dual SIM phones. This period has also witnessed a discernible surge in Post Paid SIM connections as well.

The technological trend has had direct implications on penetration of internet in valley as well as wider clientele base on the online social media platforms. The growing footprints of internet and social media platforms has been exploited by the adversarial forces to enhance their reach, carryout influence operations to strengthen confirmation bias and create echo chambers.

The terrorists' organisations and separatists have attempted to evoke local emotions and add fuel to insurgency by propagating the 'Burhanwali Aazadi' sentiment; which is presumed to have given rise to recruitment of local youths. Infatuated by their idol, this new home-grown breed of terrorists does not hesitate in romancing guns online. They are using every available digital tool for social media publicity, create sympathy for their 'cause' and manage perceptions by communicating regularly with radicalised youth of Valley, in their search for prospective recruits. By weaponising social media, they seem to have successfully etched the message of jihad on the Kashmiri mindset, lured vulnerable youth to participate in street violence and commit acts of terror,[210] This trend of rampant use of social media platforms hosting a lethal dose of radical content has given 30 years of extremism in Kashmir a methodical progression. As per reports, valley-based terrorists' organisations have extensively used social media platforms like Facebook, YouTube, WhatsApp, Twitter (X), Viber, Skype, Telegram, etc. to upload anti-India propaganda to include videos of terrorist training sessions and alleged harassment of locals by security forces to infuriate the vulnerable youth. 'Cyber jihad' has established firm roots in the Valley, churning out new-age militants to keep terror plot boiling.

Following a six-month probe into incidents of unrest in Kashmir in 2017, NIA identified 79 WhatsApp groups, having 6,386 phone numbers, used to crowdsource boys for stone pelting. Out of these numbers, around 1,000 were found active in Pakistan and Gulf nations. Remaining 5,386 numbers were found active in various parts of valley and neighbouring states. Among WhatsApp groups under scanner are the likes of 'valley of tears', 'pulwama rebels', 'daftare surat auliyan sophiyan', 'FrEEdom FigHtErz',

'Tehreek E Azaadi123', 'Mugahideen-a-Islam', 'Al Jahad', etc.[211] Many of these groups had administrators based in Pakistan. According to a media report, more than 300 WhatsApp groups were operated to crowdsource mobs to disrupt anti-terror operations in 2017.[212]

Recent trend indicates rise of virtual terrorist groups, such as The Resistance Front (TRF), Jammu Kashmir Ghaznavi Force, and People's Anti-Fascist Front (PAFF). These are front organisations for LeT and other terrorist outfits. TRF, mostly uses funding channels of LeT whereas PAAF, is a proxy of Jaish-e-Mohammed, which was responsible for deadly Lethpora suicide attack of February 2019. These groups have adroitly used social media platforms such as X, Telegram, and Facebook to push their narrative and propaganda, primarily focusing on issues like alleged conspiracy to turn Kashmir Valley into a Muslim-minority region. They have also warned locals from working as Special Police Officers (SPOs). This rising trend has also indicated emergence of 'Hybrid Terrorism' in valley; these are either trained militant or youth with no previous criminal record but radicalised through online contents. They keep a low profile evading the radar of police and at opportune time are tasked by their handlers to carry out sensational attacks on security forces or civilians. Being underage, they are tried under juvenile act and released from imprisonment after three years of probation. In recent past, there have been multiple incidents wherein hybrid terrorists were caught for committing act of terror. In one such incident, two juveniles were involved in killing of Akash Mehra, son of owner of the famous food outlet Krishna Dhaba in February 2021.

While Indian security agencies were combatting terrorists in valley in physical and digital space, ISJK was gradually making inroads in the Kashmir. Through their online propaganda and radicalisation strategy, the ISJK is targeting kashmiri youth to align with IS ideology, accord priority to global jihad and establishment of Caliphate rather pursuing merger with Pakistan or independent Kashmir. Considering unpredictable future scenario, ambitions of various non-state actors and volatile situation in immediate neighbourhood, influence of ISJK in Kashmir cannot be ignored. There is a need for a comprehensive strategy to defeat the propaganda machinery, de-radicalise misguided youth and initiate collaborative measures for conflict resolution and stability in J & K.

Analysis of these case studies reveals influence wielded by social media in shaping contours of ongoing conflicts globally. 'Arab Spring Revolution' of 2010 demonstrated the ability of social media platforms to ignite awareness and aspirations in common public to rise against oppressive regime. It would not be an exaggeration to state that social media platforms were instrumental in creating fertile ground for wide spread social activism and pioneering revolution which engulfed entire MENA Region. The protestors adroitly leveraged Facebook and YouTube accounts to garner support of population, gain viewership of population while evading scrutiny of government, coordinate protests and gain international support.

The capability to influence and shape opinion of target population demonstrated by social media platforms during 'Arab Spring Revolution', has apparently been capitalised by state and non-state actors alike in events took place in subsequent years. For instance, Russia enmeshed social media warfare strategy with its overall campaign strategy (hybrid warfare strategy) to annex Crimea in 2014 by leveraging local population and proxies against Ukrainian government and testing narrative building. During intervening period between 2014 and 2022, Russia executed its fine-tuned social media strategy to dominate information space and set stage for offensive launched to claim territory in Eastern Ukraine. During current conflict, Russia and NATO backed Ukraine have exploited social media platforms to advance their narratives, shape opinion of target population and insulate own cognitive space while dominating the same of adversary.

Influence power of social media has been instrumental in advancing radical ideology of various terrorists' organisation viz; ISIS, Al Qaida, LeT, Hizbul Mujahidin, SIMI and IM as well. These organisations have skilfully utilised social media to carryout virtual indoctrination, spread their radical ideology, recruit new members and orchestrate terror strikes. Thus, in the backdrop of evolving hybrid war scenario, it is imperative to explore plausible roles these platforms can play in influencing and complimenting main line of efforts in contemporary and future geo-political, geo-economic and military contestations. Accordingly, next chapter would focus on discerning contemporary trends of exploitation of social media in prosecution of hybrid war and visualise potential roles it can have in future competitions and conflicts.

Chapter 5

Impact of Social Media on Public Opinion and Decision-Making in Hybrid Warfare in Global and Indian Context

The examination of various case studies in the previous chapter reveals that social media has emerged as a potent weapon to achieve mass influence, impair decision-making of opponents and secure politico-military objectives. In a Hybrid threat scenario, a wide array of social media warfare tactics and cyber-attacks have been enmeshed in the overall campaign strategy to prosecute kinetic and non-kinetic operations at tactical, operational and strategic levels. It is also relevant to highlight that *operational approaches to the cyber warfare and social media warfare appear to overlap presumably due to commonality in vectors deployed. In fact, both appears to be complementing each other.*

Over wide spectrum of social media warfare and influence operations, 'Social Engineering' has captured the central space, capable of engaging and targeting diverse target population with rapidity and undetected. The effects of social engineering have been assessed to be deeper and far reaching. Thus, it is imperative to develop an explicit understanding of modus operandi of an actor carrying out 'Social Engineering'. Accordingly, in this chapter endeavor would be made to delve deep into this emerging phenomenon and ascertain role of social media in 'Social Engineering'. Various subject matter experts argues that social engineering was prevalent even before proliferation of social media. The first use of 'Social Engineering' dates back to 1842, when British economist John Gray used this term in his book titled 'An Efficient Remedy for the Distress of Nations'.[213] Later, this term migrated to cyber security domain between 1960 to 1980 and from 2007 onwards concept was referred in multiple scholarly articles and research papers. According to studies, *in the contemporary times social engineering has emerged as an art enmeshing technology with human psychology aspects.* The global reach, deep penetration in cross section of demography and rapid dissemination of contents act as force multiplier to facilitate enormous sphere of influence of the social media. Resultantly, in this era of social media dominance, the transition phase of social engineering has shorter time window and changes are unfolding with rapidity in indiscriminate and uncontrollable manner.

In this regard, it would not be incorrect to infer that social media platforms have been instrumental in people driven political movements in various parts of the world. The global trends indicate social media driven political activism has impacted conflict-stricken regions as well as other nation states alike. Refer Figure 39, a comparative analysis based on 'Varieties of Democracies Dataset 2024' project, regarding usage of SMPs by people to orchestrate offline any type of political movement indicate alarming trends. For purpose of extant study, comparison was drawn between India, Russia, Ukraine, Syria, USA, Egypt and other conflict prone nation states. It has emerged that Egypt and UAE witnessed rise in social media activism during 'Arab Spring Revolution'. In contemporary era, countries like USA and India have constantly experienced the impact of social media driven political activism, rise of extremists' ideology and radicalization. This may be attributed to increased internet network, proliferation of SMPs and even external influences applied through social media space.

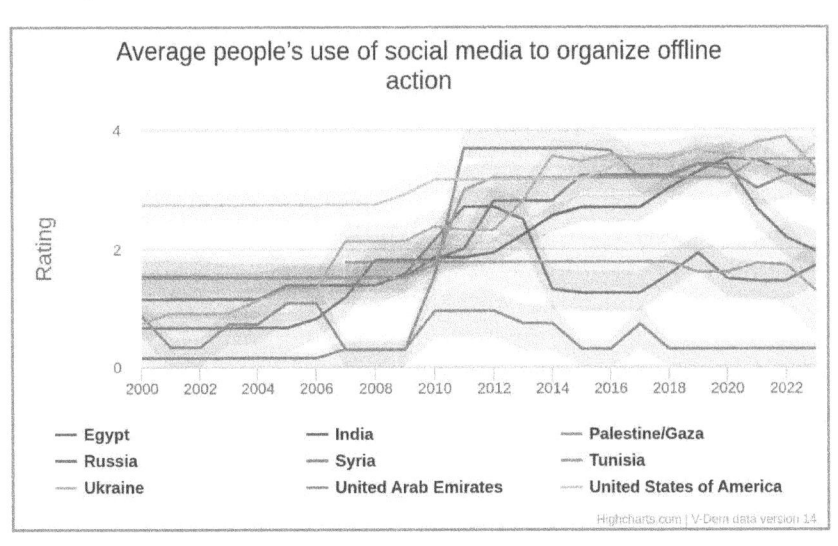

Figure 39 – Use of Social-media to organize offline action
Source - https://v-dem.net/data_analysis/VariableGraph/

Psychological Dimension of Social Engineering

Academia and subject matter experts in domains of human psychology and politics have presented their versions to define 'Social Engineering'. As per human psychology, social engineering implies *psychological manipulation to trick people into actions they wouldn't take normally*. Attackers exploit human emotions, biases, and trust to gain access to confidential information or systems. In cyber security context, social engineering actors may play with emotions, exploit trust or/ and target vulnerabilities to manipulate target's behaviour, attitude and beliefs.

In political science, social engineering has a broader meaning. It refers to the *wide array of efforts, by governments or powerful institutions, to influence attitudes and behaviours of target population/ society*. This can be achieved by deploying multifarious tactics i.e., enacting laws or policies to compel population towards desired behaviours and/ or leveraging educational systems and media to promote specific values or ideas and implement social programs aimed to change social structures or behaviours.

Christopher Hadnagy in his book titled 'Social Engineering: The Science of Human Hacking' defines *social engineering as 'any act that influences a person to take an action that may or may not be in their best interests'*.[214] *Social engineering cyberattacks are a type of psychological attack that exploits human cognition functions to persuade an individual (i.e., victim) to comply with an attacker's request.*[215] These attacks are centred around a social engineering message crafted by an attacker with the intent of persuading a victim to act as desired by the attacker. These attacks often leverage behavioural and cultural constructs to manipulate a victim into making a decision based on satisfaction (gratification), rather than based on the best result (optimisation).[216] For example, one behavioural construct is that most individuals would trade privacy for convenience, or bargain release of information for a reward.[217]

According to a study on the psychology behind social engineering, *Psychology is at the root of social engineering*. The malicious actors leverage influence techniques to trigger strong emotions such as fear. Triggering an 'amygdala hijack' or a reaction which overrides logic-based thinking thereby compelling the recipient to fall prey to their social engineering tactics.[218] The study highlights that *social engineering actors incite fear and exploit human behavioural traits such as greed, helpfulness, urgency and curiosity to manipulate their victims*. The study also emphasizes that apart from exploiting human emotions as tools to manipulate their victims, *social engineering actors also skillfully use principles of influence i.e. reciprocity, commitment, social proof, authority, liking, and scarcity to achieve desired effects.*

In the contemporary scenario, advent of Artificial Intelligence and 'Deep Fake' has enabled greater precision in content fabrication and targeting thereby making made social engineering attacks relatively more complex, sophisticated and difficult to detect. Emerging pattern reveals that malicious actors are leveraging AI technology to manipulate the victims and play with human psychology dimensions through social engineering attacks which are relatively more cunning and extremely difficult to detect.[219]

Assessing the challenges posed by social engineering to national security, individual's privacy and data protection as well as cyber security, it is imperative to understand psychological dimensions exploited by inimical elements to orchestrate social engineering attacks and shape/ influence opinion of the targeted individuals/ population. Various subject matter experts argue that social engineering attacks not only entail high level of technical skills to hack into information space but also heavily rely on deft use of human psychology. Certain psychological principles exploited to carryout social engineering in prevailing hybrid threat scenario are elucidated in succeeding paragraphs:-

> *Concept of Authority* – Attackers impersonate as public figure(s) of authority to establish credibility of contents, manipulate information and entice the target audience to fall prey to their tactics.[220] It is perceived that people fear/ trust/ respect any authoritative figures. Therefore, the attackers pose as influential political personality, leaders, think tanks, prominent celebrities or government officials and even exploit gullible social media influencers to influence the targets.[221]

> *Reciprocity* – In general, people have innate tendency to return favours and kindness extended to them. Kieran Roberts in his article titled 'Why is Social Engineering so Effective?' argues that in social engineering, reciprocity would be a threat actor extorting sensitive data or play to their plans in return for freebies offered to the victims who may feel indebted due to benefits enjoyed by them.[222] It may also be interpreted that in contemporary environment, malicious actors may lure/ blackmail the beneficiaries of social

engineering endeavors to dance to their tunes and be instrumental in enhancing range and effectiveness of their operations/ tactics.

- *Influence of Emotions and Cognitive Biases* – Manipulation of human emotions such as fear, urgency and curiosity plays a pivotal in effectiveness of social engineering tactics and cloud the judgement of target population.[223] The actors also exploit cognitive biases, termed as mental shortcuts taken by brain to process the information resulting in humans going astray from rationale decision making. One such cognitive bias is 'Conformation Bias', wherein the targets tend to seek information aligned with their existing belief system and choose to discard alternate views/ contradictory facts/ information. The actors carefully design their social engineering strategies and highly targeted messages based on the trend analysis, specific interests, demography, conformation biases, keystroke/ search patterns, ideological affiliations and identification of vulnerabilities. Under the ambit of specific strategies, actors of social engineering efforts may doctor facts/ content, build a narrative or resort to online trolling to instill fear, incite anger/ dissatisfaction and create a sense urgency so as to manipulate attitude and behavior of the target population/ society. In cyber technological realm, social media algorithms prioritize engagements/ contents designed to evoke strong emotions (positive or negative). Manipulators craft messages to trigger outrage, fear, or excitement, pushing them to the top of feeds so as to gain significant traction online.

- *Persuasion Techniques* – Persuasion techniques such as 'social proof'/ 'gamification' are used effectively to manipulate behaviors and attitude.[224] The attackers exploit indecisiveness of the target(s) related to opinion making and exercising their discretion to follow/ unfollow online trends and chatter. Invariably, they follow the actions of others influenced by quantum of likes, points or badges. The actors also attempt to create urgency by sensationalizing the issues or incite anxiety driven by fabricated time sensitivity. Further, to make their content appear legitimate and add authenticity, these actors may populate social media space with fake credentials, reviews, followership and endorsements. Further, the strategy also involves creating artificial scarcity or 'Fear of Missing Out (FOMO)' thereby compelling the target audience to become 'Click Happy' or taking action without even thoroughly examining the manufactured content(s) and examining the facts. The execution strategy encompasses amplifying the messages through fake accounts or bots so as to generate a false sense of popularity around a particular viewpoint. These inauthentic accounts can spread contents rapidly thereby creating a false impression of larger support or an issue.

> *Exploiting Trust Factor and Lack of Awareness and Education* – Normally an unsuspecting social media user(s) or target audience(s) have tendency to trust the contents shared on the social media. The perpetrators of social engineering exploit the trust factors by flooding digital space with contents supported by convincing details and impersonating the trustworthy entities. Owing to lack of awareness and education about the tactics deployed by the cyber criminals/ actors, the gullible users/ targets become easy victims and end up playing to inimical designs of adversarial elements.[225]

Vectors of Social Engineering Attacks

The orchestration of 'Social Engineering' entails deployment of various tactics having direct and indirect bearing on opinion shaping, manipulation of human minds and clouding the decision making. Based on the study of common trends in prevailing environment, the prominent tactics and vectors deployed by the actors in digital space are elucidated below:-

> *Direct Impact Vectors.* According to an article published by Terranova Security, social engineering actors exploit human nature e.g., as willingness to trust others, fear, greed and anxiety, and trick them to their pretenses or divulge sensitive information. The article asserts that in contemporary scenario social engineering has become the backbone of many cyber threats, from phishing emails to smishing and vishing attacks.[226] Direct vectors of social engineering suggested by various studies are as elucidated below: -
>   • *Spear Phishing* – Aimed to gain trust, this tactic involves targeted attacks through emails against individuals or groups based on in-depth research on potential targets. The information gleaned is exploited to craft fake news articles or propaganda aligned with recipient's interests or concerns so as to make them believe easily. The hackers usually steal login credentials of social media accounts, email addresses, or other online platforms owned by political figures/ journalists/

opinion shapers/ influencers. Fake news and propaganda to a wider audience are spread through spoofing emails originated from these compromised accounts giving semblance of a trusted source (i.e., compromised account).

- *Baiting* – A common tactics to spread fake news, misinformation/ disinformation and propaganda, executed using sensational/ provocative headlines, out of context images, or loaded questions to grab attention and trigger emotional responses like anger, fear or curiosity. Resultantly, the targets click contents and get tempted to share them rapidly thus amplifying spread of fake news and propaganda. Baiting is carefully crafted to create outrage and tailored to align with the beliefs of a specific group so as to reinforce their conformation bias and create echo chambers.

➢ *Indirect Impact Vectors.* Similarly indirect vectors of social engineering are as follows: -[227]

- *Malware* – Malware does not directly aid in spreading fake news/ propaganda but can be exploited for creating opportunities for such attempts as well as to carry out social engineering attacks. Hackers gain access to compromised devices to spread fake news and propaganda through social media accounts, email lists, or by creating fake websites. The compromised systems can appear to be legitimate sources, making misinformation more believable. *The vector can also be used to disable 'Fact Check' websites or organizations or steal their data which may obstruct the efforts to combat misinformation and propaganda campaigns.*

- *Pretexting* – Implies creating a false pretense or lie to gain trust and steal credentials of the targets. The stolen information can be utilised for impersonation and tailor fake news/ propaganda messages resonating with targets' interests, beliefs, or fears, thereby making them susceptible to believing the misinformation.

- *Water Holing* - Involves compromising legitimate websites frequented by a specific target group e.g., religious forums, news websites in a particular language, or online communities with a specific interest. Subsequent to penetrating the websites, manipulated contents are pushed to add legitimacy, achieve targets' readership and wider circulation.

Social Engineering and Opinion Shaping

The study of psychological dimensions and vectors deployed to carry out social engineering attacks provides a fair insight of modus operandi of various actors to dominate the cognitive space and carefully execute influence operations. In prevailing environment, it is observed that trend of leveraging social engineering to alter the behaviour of target population to achieve political, economic, social and military objectives is on rise worldwide. The studies point out that social engineering not only impacts the psychological space but physical space as well.

In political arena, 'Social Engineering' strategies entails demographic research, psychological profiling and sociocultural analysis to identify values, beliefs, fears, and aspirations driving voters' behaviour. Aligned with social fabric of electorate and cognitive biases, campaign strategists tailor messages and narratives resonating on a personal and emotional level, thereby fostering a deeper connection with the audience. Social proof and conformity principles, are blended in campaign strategies to gain traction and showcase widespread support to influence individuals' perceptions and behaviours. Social media platforms through direct and indirect vectors enable targeted delivery of messages, community engagement, and amplification of desired narratives. Data analytics and social listening tools are employed to continuously refine strategies based on real-time feedback and engagement metrics, thereby ensuring adaptability and responsiveness of campaign to the electorate's evolving sentiments.[228]

It is assessed that social engineering can be used effectively by security forces in influencing the population in conflict zones as well as to conduct Information Warfare (IW) operations. The forces can craft pragmatic IW strategies driven by detailed demographic analysis, social profiling and centre of gravity (COG) analysis to assuage the feelings of populace, defeat negative narrative building and showcase the efforts directed towards reconstruction, rehabilitation and restoration of peace. The narrative should be aligned with overall campaign strategy and be in consonance with people's aspirations so as to make an emotional connect and a sense of involvement in overall benign effort. Popular social media platforms can be gainfully utilised to reach out to the population. Incorporation of local prominent leaders and influential personalities from diverse background and all sections of the society would facilitate greater visibility, followership and amplification of content hosted online. Online hosting of visuals of actual work done on ground and testimonials of benefits accrued to affected population would provide 'Social Proofing' thus would add credibility and win trust of the citizens. Regular review of strategy and necessary amendments, set out as part of campaign strategy, based on sentiment analysis, performance matrices and realisation of deliverables would ensure positive opinion shaping and would deny critical cognitive space to adversarial forces in the contested zone(s).

Social Media Propaganda: Scope and Potential

Propaganda has been used since ages to spread fabricated lies and narratives, cloud the opinion and discredit the adversary/ competitors to gain a competitive advantage. Propaganda implies communication designed to disseminate biased or misleading information to promote a particular agenda or point of view thereby *influencing the people's opinions or control their behaviour and attitudes through various tactics such as name-calling, band wagoning, or inciting fear.*[229] *The likely goal(s) of propaganda, perceived as a strategy for persuasion, is to sway the public opinion, promote a specific agenda, coerce/ entice the target population to behave in a certain way and support a specific cause/ political ideology.*[230]

In military conflicts, propaganda is directed to garner support of own citizens as well as of friendly/neutral nation states to mobilise their support for own efforts. Simultaneously, propaganda strategy is also and instil trust deficit amongst populace of adversary/ hostile state so as to wean away support to their war waging efforts. *War propaganda relies on misinformation/ disinformation or name calling to achieve objectives of adversely impacting morale, create chaos and undermine trust of troops of opponent forces in their leadership.* In mass communication, propaganda is exploited to sway society or mobilise the groups to support an agenda or an ideology. In politics, propaganda is intrinsic to strategy to shape the public opinion riding on emotional appeal, name calling and scare tactics. Propaganda is also leveraged extensively in business and advertisement industry through persuasion techniques such as fear tactics and band wagoning.

In 1939, social scientists Alfred and Elizabeth Lee first classified propaganda as a collection of seven commonly used techniques in their book 'The Fine Art of Propaganda'. The seven techniques were defined as *name-calling, glittering generalities, transfer, testimonial, plain-folk,* card-stacking, and bandwagon.[231] These seven techniques are amplified as under:-

> *Name Calling.* A very precise technique, utilizes insults, stereotypes or slurs to call out perceived deficits of competitors or the opposing side. Social media platforms are increasingly exploited by various actors for 'Name Calling' the opponents, tarnish their image and evoke strong reactions of targets audience/ users. Usage of this technique by adversarial forces was demonstrated during 'Doklam' and 'Galwan' stand-off, 'Pulwama Terrorist attack' and even during 'Balakot air strikes as well as Surgical Strikes'. The study of attack patterns revealed that hackers and troll armies supported Pakistan and Chinese establishment leverage this tactic to malign image on Indian leadership, demoralise and discredit Indian armed forces and sway the public opinion.

> *Glittering Generalities.* Involves use of empty word(s) i.e., vague and often unproven statements, to make people, idea or products appear better. This technique is especially used in political campaigns wherein politicians are described as 'refreshing' or 'decent'; descriptors that are complimentary, subjective, and ultimately meaningless.

> *Band Wagon.* Encourages or manipulate the people to join group/ majority, ape majority's behaver or take part in something because everyone else is doing it without a critical thought. It plays with fear of missing out (FOMO) on something which others are enjoying. Addiction to social media, attention craving and fear of being isolated in the group and ensure their social acceptability, social media users fall prey to this online behaviour.

> *Transfer.* The technique of transfer involves transferring the positive or negative value of something onto a person, product, or cause by association. The tactics relies on symbolism to push target audiences to make illogical connect, such as images of national flags, national symbol, political heroes, etc. In this process, a particular idea or personality is deliberately shown in poor picture to make the audience form a favourable opinion about alternate thought/ another personality.

> *Testimonials.* These are endorsement by a celebrity or generally a prominent personality for a product, person, or cause. The technique is commonly used as a persuasive device in advertising.

This propaganda technique can be used effectively to convince population and mobilise public support for the intended cause or goal. In the military conflict zones, the security forces can leverage testimony of community leaders, influential personalities and people in violence-stricken regions to call for peace, shunning violence and win confidence of cross section of populace in efforts directed for conflict resolution and bringing normalcy. However, inimical forces can propagate 'Deep Fakes' and AI generated fabricated contents as testimony to support their agenda and lies, which predicts a dangerous preposition for the national security.

> *Plain Folks.* This technique exploits concept of 'real people' as an aspirational tool. Plain-folk makes 'lowest common denominator' a compliment rather than an insult. It seeks to convince audience that a certain product/ idea/ thought/ person is perfect for the average person. It is used to convince audiences to accept the idea being populist or an option exercised by majority population like them.

> *Card Stacking.* The intention is to give audiences only a small part of picture by listing all positive qualities of a product, person, or cause while downplaying negative or questionable qualities. This propaganda tool may be exploited to create conformation bias and stereo types and swing opinion of a selected segment of target population.

> According to an article authored by Arlin Cuncic for site 'Very Well Mind', certain additional techniques of propaganda are as follows: -[232]

- Appealing to Emotions: Involves emotional appeals to influence people's opinions. Propaganda might incite fear or create anger to get people to support a particular cause. In prevailing threat scenario and social media trends, trolls and hashtag are commonly used to spread fear, anxiety and incite public outrage by presenting a concocted version of story. In recent times, the hostile actors leveraged potential of this tactics to intimidate the people and incite violence in Manipur by flooding internet with fake contents to manipulate emotional quotient of people in violence affected areas as well in other parts of country.

- Scare Tactics: Used to frighten people into supporting a particular cause. For example, a campaign might warn people that if they do not vote, a dangerous criminal will be elected or elected candidate may take steps detrimental to their interests. This tactics was at display during smear campaign undertaken by inimical forces to propagate lies to instigate Kashmiri population against abrogation of Article 370. Similar trends were also witnessed wherein certain elements with vested interests attempted to even drive a wedge between tribal communities in conflict torn Manipur.

- Manipulating Information: Involves distorting or misrepresenting facts to influence people's opinions. For example, a political campaign might make false claims about opponents to make them look bad. During recently conducted Lok Sabha election of 2024, the political environment and information was vitiated by manipulated information allegedly peddled by various political parties to gain mileage as well as certain external actors to malign image of India and cast aspersion on electoral process, functioning of election commission and even mock India's democratic system.

- Using False Statistics: A common propaganda technique used to mis-represent the facts and cloud people's opinion. Manipulation of statics to suit own narratives was witnessed during recently concluded Lok Sabha election in India in 2024.

- Making Unrealistic Promises: Common technique used to mislead target population. For example, a candidate might promise to end poverty, even though this is not possible.

- Using Symbols: Symbols are often used in propaganda to represent an idea or concept. According to an article published in Britannica, symbol/ sign may have a particular meaning for a given group/ an individual (called reactor in propaganda theory). The article also suggests that two or more reactors may attach quite different meanings to same symbol. For example, for Nazis swastika was a symbol of racial superiority and crushing military might of German Volk. To some Asiatic and North American people, it is a symbol of universal peace and happiness.[233]

- Slogans: Slogans are short catchphrases used to summarize an idea or concept. For example, in the 2016 presidential campaign, 'Make America Great Again' was one of Donald Trump's slogans.

- Stereotyping: This technique uses oversimplified and often inaccurate ideas or beliefs to describe an opponent or enemy.

- Snob Appeal: Uses the idea of exclusivity to make something seem more desirable. For example, a luxury car company might use the slogan, "Only the best for you."

- Loaded Language: This technique uses language to evoke certain emotions or feelings. For example, the phrase "pro-life" is loaded with emotional and moral weight.

- Weasel Words: Designed to mislead or deceive people. For example, the phrase, "I'm not saying that X is a bad person, but..." implies that the person is bad without actually saying it.

These propaganda techniques and tactics have been used frequently in politics, marketing, business and even in military operations. In yesteryears, propaganda actors innovatively used posters, pamphlets, radio messages, songs and TV advertisements to seize critical space in information environment. The aim was to gradually shape environment, influence thinking process of the target population and manipulate human emotions to their advantage. Advent of internet and rapid proliferation of social media has been a game changer; the actors of hybrid warfare and social media warfare have harnessed the power of digital media to enhance their influence and circumvent countermeasures instituted by competitors/governments and guidelines for publication of media contents.

It is evident that in this era of digital revolution, social media provides fertile ground for different types of propaganda, with a vast potential to reach and influence audiences. Dis-information and mis-information, disguised as news/ genuine content, are wide spread and possess huge potential to sow confusion, erode trust in institutions, and manipulate public opinion through shares, likes, comments, tweets and re-tweets. 'Algorithm Biases' associated with social media allows microtargeting of specific demography and create echo chambers rapidly thereby making it difficult to counter negative narrative building. The contemporary trends of propaganda and their scope and potential are briefly discussed below: -

- Growing trends of 'Memes and Humour' have been observed to be quite impactful and effective as part of various propaganda tactics such as 'Name Calling', 'Loaded Language', 'Snob Appeal' and 'Manipulating the information'. Memes, having moderate to high potential, go viral instantaneously and have been found to be very effective at conveying messages in a relatable way. These can be used to normalize propaganda or make it more appealing, especially to younger audiences. Whereas, humour disarms defence and makes messages more memorable.

- Deep Fakes, an easily accessible emerging technology and potent threat, has already proved its effectiveness in spreading misinformation through fake videos and audios. With their high potential to cloud people's objective and rationale thinking, Deep Fakes has potential to damage reputations, create distrust, and be used to influence elections, narrative building against democratically elected establishments and malign the security forces. Deepfakes can blur the line between reality and fiction thereby can cause decision paralysis for unsuspecting and ignorant common man and even decision makers.

- A common tactics observed in social media warfare is toying with human psyche to create fear psychosis through emotional appeals. It needs no emphasis that *humans are relatively more reactive to negativity than positivity; Negative emotions often trigger a stronger response in amygdala, a part of the brain associated with fear and memory.* Various studies have also established that human brain devotes more resources to processing negative information. *Negative stimuli trigger a stronger fight-or-flight response, to obviate potential harm. Resultantly, human mind tends to pay more attention to negative information/ gloomy scenario rather than positive contents and scenario depicting ray of hope.* This explains as to why negative information and narratives gain greater traction at unprecedented pace as compared to positive posts. It may also highlight the challenges of government and security forces, who usually carry tag of oppressor, to convince its citizens and population in contested zones about inimical designs of the adversary and genuineness of their efforts. There are umpteen examples in the prevailing scenario wherein various actors have exploited this aspect cunningly to fuel unrest and turbulence in the society. Recent ethnic clashes in Manipur and fabricated unrest in J&K over Article 371 revocation were triggered by orchestrating targeted emotional appeals and inciting fear and anxiety. It is believed that targeted emotional charged appeals and contents can exploit existing social divisions, radicalize target population especially impressionable youth and demographics. They also have a very high potential to manipulate and take advantage of pre-existing biases and anxieties to create echo chambers and fuel social unrest.

➢ The actors have extensively leveraged 'Bots', trolls and inauthentic accounts (sock puppets) to artificially amplify certain messages and drown out opposing viewpoints with a view to create an illusion of widespread grass root support for a cause and spread propaganda.

Mapping Influences on Decision Making: Politico, Economic and Military Spheres

It is assessed that in the realm of social media proliferation, social engineering and propaganda tactics are complementary and work in tandem to penetrate the cognitive domain and dominate the decision-making processes. Thus, having analysed the impact of social engineering and propaganda techniques on the socio-political landscape, it is imperative to gauge the influence of 'Liberation Technology (Social Media)' on the intricacies of decision making (DM) in state craft, governance, economics, society and military affairs. It is important to establish 'How and Why' social media has been able to penetrate the decision making in all walks of life significantly. In the evolving scenario, the magnitude of social media penetration and its impact on electoral process, economic decision making and narrative building in socio and military conflict zones have been observed globally. Realising the influence wielded by social media platforms over the masses and decision makers, the actors of hybrid operations are leveraging this technological tool to further their operations in near simultaneity with their kinetic and political actions. Resultantly, the current trends predict that salience on social media in contemporary and future hybrid warfare scenario would increase manifold.

A plausible answer to 'How and Why' social media's influence over the decision-making lies in the shortcomings of the existing political set-up, functioning of traditional media and state craft. These shortcomings seemingly provided a vulnerable politico-social, politico-military and economic spaces for internet and social media to penetrate and establish a strong foothold over. In succeeding paras, the study would cover certain probable causes to explain the issue at hand.

It is assessed that amongst various plausible factors, the phenomenal penetration of social media is predominantly attributed to increased footprints of internet across the globe beyond geographical confines of nations' borders and spheres of influence of societal structure. Furthermore, the low-cost data packages, improved mobile coverage, better internet connectivity and proliferation of affordable mobile handsets have afforded the social media to become a cost effective, affordable and most preferred option even for the masses. In addition, users' choice driven contents, infotainment, social connect and real time news update have also made social media platform popular and grow at exponential pace. Moreover, absence of/ inadequate low-level barrier and content regulation, anonymity, ambiguity and ease of voicing opinion by marginalised/ neglected sections of society has strengthened its foothold. This has given significant power and influence to internet in general and social media platforms in particular. The inference is substantiated by multiple examples such as 'Arab Spring Revolution' wherein the marginalised sections of the society used Facebook and YouTube to raise voice against authoritarian and totalitarian regimes and draw attention of the world towards their sufferings.

In this regard, it is also felt that the approach of traditional print media and digital media towards independent journalism, their ideological affiliations impacting transparency and failure to address the concerns of common man also provided avenues to social media and citizen journalism to make deep inroads. As per statistics, the social media has surpassed the conventional or legacy print media, TV and radio, which predated the digital media revolution and emergence of internet, in terms of customer base and reach. *While legacy media maintain relatively stable formats, the litany of new media, which includes websites, blogs, video-sharing platforms, digital apps, and social media, are continually expanding in innovative ways.*[234] *Mass media designed to deliver general interest news to broad audiences have been joined by niche sources that narrowcast to discrete users. New media can relay information directly to individuals without the intervention of editorial or institutional gatekeepers, which are intrinsic to legacy forms.* The emerging trends of doing business through new media have introduced an increased level of instability and unpredictability into the socio-political communication process. But it has provided an effective alternate channel of communication to the population to circumvent the scrutiny by the media establishment and raise the issues which matters to them. The practice has forced the traditional media houses, political establishment and governments to change their approach and align their strategy to felt need implying increasing reliance on social media and deploying more eyes and ears at grass root level to discern the pulse of the people. This has probably also triggered the prevalence of populist journalism, appeasement politics, and neo-nationalism.

As fourth pillar of Indian Democracy, *the media or journalism has an important role of providing critical connect between government and public and act as watchdog over the functioning of government and its officials.*[235] *The execution of media's role mandates greater accountability, responsibility and transparency. Traditionally, the legacy media such as print media, radio and TV networks have been serving the crucial role of informing the public, assisting them in making thoughtful decisions about leadership and policy.* They set the agenda for public discussion of issues, and provide a forum for political expression. They also facilitate community building by helping people to find common causes, identify civic groups, and work towards solutions to societal problems.[236] The investigative journalism undertaken by traditional media sources to examine the scandals and wrong doings of authoritarian regimes and officials has acted as deterrence thereby enhanced their credibility. However, there were certain criticism related to traditional media's limitation to raise voice of the marginalised sections of the society, control of media house, their ideological affiliations and following their own agendas. Commenting upon contribution of traditional media houses in promoting participation in political discourses, Hayes and Lawless in their article argues that *although legacy media coverage of political events correlates with increased political engagement among the mass public, mainstream journalists do not believe that encouraging participation is their responsibility.*[237] Moreover, the content published/ aired on the traditional has to undergo tight scrutiny, which discouraged and at times obstructed reporting of events and issues perceived as inconsequential or less important by the media houses. However, the advent of social media has changed the rules of the game. It has provided the avenues to even a common man to voice their opinion on issues which matters to him or the society. Resultantly, the involvement of the population in political process has increased manifold forcing the political leaders, media houses and strategy makers in various domains to recognise the might of the marginalised sections. Thus, it would not be incorrect to infer that social media has become catalyst for social engineering and mobilisation of masses to raise their grievances with unprecedented pace and strength.

In the current scenario, the traditional media and social media are enjoying a symbiotic relationship. Social media needs traditional media to add credibility to their coverage, content and gain popularity, whereas traditional media is increasingly becoming dependent on social media for wider coverage and reporting of incidents. The concept of citizen journalism has facilitated multiple sources of information, wider coverage and greater reach resulting into heavy reliance of traditional media on social media even for fact checking. Though, ecosystem of citizen journalism has been instrumental in prompt and wider reporting of the events, however the concept is fraught with certain risks and compromises the ethos of truthful and objective reporting. It has made the traditional media vulnerable to fake news and propaganda and lured the unsuspecting/ ignorant social media users to 'Echo Chambers' and 'Confirmation Biases'. Diana Owen in her article related to impact of social media on politics has argued that legacy media has incorporated new media into their reporting strategies. They distribute material across an array of old and new communication platforms. They rely on new media sources to meet the ever-increasing demand for content. Cable and network television news remain the primary sources of political information for people over the age of thirty. [238]

Resultantly, the main stream media on numerous occasions has fallen prey to manufactured facts and fake news spread though social media. Recently in March 2024, Al-Jazira had aired a news accusing IDF soldiers of committing rape of Palestinian women in Al-Shifa hospital. Subsequent to an investigation by Hamas, the reporting of alleged rape was later found to be false. "The woman who spoke about rape justified her exaggeration and incorrect talk by saying that the goal was to arouse the nation's fervor and brotherhood," the *Al Jazeera* columnist explained.[239] Ironically politicians, anti-government organisations and various actors with vested interests have exploited the social media to circumvent the mainstream press' control over the news agenda, reach out to their constituents/ target population and spread their agenda (fake, manufactured, lies or half-truths) swiftly.

It is assessed that in the era of digital communication, social media has potential to satisfy textbook functions provided stringent ethics and content regulations are promulgated. However, content regulation is a much-debated topic and contested by various scholars and legal experts citing concerns related to freedom of speech and government sponsored censorship. Diana Owen in her article 'The new media's role in politics' comments that social media provides unprecedented access to information, and can reach even disinterested audience members through personalized, peer-to-peer channels, like Facebook, Twitter (X), YouTube and other social media platforms. As average people join forces with established press to perform the watchdog role, public officials are subject to greater scrutiny. Issues and events that might be outside the purview of mainstream journalists can be brought into prominence by ordinary citizens. Social media can foster community building that transcends physical boundaries through their extensive networking capabilities. The new age digital media explicitly seek to directly engage public in political activities, such as voting, contacting public officials, volunteering in their communities, and taking part in protest movements. At the same time, new media era has acerbated trends that undercut the ideal aims of a democratic press. Social media disseminates a tremendous amount of political content, but much of the material is trivial, unreliable, and polarizing. The diversity of content disseminated by social media has created opportunities, such as ability for more voices to be heard. However, questionable quality of much of this information raises serious issues for democratic discourse. *Social media is integral to political coverage in a post-truth society, where falsehoods infused with titbits of fact pass as news.* Resultantly, 'watchdog press' is being overshadowed by mouthpiece press which serves as a publicity machine for politicians. The challenges are further compounded by absence of media ethics and content regulation resulting in fake/ unsubstantiated message and news piece flooding the digital space rendering identification of truth extremely difficult. *Social media has hastened the development of echo chambers, as they facilitate people's exposure to information shared by like-minded individuals in their personal digital networks. The ability of social media to isolate people from exposure to those with differing viewpoints exacerbates political polarization.* This ambiguity, absence of accountability and attributability has been exploited by the actors of hybrid warfare to orchestrate social engineering, spread false narrative and influence the decision making by leadership at all levels.

Amidst rising uncertainty and conflicts, the growing patterns of false news, propaganda, echo chamber, polarization and information fatigue would pose a phenomenal challenge to strategic leadership in all domains. The political leadership and diplomats may have to continuously battle with confusion, opaqueness and ambiguity created by narrative building and social engineering. It would be difficult to discern the truth and counter the negative perception. The adversarial elements may be able to influence the target population to orchestrate mounting pressure on the decisions makers and incite public outrage and discontent. Resultantly, the decision makers would have to wade through troubled waters to make informed and pragmatic decisions in the national interests rather than be compelled to decide in the favour of appeasement politics and welfare state.

Earlier, technological advancements and other trends were primarily felt locally or regionally. However, owing to social media proliferation, localised events have the ability to go global in minutes or seconds. Contrary to existing hierarchical bureaucratic processes, the national leadership and diplomats cannot afford to wait for prolonged period to respond to situation/ crises.[240] They would be required to remain abreast with the evolving grand picture 24x7, anticipate the next manoeuvre and pre-empt by own actions to stay ahead in closely contested battle space.

In the military domain, the rate of change and the interaction of local, regional, and global forces are inducing increased uncertainty at all levels. It is becoming increasingly difficult to isolate events into neat, compartmentalized bins associated with the tactical, operational, and strategic levels of war. The overhang of social media over the operations and its exploitation by non-state actors and citizen journalism has presented more challenges for the security forces. During recent Manipur and Rajouri incidents the adversarial elements populated the social media with fabricated narrative to fuel public anger and gain advantage over security forces. The situation spiraled out of control before the leadership could assess the situation, gather facts and respond. Thus, owing to unforeseen turbulence of VUCA world, the leadership is mandated to strategize based on multi-vectoral approach.

The decision-making must occur at the speed of the environment, the organizations and processes must account for interconnectedness and have the agility and ability to respond appropriately.

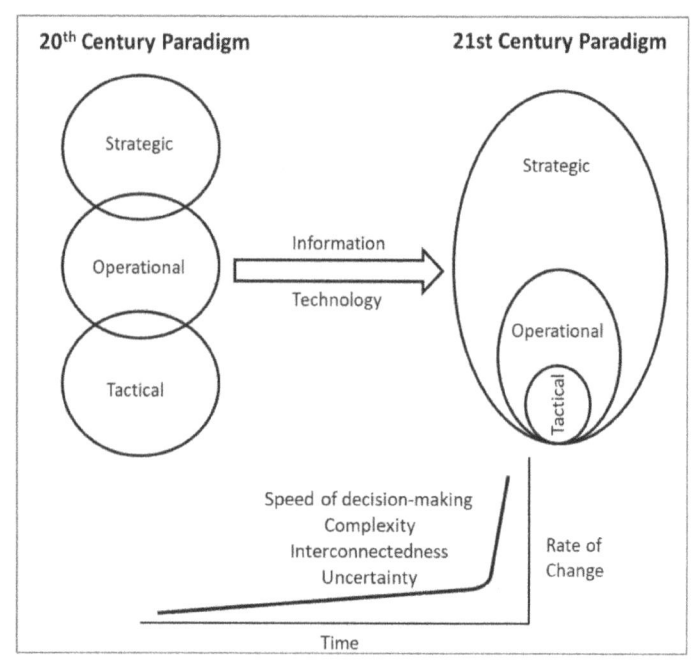

Figure 40 – Challenges of Decision making with the advent of information technology

Figure 40, depicts challenges of military decision making in 21st century vis-à-vis 20th century; consequent to revolution in information technology and proliferation of social media, interconnectedness has improved manifold, battle field changes occur at rapid pace thereby compounding complexity and uncertainty. Resultantly, decision making by the leaders in tactical, operational and strategic planes has to be done against time constraints so as to seize the initiative and deny critical space and fleeting opportunities to adversary. Failure to take timely decision may result in opportunity cost detrimental to own operations and subsequent actions may be directed to recover from the set back of sunk cost of forgone opportunities.

Key Take Aways

In the realm of digital revolution, the transmission of information has become ubiquitous. Unlike traditional media, social media has afforded greater reach, frequency, permanence and immediacy on the messages. Social media allows the interactive communication between people without spatial limits or time constraints. Social media has proved to be an amplifier of ideas, thoughts and narratives, a creator of meaning, conformation bias and echo chambers and a generator of conflicts as well. Social media is the current vector of choice for state and non-state actors prosecuting the hybrid wars. Advent of advanced technology such as artificial intelligence and machine learning and emergence of trends of Deep Fakes, voice cloning has added a complex dimension to national security.

The impact of social media activism has been witnessed on the conduct of operation in entire spectrum of conflict. In the contemporary scenario, social media warfare strategy and information operations have become increasingly crucial to campaign strategy. Evidently, social media platforms have emerged as force multiplier to orchestrate organization and mobilization of masses to protest, dissemination of fabricated messages and intelligence gathering about operations of security forces. Unarguable, as a tool for organizing operations, recruiting and mobilising people, social media and mobile phone technology provide multiple, redundant channels for conveying instructions and orders to cadres and followers by various non-state radical actors in conflict zones across the globe. For instance, ISIS, first organization to leverage social media as force multiplier, developed applications 'The Dawn of Glad Tidings' or 'Nasher' to securely share information among its members.[241] In terms of dissemination, photos, tweets, videos and Snapchats of the adversary's actions are spread across multiple social media platforms at record speed, fuelling conflict on all sides in a process that some dub 'smartphone-intifada'.

A study by World Economic Forum observes, that by extension, social media is potent platform to conduct misinformation or 'shock and awe' campaigns aimed at deterring morale, changing the direction or outcome of a war or triggering a response providing a strategic advantage. The terrorist organisation such as ISIS or Daesh has used social media to spread reign of terror by uploading videos of execution of hostages; the modus operandi has been eulogised by other terror outfit subsequently. Similarly, during the ongoing Israel-Hamas war, videos of operations, collateral damages and atrocities over the captives have been uploaded to incite fear, demoralise the public and mount pressure on the leadership.

Social media feeds have increasingly gained prominence as 'Open-Source Intelligence' for security forces and intelligence agencies, traditional media, citizens and international audience as well. As a direct consequence, it has led to greater access to ground intelligence but created cognitive paralysis on account of inability to discern truth, half-truth and fabricated lies peddled as truth. The trends of fabricated contents, manipulated facts and dis-information, have impacted the political, economical, social and military spheres thereby posed multifaceted challenges to nation security, global peace and stability and given steep rise to polarisation and extremism.

Chapter 6

Counter Measures to Mitigate Threats of Social Media

In the public domain, there are no official declarations or announcements related to India's Cyber Defence Strategy, delineation of responsibilities and intent to conduct international cyber and social media campaigns. However, based on statements of stake holders and study of various articles, it is assessed that in consonance with threat evaluation, India has gradually developed the capabilities and created various organizations to prosecute operations in the cyber space.[242] As per various reports, India has evolved a multi-pronged strategy to mitigate the cyber threats specifically, but security challenges emanating from exploitation of social media platforms and emerging trends of Hybrid Warfare are seemingly a grey area. The Indian response mechanism encompasses creation of various organizations, formulation of policies, coordination between multiple inter-ministerial agencies and private sector and coalition with international agencies. In addition, various state and central government agencies and security forces have used social media platforms to showcase development initiatives, conduct community outreach programs and counter propaganda by hostile state and non-state actors. Further, security forces deployed in conflict regions viz; J&K and North Eastern states have conducted perception management activities and projects to positively shape opinion of target population. The study would delve upon measures instituted by the Government of India (GoI) such as Cyber Security Policy and regulations, Cyber defence organizations and strategies to ascertain existing voids and shortcomings perceived to impact India's capabilities to deal with threats related to social media exploitation.

Organizations and Policy Framework

According to various studies and information available in open source, Indian government has taken various steps to address security dilemmas in cyber space. These incremental steps have facilitated creation of organisations, delineation of roles and responsibilities and gradual capacity building is this sphere.

At national level, Ministry of Electronics and Information (MEITY) and Ministry of Home Affairs (MHA) are the nodal organisations to legislate cyber policies, coordinate operations to thwart cyber-attacks, orchestrate overall perception management and narrative building campaign in the strategic plain and sanitise Indian Cyber space. In addition, Indian defence forces are also pro-actively engaged in perception management, social media campaigns and information operations to deny the freedom of action to adversarial forces and dominate cognitive space at tactical and operational levels of contested zones. As per reports, MEA also manages and coordinates India's cyber diplomacy efforts. It has a cyber diplomacy division, which is tasked with representing India at bilateral and multilateral forums. The organogram India's Cyber Defence architecture is at Figure 41 below: -[243]

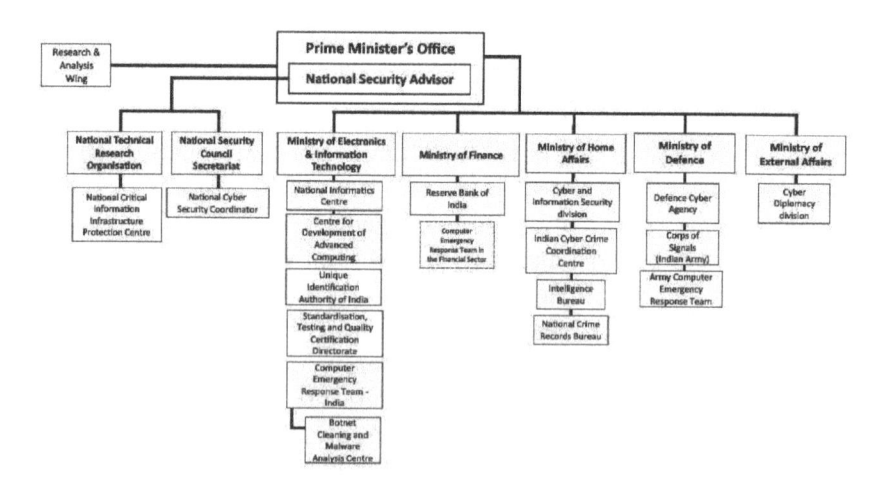

Figure 41 - India's Cyber Defence Architecture
Source- https://www.linkedin.com/pulse/gaps-national-cyber-security-policy-india-recommended-vimal-mani

India's Cyber Defence Organisations

Indian Computer Emergency Response Team (CERT-In) - CERT-In was created in 2004 in accordance with Section (70B), Information Technology Act, 2000 under Ministry of Communications and Information Technology. CERT-In under administrative control of MEITY functions as 'National

Incident Response Centre' for major computer security incidents in Indian cyber community. Its primary role is to raise security awareness among Indian cyber community and render technical assistance and advise to recover from computer security incidents.[244]

- > *Objective.* Mandated with task to ensure secure Indian cyber space, CERT-In has been assigned following objectives: -

  - Prevent cyber-attacks against the country's cyber space.

  - Respond to cyber-attacks, minimise damage and recovery time.

  - Reduce national vulnerability to cyber-attacks.

  - Enhance security awareness among common citizens.

- > *Functions.* As National Nodal Agency for incident response, the functioning of CERT-In is defined by the Information Technology (Indian Computer Emergency Response Team and Manner of Performing Functions and Duties) Rules, 2013. Information Technology Act (ITA) 2000, designated CERT-In to serve as the national agency to perform following functions in the area of cyber security: -

  - Collection, analysis and dissemination of information on cyber incidents.

  - Forecast and alerts of cyber security incidents.

  - Emergency measures for handling cyber security incidents.

  - Coordination of cyber incident response activities.

  - Issue guidelines, advisories, vulnerability notes and whitepapers related to information security practices, procedures, prevention, response and reporting of cyber incidents.

- > *Stake Holders.* To achieve its objectives and execute functions, CERT-In interacts and seek assistance from various stake-holders. Entire cyber defence eco-system includes sectoral computer emergency response teams and intermediaries, Internet Registry and Domain registrars, Industry and vendors of IT products including security products and services. CERT-In also collaborates with academia, R & D organisations, security and law enforcement agencies and individuals/ group of individuals. Globally CERT-In works in close coordination with international computer emergency response teams, forums and expert groups and agencies engaged in the protection of critical information infrastructure.

> *Incident Reporting and Level of Support.* CERT-In discloses information about cyber related incidents as per provisions of Indian Constitution. In addition to prediction, prevention and response to all Cyber security incidents, this organisation also carryout analysis and forensics of cyber security incidents and scan cyber space to detect cyber security vulnerabilities, breaches and malicious activities. Furthermore, CERT-In provides information security assurance and audits, conducts awareness and technology exposition in cyber security domain and organises training or upgrade of technical know-how for its stakeholders. The major cyber breaches reported by CERT-In are highlighted below: -

- March 2014, a critical flaw in *Android Jelly Bean's* VPN implementation.

- July 2020, Google Chrome users were warned to immediately upgrade to new Chrome browser version 84.0.4147.89. Multiple vulnerabilities that could allow access to hackers were reported.

- April 2021, *'High Severity'* rating advisory was issued on the vulnerability detected on WhatsApp and WhatsApp Business for Android prior to v2.21.4.18 and WhatsApp and WhatsApp Business for iOS prior to v2.21.32.

- As per CERT-In, India faced 11.5 million cyber-attack incidents in 2021 including attacks on corporate, critical infrastructure and government agencies. The report by Statista reveals that intensity of such attacks increased in 2022, wherein 1.3 million cyber-attacks were reported. According to a report published by NDTV, in 2023 India was ranked third amongst the countries targeted by phishing attacks after US and UK, with its technology sector facing nearly 33 per cent of all such strikes, marking it as the most targeted industry.

- December 2022, CERT-In was tasked to investigate the cyber-attack on AIIMS, Delhi.

- *Collaboration.* CERT-In collaborates with national and international organizations specialised in protecting and responding to cyber security incidents and intelligence collection, law enforcement, investigation and forensics. This organisation is also collaborating with various academia, industry, service providers and R & D institutions as well as individuals or group of individuals. Recently, CERT-In collaborated with Google Cloud to train and upskill a 'Cyber Force' of one thousand government officials and learners in Generative Artificial Intelligence (AI) and Cybersecurity. The initiatives also involve using generative AI and conducting cybersecurity AI hackathons led by front-line experts from Google Cloud and Mandiant.[245] With a view to exchange technical information, develop response strategy and solutions for cybersecurity and capacity building, CERT-In and MeitY have signed MoU with SCO, Ministry of Cabinet Office (UK), Korea, Canada, Australia, Malaysia, Singapore, Japan and Uzbekistan. In 2022, CERT-In and MeitY in collaboration with Cyber Security Agency of Singapore (CSA) conducted Cyber Security exercise 'Synergy' as part of International Counter Ransomware Initiative- Resilience Working Group.[246]

- Wide range of quality management services are provided such as security assurance framework and audit through empaneled information security auditors, vulnerability assessment and penetration test, episodic security audits of key organisations, promotion of Security Best Practices and Security Standards, Cyber Security Exercises/Drills and formulation of Cyber Crisis Management Plan (CCMP).

- CERT-In communicates through e-mail, telephone, postal communication and other possible means of communication based on urgency and sensitivity of incident and information. CERT-In provides Incident Prevention and Response services as well as Security Quality Management Services. CERT-In has now partnered with CVE Program, MITRE Corporation, USA. In this regard, Indian Computer Emergency Response Team (CERT-In) has been authorized by CVE Program, as a CVE Numbering Authority (CNA) for vulnerabilities impacting all products designed, developed and manufactured in India.

- *Cyber Swachhta Kendra.* Botnet Cleaning and Malware Analysis Centre (Cyber Swachhta Kendra – https://www.csk.gov.in) has been established by CERT-In for detection of compromised devices in India and to notify, enable cleaning and securing systems of end users to prevent further malware infections. It is working in close coordination and collaboration with Internet Service Providers, antivirus companies, academia and Industry.

National Cyber Coordination Centre (NCCC) - It was established under the aegis of National Information Board in 2013; 'Phase One' of agency became operational in 2014. The agency falls under the jurisdiction of MHA and coordinates with multiple security and surveillance agencies as well as with CERT-In. NCCC, an operational cybersecurity and e-surveillance agency, is tasked to screen communication metadata and co-ordinate intelligence gathering activities of other agencies. It has been set up to generate necessary situational awareness of existing and potential cyber security threats and enable timely information sharing for proactive, preventive and protective actions by individual entities.[247]

- ➢ As per open-source data (OSD), this agency is classified to be a project of Indian government without a legal framework, which may be counterproductive as it may violate civil liberties and human rights. Some have expressed concern that this cyber overwatch body could encroach on Indian citizens' privacy and civil-liberties, given lack of explicit privacy laws in the country.

- ➢ Under this project, the government has reportedly involved Internet service providers (ISPs) to ensure round-the-clock monitoring of Internet, while expertise of other private sector organisations would be utilised when required. It would act as India's first layer for cyber threat monitoring and all communication with government and private service providers would be through this body only.

- ➢ NCCC will be in virtual contact with control room of all ISPs to scan traffic within the country, flowing at the point of entry and exit, including international gateway. Apart from monitoring Internet, NCCC would look into various threats posed by cyber-attacks. The NCCC would also address the threats faced by computer networks of government departments and organisations handling sensitive government data and important websites[248].

Indian Cybercrime Coordination Centre (I4C) - Established by MHA in 2019, I4C is mandated to provide a framework and eco-system to prevent, detect, investigate, and prosecute cybercrime in a coordinated and comprehensive manner. I4C is envisaged to act as the nodal point for Law Enforcement Agencies (LEAs) to curb Cybercrime in the country.[249] Certain initiatives undertaken by MHA to prepare and deal with Cyber threats are as follows:-

- National Cybercrime Reporting Portal (NCRP) (www.cybercrime.gov.in) facilitates 24X7 reporting of all types of cybercrime, with special focus on cybercrime against women and children.

- Citizen Financial Cyber Fraud Reporting and Management System has been created for immediate reporting of financial cyber frauds and to prevent siphoning of funds by cyber criminals in near real time basis. A national toll-free helpline number '1930' has been operationalized to provide citizen assistance in lodging online cyber complaints.

- National Cyber Forensic Laboratory (NCFL), a 'State of the Art' facility, has been set up to train and assist the State/UT Investigation Officers in various aspects of cyber forensics under the aegis of NCTC.

- Massive Open Online Courses (MOOC) platform called 'CyTrain' portal 'https://cytrain.ncrb.gov.in' has been developed. CyTrain portal helps in capacity building of Police Officers/Judicial Officers through online courses on critical aspects of cybercrime investigation, forensics and prosecution.

- State/UT Police officials working in cyber cells across the country are being trained on Crypto currency, Dark web, Anonymization networks, Deep Fake, Banking Hacks, Forensics, Investigation, etc at NCFL and NCTC.

- A coordination mechanism of Law Enforcement Agencies of States/UTs has been established by constituting Joint Cyber Coordination Teams (JCCT) based upon cybercrime hotspots/areas and in consultation with states/UTs.

- I4C has launched CyberDost handle on various social media platforms to generate cyber awareness among citizens.

National Technical Research Organisation (NTRO) - Established in 2004 consequent to recommendations of Task Force formed to implement Kargil Review Committee Report, NTRO deals with technical intelligence and functions directly under NSA and PMO.[250] It has National Critical Information Infrastructure Protection Centre (NCIIPC) and National

Institute of Cryptology Research and Development Organization (NICRDO) under its wings. According to reports, NTRO has capabilities to take countermeasures in cyber space as well as provide technical intelligence to other agencies on internal and external security matters. The organisation undertakes hi-tech surveillance jobs considered vital for national security apparatus such as satellite, terrestrial and internet monitoring. As multi-capacity agency, NTRO specialises in remote sensing, SIGINT, data gathering and processing, cyber security, geospatial information gathering, cryptology, strategic hardware and software development and strategic monitoring.[251] According to OSINT, classified documents released by whistleblower Edward Snowden, NTRO has been one of the most proactive members of US NSA-led 10-member counter-terrorism platform called SIGINT Seniors Pacific (SSPAC) for the last 10 years.[252]

Defence Cyber Agency (DCyA) - Creation of DCyA was announced by PM Modi during Combined Commanders Conference in 2018. The tri-service organisation was raised in May 2019 under the aegis of MoD. The organisation has been staffed with personnel from all three services and DRDO representatives. As per reports, the Units of DCyA are spread across the country with its cells/ dedicated officers positioned with each formation headquarters to deal with cyber threats.[253] According to a written response to a parliamentary question by Minister of State for Defence, DCyA was set up to '*control and coordinate Joint Cyber operations*'.[254] The organisation would address challenges beyond conventional warfare and is formulating a cyber doctrine for the armed forces to formulate response strategy in cyber domain and chart out road map to integrate cyberwarfare with conventional operations.

India's Cyber Security Policy and Data Protection Regulations

National Cyber Security Policy (NCSP 2013) acts as an umbrella framework to define and design the actions to ensure safe and secure Indian cyber space. The policy provides guidelines to institutions to formulate appropriate policies and standard operating procedures for information and cyber security. It also defines broad contours of strategies and actions to be initiated by various agencies to safeguard country's interests in the cyber domain. Broadly, the objectives of Cyber Security Policy revolve around policy formulation and implementation, generating awareness, collaboration with public and private sectors for hardening IT infrastructure. It also covers risk assessment, formulation and implementation of response strategy and skill development and capacity building for creating robust cyber security framework at the national and regional levels.[255] The detailed study indicates that ibid policy deals with cyber security to protect national critical IT infrastructure and data protection. However, there is no mention of measures instituted under the ambit of NCSP 2013 to dominate the cognitive space and guard against social media warfare.

Information Technology Act (ITA) is the principal law which promulgates legal foundation for electronic governance and governs all areas of electronic communication, including social media. Cyber Appellate Tribunal and the Cyber Regulations Advisory Committee are also created under this act.[256] ITA, enacted by Parliament of India in 2000, is administered by CERT-In to provide guidelines for Indian cybersecurity legislation, institute data protection policies, and govern cybercrime. It has provisions to protect e-governance, e-banking, e-commerce and private sector. According to cyber experts, ITA is not exclusive and unitary cyber security law but in conjunction with multiple other sector-specific regulations it promotes cybersecurity standards.[257] It also provides a legal framework for critical information infrastructure in India. ITA 2008 (amended act with section 69A) was introduced to redefine terms and definitions for usage, cybercrime and validation of electronic signatures. It encourages companies to implement better data security practices and makes them liable for data breaches. ITA 2008 is applicable for wide array of users of IT, computer systems and networks in India. *The provisions of ITA 2008 are to be complied by service providers of web hosting, internet, network and telecom as well as foreign organizations having presence in India and businesses outside of the country running operations in India.* ITA 2008 aims to enhance the cyber security measures and forensic, makes it mandatory to report cyber breach to CERT-In, invokes penalties and imprisonment in cyber violation cases and has provisions for establishment of various regulatory bodies.[258] Section 69 of ITA 2008, authorises the Indian government to expeditiously intercept, monitor, decrypt, block, and remove data and content at its discretion, which can pose serious privacy concern.[259] Under this act, *social media sites are mandated to use automated methods to identify and remove illegal information, such as defamatory, vulgar, or invasive privacy. Social media networks must also post monthly compliance reports that include information about number of complaints received and the actions taken.*[260]

Under IT Act, Information Technology (Reasonable Security Practices and Procedures and Sensitive Personal Data or Information) Rules 2011 (Privacy Rules) is another important cybersecurity legislation. It includes provisions for the regulation of intermediaries, updated penalties and violation fees for cybercrime, cheating, slander, and nonconsensual publishing of private images, as well as censoring/restriction of certain speech. ITA and IT Rules govern processing of sensitive info, data protection, data retention, and collection of personal data and other sensitive information by Indian entities and organisations.

In February 2021, MeitY introduced Information Technology (Guidelines for Intermediaries and Digital Media Ethics Code) Rules, 2021 to replace IT Rules, 2011 and to cope up with the challenges of ever-changing digital landscape. The amended IT Rules published in Jun 22 aim to allow ordinary users of digital platforms to seek compensation for their grievances and demand accountability when their rights are infringed upon, as well as institute additional due diligence on organizations. The rules distinguish between smaller and significant social media intermediaries based on user numbers and places and makes them liable for personal data protection. The amended rules enforce privacy and transparency requirements for intermediaries and make it mandatory to inform users about rules and regulations, privacy policy, and terms and conditions for usage of their services. It also mandates the intermediaries to designate a grievance officer to address and resolve user complaints about violations of IT Rules, 2021.[261]

The National Cyber Security Strategy of 2020 (NCSS 2020) is long-awaited follow-up plan by the Indian government to further improve cybersecurity efforts. The draft document submitted by Data Security Council of India (DSCI) is pending review by the National Security Council Secretariat. NCSS 2020 aims to provide official guidance for stakeholders, policymakers, and corporate leaders to prevent cyber incidents, cyber terrorism, and espionage in cyberspace. Once implemented, the strategy would facilitate improved quality of cybersecurity audits and cyber security apparatus and programs, comprehensive knowledge and reviews of cybersecurity architecture of organisations.[262] The research focused on 21 areas to guarantee India's cyberspace is safe, secure, trustworthy, resilient, and dynamic. Revised National Cyber Security Strategy 2021, which takes a holistic approach to address the concerns of national cyberspace security, was presented to Parliament in 2022. Despite alarming increase in cyber assaults on India's IT networks, central government is yet to finalise and promulgate National Cyber Security Strategy.[263]

It is apparent that due emphasis has been given to formulate the policies and regulation and create organisations to deal with the cyber threats to Indian critical infrastructure, government agencies, private sectors and individual users of IT and computer systems. India has adopted multi-pronged strategy to develop requisite capability in cyber domain and take giant stride to bridge capacity deficit and magnitude of assessed threat in the cyber domain. It is a beginning in the right direction to safeguard national interests and ensure a resilient cyber space, however, a lot of work is required to be done in this direction to develop niche capabilities and achieve a credible deterrence. Apparently, threats associated with manipulation of social media have not gained proportionate attention of the stake holders and policy makers. Though, there is growing consciousness about the dangers posed by fake news, propaganda, narrative building through manipulated social media and social engineering. It is also understood that some steps have been taken to curb the menace, however, the issue has not gained requisite attention. The findings of various studies, discussed in the succeeding paragraphs point towards India's unpreparedness/ shortcomings in the response mechanism in the cyber domain in general and social media space in particular.

Global Cyber Security Index

International Telecommunication Union (ITU), a specialized **UN** organization, has undertaken drive to increase cybersecurity awareness, assess commitment of all its 194 member nations and publishes the *Global Cybersecurity Index (GCI)*; an indicator of global trend of commitment to cybersecurity. The index serves as a trusted reference depicting awareness level and understanding of cybersecurity's significance and dimensions. The GCI global ranking is evaluated based on performance on five parameters viz. *legal measures, technical measures, organisational measures, capacity development* and *cooperation*.[264]

The report advocates that subsequent to improved performance on important cyber safety metrics, *India has moved up from 37th position to 10th place in 2020 GCI ranking*. India was ranked fourth in the Asia Pacific area. The current GCI ranking is perceived as India's dedication to cybersecurity, significant overall strengthening and improvement across all cybersecurity-related metrics. The report advocates that owing to strong steps taken, India is establishing itself as a global IT giant, claiming its digital sovereignty. India's place in top ten in GCI, is attributed to strong measures instituted to defend online citizens' online rights, data privacy and achieve digital sovereignty as well as growing network of startups and rise as IT behemoth in Asia. The data depicted by Figure 42 below displays India's standing and scores according to many criteria used to calculate the Global Cybersecurity Index.[265] Based on the analysis, it has emerged that India has been able to capitalise upon its technical prowess in IT field, however, there is much left to desire in legal matters, organisational issues, capacity development and collaboration/ cooperation within state, industry and international agencies.

Overall Score	Legal Measures	Technical Measures	Organizational Measures	Capacity Development	Cooperative Measures
90.49	20.00	90.49	19.08	18.41	20.00

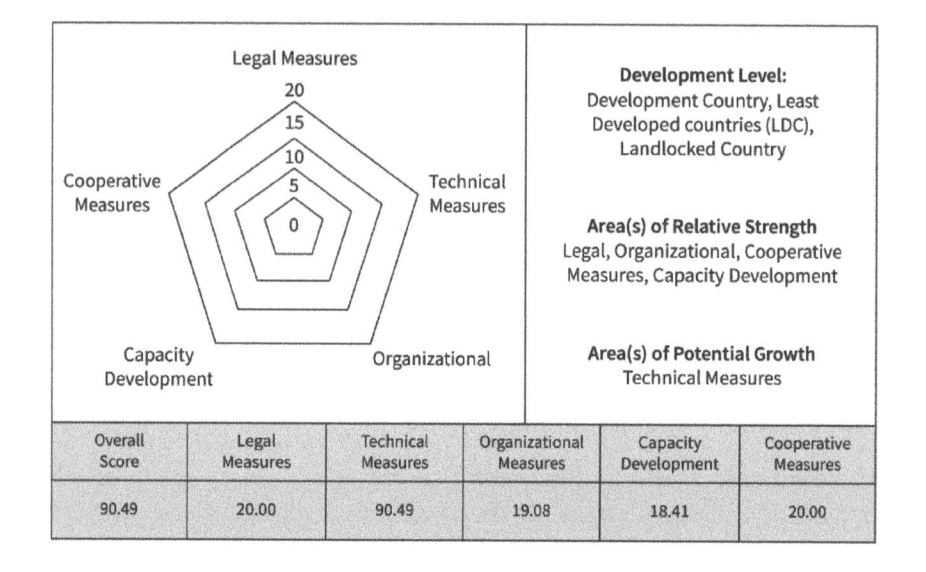

Development Level: Development Country, Least Developed countries (LDC), Landlocked Country

Area(s) of Relative Strength
Legal, Organizational, Cooperative Measures, Capacity Development

Area(s) of Potential Growth
Technical Measures

Figure 42 – India's GCI Score

The report highlights that following steps taken by India to bolster its cyber defence and tackle the cyber risks have facilitated securing higher ranking in the GCI 2020: -

➢ Formulation of Cyber Security plan.

➢ National level response mechanism and counter measures instituted by CERT-In to thwart computer security events or crises.

➢ Online web portal for reporting of cybercrimes and filing of complaints by the citizens about sexually explicit materials, child pornography, or anything depicting child sexual abuse or rape.

➢ Orchestration of cyber security plan under Indian Cyber Crime Coordination Centre (I4C) to deal with cybercrime concerns in the country in a comprehensive and coordinated way.

> **Creation of National Critical Information Infrastructure Protection Centre** (NCIIPC) to safeguard the nation›s critical information infrastructure.

It is pertinent to assess the performance of contemporary global and regional players in cyber security domain and draw lessons to improve own performance. As per report, China has strongest cyber defense capabilities, followed by USA, Israel, Netherlands, France, Canada, and UK. As per this report, with a cybersecurity score of 8.91, Denmark has most robust cybersecurity infrastructure among all nations, which indicates relatively better performance on cybersecurity exposure index. The report reveals that the Russia is the biggest short-term danger to cyber security. The analysts also opine that in longer term China would pose relatively greater threats to cyber security.

Further, the report published by MIT regarding cyber defence index for year 2022-23 has adjudged India at 17th place in global ranking. Cyber Defense Index is a ranking of 20 of the world's major economies according to their collective cybersecurity assets, organizational capabilities, and policy stances. It measures the degree to which these economies have adopted technology practices that advances resilience to cyberattacks and how well governments and policy frameworks promote secure digital transactions. The report highlights that in the domain of critical infrastructure (robust and secure digital and telecommunications networks and computing resources) India is placed at 20th position. In other spheres, the performance is relatively better. India ranks at 12th position in Cyber Security index, 13th for organisational capacity and 17th for policy commitments.[266]

It is an indicator that over the years India has made steady progress in the field of cyber security and has achieved a credible cyber resilience. However, evolving digital technology landscape and threats related to exploitation of SMPs demand a comprehensive approach and institution of robust measures including upskilling, capacity enhancement, organisational reforms and streamlining legal provisions without compromising freedom of expression.

Report on 'Cyber Capabilities and National Power' - 2021

International Institute of Strategic Studies (IISS), a London based think-tank, published a report on 'Cyber Capabilities and National Power' for the year 2021. The report has assessed cyber capabilities of 15 nation states including India.[267] The think tank conducts bi-annual qualitative study to analyse cyber ecosystem of each nation state and how it intersects with international security, economic competition and military affairs. The cyber capabilities of the nation states are analysed in seven verticals. The details are as under[268]:-

> Strategy and Doctrine. Examine evolution and quality of strategies and doctrines. Budget allocation, prioritisation, management policy and organisation change.

> Governance, Command and Control. Ascertain effectiveness of top government and military organisation and operational level organisation.

> Core Cyber-intelligence Capability. Involves assessment of 'cyber-espionage' and computer-network exploitation capability.

> Cyber Empowerment and Dependence. Assessment of capability to protect against cyber-capable adversary, vibrancy and scale of digital economy and research and usage of AI.

> Cyber Security and Resilience. Assessment of core cyber security capability to respond and recover from cyber incident, security standards, technical innovation, sector-specific risk management, effectiveness of indigenous cyber-security industry and creation of cyber specialist workforce.

> Global leadership in cyberspace affairs and offensive cyber capability. Examine global collaboration and alliances and involvement in influencing collaboration on cyber matters. It also Includes international diplomacy, formal alliances, engagement in international forums, and participation in international technical cooperation and arrangements for mutual assistance.

> Offensive Cyber Capability. Implies capability to deliver an effect. Encompasses operations designed for cognitive effects and physical destruction to civilian/ military targets in peace/ war by civilians/ military.

The countries assessed for their cyber defence capability in the report published for year 2021 are as follows.[269]

> US, UK, Canada and Australia (four of the 'Five Eyes' intelligence allies).

> France and Israel (two most cyber-capable partners of the 'Five Eyes' states) and Japan (an ally of the 'Five Eyes' states, but less

capable in the security dimensions of cyberspace, despite its formidable economic power).

- ➤ China, Russia, Iran and North Korea (the principal states posing a cyber threat to Western interests).
- ➤ India, Indonesia, Malaysia and Vietnam (in earlier stages of cyber-power development).

The countries, assessed by the report, are divided into three tiers. Categorisation of nation states assessed by the report published in 2021 is as follows: -

- ➤ Tier One - Countries having 'world-leading strengths' in all verticals. USA is the only country in Tier One.
- ➤ Tier Two - Countries have 'world-leading strengths' in some categories. It includes Australia, Canada, China, France, Israel, Russia and UK are in Tier Two.
- ➤ Tier Three - Countries have *strengths in some categories* but *significant weaknesses in others*. India, Indonesia, Iran, Japan, Malaysia, North Korea and Vietnam fall in this category.

Key Findings about India's Cyber Capabilities - In addition to verticals highlighted above, the study has also taken into account the performance and global ranking of the nation states in Global Cybersecurity Index (GCI). The report suggests that India has identified magnitude of the threat emerging in the cyber domain and acknowledged the need to upgrade its cyber defence capabilities to safeguard its national interests. However, the *progress on capacity building in cyber domain is sluggish and impeded by bureaucratic hurdles*. The key findings of the study are enumerated below: -

- ➤ Despite being cognizant of geostrategic instability and emerging cyber threats, India has made *modest progress in developing policy* and *doctrine for cyberspace security*. India released its first cyber security policy in 2013, however, owing to COVID-19, introduction of overarching and updated national cyber security strategy expected in 2020 has got delayed. The updated national cyber security strategy is appreciated 'to address developments in 5G, ransomware and Internet of Things (IOT)'.[270]

- ➤ While India's cyber policy for the civil sector continues to evolve, policy makers are reframing all areas of cybersecurity policy, including education, skills, import controls and national security.

- India's approach towards *institutional reforms of cyber governance has been slow and incremental*; the key coordinating authorities for cyber security in civil and military domains were established in 2018 and 2019 respectively. India's cyber capabilities are decentralised wherein multiple agencies play a role in cyber security related functions in close coordination with the main cyber-intelligence agency i.e. NTRO. Defence Cyber Agency, created in 2019, 'is central to the command and control of India's military cyber capabilities.' The intended function of DCyA is 'to integrate and coordinate cyber, space and special forces capabilities of three services.' Besides, Intelligence Bureau (IB), Research and Analysis Wing (RAW) and Defence Intelligence Agency (DIA) are integral parts of India's cyber intelligence capabilities.

- India's has a good regional cyber-intelligence reach but it is relatively weak when compared to global standards of Tier One and Tier Two countries. India relies on partnerships with US, UK and France for wider insights and greater cyber situational awareness as well as to develop a greater reach in future. To be able to deliver sophisticated offensive effect further afield, India needs to expand its cyber-intelligence reach and cyber capabilities with close collaboration with international partners especially USA, France and Israel.

- Based on certain evidences, the study makes a conservative assessment that India's offensive cyber capability is Pakistan-focused and regionally effective. ISS report notes that India is in the process of expanding these capabilities for wider effects. There are some indications that the focus may have shifted more to countering China.

- The country is active and visible in cyber diplomacy but has not been among the leaders on global norms, preferring instead to make productive practical arrangements with key states.

- The vibrant start-up culture and a very large talent pool are the strengths of Indian digital economy. The private sector has moved more quickly than the government in promoting national cyber security. Being a third-tier cyber power, India can progress to the second tier by harnessing great digital-industrial potential and adopting a whole-of-society approach to improve the cyber security.

Consequent to study of various policies, relevant act(s) and roles and responsibilities of various organisations mentioned above, the study has arrived at conclusion that Information Technology Act (ITA) is the principal law which governs regulation of social media in India. The ITA 2000 and 2008 and IT Rules 2021 (Guidelines for Intermediaries and Digital Media Ethics Code) in conjunction with other relevant rules and law concerning cyber space lay down the rules for users and service providers. These rules and acts also ensure cyber security, transparency, data protection of users and critical infrastructure. Cyber Appellate Tribunal and Cyber Regulations Advisory Committee established within the provisions of ibid law (ITA) are responsible to deal with cases related social media exploitation and violation cases. In 2021 the government has also rolled out explicit guidelines and rules for its officials to conceptualise and evolve their Social Media interactions and strategy.[271]

In addition, recently government has introduced stricter 'Social-Media Rules' for the users. The rules stipulate that in the event of user(s) committing mistake on one social media account, their other social media accounts e.g. Facebook and Instagram would also be deleted without any notification.[272] Further, the revised rules states that social accounts not in use for a prolonged duration would also be de-activated. IT Rules, 2021, prohibits uploading of 11 types of content on social media platforms. Intermediaries are mandated to ensure that users do not use their platform to share or transmit content violating the Rules. The IT Rules also prohibit the use of obscene, pornographic, paedophilic content and content that is invasive of a person's privacy. Highlighting threat posed by deep fakes/misinformation powered by AI, IT Rules prohibit misinformation on Indian internet. They mandate platforms to ensure that content violating provisions of these rules are removed or access is disabled upon court orders, complaints or notifications from authorised agencies. Social media intermediaries who violate the Information Technology (IT) Rules, 2021 may lose their safe harbour protection and would be liable for prosecution under IT Act and the Indian Penal Code (IPC).[273]

In this direction, a significant development is creation of 'Fact Check Units' under amended IT Rules 2021 by government to track fake and misleading news related to the government on online platforms such as Facebook and Twitter (X). The step has come under severe criticism by Editor Guild of India and News Broadcasters and Digital Association who contested that step to create and impose direction of these state-controlled fact check units amounts to censorship of media. These new rules state that an online intermediary including social media platforms such as Twitter

(X), Facebook, and YouTube and internet service providers such as Airtel, Jio and Vodafone Idea should make 'reasonable efforts' to not host content related to the central government that is 'identified as fake or misleading' by an FCU.[274] Press Information Bureau of India (PIB) in the details hosted on their web site has proclaimed that the news contents would be scrutinised for three categories i.e. fake, misleading and true, so as to dispel myths, rumours and false claims, and provides accurate and reliable information to the public.[275]

Effectiveness of Countermeasures

While Indian government has initiated multiple measures to safeguard its cyber and information space, it is prudent to assess the efficacy of these steps in protecting the national security interests in complex information environment. It becomes increasingly important considering rise in cases of fake news, rampant propaganda to spread blatant lies to tarnish India's global image, stoke controversies and create societal divide to disrupt communal harmony. Accordingly, this study would examine certain major events having potential to pose serious security threats and Indian response to thwart these threats.

Countering ISIL/ ISKP, SIMI and IM Nexus – Consequent to strikes carried out by USA and various middle east countries, the ISIS has suffered major setbacks and its cadre strength has reduced drastically. The experts claim that post Paris attack, popularity and support to the outfit has also eroded thereby resulting into declining sphere of influence. It is observed that despite India having third largest Muslim population in the world, presence of radicalized hardliners and influence of Darul Uloom Deoband ideology, ISIS, SIMI and IM triad has not been able to gain a substantial foothold in the country. For many strategists and think tanks India has long remained an enigma within the discourse on the Islamist extremism and terrorism.[276] According to various estimates, despite relentless efforts to spread radicalization and sow seeds of extremisms, the known figures of Indian youth who have joined ISIS cadres are limited to around 90. This can be attributed to resilient societal structures and multipronged strategy executed by the Government and proactive strategy adopted by its security agencies. It is assessed that countermeasures and strategy adopted by the Indian security agencies have achieved notable success in containing the triad of ISIS-SIMI-IM, however, in the realm of the evolving security scenario there is much left to be desired. The Indian strategy encompass monitoring of online chatter, identifying the SMP accounts involved in radicalizing and recruitment, intelligence gathering and apprehension of suspects and outreach program to the misguided personnel.

- As per reports, Maharashtra Police created a Media Analysis Centre and Kerla Police launched 'Operation Pigeon' to monitor online recruiting, narrative building and communication between cadres/ sympathizers of these terror outfit. The state police, NIA and central intelligence agencies have been sharing intelligence on activities of suspects and coordinate operations to dismantle terror network. Resultantly, many active cadres and recruits were apprehended, modules were busted and terror acts were foiled by the security agencies.

- In tandem, efforts directed to de-radicalize the indoctrinated youths have also borne the fruits resulting in containing the influence on misguided individuals.

- These efforts have reportedly disrupted the terror operations and forced ISIS, SIMI and IM to re-group and resolve their mutual differences. A report suggests that apprehension of Saquib Nachan's in December 2023, who was running ISIS-SIMI-IM combine module, was turning point in India's fight against these terror outfits. Nachan was reportedly involved in radicalising the youth, arranging their training, handled all foreign operations, funding and psychological operations against India. He had declared Padgha - Borivali belt as 'Liberated Zone' and directed the cadres to relocate to Padgha. Two individuals arrested from Pune revealed that this joint group working in Pune had links with modules in Hazaribagh, UP and Maharashtra and was run by handlers in Iraq/ Syria. They had a plan to carry out a major strike in India and had done the reconnaissance of Chabad House in Mumbai.

- Indian security agencies have also been attending US led summits on extremism and ISIS during Obama Administration. Reportedly, in January 2016, consequent to inputs provided by CIA as part of CIA-NIA joint counterterrorism operation, a successful operation was carried out which led to apprehension of members of a North Indian ISIS cell.[277]

- In an article, Natalie Tecimer cites Former Indian security officials claiming Intelligence Bureau's (IB) Operation Chukravyuh as India's main response to Islamic State's growing online threat. Starting in late 2014, IB officers reportedly posed as Islamic State recruiters on Twitter, communicating with hundreds of Indian youths who intended to join the Islamic State.[278]

➢ Major achievements of Indian security establishments consequent to these efforts are as summarized as under: -

- December 2014 - Bangalore police arrested Mehdi Masroor Biswas for operating Twitter account @ShamiWitness, one of the most influential ISIS Twitter handles for propaganda.

- April 2016 - Mohammad Shafi Armar, a resident of Bhatkal, Karnataka and reportedly chief recruiter for Islamic State in India, killed in US Strike in Syria.[279]

- June 2016 – NIA raided a suspected ISIS cell in Hyderabad after discovering explosive precursor chemicals ordered by the cell.

- October 2016 – NIA launched investigation into disappearance of 21 indoctrinated youths from Kerla and apprehended Subahani Haja Moideen. The reports suggest that Moideen had fought for ISIS in Syria and Iraq and had returned back to Kerala recently. In an another operation, seven members of ISIS including Moinudheen Parakadavath, a resident of Kasargod district, were arrested by NIA and Kerala Police. This operation busted 'Omar Al Hindi cell' and foiled a plot to carryout strike in crowded place in Kochi, target Israeli tourists visiting Vattakanal hill station near Kodaikanal and attack members of Ahmadiya sect and the Jamaat-e-Islami.

- March 2017 – Apprehension of four suspects revealed the source of online radicalisation. UP police ATS got engaged in a shootout in Lucknow with the terror suspect Saifullah, who was suspected to be a member of the ISKP cell.

- April 2017 – UP ATS and Delhi Police Special Cell arrested three suspects from an ISIS cell, believed to be actively recruiting, and detained six others.

- April 2017 - Shajeer Mangalassery Abdullah, 36 years old bright civil engineer from Sulthan Bathery, Wayanad district, Kerala killed in US strike in Asadkhel, Afghanistan. He was a former PFI member, handler of social media group, 'Ansar ul-Khilaaf-Kerala' and 'The Gate' on Telegram and 'Amir' of Kerala Cell of ISKP named 'Omar Al Hindi Cell'.

COUNTER MEASURES TO MITIGATE THREATS OF SOCIAL MEDIA

- December 2023 – NIA arrested 15 ISIS operatives during raids conducted across Maharashtra and Karnataka. The apprehended operatives included Saqib Nachan, who had declared Padgha-Borivali as 'Liberated Zone' (Al Sham).

ISLAMIC STATE IN INDIA

- IS incidents
- Bilateral and multilateral actions against terrorism and IS

2017

MARCH 2017
Mar. 8 Shootout with IS terror suspect Saifullah in Lucknow, linked to train blast.
Mar. 7 Train blast in Madhya Pradesh by suspected IS cell, subsequent detainment of three individuals.

OCTOBER 6, 2016
NIA arrested Subahani Haja Moideen, leading to capture of Kerala IS members.

JUNE 29, 2016
NIA raided Hyderabad IS cell.

MAY 2016
IS released video featuring Indians including Thane engineering student Fahad Tanvir Sheikh warning India.

JANUARY 20, 2016
U.S.-India joint operation led to identification of almost twenty IS operatives.

2016

SEPTEMBER 2015
Indian officials participated in Leader's Summit on Countering ISIL and Violent Extremism hosted by President Barack Obama in New York.

AUGUST 2015
Indian officials participated in U.S.-India Cyber Dialogue.

JULY 2015
Indian officials participated in U.S.-India Terrorist Designations Exchange and worked to implement UNSCRs 1373 (2001), 2178, and 2199, and sanctions under UN 1267/1989/2253 ISIL (Da'esh) and al-Qa'ida sanctions regime.

JUNE 2015
GOI appointed Special Envoy for Counterterrorism and Extremism.

MAY 2015
NIA hosted U.S.-sponsored regional dialogue on Global Counterterrorism Forum (GCTF) Marrakech Memorandum on Foreign Terrorist Fighters.

FEBRUARY 2015
Indian officials participated in U.S. CVE Summit.

JANUARY 2015
Islamic State named Hafiz Saeed Khan as wali leader of Khorasan, notice of official expansion into the region.

2015

DECEMBER 2014
Mehdi Masroor Biswas arrested for operating pro-IS twitter account that is considered one of the most influential IS accounts.

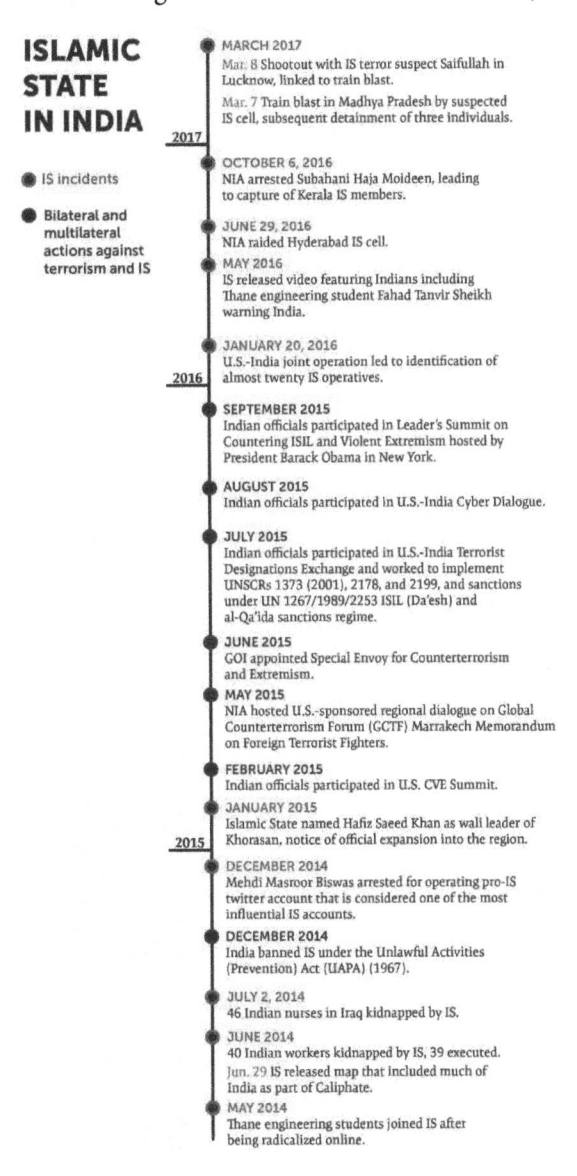

DECEMBER 2014
India banned IS under the Unlawful Activities (Prevention) Act (UAPA) (1967).

JULY 2, 2014
46 Indian nurses in Iraq kidnapped by IS.

JUNE 2014
40 Indian workers kidnapped by IS, 39 executed.
Jun. 29 IS released map that included much of India as part of Caliphate.

MAY 2014
Thane engineering students joined IS after being radicalized online.

Figure 43 – IS related incidents time line
Source - https://thediplomat.com/wp-content/uploads/2017/06/thediplomat.com-india-and-the-fight-against-islamic-state-is_india_timeline-1-768x1518.jpg

- ➢ However, despite these successes the possibility of regrouping and emergence of many other modules cannot be ruled out. The biggest challenge is to detect and monitor the ever-evolving online radicalisation and indoctrination strategy by these terror groups. The assessment is to be seen in light of call given by spokesperson of ISKP immediately after terrorist attack in Russia in March 2024 to 'Lone Wolf' to orchestrate strikes across the globe; apparently an attempt to regain its stronghold and influence.

- ➢ The Indian security establishments would continue to face serious challenges due to virtual self-radicalization of the misguided youth and their motivation to carryout terror strikes as well as exploitation of social media for indoctrination. The social media employment tactics employed by ISIS, SIMI and IM are increasingly becoming elusive thereby presenting a severe security challenge. The situation may even become more complex due to advent of AI and Deep Fakes.

- ➢ The West's experience in tackling ISIS holds lessons for India. Despite larger coffers and media specialists in play, the counter response has been lacking, says the former chief of the U.S. Center for Strategic Counterterrorism Communications. He argued that, "There is a fantasy in Washington that if you somehow put magic social media or public diplomacy pixie dust on a problem, it will go away. "It's not that ISIS is so great. It is that the response against ISIS is both limited, and weak." *He reiterated that dismantling the group's Twitter feeds was a temporary solution; the challenge remains the wide range of audiences to target with counter propaganda.*[280]

- ➢ Shruti Pandalai, a researcher and author on strategic matters, in her article published in 'The Diplomat' argues that India has worked on a multi-layered response, from surveillance and monitoring to involving religious heads in de-radicalization programs designed to reach out to disenchanted youth. Yet the scale of the challenge requires an institutionalized, not ad-hoc, response. Agencies warn that ISIS propaganda is already fueling competition between terror groups on social media, driving other non-state actors to bandwagon on the Islamic State brand and even prompting insurgent groups to copycat recruitment strategies.

Counter-Terrorism and Counter Radicalisation Division (CT-CR). According to an article by Vaasu Sharma on Research gate publications, MHA of GoI has established a Counter-Terrorism and Counter-Radicalisation Division (CT-CR) to prevent youth straying towards extremism.[281] In addition, Kerala, Maharashtra and Telangana have set up their own de-radicalisation programmes. In this endeavour, family/community and clerics played an important role, to deradicalize the youth with a new narrative in Maharashtra and Kerala respectively. 'Operation Pigeon' by Kerala state police successfully thwarted propaganda of IS, IM and LeT to radicalize 350 youths by monitoring social media. In Telangana, local officers like Rema Rajeshwari developed outreach programs to fight fake news in around 400 villages. In Kashmir, the government has employed multipronged strategy encompassing perception shaping operations, countering extremists' propaganda by Pakistan supported elements and conduct of outreach programmes. In addition, with a view to curb e-Jihad, the government has intermittently imposed internet curfews, including suspension of 3G and 4G networks and social media apps while keeping BSNL network operational, used by the administration and security forces.

Countering Pak Sponsored Disinformation Campaign

Analysing pattern of social media traffic post Pulwama incident and Balakot Strike, various think tanks have concluded that in the battle to dominate cognitive space, Pakistani agencies have seemingly enjoyed an edge over their competitors on Indian side. Alluding to the fact that developing credible capabilities to execute effective information operations and narrative building is a long-drawn process, Pakistani establishment by virtue of their involvement in fomenting insurgency in J&K for decades could mobilise their network swiftly. The simultaneous activation of vicious web of Pakistani state actors and non-state actors on both sides of Line of Control, launched an aggressive influence operation on multiple social media platforms, thereby gaining advantage in time and cognitive space. Exploiting absence of verified and genuine online reports supported by the facts, Pakistani handlers could cloud the rationale thinking and objective opinion of Indian media and certain sections in political circles. Indian media and political parties who were surfing digital space to glean information about the incident, faced the challenge of gaining first hand access to information and fell prey to designs of Pak sponsored propaganda machinery.

It is observed that during these incidents, Indian response was initially restricted to official press release and interviews. Later, Indian counter social media offensive gained momentum, however Pakistan was able to dominate the cognitive space using its strategic communication tool kit to push its own version of the incident, create confusion in the minds of Indians and discredit Indian forces and the government. *Utter chaos and confusion reigned in the cognitive space, with some Indian intelligentsia also sharing questionable information and fabricating content — to support their own political agendas against the ruling political party.*[282] It is emphasised that weaponised social media campaign realises multiple objectives in contested battle space i.e. counter and overwhelm the competitors with quantum of content, non-attributability and speed of action, gain legitimacy in absence of an equally potent counter response and disrupt counter narrative.

However, it would be incorrect to arrive at conclusion that Indian response has always been reactionary and lacked desired impact to shape opinion of people and defeat the 'Pakistan engineered Battle of Narrative'. Indian Army deployed in J&K has been at forefront to spearhead the initiatives to make impactful changes in physical space to reinforce people's trust, positively shape their attitudes and beliefs and demonstrate the armed force's commitment towards conflict termination, peace and normalcy. The efforts in physical space offered tangible social proof to support social media initiatives facilitating a befitting reply to anti-nationalist and separatist agenda. In addition, the Government of India and various other government agencies also pioneered various projects to assuage people's feelings, defeat negative narrative building and offer an alternative truth to target populace in J&K as well as in other parts of countries. The sustained efforts by armed forces and government machineries seemingly focussed on long term goals are gradually making inroads, moulding emotions and opinions favourably thereby denying freedom of action and critical space to adversarial forces.

In this context, *'Har Ghar Tiranga'* campaign launched by PM Modi under the aegis of 'Azadi Ka Amrit Mahotsav' has played a crucial role in transforming optics and strengthening the 'Idea of India' in Kashmir. A state where hoisting of tri-colour national flag has always been a matter of contestation for decades, the campaign marked significant decline in influence of adversarial forces, indicated arrival of era of stability and normalcy in state and willingness of people to be part of national celebration especially post abrogation of Article 370. It is pertinent to note that army started the initiative to hoist the national flags on government buildings in Kashmir valley almost a year prior.[283] This innovative effort by Indian army gradually gained traction, captured people's attention, challenged separatists' mindset and their reign of terror and set the stage for grand success of 'Har Ghar Tiranga Campaign'. Resultantly, the state witnessed an overwhelming response by public, tricolour was hoisted in Lal Chowk, government buildings including 23,000 schools and residential areas even in places like Anantnag, Kistwar, Kupwara and Pulwama.[284] An article analysing impact of this initiative points out that, *"This change has to be measured, not through the physical optics but the mental space it occupies. The most significant part is that it represents the moral compass of Indian leadership of the day which looks beyond the narrow political objectives"*.[285] Soon, videos of the families of terrorists hoisting Tiranga went viral. In one such video Rayees Mattoo, brother of Hizbul terrorist Javid Mattoo, hoisted the national flag at his house in Sopore.[286]

The Sadbhavana projects, 'Super-30 Scheme', 'A Day with Company Commander' a public outreach program and various programmes in areas of skill development, sports, education, health and culture have made positive contribution towards upliftment of lives of thousands of Kashmiris and garnered significant positive response.[287] Additionally, conduct of various tours and events by National Cadet Corps and country visit tours organised under Project Sadbhavana has afforded an ideal opportunity to impressionable Kashmiri students to get exposure to diverse culture and traditions of India. Recently conducted 'Khelo India Winter Games in Gulmarg', promotion of sports culture, various scholarships to meritorious students from poor financial background to pursue higher education, renovation of 20 religious sites under Smart City Project have resonated positively with the public sentiments. Such initiatives have also been successful in making impression on youth and motivated them to contribute towards nation building, join armed forces and pursue their academic goals and shunning the separatists' agenda.

The showcasing of these events and initiatives on social media platforms has made gradual positive impact on the perceptions of the Kashmiri local population. This has catapulted credibility of government driven initiatives, facilitated genuine outreach efforts and exposed the lies spread by adversarial forces. Consequent to these efforts, there are visible signs of desperation amongst the shadowy cabal, who have launched an online offensive to discredit Indian government and security agencies. In one such incident, an article published in 'Dawn' newspaper cited DG ISPR and a Stanford University study to claim that Twitter (now 'X') suspended a part of pro-India social media network on grounds of violating their Platform Manipulation and Spam Policy.[288] The article claims that narrative promoted by these accounts praised the Indian Army, and had possible links with Chinar Corps operating in valley. The article also argued that Twitter (X), Facebook and Instagram temporarily suspended official accounts of Srinagar based Indian army's Chinar Corps for 'coordinated inauthentic behaviour'. This appears to be an attempt by Pakistani establishments to spread their fake narrative, prove authenticity by quoting twisted facts and augment reinforcing cycle of beliefs of population segment vulnerable to such manipulation campaign.

To conclude, it is assessed that Indian response to such diversionary tactics and malicious social media is sub optimal. The Indian Government and State government in J&K need to formulate a comprehensive strategy to integrate efforts of all agencies operating in Kashmir, gain an upper hand over the adversarial forces and foil any attempt by them to vitiate the minds of populace.

Countering Chinese Propaganda Campaign

Various scholars have observed that China carried out a detailed analysis of Gulf War I and II, Operation Enduring Freedom and trends of RMA to discern rapidly changing character of war and deduce pragmatic lessons and inferences. Presumably, these studies have been instrumental in formulation of their strategies and military doctrines aligned with emerging threat scenarios and lay down a road map to build capacity and competencies to dominate the adversaries. The evolution of military doctrines from People's War to People's War Under Modern Conditions to Limited Local War to Limited War Under High Tech Conditions to the latest 'Local War Under Informationalised Conditions' is testimony to transition in Chinese strategic construct. The paradigm shift in strategic outlook and military doctrines is seemingly driven by their visualization of growing dominance of disruptive technology especially criticality of information technology to enhanced battle field transparency, greater situational awareness and capability to undermine adversary's combat potential and decision making. Chinese have developed credible non-kinetic capabilities, arguably the most effective means of furthering national interest in contemporary times, alongside building the conventional miliary power.

To gear up to fight battles under conditions of informationisation, China's Central Military Commission added *'san zhongzhaqia'* or 'Three

Warfare (3Ws) Strategy' to the Political Work Guidelines of People's Liberation Army in 2003. As per various experts on China, '3Ws Strategy' framework encompasses 'Strategic Psychological Operations', 'Overt and Covert Media Manipulation' and 'Exploitation of National and International Legal Systems / Legal Warfare'. 'Propaganda' and 'Dis-information' tactics have been mainstay of Chinese strategies evolved over the years. The CCP and Chinese security forces have honed their manipulative skills significantly and have leveraged the art to shape opinion of target minds to attain a decisive edge against the competitors in geo-political arena. India has been a target of Chinese propaganda campaigns since long; be it portrayal of humane image to PsOW during 1962 War or manipulation of facts during border stand-off between Indian Army and PLA troops. During Doklam and Galwan episodes, the Chinese propaganda machinery unleashed well-coordinated attacks against India. In response to Doklam standoff, the Chinese state media aired a propaganda video titled 'Seven Sins of India'. This act backfired and video was criticised for being racist. Evidently, China has adopted a multi-pronged approach in this battle of sight and sound.[289] The Chinese Strategy for battle of narratives and propaganda capitalize on various ways and means to attain desired end state. It is reported that United Front Work Department (UFWD) of CCP conducts legal warfare and influence operations with the larger aim of perpetuating the CCP rule and legitimacy. It also encourages Chinese diaspora to further the perspective of CCP on various contentious issues such as BRI, Tibet etc.[290] To disseminate CCP approved contents to global audience, China has established links with foreign media houses, academia, political organizations, NGOs and leading journalists by providing them funds, scholarship and organizing visits to China. Similar tactics was reportedly applied to lure Indian media houses also few years back. These China supported organizations act as 'Third Party Spokesperson' to propagate Chinese narrative. To control information space, the Chinese have made substantial investments in media houses with a view to regulate the news contents. China's warfare strategy has undergone a sea-change from ren hai zhan shu (human wave) to san zhong zhanfa (three wars, three tactics, or three ways of fighting) focusing on manipulating cognitive domain, the nerve-centre of decision-making.[291]

The 2017 border stand-off in Doklam, along the India–China–Bhutan Trijunction, was a crucial event for China to test its new information strategy. *The Indian response to Chinese social media strategy has received a mixed response by various think tanks and strategists. Some think tanks feel that India was initially submissive and its response did not demonstrate the* desired intent and aggressiveness. However, the contrarian views adjudged Indian response a mature and calibrated approach to tackle a volatile situation.

The strategy adopted by India to leverage social media to seize the initiative and unmask the Chinese designs during Galwan Valley clash in 2020 has had a significant impact on public opinion in India. A survey of young Indians in 2021 found that 77 % of respondents distrusted China, for example. The Indian government's nationalistic response to the clash also has trickled into the Indian media, where most outlets are critical of the Chinese government. Media organizations that published interviews with the Chinese ambassador at the time, Sun Weidong, have faced public criticism. In addition, under IT Act 2000 the Government of India imposed ban on around 300 Chinese applications to include TikTok, Weibo, WeChat, and Kwai to search engine Baidu, Alibaba's UC Browser and e-commerce sites like Alipay and Shein, as well as mobile games and dating applications. This step led to substantial decline in their customer base in India which was growing at phenomenal pace prior to 2020. In Apr 2020, in a bid to deter opportunistic take overs during COVID 2020, Indian Government came heavily while scrutinising proposals for FDI in India. This step emerged as a deterrent against Chinese investments.[292] Media reports in mid-2022 revealed that Indian government approved only 80 proposals for FDI from Chinese entities out of 382 proposals received Chinese entities which were put through a new vetting procedure. According to reports, many of these proposals involved acquisitions of minority stakes or investment in manufacturing rather than digital services. In 2019, the government announced that 26 % FDI cap would apply to digital news and current affairs outlets. This was a significant step towards protecting information environment as foreign ownership of digital-only news platforms had not previously been limited, and such firms had attracted investment from global private equity companies and other investors, including China-based corporations like ByteDance.[293]

Based on analysis of various studies, it can be deduced that Indian response was calibrated and designed to control escalation, however lacked requisite scale, intent and desired effect considering threats and vulnerabilities in internal environment and information warfare capabilities of China. It is felt that in this era of hybrid warfare and social media exploitation, India cannot afford to allow the belligerent China to seize initiative, plan fabricated narrative, create an atmosphere of uncertainty and trust deficit and incapacitate the decision makers. To counter this growing threat, India needs to create a potent force of cyber/social media warriors to gain and maintain a credible social media and cyber dominance, deny critical space in cognitive domain and develop capability to launch an aggressive social media campaign to thwart 'Battle of Narratives'. It would be prudent to sensitise Indian media houses about the Chinese social media strategy and threats posed to national security through manipulated social media feeds and propaganda campaign. It would necessitate a unified approach encompassing response from security forces, political circles, intelligentsia, academia and media houses through thousands of accounts on multiple social media platforms.

Challenges/ Shortcomings

Consequent to examining measures instituted by Indian government and analysing their efficacy, this study has attempted to discern shortcomings, identify areas of concern and improvement and forecast challenges related to protecting information and cognitive space. These challenges and shortcomings are discussed in the succeeding paragraphs.

Doctrine and Strategy – India's Cyber Security Strategy has already been presented in the Parliament. Promulgation of Cyber Security Strategy is imperative to set out a national vision and objectives for the secure, robust and resilient cyber space. In absence of national strategy, various agencies would continue to work in silos, their efforts would be devoid of synchronization and strategic orientation. It may lead to sub-optimal output with certain vulnerabilities and threats remaining unaddressed. Bureaucratic hurdles, lack of horizontal sharing of intelligence and unison in efforts would continue to obstruct the endeavours to achieve dominance of cyber space. In the context of Indian Armed forces, joint doctrine has emphatically mentioned cyber capabilities as a critical element of triad of integrated strategic forces alongside space and special operations. The joint doctrine also presaged creation of Defence Cyber Agency, which eventually became operational in 2019, task to conduct integrated operations in the digital space. Cyber operations subsumed under the rubric of information operations, have been afforded a prominent role.[294] However, it appears that social media has still not got due attention as a prominent player in ensuring a secure cyber space and denial of freedom of action to adversaries to prosecute influence operations and dominating the cognitive space.

Social Media Warfare Capability – Discerning prevailing trends and open-source evidences, it may not be incorrect to deduce that developing desired competencies to leverage social media to further national objective and secure national interests has not received the quantum of importance it deserves. However, there are very little evidences available to give fair amount of assurance on India's capability to conduct defensive and offensive social media warfare. As part of Information Campaigns, Indian army is conducting perception management operations at operational levels to show case the humane face of organization as well as defeat negative narrative building. Analysing trends of social media exploitation by adversarial forces (terrorist organizations, separatist forces and ISPR of Pakistan) in insurgency infested J&K and North Eastern States, it is observed that on many occasions Indian agencies have been reactive. Resultantly, initiative has been seized by adversarial elements/ forces, who advanced their battle of narrative to dominate critical cognitive space. Thus, there is a need to orchestrate the synergized social media operations to dominate and deny critical space in cyber domain. We need to be on 24x7 listening watch on chatter and narrative building on social media platforms as well as in dark web. Rather than being reactive we need to seize the initiative and have upper hand in this cat and mouse game.

Lack of Indigenous Social Media Platforms – As per Global Media statistics report, India has 2nd highest social media users in the world. The netizens are using all popular applications such as Facebook, Twitter (X), Instagram, YouTube, WhatsApp, Telegram, LinkedIn and other trending platforms. It is pertinent to note that none of these applications have their servers located in India. In the recent past, there have always been serious concerns regarding data protection and misuse of these platforms by inimical elements to spread manipulated contents in India's digital space. The service providers have been at logger head with the Indian agencies on issues pertaining to content regulation and providing details of accounts suspected to be involved in spreading malicious contents. It is a cause of concern that despite having a vibrant IT industry, the country does not have its own indigenous social media platform. 'Koo app' developed by an Indian company as an alternative to erstwhile 'Twitter' has lost its grip over the market resulting into sharp decline in its users' base. It is quintessential to develop multiple indigenous social media platforms as an alternative to global platforms. These suggested indigenously developed platforms should meet the requirements of domestic customers, diaspora and even customers based abroad. It is assessed that provision of such alternative application would contain external influences in internal affairs and facilitate a safe and secure digital space.

Lack of Cyber awareness – According to a report published by Global Statistics in 2024, out of 1.42 billion population of India, there are 0.692 billion internet users i.e. ,48.73% of population has internet access.[295] Interestingly, 0.672 billion users have internet access on their mobiles. The current active social media users are 0.467 billion (i.e. 32.88% of population and 69.2% of internet users). Indian netizens' average internet usage time is six hours 23 mins every day and their average social media surfing time is two hours 50 mins every day. As per statistics, top four most surfed social media platforms in India are Instagram (74.7%), Facebook (71.2%), Twitter (X) (42.90%) and LinkedIn (35.70%) in descending order. However, in absence of cyber consciousness and awareness about social media strategies for opinion shaping, the gullible users fall prey to negative narrative building online campaign and inadvertently aid wider circulation of manipulated content. Due to lack of awareness, Indian populace would continue to become target of fake news, propaganda and social engineering attempts by inimical elements to sow discord and create societal fissures. Thus, there is a need to create greater cyber awareness amongst Indian public, ensure high standards of cyber hygiene and educate the users about challenges posed by social media warfare.

Strategy for Counter Narrative and Engaging Wide Range of Audiences – The Indian response to online radicalization and indoctrination, narrative building and extremist propaganda has apparently lacked unified approach and strategic perspective. The Indian Army and Central agencies have reacted to nefarious attempts by the adversarial forces to orchestrate social engineering and manipulate cognitive space of vulnerable sections of the society. However, the response has been confined to approaching these SMPs for content removal or responding to online trolls and hashtag campaigns. The ecosystem and cohort of adversarial forces comprising of non-state actors (hackers, troll factories, terrorists' organizations, anti-national elements, separatists and over ground workers), hostile state actors, anonymous supporters and certain section of irresponsible media/ channels operate in synergy to propagate the manipulated content. Thousands of social media accounts and handles give wide publicity to such contents targeting wide range of audiences, influencing their emotions, triggering cognitive biases and creating echo chambers. By the time, such contents come under scrutiny of the government agencies, the adversarial forces are able to occupy critical contested cognitive and digital space, their fabricated narratives spreads like expanding torrents influencing substantial target population resulting in chaos, uncertainty and dilemma in the mindscape of decision makers and unsuspecting common public. To defeat such designs, there is a need to have substantial digital presence of social media experts having understanding of regional dynamics, local sensitivities and technical expertise. Such social media watch apparatus should be capable of monitoring the digital chatter constantly, discern early trendlines, patterns and battle indicators and pre-emptively flood digital space with counter narrative. In this era of hybrid warfare transcending entire spectrum of conflict, not confined by geographical borders, time-lines and morality and ethics, safeguarding the cognitive domain and digital information space should be a continuous endeavor. The opinion shaping of own citizens and maintaining a competitive edge over adversaries in battle of cognitive space/ cognitive colonization should be a well thought of strategy. The response strategy should encompass state teams operating round the clock to monitor, filter, engage with netizens and create counter-narrative contents to provide alternative perspective and messaging to mass population. Various experts and subject matter experts perceive India as a weak responder in the domain of social media warfare and cyber offensive. Consequent to threat evaluation and challenges to national security in evolving hybrid conflict scenario, it is strongly felt that India needs to develop niche capabilities and competencies to synergise it's counter online offensive capabilities well beyond the immediate borders and be able to neutralise the threat at origin. India must develop competencies to expose the inimical players and push the envelope of its counter offensive deep into their cognitive and ideological sanctuaries, attack vulnerabilities and discredit their agenda. However, in the current scenario, there appears to be a void in this aspect, wherein state governments in turbulent regions have been found to be failing in responding to online offensive of adversaries. It is emphasised that changing landscape of social media technologies and tactics, would be users' delight but security nightmare'.

Cheap Data Packages and Virtual/ e-SIM cards – According to a report, India has cheapest internet data packages in the world. Availability of internet data packages at relatively affordable prices and abundance of cheap smart mobile handsets has triggered an incredible increase in the number of internet users countrywide. For example, Between December 2016 to December 2017, Jammu and Kashmir recorded 1.85 million new wireless telephone subscribers. This 16.4% increase was the highest, recorded by any state in the same period, with an increase from 11.27 million subscribers in December 2016 to 13.12 million a year later.[296] In the meanwhile, introduction of 4G services has further improved the internet speed and mobile services. Correspondingly, number of users using internet services rose unexpectedly with extended screen time and greater exposure to online contents, thereby compounding challenges of law enforcements agencies pertaining to tracking communication and online activities of suspected users and screening malicious contents hosted on internet/ SMPs. Amidst this complex scenario, prevalence of virtual/ e-SIM cards, cloud-based SIM which does not need physical verification, have added another dimension to the security challenges. According to a report, use of virtual SIM cards has been significant, especially in the case of Jammu and Kashmir. The terrorists involved in the February 2019 attack in Pulwama used a virtual SIM card to keep in touch with their Pakistan and Kashmir based handlers. Further, the administrators of WhatsApp groups linked to militant outfits have phone numbers with area codes from countries including US, UAE, Saudi Arabia and UK. Many of these phone numbers are acquired using online services and products, such as 'VirtualPhone' or 'Sonetel', which do not require in-person registration. This helps the militant outfits evade monitoring and interception by Indian security agencies.[297] These practices hint towards growing trend and tactics of inimical actors to evade the law enforcement agencies and carry out their operations unhindered. Therefore, there is a need to enforce stringent rules to mandate verification of customers procuring virtual SIM cards and find a way out to detect and intercept communication by suspected persons taking advantage of virtual SIM cards.

Chapter 7

Future Implications of Social Media on National Security

Having studied the evolution journey of social media as game changer in communication domain and a potent tool of opinion shaping, it is deduced that this technological revolution will play an increasing role in influencing attitudes and behaviour of competitors in geo-political and geo-economic contestation. In the realm of hybrid threat environment, covert and overt exploitation of social media has become a new normal; the trends suggest that social media may even gain more prominence in future conflicts and competitions. Analysis of conflicts in last decade reveals that state and non-state actors have refined and evolved social media warfare strategy and tactics rapidly. Thus, it can be presaged that owing to greater reach, speed of dissemination, ambiguity and non-attributability, state and non-state actors would leverage social media as a low-cost option to gain and maintain a decisive edge over the adversary. The footprints of narrative warfare are visible in wide range of conflicts and competitions. It would not be an exaggeration to infer that the social media warfare strategy encompassing creating echo chambers, confirmation biases and stereotypes through direct and indirect vectors would form an essential part of overall grand strategy. The opinion shaping and propaganda through social media has added a complex dimension to national security challenges. Emergence of deep fakes, geo-tagging and voice cloning technologies has already compounded the security challenges. Owing to their features, certain innovations and futuristic trends in social media technologies knocking at the door would be nightmare for the security agencies and policy makers. Thus, to analyse impending threats of social media to India's national security, it is imperative to study the emerging trends of technology development and understand the impact of these futuristics features on exploitation of social media.

Prospective Trends of Emerging Social Media Technologies

Evolution of social media has been rapid since the early days of "MySpace and 'Friendster'. This technological innovation has occupied an important place in contemporary scenario. The impact of social media has been felt in all spheres, the analysis of recent turn of events reveals that digital revolution has played an important role in decision making and outcomes of the competitions/ contestation in the diverse domains.

In the realm of fast technological advancements, world stands at the cusp of pathbreaking developments which will shape the future of social media space. These emerging platforms and technologies promise to revolutionise the way we connect, communicate, and engage in the digital world. But it needs no emphasis that emerging social media technologies would also compound the national security challenges. Marco Labre in his article has outlined the contours of future trends of social media platforms (SMPs).[298] While some of these technology trends would act as enabler and others may be a challenge for the security agencies. Some of these emerging technology trends are discussed below.

> ➤ *Decentralised Social Networks.* These networks built on blockchain technology, offer transparency, greater control and data privacy to users and temper proof communication. Users own their data and have the power to decide who accesses it. Platforms like Diaspora, Damus, Mastodon, Peepeth and Hive are early examples, and more are likely to emerge as people seek alternatives to traditional, centralized social networks. Decentralised platforms distribute data across a network of computers, making it much more difficult for any one entity to access or control data or to enforce censorship.[299] The decentralised structure may be beneficial for individual users to keep their communication discreet and protected however makes it much more difficult for these platforms to be censored or shut down by the government agencies in case of misuse, as there is no central point of control.[300]

> ➤ *Metaverse and Virtual Reality (VR).* The concept of metaverse, a fully immersive virtual world, has been gaining traction of late. It is believed that social media will play a pivotal role in shaping metaverse by offering users ability to interact in 3D environments. VR technology is advancing rapidly, and platforms like Facebook's "Horizon Workrooms" are paving the way for a more interactive and immersive online experience. It is assessed that Metaverse

would be devoid of any government regulations, oversight or law and data control would lie with the company whomsoever owns the platforms. The technology experts caution that Metaverse and VR can potentially be used for committing crimes, disinformation campaigns and deploying 3D fakes. They advocate that learning from challenges of current generation of social media, laws and regulations need to be updated to ensure data protection, secure individual privacy rights and safeguard national security against the appreciated challenges of Metaverse and VR.[301]

➢ *Voice-Based Social Networks (VBSN).* Platforms like 'Clubhouse' have already gained popularity for their audio-only interactions. Voice-based social media adds a new layer of personalisation and intimacy to online conversations. It is likely that VBSN may use encryption to protect data, which will make it difficult for security agencies to monitor the communication, enforce censorship, gather evidences and carryout content analysis to discern the potential threats.

➢ *AI-Enhanced Social-Media.* AI is being used to enhance social media experiences. From chatbots that provide instant customer support to AI-generated content and deep data analysis, businesses can leverage AI to optimize their social media strategies. AI can help in personalizing content, predicting user behavior, and streamlining advertising efforts. However, there are certain potent threats of using AI. The technology can be used for deploying Deep Fakes and spread disinformation/ misinformation. The hostile state and non-state actors can leverage this technology to identify and radicalize vulnerable individuals or spread propaganda. It would be difficult to establish attributability of the offensive contents. Further, algorithm bias can lead to unfairly targeting certain demographics or missing threats from others.

➢ *Ephemeral Content Evolution.* Ephemeral content e.g., stories on Instagram and Snapchat, have gained significant popularity on account of longer-form stories, more interactive features, engaging content and perishability. The temporary nature of these messages would make it difficult to carry out content analysis, discern potential threats and gather evidences. It would also be difficult to identify the users/ bad actors and trace the source of misinformation.

> *NFTs and Social Tokens.* The emerging trends indicates that online content creators and users may gradually start using 'Non-Fungible Tokens (NFTs)' and 'Social Tokens' to interact on social media. NFTs can represent ownership of digital assets, and social tokens can be used for various interactions within online communities. The innovation which can gainfully be utilised for monetization and community building, presents certain threats in terms of money laundering, discreet funding to hostile actors to launch mis-information campaigns, market manipulations to cause economic losses to target nation(s) (insider trading, pump and dump tactics) and avenues for criminals to evade national laws and regulatory authorities.

> *Geo-Social Networking.* Geo-social networking combines location-based technology with social media. Platforms like 'TikTok' and 'Snapchat' are already using location data to deliver personalised content and establish connect with users based on their physical locations. However, it will expose users to certain threats in terms of targeting by criminals to carryout selective misinformation and incite violence based on demography. The security of military installations and critical assets may also get compromised due to revelation of geographical location.

> *Ethical and Privacy-Focused Platforms.* Growing concerns about privacy and data security have led to a demand for ethical and privacy-focused social media platforms. Businesses that prioritise user privacy and data protection can build trust with their audiences and gain a competitive edge. It is assessed that certain features like end-to-end encryption, limited user information and self-destruct mode of the content may make it difficult to carryout content analysis, identify the threats, and take preventive actions. The features may also be exploited for creating pseudo-anonymous accounts which will compound the challenges of security agencies.

> *User-Generated Content (UGC) Communities* - Platforms like 'Reddit' and 'Imgur' have long been hubs for user-generated content. UGC communities can be exploited for radicalisation, indoctrination, recruitment, spread false information, sow discord, or manipulate public opinion. Hate speech, violent content, and propaganda can be easily shared and spread within these communities to create echo chambers and confirmation bias. These platforms can be used by terrorists or criminals to

plan attacks, coordinate activities, or share sensitive information. Monitoring and verifying the accuracy of user-generated content to identify potential threats would also be a difficult task. Anonymity or pseudonymity on UGC platforms can make it difficult to identify the source of threats or hold individuals accountable for their actions.

Automated Journalism. 'Robot Journalism,' most controversial examples of emerging technologies, is being used by journalists, content creators, and publishers for interpreting and analysing data to produce content. Automated journalism is also used to test headlines, source information, and identify trending stories. 'The Washington Post' has developed 'Bandito', which provides real-time testing to identify the best performing content and make improvements to stories that do not quite 'hit the mark'.[302] AI-powered algorithms can be manipulated to generate fake news articles or misleading content. Malicious actors could exploit this to spread propaganda, sow discord, or manipulate public perception during critical events.

Local Targeting will Grow - Using location-based targeting helps companies attract local consumers. A common way to find locals is to use geotagging in social media content to reach a target audience. Social media users can search for posts near them, so be sure to add a location to the post. For example, Instagram has location search option. Similarly on Facebook, companies can 'boost a post' and select target locations for the audience to help narrow the reach.[303]

Proliferation of social media platforms and rapid advances in technology, have driven the concept of 'Surveillance Capitalism' and 'Attention Economy' to gain, retain and expand the users' base. To realise their interests and maintain an upper edge, social media players harness tremendous users' data and utilise the same to predict consumers' interests and tailor personalised contents. The intentional design and surveillance-driven business model of social media platforms yield a potent attack surface to be exploited by state and non-state actors. It is assessed that third-party state and non-state actors can leverage social media platforms to 'micro-target' individuals and groups and orchestrate social engineering and information operations. Psychological profiling on social media enables the construction and manipulation of target audiences, which can result in real-world consequences.[304] It needs no emphasis that amidst hybrid threat conundrum, social media ecosystem having gained a critical significance for multi-domain operations, cybercrime, and espionage, has demonstrated its potential to impact entire spectrum of conflicts. It is an established fact that propaganda, intelligence, and influence operations have been the corner stone of military conflicts and campaign planning. In contemporary and future conflicts, owing to massive potential to influence entire spectrum of conflict, social media operations present a unique threat to National Security and society and predicts the impact these operations can have on outcome of future contestation. In the same vein, *Automated Journalism, Decentralized Social Networks, Voice-Based Social Networks, Geo-Social Networking and Metaverse and Virtual Reality, would present an extremely complex security picture.*

Amidst the growing geo-political competition and hybrid threat looming large, India's internal and external security environment is not immune to potential threats of exploitative trends of social media. These threats are not confined to military conflicts alone but transcends to multiple domains in micro (internal), macro (external) and operating environments viz; geo-political, geo-economical, technology, socio-political, socio-cultural and legal. In the contemporary and foreseeable threat scenarios, India's emergence as global geo-political player would be contested by state, non-state and supranational actors in the immediate neighbourhood as well as extended neighbourhood and global arena. While toying with wide range of instruments of power and influence, these actors are leveraging social media and its potential to influence Indian population and strategic leadership. These players driven by their vested interests are also carrying out opinion shaping, narrative building and clouding decision making and rationale thinking ability of leadership and stake holders at multiple levels. The trend would continue to dominate the future conflict matrix. Thus, it is imperative to assess the challenges related to social media to India's national security.

Increasing Influence of Social Media: Threats and Risks to National Security

Lieutenant General SA Hasnain (Retired), in his article titled 'Analysing India's threat spectrum', has thrown light on emerging threats to India's national security in this era of weaponised information space. He argues that *"means of war are in transition and the outlook and doctrines of adversaries are changing, even as technologies are under rapid development. Across the Western border, Pakistan's Army Chief has stated that his country will win the Fifth Generation Warfare (5GW) hybrid conflict without naming the adversary against which the conflict will be fought"*.[305] Fifth generation of warfare defined as 'Battle of perception and information', is considered most dangerous owing to ambiguity, non-detectability and anonymity attached to it. Social media warfare, a low-cost weapon, by virtue of greater reach, affordability of internet and social media platforms and capability to deliver target specific articulated contents is able to alter thought process of target population on sensitive issues. This evolving art of warfighting has demonstrated the potential to discredit national leadership, erode people's trust in institutions and government and mobilise population to create anarchy and chaos. Social media platforms can be breeding grounds for fake news, rumours mongering and disinformation/ misinformation.

In the Indian context, Pakistan has honed the art of propaganda, disinformation and narrative building for decades. ISPR, an organisation created to prosecute 'battle of narratives' and propaganda mongering, has been orchestrating information warfare in J&K for a prolonged period. China, a Northern adversary, has also invested significantly in developing 'Three Warfare Strategy' encompassing 'Media, Psychological and Legal Warfare'. India was confronted with high density information offensive during Doklam and Galwan crisis and in the subsequent period waged by Chinese troll factories and wolf warriors. While, both mainstream adversaries would continue to threaten the India's national security. The non-state actors such as ISIS/ ISKP, IM, SIMI and Terrorists' organisations operating in J&K and North Eastern states would add complexities to Indian nation security paradox. The threats and security risks would cast shadow over the entire spectrum of conflict/competition. These trends of emerging threats and risks are briefly discussed in the succeeding paras.

In the military conflict scenario, Indian security forces deployed in counter insurgency/ counter terrorism operations in Kashmir Valley have been dealing with challenges of propaganda and narrative building curated by terrorists' organisations as well as social media handles operated by ISPR and Pakistan army. These challenges are likely to increase manifold due to Deep Fakes and AI generated content and collusive threat from nexus of hybrid terrorists, separatists' organisations and home grown and foreign terrorists' organisations. Despite, counter campaign by Indian security forces, the nexus can up the ante to fuel discontent and incite local populace against the Indian government. Their battle of narrative, propagated through multitude of social media platforms and internet, may be directed to plant fake stories and distorted facts on contentious issues such as abrogation of Article 370, alleged demographic change, UCC and perceived Hindu superiority. In the recent past these adversarial elements have used fake news, photos and videos, of violence and atrocities committed in other countries, to portray Indian security forces committing HR violation in J&K, Manipur and other parts on countries. These tactics could impact wide section of population and created a negative perception about the Indian government. The fabricated videos, pictures and deep fakes may also be used to portray the security forces and government agencies in negative light and would have potential to create a major security challenge.

The North Eastern Regions may also witness sporadic episodes of unrest and violence over societal divide and tribal issues triggered by adversarial elements through fake news and inflammatory messages spread through social media platforms. These forces may attempt to keep the region embroiled in the internal conflict and instability by keeping the pot boiling over NRC/ NPR, CAA issues.

Terrorist organizations e.g., Troika of ISIS/ ISKP, SIMI and IM and hate-mongering groups can exploit social media to recruit new members, carry out indoctrination, spread propaganda, and radicalise vulnerable individuals. The anonymity, echo chambers and reinforcing cycle created by these groups through Facebook, Twitter (now X), Telegram and YouTube can accelerate the radicalization process. These organisations are likely to mobilise their cadres and sleeper cells in Southern States of India for recruiting misguided youth from vulnerable sections of the community and lure the returnees from Middle East countries to carry out acts of violence in India or join ISIS fighters in other conflict-affected regions in West Asia.

Undisputedly, the digital space would become increasingly vulnerable to varied forms of cyberattacks, viz; ransomware, cyber extortion, cyber espionage and DODS attacks. In recent past, Indian critical infrastructure and financial institutions had come under cyber-attacks carried out by hackers suspected to be of North Korean and Chinese origin. It is assessed that in absence of credible cyber resilience and cyber hardening, these state sponsored hackers and non-state actors may resort to steal sensitive information, disrupt critical infrastructure, and launch disinformation campaigns. The cyber threat would have serious implications for military operations as well as security of critical infrastructures. Indian Startups, MSME, academia, Research Institutes and Public and Private sector units working on niche and futuristics technology development are likely to be most exposed to cyber-attacks carried out to sabotage and steal data.

As per Global Risk Report 2023, India is most threatened country in the world due to fake news and fabricated contents spread online. This report suggest that during ongoing Lok Sabha elections of 2024, Indian public would be under grave threat of narrative building, disinformation operations and 'Algorithm War' unleashed by various inbound and outbound players. Considering India having vast users' base of popular social media platforms such as Facebook, Twitter ('X') and YouTube, reported to be involved in spread of fake news globally, the magnitude of damage caused by social engineering would be grievous and detrimental to national security and social cohesion. In this context, it is pertinent to highlight that social media algorithm, based on predictive analysis of users' content and behavioural patterns, can create filter bubbles and echo chambers confirming their existing beliefs, and exacerbate social polarisation, making it harder for people to have constructive dialogue across ideological divides. The salvo of negativity and misinformation on social media can erode public trust in constitutional and government institutions, legislative, executive, judiciary and media. Such trends may render it difficult for the government to effectively address national security threats. The social engineering and intrusion in ideological space may even pose greater threat to democratic process i.e., elections and interfere with transparent and unbiased public discourses. Amidst the threat looming large on ideological scape, it would become extremely difficult for an unsuspecting and naïve citizen to differentiate between genuine and fabricated messages, which may lead to clouding of opinion. This would pose a significant challenge to national security as inimical forces may try to sow seeds of discord and drive a wedge in the society through fabricated stories.

The social media manipulation has significant potential to adversely impact India's geo-economic interests. As per a study, social media's influence on financial markets has connected the economy in unpredictable ways. Tweets from users with little to no expertise in finance have proven to be capable of triggering a ripple effect on stock value of unrelated companies.[306] The phenomenal cost of fake news on global economy has caused serious concerns for governments, markets and financial institutions. It is appreciated that Indian markets and financial institutions would be exposed to increasing threats of algorithm induced volatility and fluctuation causing substantial financial losses. Various actors may also try to create turbulence and swing opinion of share-holders and investors by planting fabricated and manipulated facts on social media platforms, which may be detrimental to financial health of companies and result in wealth drain. Indian companies may also be targeted by smear campaign by malicious actors with a view to tarnish their global image, ratings and discredit 'Brand India'.

The menace of exploitative trends of social media would also have significant impact at strategic levels in terms of adverse impact on diplomatic relations and strategic decision making by the leaders. It is evident that irresponsible messaging or deliberate online tirade by players with vested interests on issues related to bi-lateral and international relations have had serious consequences resulting into diplomatic crisis and avoidable embarrassment. During Doklam and Galwan Crisis, Balakot Strike, Maldives-India dispute and Israel-Hamas conflict, social media space was taken by storm of tweets and messaging by global audience including Indian citizens. In certain cases, content, tone and tenor of messaging by prominent personalities and public figures polarised the public opinion and triggered violent reactions by netizens and created avoidable friction. It is also emphasised that in this era of digitised world, small incidents become viral in fractions of seconds and are given twist by the opportunist players, thereby leaving little or no reaction time for the leadership and decision makers to carryout fact check for informed decision making. The flooding of digital space by fabricated content makes it difficult for media and political parties to carry out investigation prior to comment on contentious issues in public discourses. Thus, clouded by manipulated content, media and opposition mount pressure on the government, which affords opportunity to malicious actors to gain traction and earn credibility for content promoted by them online.

In view of the challenges and shortcomings of the Indian response mechanism, it is apparent that formulation of robust policies, unified approach and articulation of social media warfare strategy is a time critical task. In addition, various ministries and agencies tackling threat to cognitive space and cyber threat need to operate in unison to carry out constant vigil over information space and detect and neutralise emerging threats. The prevailing threat situation points out that India is facing a multifaceted threat in information space; wherein online radicalisation, polarisation, opinion shaping and social engineering pose a significant challenge to national security. To deter the threat and gear up to deal with future scenario, India needs to adopt a comprehensive approach in the domains of capability building, data regulation policies, organisational reforms and developing indigenous technology. Based on the findings of the study, certain strategies and measures are recommended in next chapter.

Chapter 8

Recommended Strategies and Counter Measures

The trends of escalation of intensity of competitions/ contestations and simultaneous application of all instruments of national power (DIME) in time, purpose and space to seize a competitive edge over the adversaries indicate growing challenges to global peace, stability and security. Amidst prevailing VUCA environment, hybrid warfare encompassing deploying myriad 'Ways and Means', presents a significant threat to security of nation states. It is appreciated that in future conflict scenario, the competitors and collaborators would increasingly exploit potential of non-kinetic means to influence outcome of conflicts. This probably indicate plausibility of information wave rather than human wave in determining the end state by influencing decision making of strategic and operational leadership in various domains. Unarguably, SMPs would act as force multiplier to seize critical space in cognitive domain, trigger social engineering, altering societal fabric and creating decision dilemma. In the back drop of rapidly changing character of war, India faces multi-front wide array of challenges to national security across entire PESTLEM (Political, Economy, Social, Tech, Legal, Environment and Military) construct. In over all threat matrix, social media has emerged as a potent player having capability to influence and impact entire spectrum of conflict and competitions. Owing to fragility of prevailing social, political, information, economic and military conflict situations in India, triggered by various internal and external forces, manipulated social media space is detrimental to national security. Therefore, India needs to initiate and fast track efforts to build credible capability to protect the digital and cognitive space. Measures need to be initiated in multiple verticals and pursued vigorously to achieve desired state of readiness in a time bound manner. Apropos, this study recommends certain measures and strategies related to cyber diplomacy, policy and legal frameworks, organizational structures, social media warfare strategy and technological developments. These measures and strategies are elucidated in the succeeding paragraphs.

Cyber Diplomacy

Global Leadership in Cyber and Social Media Space. India has established the reputation of being vocal on voicing concerns, aspiration and demand for participation of the third world and developing nations in decision making in international forums. In view of influence of social media in matters impacting nation states' internal and external affairs without any attributability, accountability and moral and ethical obligations, it is quintessential to mobilise global opinion to legislate binding rules of engagements (RsOE) for SMPs (Social Media Platforms).

- There is also a need to formulate a comprehensive legal framework to safeguard national interests, address privacy and data protection concerns to obviate catastrophes caused by propaganda mongering and social engineering.

- It is imperative that under UN umbrella, an international appellate body be constituted to monitor and conduct investigation and trials into incidents of manipulation of social media by the state and non-state actors. To be effective as a strong deterrence, it is suggested that such activities be tried as an act of prosecution of hybrid warfare and violation of sovereignty and national security. The perpetrators of hybrid warfare should not be allowed to unleash their tactics against target nations and societies uncontested.

- The parameters laid down by certain supra-national organisation and think tank institutions to determine indices of freedom of speech and citizens' rights have an overarching overhang of Western values and perception. There is a requirement to analyse such issues with perspective and value system of developing and third world countries. The determining parameters of these indices need to be aligned to changing character of conflicts in hybrid threat scenario. It is observed that viewing from an idealist scholarly vantage point, these organisations label such efforts as muzzling discontent and freedom of speech. It may be prudent to invite a debate on this important issue and capture diverse views to formulate broad and pragmatic guidelines to assess performance of nation states in these aspects.

- The steps in this direction may be heavily contested by certain nation states due to their vested interests, however, global peace, security and stability cannot be compromised for commercial interests and to align with skewed perceptions of few nations. Being one of the most affected country due to fake news and propaganda and having largest customer base of social media platforms developed and operated by Western countries, India would have to assume leadership role in generating a global consensus and formulate the laws and regulations governing the functioning of SMPs.

Shaping World's View. India has been a constant target of propaganda and narrative building orchestrated by various state and non-state actors. There have been numerous attempts to peddle lies, sow discord and discredit the government and India's global reputation as largest democracy, credible military power, fast emerging geo-economic players and a nation with diverse culture, religion and values. India's diversity and numerous challenges are not viewed and understood in correct perspective. The skewed perspective shaped by stereo types, colonial hangover coupled with performance assessment indices formulated based on Western values, presumably has led to sub-optimal ratings by various global organisations. Such inconsistent and biased ratings have been referred by various influencers, thinks tanks and scholars as 'Social Proof', to cast aspersions on government's policies, negative portrayal of the country per se and create conformation biases. It needs no emphasis that unsuspecting and impressionable common Indian public, diaspora and even global audiences get influenced by such fabricated narratives and form a biased opinion. In this regard, it is emphasised that while the efforts are directed to become a 'Viksit Bharat', there is an inescapable requirement to dominate this contest of optics by undertaking social media diplomacy to showcase our capabilities and value system and projecting Indian contributions in global affairs. In the recent past, India has proactively engaged global audience through various SMPs to present our perspective and shatter lies and misconception propagated in digital space. In addition, endeavors of Indian Army contingents in UN peace keeping missions, anti-piracy and humanitarian efforts by Indian Navy and strategic airlift and disaster relief operations undertaken by Indian Air Force, should be projected in social media under a well-conceived theme. For instance, large scale deployment of armed forces, such as deployment of eight submarines simultaneously in Indian Ocean Region (IOR), by Indian Navy, should be capitalised to project credibility of India's military might. While the armed forces and Ministry of Defence, would post messages in social media, however the messaging may still not achieve the desired effect on account of limited publicity and viewership. The Ministry of External Affairs (MEA), diplomatic missions and national media should work in concert to give wider publicity to such events in social media and digital media to build a positive narrative, influence greater population and defeat the narrative of adversaries.

Policy and Legal Framework, Organizational Reforms and Technology Development

Cyber and SM Resilience and Vision for 'Viksit Bharat 2047'. Securing a resilient Cyber and Social Media space is critical to realisation of India's vision for 'Amrit Kaal' and 'Viksit Bharat 2047'. The vision of 'Amrit Kaal' aims to embody a technology driven, knowledge based, empowered and inclusive economy with robust public finances and a strong financial sector.[307] In the current economic landscape, e-commerce and fintech are playing a pivotal role in driving India's growth by offering greater opportunities for expansion of business, job creation, efficient supply chain and ensuring transparency. In this endeavour, cyber and social media space act as catalyst for an efficient eco-system to realise economic goals. Assessment of India's performance on Cyber Security Index (GCI) and Cyber Security and National Power index are reminders of capability voids. The current global ranking in the cyber security index (10th in world) and India being placed with 3rd tier countries are not aligned with aspirations to become a world leader. The current capabilities are assessed to be inadequate to thwart threats posed to India's economic interests through digital space. In absence of credible deterrence and punitive measures, Indian economy would continue to be exposed to market manipulation, algorithm induced market turbulence and smear campaign by state and non-state actors with vested interests to discredit Indian companies and cause wealth drain. Thus, it is imperative for India to invest in capacity building in cyber domain and transform the legislative framework to safeguard commercial and economic interests. It should also be included in the key goals laid down to realise vision of 'Viksit Bharat 2047'.

Building Nationwide Consensus. Considering India being placed in 'Third Tier' countries for cyber defence capability and being target of attempts to cause social engineering, opinion shaping and false narrative to sway citizen's opinions, there is a need to build nationwide consensus on safeguarding national security interests and creating a resilient cyber space. In the emerging hybrid threat scenario and weaponisation of social media, we need to accord priority to national security vis-à-vis constitutional right of freedom of speech. The perpetrators of hate speech, fake news and propaganda and false narrative mongers cannot be absolved of their accountability for contents shared/ created/ hosted by them online. It is important to have provisions of punitive actions as these manipulative contents trigger catastrophe in social domain, cause financial losses, fuel unrest and anarchy, erode trust in institutions and may even cause serious damage to nation's global image and dent diplomatic ties. Achieving a shared awareness and common level of understanding is imperative to bring in appropriate legislature on privacy, data protection, instituting oversight and monitoring mechanism. Such an initiative is also necessitated to obviate unnecessary sabre rattling on rights issues, prevent infringement of citizens right to freedom of speech and counter scrutiny and interference by international organisations. To formulate a comprehensive strategy, it is recommended that a collegiate view of cross section of society to include political parties, policy makers, judiciary and legal experts, cyber experts and technocrats, representatives of media (traditional, digital and social media), security agencies, academia, thinks tanks and influential personalities be taken to formulate the policy within the constitutional frame work.

Collective Situational Awareness and Cyber and Social Media Literacy. Considering penetration of social media transcending beyond geographical boundaries, societal confines, diverse demography and strata, it is assessed that social media would continue to be a potent tool to shape and manipulate people's cognitive space and cloud their decision making. There is a need to generate greater awareness amongst Indian citizens about potential threats of social engineering and opinion shaping by adversarial forces. The need is compelling given to fact that majority of population lack awareness about exploitative trends of social media warfare and cannot discern authenticity of online contents. To instil a desired consciousness, there is requirement for multilevel and unidirectional approach at national level to educate diverse generations and cross sections of the society. The range of audience should include Gen X, Gen Millenium, Gen Z and Gen Alpha, rural and urban class, government officials, policy makers and industry as well. It may entail a multipronged-multi level approach to address wide target audience, such as: -

➢ Education on social media usage be conducted in schools and colleges to sensitise and educate the future generation about cyber threats, challenges to emotional and personal health (body shaming, trolling, depression, attention craving) and potential constructive usage for development of society.

➢ Media (Print and Digital) be dovetailed in national efforts to generate greater awareness on threats, bring accountability and attributability, formulate stringent checks for content regulation and develop shared awareness and understanding on challenges related to unabated social media exploitation.

➢ Government officials especially those dealing with policy formulation and national security matters be trained in cyber security and social media warfare. There is a need to create robust cyber defence mechanism to thwart attempts to encroach upon the nation's digital space. It is suggested that certain crucial ministries such as defence, home affairs, external affairs, information and technology, finance, commerce and law to be provided a well-trained social media and cyber watch team. The teams be tasked to carryout 24x7 surveillance over the digital space to discern, detect and deter the attempts in respective domains through digital space threatening national interests.

Amendment to Personal Data Protection Bill 2023. The provisions of data protection bill should be reviewed and legal gaps should be addressed in a comprehensive manner. The current bill does not explicitly address the challenges posed by social media. The aim of amended bill should be to protect privacy and data of the citizens and build adequate safeguards to address national security concerns without infringing upon citizens' constitutional rights. An institutionalised discussion be held with IT specialists, social media representatives, political parties, legal experts, academia and youths to consider alternate views and formulate a balanced policy frame work. It would dispel the apprehensions of environment, facilitate a vibrant and free exchange of ideas and views on regulation of social media platforms. Such an initiative would also act as deterrent against any attempt to spread rumours, propaganda and manipulation of information space. The comprehensive Data Protection Bill with provisions for appropriate penal actions would deny manoeuvre space to offenders and foreclose avenues for circumventing legal framework.

Develop Credible Capability to Counter Emerging Threats. World is currently in the midst of third technological revolution or digital revolution and gradually transitioning to era of internet 3.0 through adaption of emerging technologies such as blockchain, semantic web and artificial intelligence. Currently world is still struggling to deal with challenges posed by unregularized and uncontrolled exploitation of social media by state and non-state actors alike. The emergence of Metaverse, Virtual Reality, NFTs, Decentralised and Voice Based Social Networks, AI enabled Social Media and Robotic Journalism on the horizon predicts future threats to cognitive space. Thus, it imperative that necessary provisions be made in social media regulation and ethics policy to address existing challenges as well as lay down RsOE for futuristic trends of the technology. In addition, Government of India should collaborate with start-ups and Indian IT sector to develop effective indigenous tools and technology for social media trends analysis, content filtering, identify dangerous/ malicious contents and thwart challenges in social media space.

Roll out National Cyber Security Strategy and Social Media Regulation Policy. To ensure transparency, data protection, address privacy concerns and create a cyber resilient digital space, India should roll out National Cyber Security Strategy drafted under the aegis of National Security Council Secretariate (NSCS). The draft strategy has already been presented to Parliament in 2022, however promulgation of this strategy is pending for Government's approval. During this research, it was learnt that India has not yet drafted a Social Media Regulation Policy and Social Media Warfare Strategy. While framing Social Media Warfare (SMW) Strategy, overall responsibility may be assigned to NSCS for unified approach and greater coordination amongst all stake holders. The SMW Strategy may spell out national vision and objective, give strategic direction, lay down role and responsibilities. Based on PESTLEM and COG analysis of target entity, it may also define broad contours of SM themes and narratives, assign tasks for executing campaign for specific inbound/ outbound target audience and carryout SM Intelligence collation and sharing. It is also assessed that in consultation with experts in legal and constitutional matters, industry representatives, cyber experts and political parties, Government of India should roll out Social Media Regulation Policy. The policy should define fake news, propaganda (radical propaganda and contents endangering national security) and potential social engineering contents. The policy and regulation should take into consideration social media platforms' 'statement of rights and responsibilities' or 'community guidelines'. It is important for central government to work with state governments to help define 'dangerous content', to ensure that frameworks are universal in nature, without taking into account nature of localised conflicts. By working together with a cross section of state governments and civil society groups, the government can set agenda on what constitutes safe versus dangerous content, with controlled risk of bias mitigated among a variety of stake holders.[308]

Unified Approach and Synergy of Efforts. Efforts directed to contain influence of propaganda, fake news, narrative building and social engineering should be coordinated at national level and executed in a decentralised way at multiple levels in concert with regional dynamics and vulnerabilities identified. The information sharing should be done in real time horizontally and vertically, and procedures should be refined to remove bureaucratic hurdles. Though, roles and responsibilities of various agencies have already been laid down to deal with threats to internal security in cyber space and prosecute counter operations against hostile state and non-state actors. The synergised approach and unified strategy would facilitate threat mitigation more effectively during conflicts with our Northern and Western adversaries, and prevent conflict escalation and exploitation of critical vulnerabilities.

Dynamic Response Strategy and Counter Radicalisation Policy. Based on centre of gravity (COG) analysis and threats assessment, the government should evolve a dynamic response strategy to prosecute social media warfare to guard own critical vulnerabilities in multiple domains. The strategy should also encompass carrying out aggressive social media operations to exploit vulnerabilities and weaknesses of the adversaries so as to maintain a competitive edge. Measures should be instituted to gauge effectiveness of strategy in the realm of rapid technological developments and tactics adopted by adversarial forces encompassing state and non-state actors.

> ➤ Considering involvement of educated and rich families/individuals in web of terror and indoctrination, it is felt that India needs a dynamic National Counter Radicalisation policy dealing with host of factors including motivation and catalysts for radicalisation. The policy should also address potential breeding grounds due to unemployment, poverty and lack of education. Apart from returnees from West Asian countries, the policy should also monitor locals who are vulnerable to radicalisation through madrassas, preaching by radicals like Dr Zakir Naik and easily accessible online indoctrination material. India needs to institute

effective measures to counter fake news and online propaganda through social awakening, community out-reach programs and ground action by the government agencies. A pro-active role by government, educational institutions, civil society, media and intellectuals to push their narrative amongst youth/ society is of vital importance, which should focus on prevention and controlling the radicalisation by elements driven vested interests.

> The broad contours of comprehensive and effective 'counter radicalisation' policy to address the growing menace of religious fanatism, virtual indoctrination and radicalisation. The policy should encompass continuous monitoring of digital space to detect radicalised content hosted online and content regulation and removal in coordination with social media platforms. Simultaneously, efforts should be made to identify vulnerable sections of the society and individuals who have already been indoctrinated by various terrorists' and separatist organisations. State governments, religious institutions and influential public figures should form part of the 'de-radicalisation teams' to sensitise, educate and counsel impressionable youth and individuals who have become victims to such tactics and assist them to return to the main stream.

Creation of 24x7 Social Media Analytics Centre (SMAC). The project to constitute Social Media Analytics Centre under Ministry of Communication and Information Technology should be accorded due impetus. The agency should be staffed with personnel trained in Cyber Security, Data Analytics, Artificial Intelligence and Social Media Analysis tools and be tasked to carry out round the clock surveillance over internet and traffic on various social media platforms. The project undertaken by Government of India to create a team of 5,00,000 cyber security experts over next five years can be leveraged to create a pool of experts in domain of social media analytics. It is assessed that staff selected to work with SMAC should have requisite technological competence as well as should be well versed with regional dynamics. To achieve requisite domain expertise, SMAC should carry out detailed study of history, demographic profile, past and current trends of violence, agitation and external influences, sentiments and sensitivities of local population and clientele base of popular social media platforms. The team should discern under currents/ pattern of activities and trends of social media chatter, identify offensive contents/ hostile accounts, target fake accounts, using algorithms and artificial intelligence and take proactive actions for content regulation/ removal or banning the accounts as per law and policies. The information about social media manipulation, fake news, radicalisation, indoctrination and any plan to incite violence and unrest and mobilise the cadres by adversarial forces, collated by SMAC should be shared with concerned ministries, agencies and armed forces to initiate appropriate response. It is also recommended that SMAC should collaborate with private sector entities having expertise in sentiment and content analysis of online communication for jointly undertaking such projects including indigenously developing social media analytics tools.

Coordination with Social Media Platforms. Presently, none of the social media platforms have located their servers in India and all users' related data is being stored in their off-shore servers. This has led to confrontation between SMP companies and Government of India on matters related to content removal, differing opinion about hostile/ dissenting contents. It is recommended that these companies should be pursued to establish micro-research centres in India to carryout detailed study of the region-specific social science and internal dynamics. It would help them to develop a tacit understanding of hostile content and dissenting voices and customise their content regulation policies in concert with peculiarities of conflict prone states of India. It would also facilitate better coordination between state law enforcement agencies, central intelligence agencies, security forces and SMPs. Government should relentlessly pursue the SMPs to locate their servers in India to address the concerns related to data protection and privacy.

Developing Indigenous Social Media Platforms. The exponential growth of clientele base of social media platforms has translated into corresponding influence of these platforms in shaping decision making in global affairs. In the contemporary geo-political scenario, social media platforms have significantly impacted economies, business, politics, and even military operations. There is a growing belief that one who rules the data and decision making would rule the world. Presently, most popular social media platforms viz; Facebook, WhatsApp, YouTube, Telegram, Twitter (X) etc are controlled predominantly by US based/ Western firms. Realising potential of social media platforms, China launched its own search engine and social media platforms such as Weibo, WeChat, Baidu and Taobao to control digital space and regulate online communication. Similarly, Russia has its own search engine and indigenous social media platforms, which are used by majority of Russian population post ban on Facebook and Twitter by the government. Indian companies had also launched some social media apps such as 'Koo', however, platform could not sustain amidst tough market competition. It is recommended that Government of India should encourage Indian companies and start-ups to develop and launch technologically sustainable and economically viable social media platforms for Indian and global clientele. To achieve tangible results, the government may consider providing financial aid for R&D and render necessary assistance to create an eco-system for innovation and growth of start-ups. It would challenge dominance of western social media firms in Indian digital space and contain external influences over the cognitive space. To allay fears of censorship by government and infringement on freedom of speech, the government may institute an autonomous body to ensure protection of citizens' rights and personal data, transparency in content regulation by SMPs and prevent monopoly of private players. The core body may have representation from central and state governments, industry, legal and constitution experts, cyber experts, parliamentarians and judiciary.

Indigenous Cloud Infrastructure -   Presently, social media platforms operating in India have their servers and cloud infrastructure located offshore. Resultantly, Indian law enforcement and regulatory bodies have lesser control over data usage. There are also concerns about data privacy and its potential misuse, especially for extracting sensitive information. The data on these servers might be governed by laws of the country where servers are located. There is always an apprehension that users' data stored on these offshore servers could be accessed by foreign governments for surveillance, enforcing content regulation and censorship and disruption in the event of conflicts. Further, in absence of indigenous cloud infrastructure, Indian origin SMPs as well as Western SMPs would have dependence over cloud/ servers located abroad. Therefore, it is recommended that Government should provide funds and encourage Indian companies to develop indigenous servers and cloud infrastructure.

Regularise Fact Check Units (FCUs). Recently, the Government of India issued a notification to constitute 'Fact Check Units (FCUs)' under Information Technology (Intermediary Guidelines and Digital Media Ethics Code) Amendment Rules 2023 (IT Amendment Rules 2023). Establishment of FCUs has been planned under Press Information Bureau to identify fake news related to 'business' of Union Government on social media platforms. The government has justified creation of entity stating that statutory mechanism was found inadequate to combat viral dissemination of false content. However, on 21 March 2024, the honourable

Supreme Court of India has stayed government notification on this issue. The stay will remain in place till Honourable Bombay High Court finally decides validity of Information Technology (Intermediary Guidelines and Digital Media Ethics Code) Amendment Rules 2023 under constitutional provisions. The government notification came under criticism on account of timing of notification just prior to Lok Sabha elections 2024 and violation of constitutional right to freedom of speech. In opinion of journalists, it implies that only central government would have monopoly over the truth and sole judge and arbiter of its own affairs.[309] In this regard, it is recommended that government should reach out to all stake holders viz; political parties, state governments, judiciary, Editor Guild of India, social media platforms and legal experts to arrive at consensus. The initiative would address their concerns, generate consensus and formulate a comprehensive policy to ensure transparency, protection of constitutional right of freedom of speech, procedure to be adopted to carry out fact check and options for appeal mechanism against the orders of FCUs.

Social Media Warfare

Broadened Horizon of Social Media Listening and Social Media Intelligence Gathering. It is suggested that scope of social media listening and intelligence gathering should be enhanced to cover micro and macro environment. The strategy should be to deploy eyes and ears on internet and deep dark net to detect trends and viral narratives on multiple social media platforms. A well trained and technically proficient unified task force manned by best brains be tasked to leverage social media warfare strategy and tactics to gain valuable information, discern early indicators and viral content having potential to foment unrest in conflict regions in country. The strategy should also encompass discreet surveillance to identify accounts and bots suspected to be involved in astroturfing and amplification of fabricated messages.

Formulate Net Trolls Strategies. The global war of narratives aimed to shape perceptions occupies core of 'Net-Trolls Strategies'; a relatively new phenomenon in the context of international security. According to subject matters experts, 'Net-Trolls' are designed to initiate discussions and invite comments to discern contents deemed offensive or detrimental to the nation states, organisations and peoples and trigger counter trolls to overwhelm net space by friendly and supportive views. The tactics is an integral part of China's propaganda strategy. The data suggests that social media handlers sponsored by Chinese government fabricate and post about 448 million social comments a year, the figures may have increased manifold in the recent times.[310] Similarly, Russia has also reportedly developed advanced net-trolls strategies to secure its geopolitical and information space. Israeli Defence Force (IDF), learning from its shortcomings observed against information and psychological operations conducted by Hezbollah during 2006 Lebanon war, was trend setter in leveraging social media, as a force multiplier on the battlefield. The lessons learnt during Lebanon War in 2006 and adaptation of social media in overall campaign strategy by IDF set an example that has been emulated by armed forces of many countries. For instance, militaries of USA and UK have created 'Special Social Media Division', to engage in unconventional warfare in information age; activities of these entities though shrouded in secrecy, conducts online influence campaigns, countering disinformation, promoting certain narratives, and/ or engaging with foreign audiences. The operating environment of Indian Armed Forces is extremely complex and challenging. In contemporary scenario, advent of online activism, radicalisation, mobilisation and recruitment for anti-national outfits and battle of narrative waged on social media platforms have compounded the challenges of armed forces manifold. The emerging threat to national security demands that Indian Armed Forces enmesh social media in their campaign strategy to seize initiative, carry out round the clock surveillance over the internet and deep dark net, aggressively dominate cognitive space by engaging hostile home bound and foreign actors and neutralise challenges/ threats at an early stage. This may require legal mandate given through appropriate constitutional provisions, budgetary allocation for creation of potent force of social media and cyber warriors, upskilling, strategic direction and unified command to synergize the operations.

Social Media Warfare Strategy. In the present context, there is no document available in open domain notified as official version of 'Social Media Warfare Strategy'. Thus, it may not be incorrect to infer that despite being the target of weaponised social media tactics, India has not yet formulated/ declared a strategy for 'Social Media Warfare'. In fact, term 'Hybrid Warfare' itself has not gained significant attention of scholars, strategists and policy makers. Exploitation of social media during Russia-Ukraine and Hamas-Israel conflict to shape global opinion, create dilemma for decision makers and for precision targeting of Russian location due to geo tagging highlights the need to dovetail social media in the strategic planning to dominate the contested zones. It is recommended that social media warfare be coordinated and orchestrated at national level. Strategy be formulated to streamline roles and responsibilities of various ministries, intelligence agencies and Armed Forces so as to continuously monitor contested cognitive space throughout the blurred boundaries of peace and war periods. Based on study of various recent conflicts and modus operandi of state and non-state actors, the study suggests an approach towards strategy formulation: -

> *Institute Monitoring and Surveillance Mechanism.* Create a national level architecture to monitor and carry out surveillance over social media landscape. The step would facilitate better coordination and orchestration of 'Whole-of-Nation' efforts to thwart social media warfare waged by the adversarial forces and carry out retaliatory/ pre-emptive strike as per overall grand national strategy.

> *Mandate for SM Campaigns.* To ensure explicit demarcation of jurisdiction, better coordination and earmark 'First Responders' to threats in digital space including cyber and social media, there is a need to issue a clear mandate for various agencies. It is recommended that military strategists, policy makers and experts in legal and constitutional matters be taken on board to chalk out legal mandate and lay down jurisdiction for three services, DyCA, state police, and other security agencies. The legal mandate should lay down responsibilities of all stake holders to carry out counter propaganda operations and undertake social media listening and intelligence gathering in their respective areas of operations. This step would facilitate high degree of preparedness to tackle persistent threats, effective counter of negative propaganda, and narrative building operations as well as seamless surveillance over digital space.

> *Identify Hotspots/ Vulnerabilities.* There is a need to carry out a detailed study of regional dynamics and societal issues/ legacies having potential to impact peace and stability in conflict prone/ stricken states and regions in India. In coordination with think tanks, academia, social scientists and experts on security matters, the government can identify hot spots and driving factors which can be exploited by adversarial forces to foment unrest and anti-India sentiments. The government agencies can do a detailed trend analysis to discern tactics used by inimical elements to exploit the critical vulnerabilities and manipulate public sentiments through fabricated social media contents and propaganda. The institutionalized knowledge base can facilitate design of own

counter strategy and build a narrative to discredit negative narrative building.

- *Multi Domain Target Profiling.* Next practical step could be to form inter-ministerial teams with domain expertise in diverse verticals to identify potential targets in respective domains which can be attacked using social media warfare tactics. The list can be shared on 'Need to Know Basis' with other ministries for shared situational awareness. Towards this direction, NIA, National Technical Research Organisation (NTRO_ and other intelligence and law enforcement agencies can be tasked to design narratives and strategize in concert with their mandated roles and responsibilities. The security forces, para military forces and police deployed in the conflict regions/ states such as J&K, Manipur, Assam, Nagaland may consider to constitute region specific teams to carryout continuous 'Social Listening' of online chatter to discern local sentiments, trends of social engineering and opinion shaping, stereo types, threats and targets. The teams should be comprised of best brains with expertise in social science, cyber and social media. The teams may be employed to develop innovative and genuine themes, contents and narratives to denounce lies and fake news and spread the truth in concert with overall strategy.

- *Embedded Social Media Warriors.* During annexation of Crimea in 2014, the Russian government spent more than $19 million to fund 600 people to constantly comment on news articles, write blogs, and operate social media campaign.[311] On similar lines, India security forces, intelligence agencies and state government machinery can plan for 'embedded social media warriors' (young passionate minds, social scientists, content creators, technocrats, IT professionals and ethical hackers). These allied/ hired professionals can be tasked for 'influencer role' for developing themes and contents. These embedded SM warriors should form part of Indian ecosystem mandated to engage wide range of demography by uploading stories, parody, rap songs, memes, photos, blogs/ vlogs and opinions resonating with feelings and sentiments on multiple social media platforms.

- *Tactics and Tools.* The response tactics can be multifold i.e. troll farming, hashtag hijacking and astroturfing to expose lies, propaganda and fake news, spread facts through genuine contents supported by social proofing. The spread of lies and propaganda can be countered by persuading SMPs for removal of hostile contents and banning anonymous and fake accounts. It is important to note that manipulated contents can influence wide range of population. Removal of hostile/ objectionable content and banning of account may facilitate limited damage control, however, large section of society would continue to carry perception created by narrative building. Thus, it is imperative to create an 'amplification eco-system' of multiple accounts (genuine, hybrid, bots), content creators, social media influencers, opinion shapers and local social activists who should be able to provide desired traction to genuine and fact-based counter narrative in digital space. Simultaneously, embedded SM warriors should operate in close coordination with security personnel deployed in conflict prone/ insurgency infested areas. The aim should be to gauge impact of perception management campaign underaken by security forces on the target population, feel pulse of population and discredit negative reporting and narrative painting by inimical elements and sympathizers of anti-national forces. Meanwhile, the security forces may constitute their own SM cells manned by personnel equipped with requisite skills to upload stories and contents giving a grass root perspective through multiple accounts. These cells created at successive levels of command chain to simultaneously upload genuine content through multiple accounts of security forces, SM warriors, pro-Indian locals and netizens. This 'Kill by Volume Tactics' (Brigading Tactics) would flood digital space with viral contents showcasing hues of truth. It would also gain significant traction on multiple social media sites owing to content supported by social proofing and testimonials. The genuine content would gain confidence of intellectuals, prominent public figures and even 'Plain Folks' and expose the adversary's designs.

➤ *Social Listening, Data Analysis and Targeting.* Based on socio-cultural analysis and 'Social Media Analytics Tools', dedicated monitoring mechanism established by security forces and intelligence agencies can discern stereotypes, carryout sentiment analysis, identify influential actors and their pattern of operations and formulate social media targeting strategies. To achieve desired objectives and end states, these dedicated cells created at successive levels of command with subject matter experts handling the regional desks can gather insights and data from 'social listening' over the communication on social media platforms. By using social listening tools, such as Clarabridge, HubSpot, Lately, Sprout Social and Hootsuit,[312] these dedicated teams can monitor conversations on social media and understand reactions. Social listening would provide understanding of impact of campaigns, narrative and themes and help in discerning aspiration of environment/ target population. Akin to marketing strategies of companies, these cells can use tailored hashtags and relevant keywords in social media feeds to see the results. It would also facilitate in specific targeting/ engagement of audiences with diverse demographic and socio-cultural background.

> *Anti-Propaganda Strategy.* Teams formed for 'social media listening' and 'social media intelligence' gathering can be deployed to identify early signs of social engineering. These teams can also be employed to detect attempts to sow discord in society by adversarial elements, discern online behavioral patterns and shortlist accounts propagating propaganda mongering. These teams can be effectively employed for proactive attack on online *'Troll Campaigns'.* Proactive measures would defeat the propaganda and false news and avert any potential crises in country.

> *Content Design and Targeting.* Region specific themes, social media content and narrative be designed in concert with ground conditions viz; demography, ideology, societal fissures/ vulnerabilities and socio-cultural and sentiment analysis. The messages be carefully carved to *target vulnerability of target audience and discredit ideology* binding target population and acting as driving force. The leadership at various levels should constantly review the impact of strategy as per evolving grand picture.

- Sentiment analysis is the technique of using natural language processing, machine learning, and text analytics to identify and extract emotional tone, attitude, and opinion of users from social media posts, comments, reviews, and feedback. Sentiment analysis can help in developing understanding of feelings and emotions of audience towards narratives, local issues and concerns, and how their sentiments change over time or across different channels.[313]

- In this regard, AI can be leveraged to automate and optimize various aspects of social media data analytics, such as data collection, cleaning, processing, analysis, visualization, or reporting. AI can also help to enhance and personalize social media experience, such as content creation, curation, recommendation, or delivery platforms.

- Based on detailed analysis and review of situation, contents (memes, jokes, rap songs, parody, memes, videos, tweets, stories, hashtags) should form part of weaponry to engage audiences of different age groups, strata and wide range of domains. The content can be uploaded on multiple social media platforms (Facebook, Twitter ('X'), YouTube, Telegram, Instagram, Reditt) depending upon clientele base for maximum traction and visibility.

- For example, teams deployed in J&K can create content to promote diverse religious ideologies and rich cultural heritage, development initiatives, infrastructure development, employment generation and progress in education fields. The facts related to current economic disparity, government apathy, hardships, lack of infrastructure and suppression of dissent by locals in Pakistan occupied Kashmir can be highlighted to influence opinion of Kashmiri population.

➢ *Develop Inhouse Influencer Analytics Tools.* There is a need to gauge the impact of content uploaded on the social media platforms in countering the narrative of adversarial elements. The assessment may also help in revisiting own strategy so as to achieve optimum traction and make perceptible change in attitude and beahaviour of people. 'Influencer Analytics' is the process of measuring and evaluating performance, impact, and ROI of campaigns on social media platforms. Influencer analytics can identify and select right influencers, based on their relevance, reach, engagement, authenticity, and trustworthiness. Influencer analytics can also assist in tracking and comparing results and outcomes of influencer collaborations and contents, awareness, acceptability, and optimize influencer strategy accordingly.[314] This is found to be a valuable trend because it provides measurable insights into the impact of influence campaigns. It allows tracking of key performance indicators (KPIs) like engagement rates, reach, and conversion rates. This data-driven approach helps in identifying effective influencers, optimizing strategies, and maximizing ROI. It also enables informed decisions, build authentic content which resonates with the target audience.[315] It is recommended that DRDO to undertake initiative along with private sector and IT incubation hubs to develop indigenous SM influencer analytical tools and create SM monitoring boards at appropriate levels.

- ➤ *Develop Niche Capabilities.* The services need to invest in niche IT technology to contain negative influence of social media and leverage its features to gain and maintain competitive advantage over adversary. It is recommended that *customized 'Large Language Models (LLM)' be procured/ developed for carrying out 'Sentiment Analysis'* of social media contents to discern patterns of under current. Creation of *'social media analysis board and world cloud'* using various application would assist in a great way in this regard.

- ➤ *Defeating False News and Social Engineering.* Synergised multi agency operations can facilitate identification of accounts and actors involved in spreading rumours, false news and social engineering. To defeat nefarious designs, social media teams can be tasked to forecast potential future events and narrow down on actors who may resort to *hashtag hijacking and rage farming* and creating *'echo chambers and confirmation biases'*. The security agencies should be able to pick up such trends and launch counter campaigns. To turn the tables, we need to bolster the capability to engage the target population through various tactics such as *'amplification'* through multiple accounts, bots and *'Astroturfing'*.

- ➤ *Surveillance of Advance Persistent Threat (APT).* Amidst growing tension with China, Indian companies, institutes and media outlets have been targets of increased cyber-attacks from *Advance Persistent Threat* groups. APT 40/ 41 are reportedly state sponsored groups who have been carrying out cyber attacks in India. The involvement of the group was also reported in Bhima Koregaon case. Though, involvement of APT 40 has not been reported in peddling of false news, narrative building and propaganda, however possibility of the group being complicit in any such misadventure in future cannot be ruled out. Therefore, it is imperative that government agencies keep a constant vigil on activities of the group in digital space and develop capabilities to counter the threat.

- ➤ *Strategic Deterrence and Coercion.* It is assessed that in this era of weaponised information space, it is imperative to adopt a proactive and aggressive stance to counter threats posed to national security through disinformation campaigns, fake news, narrative building and social engineering carried out by external forces. Realising trends and extent of interference by external actors in India's internal affairs and endeavours to stunt India's growing global influence, it becomes quintessential to take cognizance of these challenges and accordingly align own strategies. The gravity of security situation and emerging threat dynamics have left India with no other option than to acquire credible deterrence capability in social media space. The strategic deterrence and coercion should entail exploiting vulnerabilities of hostile actors, discredit and undermine their influence by penetrating their ideological support base and sow distrust amongst their followers. It also mandates shaping and dominating global information space, present alternate truth to global audience, refute fake claims and narratives and decimate potential challenge/ threat at an early stage. Thus, situation demands that India should extend envelope of fight against intrusion in its cognitive space to home turf of adversaries in external environment. In this regard, suggested organogram of these proposed cells and recommended measures as follows: -

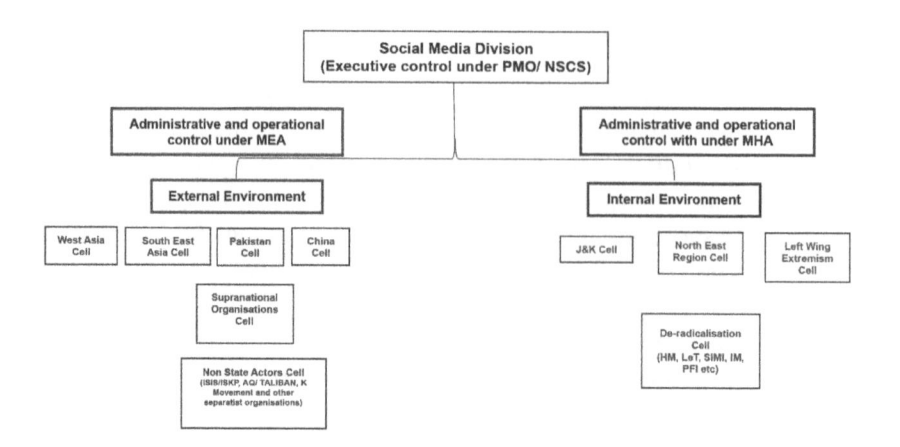

Figure 44 – Proposed Social-Media Division
(Suggested organisation is author's personal view)

Recommended Strategies and Counter Measures

- Scope of India's influence operations and social media warfare campaigns be enhanced beyond Pakistan. India should build credible capabilities to orchestrate effective information operations and dominate and shape cognitive space of China as well as other state and non-state actors and supranational organisations covertly or overtly nursing anti-India feelings.

- Target audience of social media warfare should include hostile actors (state and non-state) and ecosystem of their sympathisers, followers and proxies. Target profiling should preferably address threats in both conventional and unconventional domains.

- Dedicated cells be tasked to develop in-depth domain knowledge of their designated targets in India's external environment (both state and non-state actors, organisations etc,). Build explicit understanding of their modus operandi, tactics and identify organisations, social media accounts and bots supporting and advancing their operations. Focus be laid on developing strategies to eliminate threats and create challenges for India's traditional adversaries as well as other countries which generally have anti-India stance or likely to be coerced by adversaries to strangulate or isolate India geo-politically.

- Foreign extremist organisations, hardliners and terrorists' organisations such as ISIS/ ISKP, Taliban, K-movement outfits etc, should also be included in the target list.

- Develop competencies to leverage coercive tactics through social media viz; microtargeting, doxing, fear psychosis, emotional manipulation and isolation, echo chambers, conformation bias and astroturfing.

- Create themes and narratives to exploit divisions, ideological rifts and vulnerabilities of hostile targets. The verticals wherein social media campaigns may be directed to create vulnerabilities can be politics, economy, societal structure, internal and external security and diplomacy.

- Create self-sustaining ecosystem for own social media warfare campaign. Ecosystem for strategic deterrence and coercion through social media may include, diplomats, intelligence agencies, intelligentsia, IT experts, historians, economists, social scientists, and defence forces. This support system can execute their operations through an intricate web of real, hybrid, fake, anonymous, pseudo anonymous accounts, bots and hashtags.

- The objective of these campaign could be to fan anti-establishment & separatists' ideology amongst audience in target nation/ organization, erode trust of target population in their leadership and support people's demands for equality, social justice, autonomy and opportunities. Economic coercion, political isolation and grassroot movement against government unjust policies can also be manifested through aggressive social media campaigns.

- Most importantly, objectives of social warfare strategy would conform to grand strategy formulated to project India's global image, enhance geo-political influence, align national diplomacy manoeuvre and protect national security objectives.

- *Suggested Themes.* The themes of social media warfare strategy are suggested as under: -

    - Draw analogy between challenges faced by India due to terrorism, spread of fanatic and extremist ideology and influx of Rohingya immigrants with refugee crisis and hate crimes associated with immigrants witnessed by western world.

    - Relate K-movement, terrorists' organization operating in J&K and North Eastern states with ideology of various hardliner outfits operating in EU nations, USA and other conflict-stricken countries.

    - Highlight plight of people in Baluchistan and Pakistan occupied Kashmir.

    - Expose predatory practices of Western and Chinese corporates and think tank organisations.

    - Promote idea of strategic autonomy, equality, and respect of values and traditions of countries in Global South.

- Interference in democracy and electoral process (through fake news, narrative building and propaganda as witnessed in run up to Lok Sabha elections in 2024) be challenged on account of denial of political rights and right to self-determination and erosion of sanctity of Indian constitution and democratic institutions.

• Based on the anlaysis of social media warfare strategy of various state and non-state actors engaged in ongoing contestation globally, a flow chart depicting suggested ecosystem for India's campaign is as under: -

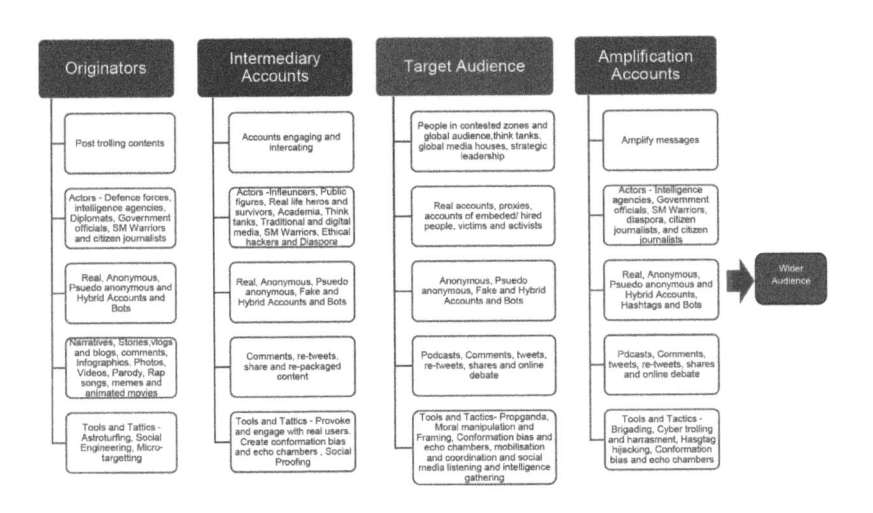

Figure 45 - Suggested Ecosystem of Social Media Warfare Campaign – External Environment

Conclusion

Despite there being a lack of unanimity over the concept of Hybrid Warfare amongst think tanks, academia and military strategists, this war-fighting concept prevails over all ongoing conflicts and competitions. It may be inferred that hybrid warfare blurs the distinction between peace and war, blends political warfare and conventional warfare to shape behaviour of adversary. Under ambit of hybrid warfare, all *instruments of national power are unleashed simultaneously across the spectrum of conflict with unified strategy. It entails involvement of state and non-state actors operating in synergy to achieve the desired end state.* The study of ongoing conflicts and contestations reveals that state and non-state actors prosecuting hybrid warfare endeavour to make an effective use of propaganda, psychological operations and disinformation/ misinformation campaigns to wage 'Battle of Narratives'. This strategy aims to dominate cognitive space, break the will of adversary to fight and influence decision making by leadership at all levels and cloud opinion of public. The study of geo-political and military contestations across the globe suggests that hybrid warfare would dominate the entire spectrum of future conflicts. In the backdrop of trends of hybrid warfare, the state and non-state actors would in fact progressively refine and evolve their war fighting strategies and dovetail emerging technologies to gain and maintain domination over the critical contested space. Exploiting global reach, absence of low level barriers and anonymity, various actors, have innovatively used social media in tandem with kinetic and non-kinetic means to prosecute the hybrid wars.

It is evident that these actors have exploited social media platforms and internet to propagate the propaganda campaign, circumvent scrutiny of government, international watch dog organisations and law enforcement agencies. Through carefully curated customised narrative and contents, these actors have engaged wide range of target population effectively and swiftly and triggered mass mobilization leading to unrest, agitations and violence. 'Arab Spring Revolution', 'Russia-Ukraine Conflict and 'Israel-Hamas Conflict' are an apt testimony. In Indian context also, social media platforms have been used by cohort of inimical actors to spread disinformation, plant fabricated narratives and spread extremists/ separatist ideology to vitiate cognitive space and mobilise public sentiments in conflict prone regions.

In future conflict scenarios also, the trend of exploitative use of 'social media' to influence ideological landscape, cripple decision making and manipulate opinion of target population would continue. In fact this 'New Normal' is likely to gain traction in foreseeable future. Popular SMPs Facebook, Twitter ('X'), YouTube, Telegram and Instagram would be exploited increasingly to plant fabricated contents targeting Indian populace. Considering reach and capability of these SMPs to disseminate messages swiftly and at mass scale, these platforms would become a tool of coercion, indoctrination and social engineering for India's conventional competitors i.e., Pakistan and China as well as non-state actors viz; Hizbul Mujahidin, Jaish-e-Mohammad, Lashkar-e-Toiba, ISIS/ISKP, Indian Mujahidin, Students Islamic Movement of India and Popular Front of India.

It is established that impact of social media warfare amidst hybrid threat environment would not be confined to war time scenario or military domain only; the Indian national security would continue to be threatened throughout peace and war time and ripple effects would be multi-domain. The menace of social media warfare would pose a significant threat to national security in political, military, socio-political and legal domains. To curb this menace and thwart threats to national security, there is a requirement for paradigm shift in our national security strategy. Policy makers and security establishment need to take cognisance of growing threats and affect changes in policy, procedures, skill development of personnel dealing with portfolios related with national security and ambiguity and ensure seamless cooperation between multiple agencies and ministries.

The shortcomings and challenges of existing policy framework and organisations and strategies to develop competencies to deal with complex security scenario have been deliberated in this study. Broadly, it is recommended that Government of India should come out with a comprehensive data protection and social media regulation policies to safeguard national interests and insulate information sphere from external influences. It would be pragmatic that such policies be introduced post discussion with cyber and legal experts, political parties, industry representatives, judiciary and media. While implementing the policy, constitutional rights of freedom of speech and democratic values should be upheld without compromising national security. Unveiling long pending National Cyber Security Strategy and formulation of Social Media Warfare Strategy would be an important step towards ensuring cyber and cognitive autonomy.

India should also leverage blooming start-ups, micro, small and medium enterprises and IT sector to develop indigenous software, SMPs and analytical tools to detect and discern the online behavioural trends. This technological ecosystem can also be leveraged to initiate pre-emptive measures to foil any attempt by adversarial forces to exploit vulnerabilities and socio-political sensitivities. There is a need for unified strategy and response mechanism encompassing involvement of all agencies dealing with national security to carry out 24x7 monitoring of social media space, social media intelligence gathering, discern patterns and signs of narrative building, real time information sharing and take commensurate actions. This would necessitate creation of an inter-ministerial, inter agency and multi domain agency tasked to prosecute social media warfare to defeat anti-India agenda.

The analysis of incidents of social engineering indicates that narrative building and themes are crafted carefully taking into consideration various dimensions of human psychology. These narratives and fabricated contents are designed for specific target demography and propagated through multitude of direct and indirect vectors on various social media platforms. Thus, it can be deduced that formulation of social media strategy necessitates blending of human psychology, art of content creation, technological expertise and tactical acumen. Therefore, it is recommended that India should invest in preparing a team of experts in domains of social science, regional dynamics, technology, human psychology, legal matters and military operations to prepare a comprehensive strategy and lead coordinated operations to dominate the digital space.

Amidst challenges of social engineering and narrative building, the Indian army should consider dedicated social media task force assigned to monitor social media chatter and discern under currents. The teams should have in-depth knowledge of conflict prone regions and be able to formulate an effective social media strategy and discredit negative perception shaping.

In this context, it is suggested that future studies be undertaken in domains of socio-political analysis of conflict prone areas so as to discern fault lines and vulnerabilities and formulate comprehensive strategies to address the challenges. In addition, study should also be undertaken by subject matters experts to recommended provisions of social media regulations within the confines of constitutional frame work and draft a fool proof policy.

Finally, seamless coordination and synergy amongst the national security agencies is an imperative. There is a need to carry out review of existing structures and coordination mechanism and recommend a joint organisation structure and protocol for social listening, social intelligence gathering and carry out unified information operations.

Endnotes

1. Deaths in armed conflicts, Our world in Data, https://ourworldindata.org/grapher/deaths-in-armed-conflicts-by-type
2. https://acleddata.com/dashboard/#/dashboard
3. HYBRID WARFARE The Changing Character of Conflict, Edited by Vikrant Deshpande, Institute For Defence Studies and Analyses New Delhi, book-hybrid-warfare-vdeshpande.pdf
4. New Messengers: The Role of Traditional and New Media in China's External Messaging During India–China Border Crises, By Ananth Krishnan, 3 May 2023, https://csep.org/reports/new-messengers-the-role-of-traditional-and-new-media-in-chinas-external-messaging-during-india-china-border-crises/
5. Guidance of public opinion. China Media Project, 14 Apr 2020, By D Bandurski. Retrieved from https://chinamediaproject.org/the_ccp_dictionary/guidance-of-public-opinion/
6. China Global Television Network. (n.d.). Home [YouTube Channel]. YouTube. Retrieved from https://www.youtube.com/channel/UCgrNz-aDmcr2uuto8_DL2jg
7. http://timesofindia.indiatimes.com/articleshow/75321469.cms?from=mdr&utm_source=contentofinterest&utm_medium=text&utm_campaign=cppst
8. In India's strife-torn Manipur, narrative battle is fought on social media, By Angana Chakrabarti, Published On 27 Oct 2023, https://www.aljazeera.com/features/2023/10/27/in-indias-strife-torn-manipur-narrative-battle-is-fought-on-social-media#:~:text=In%20at%20least%20two %20instances,being%20spread%20over%20social%20media.
9. In India's strife-torn Manipur, narrative battle is fought on social media, By Angana Chakrabarti, Published On 27 Oct 2023, https://www.aljazeera.com/features /2023/10/27/in-indias-strife-torn-manipur-narrative-battle-is-fought-on-social-media#:~:text=In%20at% 20least%20two%20 instances,being% 20spread%20over%20social%20media.
10. In India's strife-torn Manipur, narrative battle is fought on social media, By Angana Chakrabarti, Published On 27 Oct 2023, https://www.aljazeera.

com/features/ 2023/10/27/in-indias-strife-torn-manipur-narrative-battle-is-fought-on-social-media#:~:text=In%20at%20least%20two %20 instances,being%20spread%20over%20social%20media.

11 National Security | Definition, Policy and Importance, https://study.com/academy/lesson/the-economics-of-national-security-policy.html#:~:text=National%20Security%20Policy%20Definedandtext=National%20security%20is%20the%20 protection,%2C%20environmental%2C%20and%20political%20threats.

12 Media as an instrument of Hybrid Warfare, Mar 21, By Haseeb ur Rehman Warrich, Muhammad Waqas Haider and Tahir Mahmood Azad, Global Mass Communication Review (GMCR), Research Gate, https://www.researchgate.net/publication/351775179

13 Sameer Patil, Shourya Gori, Deep fake, disinformation, and deception, 25 Aug 23, https://www.orfonline.org/expert-speak/deep-fake-disinformation-and-deception

14 Discussing conflict in social media: The use of Twitter in the Jammu and Kashmir conflict, Dec 2020, https://journals.sagepub.com/doi/10.1177/1750635220970997

15 Sameer Patil, Shourya Gori, Deep fake, disinformation, and deception, 25 Aug 23, https://www.orfonline.org/expert-speak/deep-fake-disinformation-and-deception

16 Ekaterina Zhuravskaya, Maria Petrova and Ruben Enikolopov, Political Effects of the Internet and Social Media, Annual Review of Economics, Aug 2020, Political Effects of the Internet and Social Media | Annual Review of Economics (annualreviews.org)

17 Ajinkya B Metkara and Aakash A Aade, 13 Aug 23, Role of Social Media in Political Management in India, Dr. Ambedkar Institute of Management Studies and Research, Nagpur, https://journals.sagepub.com/doi/10.1177/17427665231186252

18 Maria Cristina Arcuri, Gino Gandolfi, and Ivan Russo, Does fake news impact stock returns? Evidence from US and EU stock markets, Journal of Economics and Business, Jun 23, https://www.sciencedirect.com/science/article/pii/S0148619523000231#:~:text=However%2C%20the%20representative%20agent%20model,based%20on%20this%20misleading%20 information.

19 Jonathan Clarke, Hailiang Chen , Ding Du and Yu Jeffrey Hu, 23 Jul 2020, Fake News, Investor Attention, and Market Reaction, https://pubsonline.informs.org/doi/10.1287/isre.2019.0910

20 Fake News and its Impact on the Economy, 11 Aug 2020, Fake News and its Impact on the Economy | We Live Asia (priorityconsultants.com)

Endnotes

21 https://economictimes.indiatimes.com/markets/ stocks/news/social-media-scam-artists-prey-on-indias-amateur-investors/articleshow/ 93176552.cms?utm_source=contentofinterestandutm_medium=textandutm_campaign=cppst

22 Anurag Bana , Colette Allen, 19 May 2020, Social Media and the Judiciary, Social Media and the Judiciary (barandbench.com)

23 Lobby targeting judiciary via sponsored articles: Justice Arun Mishra - The Hindu

24 A Guide to Activism in the Digital Age, 25 Nov 19, https://online.maryville.edu/blog/a-guide-to-social-media-activism/

25 Hybrid Warfare: Fighting Complex Opponents from the Ancient World to the Present, by Williamson Murray, June 14, 2012

26 'Conflicts in 21st Century: The Rise of Hybrid Wars', by Frank G Hoffman, 2007, pg 14

27 Conflicts in 21st Century: The Rise of Hybrid Wars', by Frank G Hoffman, 2007, pg 30

28 'Commanding the Contested Zones' by Robert E Schimidle and FGH Hoffman, Sep 2004

29 MCDC Countering Hybrid Warfare Project: Countering Hybrid Warfare, March 2019, Dr Patrick Cullen and Dr Njord Wegge, Senior Research Fellow, NUPI, MCDC Countering Hybrid Warfare Project: Countering Hybrid Warfare (publishing.service.gov.uk)

30 'Hybrid Threat Concept: Contemporary War, Military Planning and the Advent of Unrestricted Operational Art', Brian P. Fleming, 2011, The Hybrid Threat Concept: Contemporary War, Military Planning and the Advent of Unrestricted Operational Art (dtic.mil)

31 Hybrid Warfare, by Lieutenant Colonel Juan Jose Terrados, Spanish Air Force, Former Joint Targeting Subject Matter Expert NATO Joint Warfare Centre, Three Swords Magazine, 2019

32 "The Islamic State is a Hybrid Threat: Why Does That Matter?". By Jasper Scott Moreland, *Small Wars Journal*, Small Wars Foundation

33 EU. European External Action Service. Working Document EEAS (2015) 731, Food-for-thought paper "Countering Hybrid Threats". 13 May 2015. http://www.statewatch.org/news/2015/may/eeas-csdphybrid-threats-8887-15.pdf

34 Sergey Chekinov, Sergey Bogdanov, "Evolution of the Essence and Content of the Concept of "War" in the 21st Century," Military Thought, January 2017, https://dlib.eastview.com/browse/doc/50724910

35   Alexander Bartosh, "Strategy and Counter Strategy in Hybrid Warfare," Military Thought, October 2018, https://dlib.eastview.com/browse/doc/53754116

36   V. Kiselev, "Hybrid War as a New Type of War of the Future," Army Collection, December 2015, https://dlib.eastview.com/browse/doc/45952340

37   V. Kiselev, "Hybrid War as a New Type of War of the Future," Army Collection, December 2015, https://dlib.eastview.com/browse/doc/45952340; Alexander Bartosh, "Strategy and Counter Strategy in Hybrid Warfare," Military Thought, October 2018, https://dlib.eastview.com/browse/doc/53754116; Sergey Chekinov, Sergey Bogdanov, "Evolution of the Essence and Content of the Concept of "War" in the 21st Century," Military Thought, January 2017, https://dlib.eastview.com/browse/doc/50724910

38   Alexander Bartosh, "Strategy and Counter Strategy in Hybrid Warfare," Military Thought, October 2018, https://dlib.eastview.com/browse/doc/53754116

39   https://brggdotfudan.edu.cn/articleinfo_4769.html

40   http://www.81dotcn/jfjbmap/content/2020-01/02/content_251236.html

41   http://www.81dotcn/jfjbmap/content/2020-01/02/content_251236.html
     http://www.81dotcn/jfjbmap/content/2021-09/02/content_298119.html

42   http://www.81dotcn/jfjbmap/content/2021-08/19/content_296897.html

43   An overview of the three warfares, https://jamestown.org/program/the-plas-latest-strategic-thinking-on-the-three-warfares/, https://www.usip.org/publications/2023/08/china-and-space-next-frontier-lawfare

44   Hybrid Warfare With Chinese Characteristics, By Benjamin David Baker, 23 Sep 2015, Hybrid Warfare With Chinese Characteristics – The Diplomat

45   "The blurring of war and peace," *Survival* 61, By Elie Perot, No 2 (2019): 101-110, The Blurring of War And Peace: Hybrid Warfare – Analysis, By Haleema Zia, 19 Apr 21, The Blurring Of War And Peace: Hybrid Warfare – Analysis – Eurasia Review

46   Reichborn-Kjennerud, Erik, and Patrick Cullen. *What is hybrid warfare?*. Norwegian Institute for International Affairs (NUPI), 2016, https://brage.bibsys.no/xmlui/bitstream/id/411369/NUPI_P

47   "The US concept and practice of hybrid warfare," *Strategic Analysis* 41, By Vladimir I. Batyuk, No 5 (2017): 464-477

48   Hybrid Warfare, By Lieutenant Colonel Juan Jose Terrados, Spanish Air Force, Former Joint Targeting Subject Matter Expert NATO Joint Warfare Centre, Three Swords Magazine, 35/2019

49   "The blurring of war and peace," *Survival* 61, By Elie Perot, No 2 (2019): 101-110

50. International Security Advisory Board, Report on Gray Zone Conflict, Washington, D.C.: U.S. Department of State, 03 Jan 2017; Nathan P. Freier, Outplayed: Regaining Initiative in the Gray Zone, Carlisle, US Army War College, Strategic Studies Institute, Jun 2016; and Michael J. Mazarr, Mastering the Gray Zone, Carlisle, US Army War College, Strategic Studies Institute, Dec 2015.

51. War's Future: The Risks and Rewards of Grey-Zone Conflict and Hybrid Warfare, By David Carment and Dani Belo, Canadian Global Affairs Institute, War's Future: The Risks and Rewards of Grey-Zone Conflict and Hybrid Warfare - Canadian Global Affairs Institute (cgai.ca)

52. Worldwide digital population 23, Published by Ani Petrosyan, Oct 23, https://www.statista.com/statistics/617136/digital-population-worldwide/#:~:text=Worldwide%20digital%20population%202023andtext=As%20of%20October%202023%2C%20there,population%2C%20were%20social%20media%20users.

53. What is Social Media Warfare?, https://prevency.com/en/what-is-social-media-warfare/

54. Grey is the new black: Covert action and implausible deniability, by Rory Cormac and Richard J. Aldrich, 2018

55. Russian hybrid warfare and extended deterrence in Eastern Europe, Alexander Lanoszka, *International Affairs*, Volume 92, Issue 1, January 2016, Pages 175–195, https://doi.org/10.1111/1468-2346.12509

56. What is social media warfare?, https://prevency.com/en/what-is-social-media-warfare/

57. Towards a typology of non-state actors in 'hybrid warfare': proxy, auxiliary, surrogate and affiliated forces, By Rauta, Vladimir (2020), https://doi.org/10.1080/09557571.2019.1656600 Available at https://centaur.reading.ac.uk/86256/

58. 7 Types of Cyber Threat Actors and Their Damage, by RedLegg Blog, 09 Apr 2023, https://www.redlegg.com/blog/cyber-threat-actor-types

59. Cyber organized crime activities, E4J University Module Series: Cybercrime, https://www.unodc.org/e4j/zh/cybercrime/module-13/key-issues/cyber-organized-crime-activities

60. Non-State Actors in Computer Network Operations, Jason Andress, Steve Winterfeld, in Cyber Warfare (Second Edition), 2014, https://www.sciencedirect.com/topics/computer-science/hacktivist#:

61. What Is Cyber Extortion?, https://www.proofpoint.com/us/threat-reference/cyber-extortion#

62. https://www.drishtiias.com/daily-updates/daily-news-analysis/state-sponsored-cyber-attacks#

63   The Weaponization of Social Media, How social media can spark violence and what can be done about it?, Mercy Corps, 2019,

64   Mueller Report (2019) - https://www.politico.com/news/ 2020/03/16/russia-election-justice-department-132875; Justice Department drops plans for trial over Russian interference in 2016 U.S. election, by Josh Gerstein, Mar 2020, https://www.politico.com/news/2020/03/16/russia-election-justice-department-132875

65   Talha Latief Tantray, Research Scholar, J and K Central University, Social Media and Online Radicalization- A Case Study of Jammu and Kashmir, 23 Jun 22, http://www.socialresearchfoundation.com/new/publish-journal.php?editID=1261

66   ET Bureau, "Behind the Information Curtain: Kashmir Has Learnt To Work around Social Media Ban", 2020, p. 7

67   Basharat Reshi, "Changing Nature of Insurgency in Kashmir: Its Impact on the Kashmiri Cause of Self-Determination with Special References to 2008 And 2010 Agitations", European Academic Research, 2.11 (2015), 13 <https://doi.org/2286-4822

68   Ab Rouf Bhat, PhD Scholar and Dr. Syeda Afshana , Associate Professor, Media Education Research Centre, University of Kashmir, Fake News in Kashmir: A Case Study, 13 March 2019, https://www.researchgate.net/publication/333016835_Fake_News_in_Kashmir_A_Case_Study

69   Attorney Matthew Bergman, What Is Trolling on Social Media?, 4 Dec 2023, https://socialmediavictims.org/cyberbullying/types/trolling/

70   Luis Assardo, Investigating Digital Threats: Trolling Campaigns, 24 May 23, https://gijn.org/resource/investigating-digital-threats-trolling-campaigns/

71   Luis Assardo, Investigating Digital Threats: Trolling Campaigns, Global Investigative Journalism network, May 24, 2023, https://gijn.org/resource/investigating-digital-threats-trolling-campaigns/

72   Rage Farming, What is Rage Farming on Social Media? | Reality Team

73   Abu Muna Almaududi Ausat, The Role of Social Media in Shaping Public Opinion and Its Influence on Economic Decisions, Technology and Society Perspectives (TACIT) Vol. 1, No. 1, 01 Mar 2023, https://scholar.google.co.in/scholar_url?url= https://journal.literasisainsnusantara.com/ index.php/tacit/ article/download/37/53andhl=enandsa=   Xandei=bVmnZcKAL6mu6rQPqourg Aoandscisig= AFWwaeZFuPH3bptqTxB6b GmTgywJandoi=scholarr

74   Guo, Lei; A. Rohde, Jacob; Wu, H. Denis (28 January 2020). "Who is responsible for Twitter's echo chamber problem? Evidence from 2016 U.S. election networks". *Information, Communication and Society*. **23** (2): 234–251. doi:10.1080/1369118X.2018.1499793. ISSN 1369-118X. S2CID 149666263

Endnotes

75 Chater, James (6 July 2016). "What the EU referendum result teaches us about the dangers of the echo chamber". New Statesman

76 Verena K. Brändle, Charlotte Galpin and Hans-Jörg Trenz, 07 Jun 2021, Brexit as 'politics of division': social media campaigning after the referendum, https://www.tandfonline.com/doi/full/10.1080/14742837.2021.1928484

77 Zara Abrams, June 1, 2022, The role of psychological warfare in the battle for Ukraine, American Psychological Association, The role of psychological warfare in the battle for Ukraine (apa.org)

78 International Crisis Group (2018) - https://www.crisisgroup.org/middle-east-north-africa/east-mediterranean-mena/syria

79 Javier Lesaca, November 19, 2015, Fight against ISIS reveals power of social media, Brookings Institution (2017) - https://www.brookings.edu/articles/fight-against-isis-reveals-power-of-social-media/

80 Carnegie Endowment for International Peace (2013) - https://carnegie-mec.org/specialprojects/arabspring2.0/all/2742?lang=enandpageOn=2

81 What is Social Media Warfare?, https://prevency.com/en/what-is-social-media-warfare/

82 Marc Ambinder, Jan 09, 2015, How the NSA uses your telephone records, New York Times (2018) - https://theweek.com/articles/463482/how-nsa-uses-telephone-records,

83 Hannah Macready, September 14, 2023, What is social media intelligence?, https://blog.hootsuite.com/social-media-intelligence/#:~:text=Social%20media%20 20intelligence%20is%20the,data% 20to%20inform%20decision%2Dmaking.

84 Social Media Users And Statistics For 2024 (Latest Data), By Rohit Shewale / January 1, 2024, https://www.demandsage.com/social-media-users/

85 Social Media Users And Statistics For 2024 (Latest Data), By Rohit Shewale / January 1, 2024, https://www.demandsage.com/social-media-users/

86 https://www.oberlo.com/statistics/fastest-growing-social-media-platforms#:~:text=What%20is%20the%20fastest% 2Dgrowing, than%20 quadrupled%20over%20this%20period.

87 Social Media Users And Statistics For 2024 (Latest Data), By Rohit Shewale / January 1, 2024, https://www.demandsage.com/social-media-users/

88 Social Media Users And Statistics For 2024 (Latest Data), By Rohit Shewale / January 1, 2024, https://www.demandsage.com/social-media-users/

89 https://www.researchgate.net/figure/World-map-depending-on-the-use-of-social-media-3_fig1_336265669

90 ARABS SEE DAESH, HOUTHIS AS BIGGEST SECURITY THREAT, 10 Oct 2022, https://sawabcenter.org/surveys/arabs-see-daesh-houtis-as-biggest-security-threat/

91 Malaysia: Extremism and Terrorism, Counter Extremism Project, https://www.counterextremism.com/countries/malaysia-extremism-and-terrorism

92 Top Social Media Statistics And Trends Of 2024, By Belle Wong and Aashika Jain, Forbes Advisor, https://www.forbes.com/advisor/in/business/social-media-statistics/#:~:text=Active% 20Social%20Media %20Penetration%20 in,of%20the%20country's%20entire%20population.

93 https://www.forbes.com/advisor/in/business/social-media-statistics/#sources

94 https://www.forbes.com/advisor/in/business/social-media-statistics/#sources

95 Michael Holloway, 10 May 2017, How Russia Weaponized Social Media in Crimea (thestrategybridge.org)

96 Bhumika Khatri, 08 Jun 18, Indian Government Issues Third Notice To Facebook Over Data Sharing, https://inc42.com/buzz/indian-government-issues-third-notice-to-facebook-over-data-sharing/

97 Mark Travers, 21 Mar 2020, Facebook Spreads Fake News Faster Than Any Other Social Website, According To New Research, https://www.forbes.com/sites/traversmark/2020/03/21/facebook-spreads-fake-news-faster-than-any-other-social-website-according-to-new-research/?sh=296e2cde6e1a

98 Karen Hao, 11 Mar 21, How Facebook got addicted to spreading misinformation?, MIT Technology Review, https://technologyreview.com/2021/03/11/1020600/facebook-responsible-ai-misinformation/

99 David Klepper, 30 Nov 23, Thousands of fake Facebook accounts shut down by Meta were primed to polarize voters ahead of 2024, https://apnews.com /article/meta-facebook-2024-election-misinformation-china-956019723463918043e060ac577270f7

100 Daniel Pereira, 04 Oct 2023, Twitter SWOT Analysis, https://businessmodelanalyst.com/twitter-swot-analysis/

101 Daniel Pereira, 04 Oct 2023, Twitter SWOT Analysis, https://businessmodelanalyst.com/twitter-swot-analysis/

102 Sara Hamad Alqurainy, Hamedi M. Adnan, ISIS Use of Twitter to Appeal to Saudis: Experts' Views on Saudi Counter-Measures, https://dialnet.unirioja.es/descarga/articulo/8355750.pdf

103 Amanda Macmillan, 25 May 2017, Why Instagram Is the Worst Social Media for Mental Health, https://time.com/4793331/instagram-social-media-mental-health/

Endnotes

104 Thomas Perkins and David Robinson, 17 Jul 22, TIKTOK — WHITEPAPER, https://internet2-0.com/tiktok/

105 Andrew Williams, 26 Sep 2023, Is TikTok safe to use? Concerns raised about harmful content and data privacy, https://www.standard.co.uk/news/tech/tiktok-safety-content-misinformation-data-children-government-china-b1047589.html#:~:text=A%20paper%20by%20cybersecurity%20firm,on%20servers%20in%20mainland%20China.

106 Emily Baker-White, 20 Oct 2022, TikTok Parent ByteDance Planned To Use TikTok To Monitor The Physical Location Of Specific American Citizens, https://www.forbes.com/sites/emilybaker-white/2022/10/20/tiktok-bytedance-surveillance-american-user-data/?sh=ae1e2d36c2db

107 https://www.standard.co.uk/optimist/vaccine-world/tik-docs-medics-social-media-debunk-vaccine-myths-b939719.html

108 Gabriel Weimann and Natalie Masri, 15 Nov 21, TikTok's Spiral of Antisemitism, https://www.mdpi.com/2673-5172/2/4/41

109 https://www.standard.co.uk/news/tech/tiktok-safety-content-misinformation-data-children-government-china-b1047589.html#:~:text=%20paper%20by%20cybersecurity%20firm,on%20servers%20in%20mainland%20China.

110 Pace, Michelle. 2013. An Arab 'spring' of a different kind? Resilience and freedom in the case of an occupied nation. Mediterranean Politics 18(1). 42–59. https://doi.org/10.1080/13629395.2012.745705

111 TikTok Intifada: Analyzing Social Media Activism Among Youth, https://www.degruyter.com/document/doi/10.1515/omgc-2022-0014/html?lang=en

112 Developing Effective Counter-Narrative Frameworks for Countering Violent Extremism, Sep 2014, https://www.dhs.gov/sites/default/files/publications/Developing%20Effective%20Frameworks%20for%20CVE-Hedayah_ICCT%20Report.pdf

113 Global Risks Report 2024, World Economic Forum, 10 Jan 2024, https://www.weforum.org/publications/global-risks-report-2024/digest/

114 Global Risks Report 2024, World Economic Forum, 10 Jan 2024, https://www.weforum.org/publications/global-risks-report-2024/digest/

115 Anna Fleck, Where False Information Is Posing the Biggest Threat, 19 Jan 2024, https://www.statista.com/chart/31605/rank-of-misinformation-disinformation-among-selected-countries/

116 Forecast of the social network user penetration rate in Ukraine from 2018 to 2027, https://www.statista.com/statistics/1134664/predicted-social-network-user-penetration-rate-in-ukraine/

117 https://explodingtopics.com/blog/countries-internet-users

118 https://blog.miappi.com/social-media-use-uk-versus-usa#:~:text=With%20 87% 20percent%20of%20internet, enterprises%20are%20using% 20social% 20networks.

119 Jeannie L. Johnson, Strategic Culture: Refining The Theoretical Construct, 31 Oct 2006, Advancing The Strategic Culture Paradigm: (fas.org), https://irp.fas.org/agency/dod/dtra/strat-culture

120 *By Nayef Al-Rodhan, 22 July 2015,* Strategic Culture and Pragmatic National Interest, Strategic Culture and Pragmatic National Interest | Global Policy Journal

121 Dr. Patrick J. Cullen and Erik Reichborn-Kjennerud, Understanding Hybrid Warfare, MCDC Countering Hybrid Warfare Project: MCDC January 2017, https://wss.apan.org/s/ME/mcdc2015-2016/CHW/SitePages/Home

122 Critical function Definition | Law Insider,

123 Dr. Patrick J. Cullen and Erik Reichborn-Kjennerud, Understanding Hybrid Warfare, MCDC Countering Hybrid Warfare Project: MCDC January 2017, https://wss.apan.org/s/ME/mcdc2015-2016/CHW/SitePages/Home

124 Dr. Patrick J. Cullen and Erik Reichborn-Kjennerud, Understanding Hybrid Warfare, MCDC Countering Hybrid Warfare Project: MCDC January 2017, https://wss.apan.org/s/ME/mcdc2015-2016/CHW/SitePages/Home

125 Dr. Patrick J. Cullen and Erik Reichborn-Kjennerud, Understanding Hybrid Warfare, MCDC Countering Hybrid Warfare Project: MCDC January 2017, https://wss.apan.org/s/ME/mcdc2015-2016/CHW/SitePages/Home

126 Isabel Gan, 09 Mar 2021, Mental Models and Product #5: Second-Order Thinking, https://medium.com/mental-models-product/mental-models-product-5-second-order-thinking-893e510c428c#

127 Marvin Kalb and Carol Saivetz, The Israeli-Hezbollah War of 2006: The Media as a Weapon in Asymmetrical Conflict, 18 Feb 2007, https://www.brookings.edu/wp-content/uploads/2012/04/2007islamforum_israel-hezb-war.pdf

128 Daniel Byman and Emma McCaleb, 31 Jul 23, Understanding Hamas's and Hezbollah's Uses of Information Technology, https://www.csis.org/analysis/understanding-hamass-and-hezbollahs-uses-information-technology

129 Daniel Byman and Emma McCaleb, 16 Jun 24, Center for Strategic and International Studies (CSIS), Understanding Hamas's and Hezbollah's Uses of Information Technology, https://www.jstor.org/stable/pdf/resrep52622.pdf?refreqid=fastly-default%3Afe878ee6e20a2e2d9dae6afa5718d70aand ab_segments=andorigin=andinitiator=andacceptTC=1

130 Yousef al-Helou, 12 Feb 2015, Social media: The weapon of choice in the Gaza-Israel conflict, Middle East Eye, https://www.middleeasteye.net/news/social-media-weapon-choice-gaza-israel-conflict

131   Antony Loewenstein, 01 Nov 2023, Social media is a warzone: the IDF's strategy for war as online spectacle, https://www.versobooks.com/en-gb/blogs/news/social-media-is-a-warzone-the-idf-s-strategy-for-war-as-online-spectacle

132   Jonathan Conn, 13 Jun 21, Did Israel Lose the Social Media War over Gaza?, https://jcpa.org/article/did-israel-lose-the-social-media-war-over-gaza/#_edn6

133   Uppsala Conflict Data Program (UCDP), the Armed Conflict Location and Event Data (ACLED) Project, the United States Institute of Peace (USIP), www.understandingconflict.org

134   https://en.wikipedia.org/wiki/Arab_Spring#:~:text=

135   Arab Spring pro-democracy protests, 08 Dec 23, Arab Spring | History, Revolution, Causes, Effects, and Facts | Britannica

136   Bülent Aras and Şaban Kardaş, 18 Feb 21, Geopolitics of the New Middle East: Perspectives from Inside and Outside, Journal of Balkan and Near Eastern Studies, Geopolitics of the New Middle East: Perspectives from Inside and Outside (tandfonline.com)

137   Arab Spring pro-democracy protests, Arab Spring | History, Revolution, Causes, Effects, and Facts | Britannica

138   Hussein Solomon, Arno Tausch, Arab MENA Countries: Vulnerabilities and Constraints Against Democracy on the Eve of the Global COVID-19 Crisis, Arab MENA Countries: Vulnerabilities and Constraints Against Democracy on the Eve of the Global COVID-19 Crisis | SpringerLink

139   Arab Spring pro-democracy protests, Arab Spring | History, Revolution, Causes, Effects, and Facts | Britannica

140   Stepanova, Ekaterina, May 2011, "The Role of Information Communication Technologies in the "Arab Spring", https://pircenter.org/kosdata/page_doc/p2594_2.pdf

141   Marwa Fatafta, December 17, 2020, From Free Space to a Tool of Oppression: What Happened to the Internet Since the Arab Spring?, https://timep.org/2020/12/17/from-free-space-to-a-tool-of-oppression-what-happened-to-the-internet-since-the-arab-spring/

142   Khamis, Sahar and Katherine Vaughn. "Cyberactivism in the Egyptian Revolution: How Civic Engagement and Citizen Journalism." Arab Media and Society. Summer 2011 and Lim, Merlyna. «Clicks, Cabs, and Coffee Houses: Social Media and Oppositional Movements in Egypt, 2004-2011.» Journal of Communications. April 2012

143   Marc Lynch, Deen Freelon and Sean Aday, Jan 14, Syria's Socially Mediated Civil War, United State Institute for Peace,

144 Kali Robinson and Will Merrow, 03 Dec 20, The Arab Spring at Ten Years: What's the Legacy of the Uprisings?, published on Council on Foreign Relations, https://www.cfr.org/article/arab-spring-ten-years-whats-legacy-uprisings

145 Analysis Of Russia's Information Campaign Against Ukraine, Riga, 2015, russian_information_campaign_public_12012016fin.pdf

146 The 1990s were a period of economic turmoil in Ukraine: by the end of the decade, the economy had shrunk to one third of its pre-1991 level. Serhy Yekelchyk, *Ukraine: Birth of a Modern Nation* (Oxford: Oxford University Press, 2007), p. 43, http://www.inquiriesjournal.com/articles/986/the-euromaidan-revolution-in-ukraine-stages-of-the-maidan-movement-and-why-they-constitute-a-revolution

147 Elias Kuhn von Burgsdorff, 2015, The Euromaidan Revolution in Ukraine: Stages of the Maidan Movement and Why They Constitute a Revolution, http://www.inquiriesjournal.com/articles/986/the-euromaidan-revolution-in-ukraine-stages-of-the-maidan-movement-and-why-they-constitute-a-revolution

148 EU or IMF conditions on loans would not have favoured President Yanukovych's increasingly authoritarian leadership. What is more, Russia's President Vladimir Putin had ambitions to create a Eurasian Union, and Ukraine could not be both a member of both Putin's union and the European Union. Peter Leonard, "IMF offers Ukraine up to $18 billion in loans," Yahoo News, March 27, 2014, accessed April 2, 2014, http://news.yahoo.com/imf-offers-ukraine-18-billion-loans-082715644.html

149 Analysis Of Russia's Information Campaign Against Ukraine, 2015, NATO COE, russian_information_campaign_public_12012016fin.pdf (stratcomcoe.org)

150 Analysis Of Russia's Information Campaign Against Ukraine, 2015, NATO COE, russian_information_campaign_public_12012016fin.pdf (stratcomcoe.org)

151 Russian "Hybrid Warfare": Resurgence and Politicization Ofer Fridman (Oxford University Press, 2022), 261 pages. Reviewed by Christopher Bort, Review: Russian "Hybrid Warfare": Resurgence and Politicization (cia.gov)

152 Arsalan Bilal, 26 Apr 24, Russia's hybrid war against the West, NATO Review - Russia's hybrid war against the West

153 Russia's war on Ukraine: Timeline of cyber-attacks, https://www.europarl.europa.eu/RegData/etudes/ BRIE/2022/733549/EPRS_BRI(2022)733549_EN.pdf

154 Kseniya Kizilova and Pippa Norris, 17 Mar 2022, What do ordinary Russians really think about the war in Ukraine?, What do ordinary Russians really think about the war in Ukraine? | EUROPP (lse.ac.uk)

Endnotes

155 Christian Perez, Senior Policy and Quantitative Analyst and Anjana Nair, Policy Fellow, FP Analytics, Information Warfare in Russia's War in Ukraine, Information Warfare in Russia's War in Ukraine – Foreign Policy

156 Christian Perez, Senior Policy and Quantitative Analyst and Anjana Nair, Policy Fellow, FP Analytics, Information Warfare in Russia's War in Ukraine, Information Warfare in Russia's War in Ukraine – Foreign Policy

157 DFRL Lab, 04 May 22, How Russia employs fake fact-checking in its disinformation arsenal, How Russia employs fake fact-checking in its disinformation arsenal | by @DFRLab | DFRLab | Medium

158 Disinformation and Russia's war of aggression against Ukraine: Threats and governance responses, 03 Nov 22, https://www.oecd.org/ukraine-hub/policy-responses/disinformation-and-russia-s-war-of-aggression-against-ukraine-37186bde/

159 Wahlstrom A, 2022, *The IO Offensive: Information Operations Surrounding the Russian Invasion of Ukraine*, https://www.mandiant.com/resources/information-operations-surrounding-ukraine.

160

161 Undermining Ukraine: How Russia widened its global information war in 2023, Atlantic Council, DFRL Lab, Undermining Ukraine: How Russia widened its global information war in 2023 - Atlantic Council

162 Undermining Ukraine: How Russia widened its global information war in 2023, DFRL, Atlantic Council, Feb 2024, Undermining Ukraine: How Russia widened its global information war in 2023 - Atlantic Council

163 Disinformation and Russia's war of aggression against Ukraine: Threats and governance responses, 03 Nov 22, https://www.oecd.org/ukraine-hub/policy-responses/disinformation-and-russia-s-war-of-aggression-against-ukraine-37186bde/

164 Institute of Mass Information, 2021, *Compliance with Professional Standards in Online Media. The 1st Wave of Monitoring in 2021*, https://imi.org.ua/en/monitorings/ compliance-with-professional-standards-in-online-media-the-1st-wave-of-monitoring-in-2021-i38434

165 Matyushenko, Y. (2021), "Zelensky Approves Regulation on Center for Countering Disinformation", *Unian*, https://www.unian.info/politics/center-for-countering-disinformation-zelensky-approves-regulation-11413858.html

166 Dyczok, M. Mar 2022, "Ukraine's Information Warriors", *Journal of Democracy*, https://www.journalofdemocracy.org/ukraines-information-warriors/

167 Disinformation and Russia's war of aggression against Ukraine: Threats and governance responses, 03 Nov 22, https://www.oecd.org/ukraine-hub/

policy-responses/disinformation-and-russia-s-war-of-aggression-against-ukraine-37186bde/

168 Megan Specia, 25 Mar 22, 'Like a Weapon': Ukrainians Use Social Media to Stir Resistance, https://www.nytimes.com/2022/03/25/world/europe/ukraine-war-social-media.html

169 A Private Company Is Using Social Media to Track Down Russian Soldiers, 02 Mar 2023, https://foreignpolicy.com/2023/03/02/ukraine-russia-war-military-social-media-osint-open-source-intelligence/

170 Col Vinayak Bhatt, 09 Oct 2020, How China's propaganda machinery is trying to get into the heads of Indians, https://www.indiatoday.in/news-analysis/story/ how-china-s-propaganda-machinery-is-trying-to-get-into-the-heads-of-indians-1729655-2020-10-08

171 Ananth Krishnan, 03 May 2023, New Messengers: The Role of Traditional and New Media in China's External Messaging During India–China Border Crises,https://csep.org/ reports/new-messengers-the-role-of-traditional-and-new-media-in-chinas-external-messaging-during-india-china-border-crises/

172 Bei Qin, David Strömberg, Yanhui Wu, 2017, *The Journal of Economic Perspectives*, Vol. 31, No. 1 (Winter 2017), pp. 117-140 (24 pages), Why Does China Allow Freer Social Media? Protests versus Surveillance and Propaganda, https://www.jstor.org/stable/44133953?seq=1

173 Ananth Krishnan, 03 May 2023, New Messengers: The Role of Traditional and New Media in China's External Messaging During India–China Border Crises,https://csep.org/reports/new-messengers-the-role-of-traditional-and-new-media-in-chinas-external-messaging-during-india-china-border-crises/

174 Charlotte Gao, 10 Aug 2017, Fake News: Chinese National Media on the Doklam Standoff, https://thediplomat.com/2017/08/fake-news-chinese-national-media-on-the-doklam-standoff/

175 Sarthak Ahuja and Samridhi Diwan, India's two-front information war, 10 May 2023, ORF, India's two-front information war (orfonline.org)

176 Sarthak Ahuja and Samridhi Diwan, India's two-front information war, 10 May 2023, ORF, India's two-front information war (orfonline.org)

177 Arun Anand, 06 Mar 2020, Imran Khan party wing showed Delhi riots as anti-Muslim, spread fake news: Delhi Police, Imran Khan party wing showed Delhi riots as anti-Muslim, spread fake news: Delhi Police (theprint.in),

178 Kinjal, 04 Mar 2020, Old images from Syria, Bangladesh shared as Delhi riots, Old images from Syria, Bangladesh shared as Delhi riots - Alt News

179 Sarthak Ahuja and Samridhi Diwan, India's two-front information war, 10 May 2023, ORF, India's two-front information war (orfonline.org)

Endnotes

180 India's War Crimes in Kashmir: Violence, Dissent and the War on Terror, 20 Jan 22, India's War Crimes in Kashmir: Violence, Dissent and the War on Terror (swiunit.com)

181 Raffaello Pantucci, a senior associate fellow at Britain's Royal United Services Institute, 08 Oct 2020, Indians and Central Asians Are the New Face of the Islamic State, https://foreignpolicy.com/2020/10/08/isis-indian-kyrgyzstan-tajikistan-uzbekistan-central-asians-are-the-new-face-of-islamic-state/

182 Abhishek Bhalla, 27 Aug 21, From Kerala to Kabul to Kashmir— how Islamic State Khorasan poses threat to India, https://www.indiatoday.in/india/story/kerala-kabul-kashmir-islamic-state-khorasan-threat-india-1846161-2021-08-27

183 Adam Zeidan, 27 Mar 2024, Islamic State–Khorasan Province- jihad movement, https://www.britannica.com/topic/Islamic-State-Khorasan-Province

184 Raffaello Pantucci, a senior associate fellow at Britain's Royal United Services Institute, 08 Oct 2020, Indians and Central Asians Are the New Face of the Islamic State, https://foreignpolicy.com/2020/10/08/isis-indian-kyrgyzstan-tajikistan-uzbekistan-central-asians-are-the-new-face-of-islamic-state/

185 Antonia Ward, 10 Dec 2018, ISIS's Use of Social Media Still Poses a Threat to Stability in the Middle East and Africa, Georgetown Security Studies Review, https://www.rand.org/pubs/commentary/2018/12/isiss-use-of-social-media-still-poses-a-threat-to-stability.html

186 Hashtag Terror: How ISIS Manipulates Social Media, 07 Nov 2014, https://www.adl.org/resources/report/hashtag-terror-how-isis-manipulates-social-media

187 Shruti Pandalai, ISIS in India: The Writing on the (Facebook) Wall, 06 May 2016, https://thediplomat.com/2016/05/isis-in-india-the-writing-on-the-facebook-wall/

188 Hillary Mann Leverett, 17 Feb 2015, ISIS sends out "90,000 social (media) messages a day.", https://www.politifact.com/factchecks/2015/ feb/19/hillary-mann-leverett/cnn-expert-islamic-state-posts -90000-social-media-/#:~:text=Leverett% 20said%20the%20Islamic%20State% 20group%20sends%20out, includes%20re-tweets% 20and%20some% 20generated%20 by%20computer%20programs.

189 Regina Mihindukulasuriya, 20 May 2019, ISIS influence growing in South India, particularly Kerala: Social media monitoring firms, https://theprint.in/india/isis-influence-growing-in-south-india-particularly-kerala-social-media-monitoring-firms/234953/

190 Regina Mihindukulasuriya, 20 May 2019, ISIS influence growing in South India, particularly Kerala: Social media monitoring firms, https://theprint.

in/india/isis-influence-growing-in-south-india-particularly-kerala-social-media-monitoring-firms/234953/

191 MK Madhusudan and Chetan Kumar, 13 Dec 2014, Mehdi Masroor arrested, confesses to operating ISIS Twitter, http://timesofindia.indiatimes.com/articleshow/45503070.cms?utm_source=contentofinterestandutm_medium=textandutm_campaign=cppst

192 Natalie Tecimer, 14 Jun 2017, India and the Fight Against Islamic State, https://thediplomat.com/2017/06/india-and-the-fight-against-islamic-state/

193 Moran Yarchi, 18 Mar 2019, Sage Journal, Volume 4 Edition 1, ISIS's media strategy as image warfare: Strategic messaging over time and across platforms, https://journals.sagepub.com /doi/full/10.1177/2057047319829587

194 Saikiran Kannan, 03 Sep 2021, Explainer: ISKP and other factions of Islamic State, https://www.indiatoday.in/world/story/explainer-iskp-and-other-factions-of-islamic-state-1846544-2021-08-28

195 Jeemon Jacob, 11 Sep 2017, The Jehadis of the south: Why Kerala became fertile ground for new ISIS recruits, https://www.indiatoday.in/magazine/nation/story/20170911-omar-al-hindi-isis-module-kerala-jihad-simi-operation-pigeon-1034806-2017-09-02

196 ISIS Spreading its Base, Most Active in 12 Indian States: Government to Parliament, 16 Sep 2020, https://www.news18.com/news/india/isis-most-active-in-12-indian-states-government-to-parliament-2881679.html

197 Jeemon Jacob, Sep 2017, The Jehadis of the south: Why Kerala became fertile ground for new ISIS recruits, https://www.indiatoday.in/magazine/nation/story/20170911-omar-al-hindi-isis-module-kerala-jihad-simi-operation-pigeon-1034806-2017-09-02

198 Raffaello Pantucci, a senior associate fellow at Britain's Royal United Services Institute, 08 Oct 2020, Indians and Central Asians Are the New Face of the Islamic State, https://foreignpolicy.com/2020/10/08/isis-indian-kyrgyzstan-tajikistan-uzbekistan-central-asians-are-the-new-face-of-islamic-state/

199 Natalie Tecimer, 14 Jun 2017, India and the Fight Against Islamic State, https://thediplomat.com/2017/06/india-and-the-fight-against-islamic-state/

200 Natalie Tecimer, 14 Jun 2017, India and the Fight Against Islamic State, https://thediplomat.com/2017/06/india-and-the-fight-against-islamic-state/

201 Joe Khalil, ISIS-K calls for lone wolf attacks across US, Europe, Israel, https://www.msn.com/en-us/news/world/isis-k-calls-for-lone-wolf-attacks-across-us-europe-israel/ar-BB1kLAaJ#:~:text=WASHINGTON%20%28NewsNation% 29%20%E2%80%94% 20A%20new%20warning%20 from% 20ISIS,people.%20The% 20Islamic% 20State%20offshoot%2C% 20ISIS-K%2C%20claimed%20responsibility.

202 Animesh Roul, "Students Islamic Movement of India: A Profile", Terrorism Monitor 4(2006), Accessed March 25, 2015, http://www.jamestown.org/single/?tx_ttnews%5Btt_news%5D=728andno_cache= 1#.VRK9A_yUdEw

203 Praveen Swami, "SIMI and the cult of the Kalashnikov", The Hindu, November 28, 2007

204 Taruni Kumar, ORF Issue Brief, Youth and Radicalisation: The Threat to India, Jun 2015, https://www.orfonline.org/wp-content/uploads/2015/06/IssueBrief_92.pdf

205 Animesh Roul, 29 Apr 2016, How Islamic State Gained Ground in India Using Indigenous Militant Networks, Jamestown Foundation, https://webarchive.archive.unhcr.org/20230520084125/https://www.refworld.org/docid/573573764.html

206 Animesh Roul, 29 Apr 2016, How Islamic State Gained Ground in India Using Indigenous Militant Networks, Jamestown Foundation, https://webarchive.archive.unhcr.org/20230520084125/https://www.refworld.org/docid/573573764.html

207 Vasu Sharma, Dec 2021, Online Radicalization in India, https://www.researchgate.net/publication/357577438_Online_Radicalization_in_India

208 Vasu Sharma, Dec 2021, Online Radicalization in India, https://www.researchgate.net/publication/357577438_Online_Radicalization_in_India

209 Najeeb Network, 'Kashmir Ki Azadi Tak | Raja Rapstar | Official Video | 2016 Latest', 3 September 2016, , accessed 3 May 2019

210 Varinder Bhatia, 05 Sep 2017, Cyber Jihad: The biggest challenge in Kashmir, 13 Jul 2018, WhatsApp used to gather stone pelters, many admins abroad: NIA | India News - The Indian Express, https://www.orfonline.org/expert-speak/42391-cyber-jihad-biggest-challenge-kashmir

211 WhatsApp used to gather stone pelters, many admins abroad: NIA, https://indianexpress.com/article/india/whatsapp-used-to-gather-stone-pelters-many-admins-abroad-nia-4828984/

212 Cyber Jihad: The biggest challenge in Kashmir, 13 Jul 2018, https://www.orfonline.org/expert-speak/42391-cyber-jihad-biggest-challenge-kashmir

213 Joseph M. Hatfield, Mar 218, Social engineering in cybersecurity: The evolution of a concept, https://www.sciencedirect.com/science/article/abs/pii/S0167404817302249

214 Christopher Hadnagy, Social Engineering and Psychology, 03 Feb 2021, https://www.psychologytoday.com/us/blog/human-hacking/202102/social-engineering-and-psychology

215 Anderson R J, 2008, Security Engineering: A Guide to Building Dependable Distributed Systems, 2nd Edn. New York, NY: Wiley Publishing, https://www.ncbi.nlm.nih.gov/pmc/articles/PMC7554349/

216 Kahneman D. (2011). Thinking, Fast and Slow. New York, NY: Farrar, Straus and Giroux, Indrajit R. E. (2017). Social engineering framework: Understanding the deception approach to human element of security. Int. J. Comput. Sci. Issues 14, 8–16. 10.20943/01201702.816, https://www.ncbi.nlm.nih.gov/pmc/articles/PMC7554349/

217 Acquisti A., Grossklags J. (2005). Privacy and rationality in individual decision making. IEEE Secur. Privacy 3, 26–33. 10.1109/MSP.2005.22

218 The Psychology Behind Social Engineering, 13 Feb 2024, https://www.social-engineer.com/the-psychology-behind-social-engineering/

219 AI Assisted Social Engineering Attacks, 27 Fen 2024, https://www.social-engineer.com/ai-assisted-social-engineering-attacks/

220 Pia Bogush, Social Engineering Principles: Understanding social engineering techniques, 25 Sep 2023, Business-tech weekly, https://www.businesstechweekly.com/cybersecurity/social-engineering/social-engineering-principles/

221 What is social engineering?, https://www.ibm.com/topics/social-engineering

222 KIearn Roberts, 15 Nov 21, Why is Social Engineering so Effective?, https://www.bulletproof.co.uk/blog/why-is-social-engineering-so-effective

223 Pia Bogush, Social Engineering Principles: Understanding social engineering techniques, 25 Sep 2023, Business-tech weekly, https://www.businesstechweekly.com/cybersecurity/social-engineering/social-engineering-principles/

224 Pia Bogush, Social Engineering Principles: Understanding social engineering techniques, 25 Sep 2023, Business-tech weekly, https://www.businesstechweekly.com/cybersecurity/social-engineering/social-engineering-principles/

225 Pia Bogush, Social Engineering Principles: Understanding social engineering techniques, 25 Sep 2023, Business-tech weekly, https://www.businesstechweekly.com/cybersecurity/social-engineering/social-engineering-principles/

226 9 Examples of Social Engineering Attacks, https://terranovasecurity.com/blog/examples-of-social-engineering-attacks/

227 9 Examples of Social Engineering Attacks, https://terranovasecurity.com/blog/examples-of-social-engineering-attacks/

228 Kiran V, 16 Jun 2020, Social Engineering Strategy for Political Campaigns, https://politicalmarketer.com/social-engineering-strategy-for-political-campaigns/

229 Arlin Cuncic, 29 Nov 23, How Does Propaganda Work?, https://www.verywellmind.com/how-does-propaganda-work-5224974

230 Arlin Cuncic, 29 Nov 23, How Does Propaganda Work?, https://www.verywellmind.com/how-does-propaganda-work-5224974

231 The ultimate guide to propaganda, 15 Sep 22, https://www.adobe.com/express/learn/blog/ultimate-guide -propaganda#:~:text=In%20 1939%2C%20social% 20scientists%20Alfred,card% 2Dstacking%2C%20 and%20bandwagon

232 Arlin Cuncic, 29 Nov 23, How Does Propaganda Work?, https://www.verywellmind.com/how-does-propaganda-work-5224974

233 Bruce Lannes Smith, 30 May 2024, Signs, symbols, and media used in contemporary propaganda, Propaganda - Signs, Symbols, Media | Britannica

234 Diana Owen, The New Media's Role in Politics, The New Media's Role in Politics | OpenMind (bbvaopenmind.com)

235 Abhrajita Mondal, 25 Apr 2022, Four Pillars of Democracy, https://thecreativepost.co.in/four-pillars-of-democracy/

236 Diana Owen, The New Media's Role in Politics, The New Media's Role in Politics | OpenMind (bbvaopenmind.com)

237 Hayes, Danny, and Jennifer L. Lawless. 2015. "As Local News Goes, So Goes Citizen Engagement: Media, Knowledge, and Participation in U.S. House Elections," The Journal of Politics, vol. 77, no. 2: 447-462

238 Barthel, Michael, Amy Mitchell, and Jesse Holcomb. 2016. "Many Americans Believe Fake News Is Sowing Confusion." Research Report. Washington, D.C.: Pew Research Center. http:// www.journalism.org/ 2016/12/15/many-americansbelieve-fake-news-is-sowing-confusion/

239 Hamas admits women not raped by IDF at Shifa hospital, following deleted Al Jazeera report, 25 Mar 24, i24NEWS, https://www.i24news.tv/en/news/israel-at-war/artc-hamas-admits-women-not-raped-by-idf-at-shifa-hospital-following-al-jazeera-report

240 Daniel H. McCauley, Sadi Sadiyev, and Col Rashad Tahirov, 11 Jan 2020, More Than A "Given:" Professionalizing Military Strategic Leadership, More Than A "Given:" Professionalizing Military Strategic Leadership | Small Wars Journal

241 The global war of narratives and the role of social media, Jul 2016, World Economic Forum, https://www.weforum.org/agenda/2016/07/ the-global-war-of-narratives-and-the-role-of-social-media/

242 Arindrajit Basu, India's International Cyber Operations: Tracing National Doctrine and Capabilities, https://unidir.org/files/2022-12/UNIDIR_India_International_Cyber_Operations.pdf

243 Vimal Mani, 23 Aug 23, Gaps in National Cyber Security Policy Of India and Improvements recommended, https://www.linkedin.com/pulse/gaps-national-cyber-security-policy-india-recommended-vimal-mani

244 https://cert-in.org.in/PDF/RFC2350.pdf

245 Peerzada Abrar, 07 Sep 23, Google Cloud partners with CERT-In to train government officials in cybersecurity, https://www.business-standard.com/india-news/google-cloud-partners-with-cert-in-to-train-government-officials-in-cybersecurity-123090700723_1.html

246 Arpit Gupta, 01 Sep 22, CERT-In conducts cyber security exercise 'Synergy' for 13 countries in collaboration with CSA, Singapore, https://government.economictimes.indiatimes.com/news/digital-india/cert-in-hosts-cyber-security-exercise-synergy-for-13-countries-in-collaboration-with-csa-singapore/93922255

247 https://pib.gov.in/PressReleaseIframePage.aspx?PRID=1556474

248 Joshi, Sandeep, 10 June 2013. "India gets ready to roll out cyber snooping agency", *The Hindu*. ISSN 0971-751X

249 Indian Cybercrime Coordination Centre (I4C), https://i4c.mha.gov.in/mission.aspx

250 RS Bedi, 23 Apr 2015, NTRO: India's Technical Intelligence Agency, Indian Defence Review, https://www.indiandefencereview.com/spotlights/ntro-indias-technical-intelligence-agency/

251 Cherian Samuel and Munish Sharma, 2019, India's Strategic Options in a changing Cyber Space, IDSA, https://idsa.in/system/files/book/book_indias-strategic-options-in-cyberspace.pdf

252 Arindrajit Basu, India's International Cyber Operations: Tracing National Doctrine and Capabilities https://unidir.org/files/2022-12/UNIDIR_India_International_Cyber_Operations.pdf

253 Apr 19, https://www.firstpost.com/india/india-all-set-to-have-defence-cyber-agency-next-month-to-tackle-hackers-rear-admiral-mohit-gupta-to-head-service-6542791.html

254 Government approves setting up of defence cyber agency, PTI, https://timesofindia.indiatimes.com/india/government-approves-setting-up-of-defence-cyber-agency/articleshow/72264836.cms

255 National Cyber Security Policy (draftv1), https://www.meity.gov.in/writereaddata/files/downloads/National_cyber_security_policy-2013%281%29.pdf

256 Sanket Kumar, 3 Aug 23, Social Media Regulation :India Perspective, https://www.linkedin.com/pulse/social-media-regulation-india-perspective-sanket-kumar#:~:text=The%20Information%20Technology%20Act%20is,the%20Cyber%20Regulations%20Advisory%20Committee.

257 Kyle Chin, Top Cybersecurity Regulations in India [Updated 2024], 18 Jan 2024, UpGuard, https://www.upguard.com/blog/cybersecurity-regula-

Endnotes

tions-india#:~:text=The% 20goal%20behind%20the%20 National,through% 20skill%20development%20and%20training.

258   https://eprocure.gov.in/cppp/rulesandprocs/kbadqkdlcswfj delrquehwux-cfmijmuixngudufgbuubgubfugbububjxcg fvsbdihbgfGhdfgFHytyhRtMT-k4NzY=

259   Namrata Maheshwari, Ria Singh Sawhney and Akhil Thomas, 22 Aug 21, How the Modi government's new IT rules jeopardise the right to privacy and free speech, How the Modi government's new IT rules jeopardise the right to privacy and free speech (scroll.in)

260   Sanket Kumar, 3 Aug 23, Social Media Regulation :India Perspective, https://www.linkedin.com/pulse/social-media-regulation-india-perspective-sanket-kumar#:~:text=The%20Information%20Technology%20Act%20 is,the%20Cyber%20Regulations%20Advisory%20Committee

261   https://www.upguard.com/blog/cybersecurity-regulations-india#:~:text=The%20goal% 20behind%20the% 20National,through%20skill% 20development%20and%20training.

262   Maj Gen PK Mullick, Apr 2020, IB-222_Indias-National-Cyber-Security-Strategy.pdf, https://www.claws.in/static/IB-222_Indias-National-Cyber-Security-Strategy.pdf

263   National Cyber Security Policy - Recent Update, Objectives, Main Components and Cyber Security in India, 31 May 23, https://testbook.com/ias-preparation/national-cyber-security-policy

264   https://www.scaler.com/topics/global-cybersecurity-index/

265   Global Cybersecurity Index [GCI] by ITU, https://www.scaler.com/topics/global-cybersecurity-index/

266   The Cyber Defense Index 2022/23, MIT Technology Review, https://www.technologyreview.com /2022/11/15/1063189 /the-cyber-defense-index-2022-23/

267   Dr Sankalp Gurjar, 15 Jul 21, India's Cyber Security: A look at the Approach and the Preparedness, Indian Council of World Affairs, https://www.icwa.in/show_content.php?lang=1andlevel=3andls_id=6172andlid=4236

268   Cyber Capabilities and National Power Volume 2, 07 Sep 2023, https://www.iiss.org/en/research-paper/2023/09/cyber-capabilities-national-power-volume-2/

269   Cyber Capabilities and National Power: A Net Assessment, 28 Jun 21, https://www.iiss.org/research-paper//2021/06/cyber-capabilities-national-power

270   Dr Sankalp Gurjar, 21 Jul 21, India's Cyber Security: A look at the Approach and the Preparedness - Indian Council of World Affairs (Government of India) (icwa.in)

271 Framework and Guidelines for Use of Social Media for Government Organisations, https://www.meity.gov.in/writereaddata/files/Approved%20Social%20Media%20Framework%20and%20Guidelines%20_2_.pdf

272 One Strike and You're Out! Government Introduces New Social Media Regulations, 30 Dec 23, https://news24online.com/tech/one-strike-and-you-are-out-government-introduces-new-social-media-regulations-instagram-facebook-youtube/205752/

273 Social media intermediaries who violate IT Rules may lose safe harbour protection: Union Minister Rajeev Chandrasekar, 16 Dec 23, https://www.thehindu.com/news/national/tamil-nadu/social-media-intermediaries-who-violate-it-rules-may-lose-safe-harbour-protection-union-minister-rajeev-chandrasekar/article67644694.ece

274 Centre's fact-check unit: What is it and how does the Union government defend it?, 16 Mar 2024, https://www.business-standard.com/india-news/centre-s-fact-check-unit-what-is-it-and-how-does-the-union-government-defend-it-123060800416_1.html

275 PIB Fact Check Unit, https://pib.gov.in/aboutfactchecke.aspx#:~:text=Through%20an%20established%20rigorous%20fact,reliable%20information%20to%20the%20public.andtext=The%20PIB%20Fact%20Check%20Unit%20is%20headed%20by%20a%20senior,Indian%20Information%20Service%20(IIS).

276 Ajay Sahni, Jan 2015, Vulnerabilities and Resistance to Islamist Radicalization in India, https://www.mei.edu/publications/vulnerabilities-and-resistance-islamist-radicalization-india

277 By Natalie Tecimer, 14 Jun 2017, India and the Fight Against Islamic State, India and the Fight Against Islamic State – The Diplomat

278 Natalie Tecimer, 14 Jun 2017, India and the Fight Against Islamic State, https://thediplomat.com/2017/06/india-and-the-fight-against-islamic-state/

279 http://timesofindia.indiatimes.com/articleshow/51972203.cms?utm_source=contentofinterestandutm_medium=textandutm_campaign=cppst

280 Shruti Pandalai, https://thediplomat.com/2016/05/isis-in-india-the-writing-on-the-facebook-wall/

281 Online Radicalization in India, Vaasu Sharma, https://www.researchgate.net/publication/357577438_Online_Radicalization_in_India

282 Debasis Das, May 2019, FACING A FUTURE WITH ORGANIZED WEAPONIZATION OF SOCIAL MEDIA - War Room - U.S. Army War College,

283 Nazir Masoodi, 14 Aug 2021, National Flag To Be Hoisted In 23,000 Schools In J&K On Independence Day, Independence Day 2021: National Flag To Be Hoisted In 23,000 Schools In J&K On Independence Day (ndtv.com)

Endnotes

284 Aljazeera, 04 Aug 2022, 'Har Ghar Tiranga' campaign – a big hit in Jammu and Kashmir, 'Har Ghar Tiranga' campaign – a big hit in Jammu and Kashmir | AlJazeera

285 Arun Joshi and Sameer Khan, 04 Aug 22, Har Ghar Tiranga, what it means for Kashmir, Har Ghar Tiranga, what it means for Kashmir (siasat.com)

286 Kavya Mishra, 14 Aug 2023, Families of Hizbul Terrorists Join PM Modi's 'Har Ghar Tiranga' Movement, Unfurl National Flag in Kashmir | WATCH, Families of Hizbul Terrorists Join PM Modi's 'Har Ghar Tiranga' Movement, Unfurl National Flag in Kashmir | WATCH - News18

287 Army begins public outreach program 'A day with company commander' in J&K's Baramulla', 27 Feb 21, https://economictimes.indiatimes.com/news/defence/army-begins-public-outreach-program-a-day-with-company-commander-in-jks-baramulla/articleshow/81244475.cms?utm_source=contentofinterestandutm_medium=textandutm_campaign=cppst

288 Abdul Sattar Abbasi, 23 Sep 22, Tactics behind pro-India Twitter drive against Pak Army revealed, https://www.dawn.com/news/1711531

289 Kanchana Ramanujam, 03 Jul 19, From Human Wave to Info Wave: China's Propaganda Warfare, https://www.claws.in/from-human-wave-to-info-wave-chinas-propaganda-warfare/

290 Beaumelle, M. (2017). The United Front Work Department. "Magic Weapon" at Home and Abroad -Jamestown. [online] Jamestown. Available at https://jamestown.org/program/united-front-work-department-magic-weapon-home-abroad/

291 Beaumelle, M. (2017). The United Front Work Department. "Magic Weapon" at Home and Abroad -Jamestown. [online] Jamestown. Available at https://jamestown.org/program/united-front-work-department-magic-weapon-home-abroad/

292 Antara Ghosal Singh and Sarah Cook, Freedom House, https://freedomhouse.org/country/india/beijings-global-media-influence/2022

293 Antara Ghosal Singh and Sarah Cook, Freedom House, https://freedomhouse.org/country/india/beijings-global-media-influence/2022

294 Cyber Capabilities and National Power: A Net Assessment, Institute for Strategic Studies, 28 Jun 21, https://www.iiss.org/research-paper//2021/06/cyber-capabilities-national-power

295 India Social Media Statistics 2024, India Social Media Statistics 2024 | Most Used Popular Top Platforms – The Global Statistics

296 Telecom Regulatory Authority of India, 'Yearly Performance Indicators of Indian Telecom Sector (Second Edition) 2017', 4 May 2018, , accessed 15 May 2019, https://static.rusi.org/20190807_grntt_paper_11.pdf

297 The Hindu, 'Virtual SIMs Used in Pulwama Terror Attack; India to Approach U.S. for Help', 24 March 2019, , accessed 1 May 2019.

298 Marco Labre, 30 Oct 2023, CEO, SouthAmConnect, The Future of Social Media: Emerging Platforms and Technologies, https://www.linkedin.com/pulse/future-social-media-emerging-platforms-technologies-marco-labre-hdhdf

299 Jackson Hedden, 25 May 2023, How Decentralized Social Media Platforms Can Benefit Your Business, How Decentralized Social Media Platforms Can Benefit Your Business (forbes.com)

300 www.coingecko.com/learn/decentralized-social-media-platforms

301 Vincent Mosco, 21 Apr 23, Into the Metaverse: Technical Challenges, Social Problems, Utopian Visions, and Policy Principles, Full article: The role of (social) media in political polarization: a systematic review (tandfonline.com)

302 Thiago Veloso, 08 Sep 22, 10 examples of emerging technologies that are revolutionizing the media industry, https://www.wibbitz.com/blog/examples-of-emerging-technologies-revolutionizing-media-industry/

303 Amanda Hetler, 27 Dec 22, 10 social media trends in 2023https://www.techtarget.com/whatis/feature/9-social-media-trends

304 Brendan M. Cullen University of South Carolina – Columbia, 2023, Assessing the Threat of Social Media to National Security: Information Operations in the 21st Century, https://scholarcommons.sc.edu/cgi/ viewcontent.cgi?article=1665andcontext=senior_theses

305 Lt Gen SA Hasnain (Retd), Analysing India's threat spectrum, 16 Nov 21, https://www.newindianexpress.com/opinions/columns/ 2021/Nov/16/analysing-indias-threat-spectrum-2383998.html

306 Alysha A. Cunningham, Understanding Social Media's Influence on the Economy, https://newsroom.carleton.ca/story/economy-social-medias-influence/

307 Madhavi Gaur, 19 Sep 23, What is Amrit Kaal? Origin, Vision And Growth, https://pwonlyias.com/amrit-kaal/#amrit-kaal-vision

308 Kabir Taneja and Kriti M Shah, The Conflict in Jammu and Kashmir and the Convergence of Technology and Terrorism, Global Research Network on Terrorism and Technology: Paper No. 11, https://static.rusi.org/20190807_grntt_paper_11.pdf

309 Indu Bhan and Suraksha P, Supreme Court puts on hold government's fact-check unit notification, 22 Mar 24, https://economictimes.indiatimes.com/tech/technology/ supreme-court-puts-on-hold-governments-fact-check-unit-notification/articleshow/108684634.cms? utm_source=contentofinterestandutm_medium=textandutm_campaign=cppst

310 World Economic Forum, 08 Jul 2016, The global war of narratives and the role of social media, https://www.weforum.org/agenda/2016/07/the-global-war-of-narratives-and-the-role-of-social-media/

311 Patrick Duggan, "Harnessing Cyber-technology's Human Potential," *Special Warfare*, 28, No.4 (Oct-Dec 15), http://www.soc.mil/swcs/SWmag/archive/SW2804/October%202015%20Special% 20Warfare.pdf; Michael Holloway, 10 May 2017, How Russia Weaponized Social Media in Crimea, How Russia Weaponized Social Media in Crimea (thestrategybridge.org)

312 Amanda Hetler, 27 Dec 22, 10 social media trends in 2023https://www.techtarget.com/whatis/feature/9-social-media-trends

313 What emerging trends and technologies should you know in social media data analytics?, https://www.linkedin.com/advice/3/what-emerging-trends-technologies-should-you-know

314 What emerging trends and technologies should you know in social media data analytics?, https://www.linkedin.com/advice/3/what-emerging-trends-technologies-should-you-know

315 Robert Jordan, Founder Rojo Media, https://www.linkedin.com/advice/3/what-emerging-trends-technologies-should-you-know?utm_source=shareandutm_campaign=copy_ contribution_linkandutm_medium=guest_desktopandcontributionUrn= urn%3Ali%3Acomment%3 A%28articleSegment%3A% 28urn%3Ali%3 AlinkedInArticle%3A7110680889554083841% 2C7110680891374411777%29%2C7 113019075202572288%29andarticleSegmentUrn=urn% 3Ali%3 AarticleSegment%3A% 28urn%3Ali%3 AlinkedInArticle%3A7 110680889554083841 %2C7110680891374411777 %29anddash Contribution Urn=urn %3Ali%3Afsd_comment%3A% 287113019075202572288%2CarticleSegment% 3A%28urn %3Ali%3 AlinkedInArticle% 3A711068088955408 3841%2C7110680891374411777% 29%29

Index

A

Abu Bakr al-Baghdadi 164, 170
al-Isabah Media 170
Al-Qalam 171
Ansar-ut-Tawhid fi Bilad al-Hind 170
Application Programming Interface (API) 91
Arab Spring viii, 9, 16, 25, 64, 65, 84, 116, 117, 119, 120, 123, 124, 125, 126, 127, 130, 174, 175, 177, 191, 266, 279, 280
Artificial Intelligence 60, 179, 203, 251
Atlanta Ransomware Attack 52
Ayodhya 157, 171

B

Babri Masjid 165, 169
BeReal 69
Burhan Wani 3, 15, 56, 172
ByteDance 88, 89, 226, 277

C

Centre on Countering Disinformation (CCD) 147
Citizenship Amendment Act (CAA) 25, 155
Colonial Pipeline Attack 52
Comprehensive National Power 40
Cyber Attacks and Hacking 96
Cyberbullying 86, 93
Cyber Diplomacy 244
Cyber Extortionists 52
Cyber-operations 42
Cyber Trolling 58
Cyber-warfare 42
CyTrain 205

D

Darul Uloom Deoband 170, 216
Deepfakes 60, 189
Defence Cyber Agency 206, 214, 227
Doklam vii, viii, 6, 9, 10, 97, 109, 150, 151, 152, 153, 154, 185, 225, 238, 241, 282
Doklam Standoff viii, 9, 282
Douyin 69, 88

E

Echo Chambers 25, 63, 83, 86, 87, 93, 193
Ephemeral Content Evolution 234

F

Facebook 11, 15, 17, 18, 56, 58, 63, 64, 65, 66, 69, 70, 74, 75, 77, 78, 80, 83, 84, 86, 87, 106, 109, 114, 115, 116, 120, 121, 122, 123, 124, 125, 138, 140, 143, 144, 147, 149, 160, 161, 164, 170, 172, 173, 174, 175, 191, 194, 215, 216, 224, 228, 229, 233, 236, 239, 240, 252, 260, 266, 276, 283
Fake News 22, 85, 87, 90, 270, 274, 276, 282, 287

Fear of Missing Out 86, 180

G

Galwan Crisis 10, 241
Gen Millenium 75, 80, 247
Gen Z 69, 71, 75, 80, 88, 247
Global Risks Report 104, 277
Grey Zone 35, 36, 40, 42
Gullible Social Media Users 53
Gyanvapi Mosque 6, 157, 171

H

Hacktivism 51, 52
Hashtag Hijacking 59
Hate Mongering 85
Hijacking Hashtags 98
Hizbul-Mujahideen 56
Hybrid Warfare v, vii, 1, 3, 4, 9, 12, 25, 27, 29, 31, 32, 33, 34, 35, 36, 37, 40, 42, 43, 45, 46, 48, 51, 55, 68, 107, 110, 112, 139, 176, 199, 255, 265, 270, 271, 272, 273, 278, 280

I

Indian Cybercrime Coordination Centre 204, 288
Indian Mujahideen 166, 168, 169
Indian Ocean Region (IOR) ix, 1, 5, 245
Information Technology Act 200, 201, 207, 215
Information Warfare 94, 183, 281
Instagram 18, 66, 69, 70, 74, 75, 80, 86, 87, 114, 115, 116, 143, 149, 160, 215, 224, 228, 229, 234, 236, 260, 266, 276
Institute for Study of War 32
Institute of Strategic Dialogue 99, 100, 101
Intelligence Gathering 65, 254
International Bar Association Legal Policy and Research Unit 24
Internet of Things 213
Internet Research Agency (IRA) 56
Islamic Research Foundation 170
Islamic State in Iraq and Syria ix
Islamophobic hegemonic coalition 115
Israel-Hamas conflict vii, 2, 4, 8, 39, 43, 45, 46, 97, 109, 197, 241, 266

J

Jaish-E-Mohammad 171
Jamaat-e-Islami-e-Hind 169
Janood-ul-Khalifa 170
Joint Cyber Coordination Teams 205

K

Kumpulan Mujahidin Malaysia 76

L

Lashkar-e-Taiba (LeT) ix, 56, 169, 267
Law Enforcement Agencies 205
Lipulekh area 6

M

Machine Learning 60
Malware 182, 203
Manipulated Media 60
Masood Azhar 171
Massive Open Online Courses 205
Metaverse and Virtual Reality 233, 237
Middle East and North Africa (MENA) ix, 17, 116
Military, Political, Economic, Civilian

and Informational (MPECI) 30
Moral Manipulation and Framing 64
Multinational Capability Development Campaign (MCDC) 29, 110

N

Narrative Designing 99
National Critical Information Infrastructure Protection Centre 205, 211
National Cyber Coordination Centre 204
National Residents Census (NRC) 155
National Security and Defense Council (NSDC) 147
National Technical Research Organisation 205, 257

O

Online Social Networking 24
Open Source Intelligence x
Operation Secondary Infektion 144

P

Pak Occupied Kashmir (POK) 7
Pinterest 69, 74, 81
Psychological Warfare 97

R

Reddit 74, 92, 116, 235
Role of Social Media in Hybrid Wars 44
Russia-Ukraine conflict 1, 2, 4, 8, 15, 39, 43, 45, 46, 48, 91, 97, 103, 108, 133, 134, 138, 139, 143, 144, 150, 255, 266
Russia Ukraine Conflict 139

S

Security Service of Ukraine (SBU) 149
Shadowcrew 51
Snapchat 69, 74, 234, 235
Social Media Intelligence x, 66, 254
Social Media Warfare 44, 45, 46, 47, 48, 51, 103, 144, 227, 249, 254, 255, 265, 267, 273, 275
Students Islamic Movement of India x, 168, 267, 285

T

Tanzim Islahul Muslimeen 169
TikTok 69, 70, 74, 80, 88, 89, 90, 91, 116, 143, 146, 149, 226, 235, 277

U

Uniform Civil Code (UCC) 155
Uppsala Conflict Data Program 2, 279

V

Virtual Private Network x
Volatile, Uncertain, Complex, Ambiguous (VUCA) x, 3, 8, 35, 195, 243

W

Weaponisation of Information 55
Weaponisation of Social-media 107
WeChat 75, 93, 94, 153, 226, 252
WhatsApp 18, 22, 56, 69, 70, 74, 75, 92, 106, 109, 114, 164, 172, 173, 174, 202, 228, 231, 252, 285
World Economic Form 103

X

Xinxiang 7

Y

Yemen Crisis viii, 9

YouTube 11, 15, 17, 56, 65, 69, 70, 80, 81, 87, 88, 109, 116, 124, 125, 143, 147, 159, 172, 173, 175, 191, 194, 216, 228, 239, 240, 252, 260, 266, 269

Z

Zeus 51

Milton Keynes UK
Ingram Content Group UK Ltd.
UKHW041004111124
451035UK00002B/309